THE TRAGIC
QUEEN

Marie Antoinette

THE TRAGIC QUEEN

Marie Antoinette

Dorothy Moulton Mayer

WEIDENFELD AND NICOLSON
5 Winsley Street London W1

© 1968 by Dorothy Moulton Mayer

SBN 297 76418 7

Printed in England by
Cox & Wyman Ltd.,
London, Reading and Fakenham

To all brave women

Though a King may abdicate for his own person, he cannot abdicate for the monarchy. The constituent parts of a State are obliged to hold their public faith with each other . . . otherwise competence and power would soon be confounded, and no law be left but the will of a prevailing force.

EDMUND BURKE

Qui ne sent que l'amour ne sent pas ce qu'il y a de plus doux dans la vie. Je connais un autre sentiment, moins impétueux peut-être mais plus délicieux, mille fois, qui quelquefois est joint à l'amour, et qui souvent en est séparé.

JEAN-JACQUES ROUSSEAU,
Confessions

Contents

Illustrations

ILLUSTRATIONS

The author and publishers are grateful to all of the copyright owners for permission to reproduce the pictures.

Foreword

IN undertaking yet another biography of Queen Marie Antoinette considerable courage is needed; so much ink has been spilled in praise or blame, one invites so much comparison with other biographers. And yet in the case of a personage who presents an enigmatic figure to the world, there may still be room for a new appraisal. In France she is even today not dead, her name need only be mentioned for a lively discussion to break out. In England she is still remembered, if only for the height of her hats and the one remark, 'If the people have no bread let them eat cake', for which no authenticity can be discovered. So I have endeavoured as a woman to present the picture of a woman who was loved and hated, praised or criticized, who has been called traitress, martyr, and even saint, but who has never sunk into oblivion.

I would like to thank the many people who have helped me in writing this book. First in Vienna, Dr F. Rennhofer, Ober-Staatsbibliothekar, National Bibliothek, Österreich; Fräulein Rauch, Bild und Porträts Archiv; Frau Dr Anna Coreth, Ober-Staatsarchivar, Haus Hof und Staats Archiv. In Paris: Monsieur Jean Pierre Babelon, Conservateur du Musée d'Histoire de France; Mademoiselle Marguerite Jallut, Conservateur au Musée de Versailles; The Directeur Général des Archives de France for exceptional permission to inspect the original documents in the 'Armoire de fer'. I thank particularly Monsieur van der Kemp who gave permission for the Petit Trianon to be opened for me, and Monsieur Pierre Lemoine who showed me round the Queen's exquisite apartments and her theatre. Also the Comtesse de Chambure, Conservateur du Musée des Instruments Anciens. I am also indebted to Dr Roger Mettam of the Department of History, University of York, for his help in reading the manuscript; to Mr John O'Donovan, Mr James Laver and Dr Monk Gibbon for their constant interest and encouragement; and to Sir Frank Francis, Director of the British Museum, and to the invaluable London Library and its directors. Lastly to the late HRH Prince Ludwig of Hesse and the Rhine; to the Princesse Amadée de Broglie; to the Director of the Hotel Bristol for permission to reproduce pictures in their collections; to the Librairie Académique Perrin for permission to reproduce the map on page 229 which appeared in André Castelot's *Marie-Antoinette*; and to my friend, Miss Joan Smith, for her translations of the poetry.

1
Background and Childhood

ON 2 November 1755 the Empress Maria Theresa of Austria was brought to bed of her fifteenth child, a girl, who was baptized Marie Antonia; her arrival in the world was heralded by one of its greatest catastrophes, the Lisbon earthquake. The whole of Europe felt the reverberations of this shock, which destroyed the town of Lisbon and killed more than thirty thousand of its citizens. It also affected the life of the newly-born child inasmuch as the King and Queen of the unhappy country were the godparents of the baby Antonia; driven from their ruined palace they could hardly have given thought to such a faraway event, but later in the life of the French Queen people added this inauspicious beginning to the unhappy events which crowded upon her through life. At the moment nothing further from this could be supposed; she slept unwitting in her cradle in charge of the nurse who had been carefully chosen for her, while her mother, following her custom, was already busy signing the State documents which had been prepared before she took to her bed.

The Empress had ascended the Habsburg throne on 20 October 1740 as a result of the Pragmatic Sanction arranged by the Emperor Charles VI in order that it might be inherited through the female line. All the European powers had agreed to this, some exacting a considerable price; as a true Habsburg he believed in negotiation rather than war, and he thought, with some justice, that he had safeguarded his daughter. However, immediately on his decease Saxony demanded for its support of the Empress her voice in the claim of the Elector to the throne of Poland, while France insisted on its being occupied by the father-in-law of King Louis xv, Stanislaus Lecynski. War, which Charles vi had hoped to evade, broke out, and at its end Austria found itself bereft of all its Italian possessions with the exception of Mantua. And worse, France demanded the cession of the Duchies of Bar and Lorraine, the hereditary territories of their Duke, Francis; in exchange the Duke would receive the Duchy of Tuscany, of far less account to a family who had been hereditary rulers of their lands for seven hundred years. The Duchess and her son protested but were forced to acquiesce and the exchange was made a little sweeter by the marriage of Francis to Maria Theresa of Austria.

When Charles vi died she had been married four years and had borne her first child. It had been a love-match, for the bonds between their two houses were close and Francis had lived at the Court of Vienna since his fifteenth year; the Emperor had done what he could to assure the throne for his daughter, but he had omitted to give her any instruction in the art of governing her far-flung empire which stretched at that time from the Netherlands through the Rhineland to the borders of Wallachia, and down into Italy.

On the day after her father's death the nineteen-year-old Empress faced her first Privy Council, a group of six men whose combined ages totalled 410 years; most of them noble, some venal, all convinced that the Habsburg dynasty existed in a world which owed it perpetuity and respect. This guiding principle admitted neither the claims of genius nor the possibility of change. The difficulties which faced her were immense; as she said, she was without money, credit, experience or army, and surrounded by councillors without counsel. But she impressed everyone by her dignity and the quickness of her judgment; she was fair, with bright blue eyes and a broad open forehead and a fine air of nobility. She was profoundly religious, her days began and ended with prayer, and the needs of her beloved husband and her ever-growing family were never neglected. In short she was loving, open, of fabulous energy and the highest principles, beautiful and gay, and her Court was the home of culture, art and music, the home in which the little Marie Antonia was to grow up.

Throughout the war which followed her accession, in which she fought her rival Frederick II of Prussia, Maria Theresa made what resistance she could against better armies more adequately commanded. On the thinnest of excuses he had invaded Silesia. She detested him for his bad faith and Machiavellian juggling with treaties and alliances. He outraged every principle of her being; her firm belief that God must defend the right was opposed to his cynicism and conviction that God was on the side of the biggest battalions. During the years 1741-4 Europe presented nothing but an immense battlefield, and though this may seem to have little bearing on the life of the small Antonia, it was the Europe she would inherit, when her turn came to hold the reins of power, equally untrained, but not equally endowed with the qualities which could make her an efficient Queen. And yet there was so much of her mother in her, the same open beauty, the same gaiety and candour. Maria Theresa loved to leave the magnificence of Vienna with its exuberant baroque Hofburg, and to enjoy the comparative simplicity of life in her Schönbrunn which she embellished after a less flamboyant manner. Just so would her daughter enjoy her little Trianon with her pretended milkmaids and shepherds. But this was far in the future and meanwhile her mother could work all day harder than her ministers, and at night play cards till the early hours, or throwing on a domino betake herself to one of the dance halls where she believed she would not be recognized. To please her the incognito would be respected, but she was always easily known by her rapid gait. The morning found her at her work table, as fresh as ever.

Shortly before her confinement Maria Theresa had taken as her Chancellor the Count Kaunitz, and in him she had for the first and last time in her reign a man of really extraordinary ability. Realistic and far-seeing, he did not hesitate to recommend to his royal mistress measures which might displease her. He had been for eighteen months Ambassador to the Court of France and while there had managed not only to reach an intimate understanding with the Foreign Minister, the Duc de Choiseul, but also to insinuate himself into the good graces of the French king's favourite, Madame de Pompadour. He saw clearly that the way to King Louis XV lay through this lady's boudoir, and he took immense trouble to make himself acceptable to her and her entourage. 'All this,' he wrote to the Empress, 'has for the moment no influence on actual affairs, but such personal relations may have considerable consequences at a favourable moment.'

So a few weeks after the birth of the little Grand Duchess we find Kaunitz home in Vienna and writing to Starhemberg, the Ambassador in Paris: 'Her Majesty is not accustomed to stay long in bed and only too soon takes up the affairs of State. I hope therefore to give you an answer in a few days.' The affairs on which they were engaged were the intricate questions of the relations between Austria, England and France. In particular France was beginning to ask herself whether Frederick II of Prussia, with whom she had had temporary alliances, was not in fact more dangerous than either of the others. Bourbons and Habsburgs were traditional enemies, but in the pressure of a changing world old enmities and friendships were forced into reconsideration.

It seemed that the moment had arrived; England and France were fighting each other in the American colonies and there was immediate danger that the war might extend to Europe, in which case it would inevitably be fought in the Low Countries. In that case Austria's neutrality would be impossible, and Maria Theresa, who feared war more than anything else, was disposed to listen to Kaunitz, whose grand design was to form an alliance with France. Her overtures to Louis XV had so far been received with apathy but on 6 January 1756 Frederick signed a treaty with England, secret it is true, but secrets are soon leaked out in the Chancellories. The effect in France was immediate, and on 19 February Count Starhemberg received a declaration that the King had decided, for the maintenance of peace in Europe and the defence of the Catholic Faith, to enter into a durable accord with Austria. Frederick had drawn upon himself the hatred of three women, all of whom he despised, the Tsarina, the Pompadour and Maria Theresa. The conflict was now certain, and the year 1756 saw the opening of the Seven Years' War.

The little girl born the year before was thus destined to live the first years of her life with this background, a continuing anxiety which engaged a great part of her mother's time and thought. Nevertheless, Marie Antonia enjoyed a very carefree existence. As she grew older she began to join her brothers and sisters in their lessons and their play, though each of the royal children had his own court, and instructors, a fact which made the yearly transition from the Hofburg to Schönbrunn somewhat exasperating. This exquisite country palace was the one which all the family loved best, and here the Empress stayed until far into the autumn, to the distress of the officials and ambassadors who were forced to make the journey over country roads thick in mud or dust. It is lovely at any season, but when the last September sun paints the beech alleys with red and brown and the whole long façade glows golden in the light, one can imagine the romping children with their dogs and ponies, and the happy family life around them.

So when, in 1762, Leopold Mozart brought his two young prodigies to Court the little Wölferl, his playing done, could enjoy himself, after he had climbed on to the Empress's knee and given her a kiss, and tell the laughing Archduchess, 'When I am grown up, you are the only girl I will marry.'

Her first Governess was the Gräfin Brandeiss, and in her tenth year she wrote: 'My dear Brandeiss, I salute you. Please believe that the good wishes I send you are dictated by my grateful heart, I hope that in future my docility will repay you for all the trouble which my education has given you. Do continue in the same way, my dear friend, and rest assured of the tender affection of your grateful pupil.' It is a dutiful letter, and one may infer that the Gräfin had had considerable difficulty in teaching her wilful charge anything. But she was such a loving and charming child that her attendants all spoiled her. So her second governess, Frau von Lerchenfeld, was chosen because she was much stricter, and the subject of the Archduchess's education became of more importance. Children learn in their early years perhaps more from observation than from books, and Marie Antonia was no exception. She saw her home in Vienna with its opulent magnificence, and the city with its wealth and gaiety, above all she felt the influence of her mother, a personage, who, even when she showed the greatest kindliness to all who served her, always kept an unexpressed but strongly intimated sense of her position and authority. She could fling a cloak around her when she heard of the birth of her first grandson, and rushing to her box at the opera halt the play crying 'Leute, Leute, der Poldi hat'n Buberl* without the people ever forgetting that it was the Empress who included them in her joy.

* People, people, Poldi has a son (the Archduke Leopold).

When Marie Antonia was five years old a great event occupied the House of Habsburg, the marriage of Joseph, the heir to the throne. He was nineteen, and his bride was the lovely Princess Isabelle, daughter of the Duke of Parma, Infant of Spain. Joseph loved her at first sight, and the whole Court raved about her beauty. The moment of his marriage coincided with the efforts of France to terminate the war, but Maria Theresa could not reconcile herself to the total loss of Silesia and the Ambassador Starhemberg was forced by Kaunitz to persuade the French Foreign Minister, the Duc de Choiseul, to continue the conflict. His reply was despairing: 'What do you want us to do?' he asked, 'we have no army or resources, no navy, no generals, no head, and no ministers, and I assure you I shall make peace as soon as possible.' To such a pass was the magnificent France of Louis XIV reduced. Almost the same thing might have been said of Austria except that the State *had* a head, its Empress.

Louis XIV had left a bankrupt State, and the glory of his early reign had been eclipsed by the questionable revocation of the Edict of Nantes with its resulting exodus of the Protestants from the country, taking with them treasures of experience in the silk and textile industries. Further, his policy of drawing to his Court at Versailles all the leading aristocrats and landowners, all of whom hoped for preferment, had the result of denuding the countryside of the very men who should have developed husbandry and agriculture; only those who were exiled under a *lettre de cachet* rebuilt their châteaux and for want of something better to do interested themselves in the improvement of their estates. Under Louis XV things were little better, and in his reign the financial condition of the country suffered and he left it with a formidable deficit. The roads were splendid, and the men who were forced to build them had the pleasure of walking on them but without shoes and stockings; and indeed they were in general deserted except for the occasional coach, for the taxes lay heaviest on the poor; the nobles and the clergy were exempt. The enormous forests, like that of the Duc de Condé at Chantilly, said to be one hundred miles in circumference, were stocked with game, but only for the hunting of the owner, the King, and his friends. In all but a few districts, or under a landlord like the Duc de Liancourt, the people lived worse than beasts; they hired the land with no means of stocking it, and yet Arthur Young, travelling there, observed that it was all highly improvable if they had known what to do with it.

Young remarked that he had seen 'the property perhaps of some of the glittering beings I saw at Court. Heaven grant me patience,' he continues, 'while I see a country so deserted and neglected – and forgive me the oaths I swear at the absence and ignorance of the possessors.' In the thirty-seven miles of the country lying between the great rivers, the Garonne, the Dordogne and the Charente, blessing the land they flowed through, the quantity of wastes was surprising to the traveller, but he need not have been astonished, for it belonged to the magnificent Duc de Soubise, whose palace overwhelms us in Paris today. As for education, it was of course non-existent, small wonder then that these sick, unlettered, uncared-for peasants at last revolted, and followed anyone who promised them freedom and a better life.

Austria and Hungary were in a somewhat better case and at least they had a ruler who was loved by her people and who kept in closer touch with them. She responded to the superhuman efforts made by the nation to raise and sustain the armies by pawning her jewels and curtailing the expenditure on fêtes and amusements; reform, public prayers and national fasts occupied her thoughts. After two more years of sporadic conflict all the monarchs were at the end of their resources, and their subjects crippled by the unremitting taxation. The Peace of Hubertsberg in 1763 brought an end to the senseless misery, and the worst fears of Austria were confirmed; Frederick alone benefited. Prussia emerged as a great power and the House of Habsburg was effectively weakened.

During the next few years Maria Theresa sought to strengthen the shaken fortunes of the Austrian Empire by means other than war. In 1764 Joseph was crowned King of the Romans in Frankfort; since his wife had died in 1763 a second match was suggested and strongly supported by France. Joseph reacted so forcibly against the Princess Cunégonde of Saxony that his mother was forced to give in, and he finally married the Princess Josepha of Bavaria, a choice urged by Kaunitz who wished for a German alliance.

It was then the turn of Leopold the second son. In furtherance of a project to remove the succession of the Duchy of Tuscany from Joseph to his brother, with the consent of the King of Spain, it was arranged that Leopold should take the Infanta Louisa to wife, whilst the third brother chose Princess Beatrice, daughter of the Duke Hercules of Modena. The whole Court transferred itself to Innsbruck to meet the Spanish bride, and rejoicings of the utmost splendour were in progress when they were marred by the bridegroom's sudden illness. But even this disappointment was obscured by an event far more tragic, the death of the Emperor Francis I on the night of 19 August. He had left Laxenburg, the charming hunting castle in the neighbourhood of Schönbrunn, but had turned back to say goodbye to his dearly loved little daughter Marie Antonia; clasping her in his arms he had wept; was it a premonition, was he already ill? Certain it is that the heat in the Tirol was almost unbearable and the pressure of public and private entertainment fatiguing. After a long evening of opera and ballet a heart attack killed him so suddenly that his wife could not even reach him in time.

With this frightful shock the whole personal life of the Empress was changed. At first she had been frozen into a stupor. By the standards of the day it had been a perfect marriage; his placidity matched her energy, he had a good head for finance and had rendered service to the State. And he had supported the difficult position of a consort with good humour and tact. He was a connoisseur of art and good living, a real Lorraine, laughing, loving late nights and good fare. And when he had a really serious love-affair the Empress kept her own counsel, only sighing, 'How difficult it is to keep a husband happy who has nothing to do.' In spite of this small peccadillo their home had been happy and the children, especially the small Antonia, profited from their father's patronage of art. Beauty lay all around them and music was never far away.

All that was now over: in future the Empress would be exclusively devoted to the future of her children and the maintenance of her dynasty. The little Antonia had been left behind in Schönbrunn and when her mother returned it was a very different person whom she met. Maria Theresa had cut off her hair and was in deepest mourning, as was the whole Court; she gave away her wardrobe and for the rest of her life wore no jewels, and lived in rooms draped in grey or black. And her son Joseph, now Emperor, set an example of parsimony which was followed by the Court and aristocracy. Mozart returning to Vienna in 1768 felt the change so much that he quickly left for Italy. By no one could it have been more deeply felt than the tomboy Marie Antonia; it was the first shock in the life of a child whose loving heart had been satisfied by the father whom she adored: it had been to him she had turned when the more formal affection of her mother did not satisfy her. Maria Theresa was the Altissima, the highly honoured parent; her own youthful gaiety in the course of a long and demanding reign had been transformed into the dignity of a loved but remote personage. And besides, having now raised the heir Joseph to a co-regency with herself, she was principally concerned with restraining the young man's reforming ardour. We may for a moment consider the nature of this prince destined to play such an important part in the life of Marie Antoinette.

He had been strictly brought up, for his mother knew that one day he would take her place as Emperor; his curriculum was all-embracing and was designed to develop every physical and moral virtue. But as is often the case with children too narrowly held, he became silent and obstinate in the effort to preserve something of his own personality. As he grew older his constant companion was a young Hungarian nobleman, Count Bathyanyi, who had all the stormy nature of his race with a passion for the open air and strenuous sports. With him the Prince loved to explore the great forests and visit the soldiers' encampments. His mother, having rigorously excluded the flattery and obsequiousness of courtiers, was surprised and hurt to find that at the age of fifteen he showed a desire for reform and admiration for her enemy Frederick.

At the end of the Seven Years' War Joseph was twenty-two, and already showed signs of the man he was to become; sceptical but believing with a fanatical ardour in the power of reason, he did not hesitate to argue with his mother. He wished to curtail the power of the useless aristocracy, to suppress their freedom from taxation – here his mother was with him – to use the money for the benefit of education and the poorer classes. Of what use, he asked in a long and critical *mémoire* to the Empress, was the brilliance and frivolity of the Court? The glory of a reign resides in the securely founded State and impeccable finance, in the integrity and impartiality of its laws, and a flourishing industry.

From this it is quite clear that the new ideas were penetrating even to the Habsburgs.

There is a portrait of Marie Antoinette as she probably was at the age of nine in 1764, when the plan suggested by Kaunitz for his grand design for a Franco-Austrian alliance first began to take shape in Maria Theresa's mind. Her elder daughter Marie Christine had been married in the April following her father's death to Prince Albert of Teschen – the only happy marriage among the five daughters – she was the nearest to her mother's heart, nothing was too good for her. Albert was given the Governorship of Hungary and it was he who made the wonderful collection of drawings and works of art which bears his name today, the Albertina Museum. But in thinking of a suitable match for the heir to the French throne, the Empress chose for her purpose the youngest of her girls, Marie Antonia. The portrait shows us a charming child, visibly on her best behaviour for this important moment, her first portrait. She is formally dressed, but has a delightfully childish expression; her pure oval face, blue eyes and small rosy mouth, not too Habsburg in shape, and her powdered hair all combine to give a feeling of liveliness, of gaiety held in check for the occasion. Her tiny hands holding her dress and the bird are those of a child still.

She was one year younger than the Dauphin, and there would still be time to remedy any lack of education and style in order to make her acceptable to that connoisseur of feminine beauty, Louis xv. At first the project was only in the air, and the French did not show any great enthusiasm for the match, but gradually through the understanding which Kaunitz had established with the Foreign Minister Choiseul, it took shape. In 1767 the French Ambassador the Marquis de Durfort was instructed to begin informal discussions. Special attention was paid to Madame Antoine as she was then called, and on her twelfth birthday presents of fruit out of season were sent accompanied by a little figure of a dolphin. Her mother remarked that although she was lazy and a tomboy she had a gift of tact, of receiving everyone with a smile and a graceful word. In the month of November 1768 Maria Theresa instructed Count Mercy Argenteau in Paris to send her without delay an ecclesiastic who would direct the education of her daughter. 'I am impatient,' she wrote, 'to know who will be chosen as the Confessor of my daughter. I would also like to have a hairdresser, but I leave all to the discretion of Choiseul.' She might well be impatient; during the last years she had been unable to pay her customary attention to the child, for in 1767 a terrible epidemic had hit the Court; Joseph's wife had died, and the Empress herself had been near death, while the Archduchesses Elizabeth and Josepha and Prince Albert, husband of Marie Christine, had been in danger. Under the circumstances the youngest children had run even more wild than usual and Marie Antonia had had a splendid time. Choiseul chose for the post the Abbé Vermond, a man of thirty-five, the Librarian of the Mazarin College, whose name has always been associated with that of the little Archduchess.

Vermond had started his work in a manner calculated to awaken the dormant faculties of his friendly pupil, giving her at first only one hour of instruction and that principally in French conversation. Gradually he went on to history and geography, again principally French. Her little exercise book shows her copy-book hand while her essays reveal what he had suspected, that she was not without natural judgment. At the end of an essay on Louis XIV in which she described an operation performed on the King without his son's knowledge, she writes: 'In my opinion I find that the Dauphin must have suffered cruelly in finding himself so disdained, and I think I would do all in my power to gain the friendship and esteem of everybody so that no one would ever want to hide such accidents from me.' Her teacher's comment was: 'Her essays show some penetration and a good deal of sense.' But he found too that though she learned quickly she retained very little, and she had a regrettable taste for turning his remarks into ridicule. She was much too fond of making fun of people, this could lead her into trouble if she was not careful.

He wrote: 'She is very capable of judgment especially on the subject of conduct. She now speaks fairly good French, apart from some undesirable expressions which she will quickly forget when she hears no more German, nor the bad French spoken here.' But he insisted on her charm 'which grows from day to day. Every day her physiognomy acquires new graces. One can find faces more regularly beautiful, but I believe none more agreeable. The way she holds herself and walks have a note of nobility and majesty which is astonishing for her age. If she grows a little the French will need little else in order to recognize their sovereign.' In short, a child who seemed singularly gifted for the place destined for her.

The seriousness of her life was beginning to be apparent to the twelve-year-old Archduchess and the departure of her best loved sister Marie Caroline for Naples, to whose King she had already been married by proxy, cast a shadow of coming events. Marie Caroline was her favourite sister, and had in some sort replaced the lost father in the loving child's heart; this affection was so matched by the elder girl's care that the shock of her loss, the second in Marie Antonia's life, must have been disturbing in the extreme. She watched as her sister threw her arms round the Gräfin Lerchenfeld, imploring her to write 'everything, even the smallest trifle about my darling Antonia'. But Maria Theresa had written years before, when the governess was appointed, 'I regard her as a sacrifice to politics; if she does her duty to God and to her husband, and assures the safety of her soul, I will be satisfied, even if she is unhappy.' Hard words, and only too accurately fulfilled, for Marie Caroline wrote from Naples, 'I pray that my little Antonia will never have to suffer what I have suffered in the first weeks of my marriage.' All Maria Theresa's daughters except one might have echoed these words.

Although no definitive word had yet been pronounced, the marriage became every day more certain. Louis xv, interested by Vermond's reports, sent an artist, Ducreux, to Vienna for Marie Antonia's portrait and at the same time by the hand of Count Esterhazy a picture of the Dauphin 'in working clothes', which must have surprised his prospective spouse. The Empress redoubled her efforts to render her daughter acceptable to the King and the Court of Versailles, her dancing master instructed her in the fashionable way of walking at Versailles with tiny quick steps so that the folds of the gown were not disarranged; her teeth were made straight by a French dentist, she learned to wear a corset and on top of all this she was drilled in the sort of conversation she might expect to hold there. History does not tell us however how much her mother revealed as to the way of life of the King and his mistresses, a very difficult subject to approach with a well brought up young girl accustomed to a severely moral home.

From France the Count Mercy Argenteau watched with anxiety the training of the future Queen of France and when

Vermond wrote that she would be everything that could be desired he remembered the King's inquiry 'has she a bust?' to which the embarrassed courtier replied that the Archduchess was very well made. 'I am sure she is,' went on the King. 'All the Archduchesses are lovely and I expect ours will be no less.' In the summer of 1769 the pourparlers were finished and the King formally asked for the Archduchess's hand for his grandson the Dauphin, and proposed Easter 1770 for the marriage. To the delight of the Empress, her Minister's Grand Design seemed assured: she had been extremely disturbed by the desire expressed by her son the Emperor for a meeting with Frederick II, a plan which had even been approved by Kaunitz. Nothing would convince Maria Theresa that every move of Frederick did not hide some ulterior disaster for Austria, and she welcomed any alliance which would buttress her Empire against her enemy. Now the preliminaries of the great event could really be set in motion. The officials of both Courts were in the coming months to wade through mountains of papers to establish the thorny questions of precedence, of protocol. Who was to sign first the betrothal contract, who decide the amount of the dowry, how was the departure from Vienna to be arranged, who should ride with the bride, who receive her on each of her stops on the journey? What presents were to be given, and last but not least, who was to be invited to the fêtes arranged for the wedding by proxy?

On 4 April 1770 the contract was signed, and Marie Antoinette, as she would in future be known, received the congratulations of the Court. On the 15th the Marquis de Durfort, having left the town an hour previously, returned as Ambassador extraordinary 'as if he came from France'. His carriages escorted the two immense berlins which Louis XV had sent to bring his granddaughter-in-law to her new home. Marie Antoinette, hidden behind the curtains of a neighbouring palace, could join the Viennese public in admiring these vehicles of unusual splendour. They were made of rare wood lined with satin and ornamented, one with embroideries of the four seasons, the other bore bouquets of golden flowers which swayed with every breeze. They had cost 40,000 frs. In spite of the poverty of both countries their sovereigns were determined to spare no expense and in both Vienna and Paris it was a heyday for the Court costumiers; new dresses were ordered by the royal families, all the

Court ladies vied with each other in elegance, and Maria Theresa determined that her daughter's trousseau should outshine them all. On the next day the Marquis de Durfort was received in public audience by the Empress and her son the Emperor Joseph II; passing through a double row of Austrian and Hungarian nobles he presented a letter from the Dauphin for the Archduchess together with yet another portrait, the sixth. The child was waiting in the next room and ran in, all excitement, and pinned the miniature on her breast.

On 17 April she made her first political gesture, the renunciation of the hereditary succession to the throne of Austria. It must be remembered that she had lived all her life in regal splendour; although little more than a child she was old enough to feel pride in the traditions of her House, in the name of Habsburg and in the Kings and Emperors who had borne it before her. For her had been reserved the highest honour. She would be a Queen of an equally splendid throne, that of France. For the past two months she had occupied the room next that of her mother and had listened to the counsel and the warnings of that remarkable woman who had experienced the pitfalls which such a position might bring. Before the altar, and on the Holy Bible, Marie Antoinette gave her oath and signed the act, which would be later countersigned by Louis XV and by the Dauphin. The solemn ceremony was followed in the evening by a grand supper offered by her brother the Emperor and followed by a masked ball in the exquisite palace of the Belvedere for which the Empress had made quite unusual preparations. She was determined that all the people of Vienna should participate in this festivity and to this end she had issued five thousand invitations, all named. They included all officials, with their wives and daughters, professors, magistrates, lawyers. Also businessmen and tradesmen, the bourgeoisie and artists, musicians, painters and sculptors. And when the invitation cards were presented to her for her approval, with the printed words 'The exchange of this invitation is strictly forbidden', she wrote under it, 'No threats'. All the leading aristocracy were included naturally, but the common people could enjoy the fête as well, for from the Kärntner gate to the Belvedere there were five hundred lanterns suspended. The crowds could admire the carriages filled with nobility in their best gala attire, while in the ballrooms three thousand five hundred candles lit up the scene. Buffets loaded with the choicest viands and delicatessen for which Vienna was – and is – famous, tempted the guests, and of course wine was not wanting, nor the good Viennese coffee. The diamonds sparkled, the golden decorations flamed, and music added to the general excitement and rejoicing.

For her daughter the Empress had prepared, as was her custom, a long memorandum on the way in which she was to conduct her life, and extorted from her a solemn oath that she would read it at least once a month. She wrote:

You will begin every day by saying your prayers and by a few minutes of devotional reading. Everything depends on a good start to the day.... You will practise meditation as often as possible, above all at Holy Mass. But you must not think of introducing new customs nor should you ask for the adoption of our Viennese ways. Read no book or even a brochure without the approbation of your confessor. This is all the more necessary in France because among the flood of publications many are hostile to religion and morals beneath a veneer of respectability.

She passed on to more worldly advice: 'Do not ask for favours, listen to no one if you wish for peace. Always ask M. and Mme de Noailles what you should do in every case since it is your wish to please the nation, and let them tell you if there is anything amiss in your talk or conduct. Reply affably to everyone, but you must know how to refuse.' Marie Antoinette was to write to her mother once a month, and she was permitted to correspond with her sister the Queen of Naples, who should be her model. And she ended the sermon: 'The only thing I am afraid of is that you may sometimes be backward in your prayers and may in consequence grow negligent and lazy. Fight against these faults. Do not forget your Mother who, though far away, will always watch over you till her last breath.'

On 21 April she held her daughter for the last time in her arms. Bathed in tears and half fainting the child clung to her mother and was with difficulty separated from her and lifted into the carriage; the final farewells were said, and the agonized woman watched until the last carriage of the cortège of three hundred and seventy had disappeared. How could she rejoice? She went to church and prayed long and desperately for her child's happiness and her uncertain future.

The heavy carriages rumbled on over the familiar way led by three postilions sounding their horns. Now they were passing Schönbrunn, and the tears flowed again as she remembered that it was here she had seen her father for the last time. She thought too of her happy childhood there, in the lovely palace which the exquisite taste of her parents had embellished, of her romps with her brothers and sisters up and down its allées, in the winter with their sledges, in summer with their horses and dogs. But once past, her mind was quickly diverted when she thought of the glory which awaited her. She was only fourteen and a half, and the magnificence of her entourage was stunning; one hundred and thirty persons and three hundred and forty horses, the latter to be changed at every halting station, the whole under the escort of noble guards commanded by the Prince of Paar. Everywhere the people were out on the roads and in the streets of the towns: such a show was not to be seen every day.

At Melk, where she passed the night in the beautiful monastery high above the Danube, her brother Joseph II had organized an operatic performance for her, doubtless to cheer her up. It had however the opposite effect, for it was very bad, and Durfort, who had accompanied her so far, reported that she was very bored and sad. Then on to Emms and Bavaria; all along the route she was entertained by her princely relatives. Through Ulm and Donaueschingen the cortège drove, through the Black Forest until at last she arrived at Schüttern, where she received the Comte de Noailles, sent by the King to greet her at this last stopping place and to introduce himself, and most important of all, to confer with her Austrian companion, Prince Starhemberg, on the weighty problems of etiquette.

The Comte de Noailles, who had badgered Louis XV into granting him this favour, had been busy, with the aid of his wife, in the endeavour to surround the new Dauphine with creatures of their own choosing; the intrigue and jockeying for position and power which were to bedevil the next twenty years of Marie Antoinette's life had already begun. The Duchesse de Noailles had a protégé, the Abbé Moreau, who had been attached to the Ministry of Foreign Affairs and had collaborated with the Duc de Vauguyon, the Dauphin's Governor. They now proposed to solicit for the Abbé the post of Librarian to the new Dauphine, but two weeks before her arrival the Duchesse called her friend and informed him that they had lost, for she was bringing with her the man who had taught her during the last three years, the Abbé Vermond. Moreau was in despair, for he had already concocted a loyal address and under the direction of Vauguyon compiled a list of books. And, said Madame de Noailles, 'You have the title of a man of letters, the library is created, you will be the Librarian, you will have the entrées, and sooner or later they will know what you are worth.' The King conferred the desired title of 'Librarian to the Dauphine' and their spy was safely in.

It had been established that the handing over of Marie Antoinette would take place on an island in the Rhine, a sort of no-man's-land between France and Germany. Here the carpenters and furnishers had been busy for months building and decorating a wooden pavilion for the ceremony. It would have two entrances, one on the German side, the other on the French, two anterooms, two robing rooms, and between, one great hall. It was richly garnished and hung with the finest tapestries from the Archiepiscopal Palace of Strasbourg and filled with the costliest furniture from the houses of the wealthy burghers of the city. For weeks before the townspeople had watched the work and it happened that a group of students visiting the island had managed to penetrate the inner sanctum to admire the decorations. But one of them, a very lively and observant young man, had exclaimed in horror at what he saw. What, had they really taken the hangings with the woven story of Jason and Medea, was this ghastly tale the right thing for a young bride to feast her eyes upon? The record of the unhappiest marriage in history? His companions had difficulty in restraining the young Goethe, for it was he, and in getting him away without further outcry.

Now the great day had arrived. Marie Antoinette was to bid farewell to all the friends and ties which had linked her to the House of Habsburg, she was to become formally and forever French. The easier-going ways of Vienna were to be forgotten, the ceremonial had been organized down to the minutest detail. She entered the pavilion by the Austrian entrance and in the robing room she was divested of all her Viennese clothes. So says Madame Campan,* but later researches assert that the story is

* She was the wife of the Queen's Librarian and was engaged as Reader to Her Majesty. Her record is useful in all which concerned the daily life of Marie Antoinette, to whom she was devoted.

not accurate, she simply put on a ceremonial dress and was allowed to keep her personal jewels. Thus attired, and followed by her Austrian ladies-in-waiting, she passed into the great hall and stood before the table which symbolized the frontier; on the other side of it stood the Comte de Noailles and the commissioners, Bouret and Gérard. Behind her the door into Germany was still open, the French door being still shut. Taking the hand of Starhemberg, the trembling girl listened to an address by Noailles, the marriage contract was read, she relinquished her hold and gave the Comte her hand and he led her round the table. At the same time, in stately measure the Austrian suite retired, their exit according precisely with the moment when she reached the members of her new suite. But now it was too much, she had kept her head, had behaved with the dignity the occasion demanded in spite of her beating heart; she could no longer contain her tears, sobbing she threw herself into the arms of the Comtesse de Noailles, the German door was shut and Madame la Dauphine was French.

It must be said that the Comtesse was the last person to comfort a terrified child. Rigid with formality, she proceeded to introduce the ladies of her Court. Her chief lady, the Duchesse de Villars, the two second ladies, the Duchesse de Péquigny and Madame de Duras, and finally the Comtesses de Mailly and de Saulx-Tavannes. All of them had been in the Court of the late Queen Marie Leczynska; none of them were young, all were steeped in the rigorous punctilio of the Court of Versailles. But mastering herself, Marie Antoinette remembered her mother's lessons, 'be charming, do not show your feelings'; smiling and composed she turned towards the other, now open door, to France and her destiny.

She was greeted by the thunder of artillery and the pealing of all the bells. The old city of Strasbourg had outdone itself in decorations, crowds lined the roads, bevies of young girls strewed garlands in her path, and of course all the dignitaries of the town were there with addresses of welcome – in German. Legend has it that the gracious child exclaimed: 'Do not speak German, gentlemen, from this day I shall only understand French.' If it is not true it is nevertheless in keeping with her usual tact. On all sides was heard a murmur of admiration. The French people had been very little informed as to the nature or appearance of their new Dauphine and what they now saw ravished them. She was

The Empress Maria
Theresa and Emperor
Franz I with their youngest
children on the evening
of St Nicholas, an
intimate family scene

A portrait of Marie
Antoinette aged about
nine

An early portrait of Marie Antoinette by Krantzinger

slender and well proportioned except for a slight imperfection of her shoulder line, unnoticeable in her carriage which was elegant and noble. Her hands and feet were exquisitely formed and her skin was brilliantly white. Her face was a pure oval, and her rather high forehead was crowned by a mass of fair hair, worn with very little powder, her eyes of a particularly light and sparkling blue were most expressive and above all her smile conquered all hearts. But it was her colouring which bewitched the most, roses and lilies together, said one contemporary. Among the painted ladies of her suite she shone like Aurora, or one of the Graces. 'Our Archduchess,' wrote Mercy, 'in her debut at Strasbourg has surpassed all our hopes, as much by her bearing as by the wisdom and unaffectedness of all her remarks.' She smiled through the dinner and the interminable fêtes organized for her, she smiled when the Marshal led her to the Episcopal Palace from where she could see the fireworks and admire the decorations of the park. And when the last spark had exploded and she was taken, long past midnight to the ball, she seemed still fresh and smiling and ready to dance several times before being mercifully allowed to go to bed. 'If we judge the health of the Dauphine by her exterior,' wrote Noailles to Choiseul 'we need not fear for her health.'

On the next morning going to Mass, she was received at the door of the Cathedral by a very strange prelate indeed, the young bishop co-adjutor who in the absence of his uncle the Cardinal de Rohan was in charge of the ceremony. Perfumed, bejewelled and be-mitred with gold he led her into the church and there delivered the speech of welcome, flowery and insincere. She must have taken an instant and apparently unreasonable dislike to him although when he spoke of her mother she was visibly moved. Mass heard, he gave her his benediction, and she could set out on the last part of her journey.

Who were the people who met her? First the King Louis xv, now in his sixtieth year. He had begun his reign as a beautiful but rather timid boy. The manners of the time demanded that the King should have a *maîtresse en titre*, but for twelve years he was faithful to his dull wife, Marie Leczynska, who bore him during that time eleven children – 'always in bed, always being brought to bed' she remarked bitterly. But the decline of Louis the Well-Beloved was abrupt and total; debauched by a Princess of the Blood, Mademoiselle de Charolais, called 'the King's procuress' for her infamous activities, he took in quick succession as mistresses the Demoiselles de Nesle, two by two. His greed for constant amusement and sensual satisfaction was equally well ministered to by a more important mistress, Madame de Pompadour, who had been replaced on her death by the current favourite, the Comtesse Du Barry. His pleasures were as well known to his subjects as to his courtiers, and the lampoons and scurrilous verses which ran from hand to hand astound us by their grossness and open allusion to the King's vices. But he preserved in spite of all a superficial outward dignity and elegance of manner, and was rigid on points of etiquette. He was the King, and Maria Theresa had repeatedly insisted that her daughter should love him, be obedient to his wishes, and in return he would be a tender father to her and her friend. Nothing could be further from the truth. The King's well known interest in little girls was not that he might be a father to them.

Then there was the Dauphin. Louis August was the son of the Dauphin, son of Louis xv, and of his second wife Marie Josèphe of Saxony. So like Marie Antoinette, he was half of German blood, and although it is unwise to draw conclusions too far, this may have accounted for his heaviness of temperament and his greediness in eating. He had received in baptism the ancient French title of Duc de Berry, and had two brothers younger than himself, the Comte de Provence, or Monsieur as he was styled, and the Comte d'Artois. He was given as governess Madame de Marsan, of the great family of Rohan, and unimpeachable in her sense of duty and responsibility. She took the baby with her to the country château of Bellevue, for he was a somewhat weakly boy, and there he developed as a happy child with strong feelings of affection and sensitiveness.

At the age of six, in accordance with custom he was taken away from petticoat care and given to a governor, chosen with discrimination by his father who had taken the precaution to obtain from the King permission to direct his son's education without interference. When the little boy was told that he was to leave his governess he would not be comforted, not even by the present of a complete battery of cannon and soldiers to play with. His tears could not be stopped, and his father said, 'Why, these childish tears please me; they show that my son has a good heart and will keep it so.' His teachers were the Duc de la Vauguyon as governor, for religion the Bishop of Limoges, the Marquis de Sinety as under governor and the Abbé de Radonvilliers, a member of the Académie Française, as preceptor. All were men of quality, able to direct his studies as his father wished, and the Dauphin himself corrected his son's work twice a week in accordance with his desire that there should be no superficiality, but a consistent emphasis on serious study in all subjects. The works of the Cambresian philosopher Fénelon enjoyed a great vogue at the time and of them all *Télémaque*, the story of the son of Ulysses, was prized for its moral teaching and for its picture of the perfect education of the young prince through Mentor, the disguised goddess Minerva. The story of the trials of the young Telemachus in his search for his father could interest a growing boy, while the discourse of this wise teacher whom he could also admire for his courage and prowess in battle would influence his thinking as he grew old enough to understand it. Fénelon presents Mentor as saying:

Happy the people who are ruled by a wise King; they have abundance and love him from whom they draw their contentment. It is thus, oh Telemachus, that you should live if ever the gods restore to you the kingdom of your father. Love your people as your own children, enjoy the pleasure of being loved by them, and behave so that they may never enjoy peace and happiness without remembering that it is a good King who gives it all to them.

It will be seen later what an enormous influence this teaching had on the thought of Louis August.

However, the programme which led to a really valuable attitude towards knowledge in the young prince had its bad side; it accentuated his tendency to efface himself, his natural timidity prevented him from spontaneous friendship and this in turn led to distrust. The courtiers seeing his lack of response turned from him to his brothers and this of course led to further discouragement. Only with his godmother, the Princess Adélaïde, the elder daughter of Louis xv, was he at ease. With her he could, as she said, talk, shout and make all the noise he liked, she gave him free rein. One day, when a provincial visitor complimented him on his precocious ability, he replied 'You are making a mistake, Monsieur, it is not I who am clever, it is my brother Provence.'

He grew up persuaded that he was less than the others. One day playing at lotteries, a game in which the winner had to offer a prize to the person he loved the most, his brothers, winners most of the time, found the required persons, but when it came to the turn of Louis August he put his prize in his pocket. 'Why,' asked Vauguyon, 'will you not offer it to someone?' 'But, Monsieur,' answered the child – he was only seven – 'how can I love someone here when I see that no one loves me?'

On 22 March 1761 his elder brother, the Duc de Bourgogne died, leaving him second from the throne, and the Dauphin took more care than ever over his education, preparing him as much as possible for the high position which one day would be his. But another blow fell shortly afterwards: his father died. The Duc de Berry was overwhelmed by the loss, for he loved his father, and the first time he heard himself announced as Dauphin his grief was intense. Now his mother took up the work of preparation and the Duc de Vauguyon was more than ever penetrated with the weight of his responsibility. It was answered by the application and the real taste for learning which the boy possessed. He had a first class memory, he read with pleasure in four languages; he amused himself with the *Gazettes* from London and he translated Hume's life of Charles I which was to have a remarkable influence on his future policy. He also translated the *Doubts on the Crimes attributed to Richard III* by Horace Walpole, and the first five volumes of Gibbon, all of which satisfied his curiosity and interest in history.

He wished to have these translations printed and in addition a work of his own *Maximes Morales et Politiques tirées de Télémaque* by Louis August, Dauphin, and for this purpose engaged one of his Readers to commission the work. It was to appear 'At the Printing House of M. le Dauphin 1766'. Twenty-five copies were printed and the first was presented to the King, which must have surprised his grandfather considerably. To all this was added an interest in agriculture and the mechanical arts. He had grown into a sturdy healthy boy with open-air and somewhat bourgeois tastes, he loved eating and drinking, had a voracious appetite and passed his hours of leisure in his carpenter's shop. He had inherited from his Saxon mother a simplicity which accorded ill with the sophistication and extreme luxury of the Court of Louis xv, and thus the courtiers and his grandfather too wrote him off as an inevitable but bad entrant for the royal stakes.

Marie Antoinette when she met him could naturally not appreciate any of his virtues, she saw only an ungainly lout of a youth a couple of years older than herself. He was badly made and awkward, lacking in charm, with a rather raucous voice and slovenly in his dress. He was even more short-sighted than she and his difficulty in distinguishing people gave him a sort of sideways glance which unfortunately hid the rather melancholy gentleness of his eyes. The mockery of the courtiers and the gibes of his grandfather paralysed him, all the more because, having once been admitted to a supper party in the King's *petits cabinets* he had been so horrified by what took place there that he shunned feminine society.

It remains for us to note the three daughters of the King, the formidable aunts to whom Maria Theresa had looked as the best friends for her child. They had been four, but the youngest had recently entered the convent of the Carmelites there, it was said, to expiate by a lifetime of prayer and dedication the sins of her father. There remained Madame Adélaïde, Madame Sophie, and Madame Victoire, of whom only Madame Adélaïde really counted. A big rawboned spinster, she had been fine-looking in her youth but her overweening pride as Daughter of France had led her to disdain any overture of marriage, even from a reigning prince, and she now existed, bitter and domineering, at Versailles. She had been violently opposed to the Austrian alliance, for she hated Choiseul, and it remained to be seen what attitude she would adopt to the intruder.

Surrounded by the dignitaries of the Church and State, all these people waited for the young Archduchess on the morning of 14 May at Compiègne. By a special favour Choiseul had been allowed to meet her and to conduct her on the last stage of her journey. He was presented to her by Starhemberg. 'I shall never forget, Monsieur,' said the tactful child, 'that I owe my happiness to you.' 'And that of France,' said the equally adroit Minister. He entered her coach and together they drove the last few miles of the way. When the head of the cortège was seen, the King descended from his carriage and accompanied by the Dauphin took a few steps towards the Archduchess, but she was before him; springing lightly to the ground she ran and sank to her knees, he raised her with a kiss, and presented her to the young man who touched her cheek with his lips. Amidst the acclamations of the crowds assembled from all the countryside they remounted and proceeded to the château.

Here Marie Antoinette met the people with whom she would live in this new world. First the Princes of the Blood, the Duc d'Orléans, grandson of the late Regent, the Duc de Penthièvre, grandson of Louis xiv, the princes of Condé and Conti, then the cousins, the Dukes of Chartres and Bourbon, almost her own age. The last Princess was Marie-Thérèse, of Savoie-Carignan, already a widow at twenty-one, living in retirement with her father the Duc de Penthièvre. Now came the turn of the ladies and gentlemen who had accompanied the King to Compiègne, after which supper was served to the royal family, while doubtless the palace buzzed with the comments of the courtiers, their impressions of the bride, the King's reactions and the Dauphin's lack of interest. For after the last of the ceremonies had come to an end, and the Dauphine had been led to her chamber and put to bed, he waited in his room at the hôtel of Monsieur de St Florentin until his gentlemen had left him and in his journal wrote the brief remark 'Interview with Madame the Dauphine'.

On 15 May the royal family set forth on its way to Paris, pausing only at St Denis so that the Dauphine could visit her aunt in the Carmelite convent. Arrived at La Muette they prepared for a grand supper, and here took place an event which had been bedevilling the days and nights of Mercy for the last month – the King had allowed it to be known that his mistress, Madame Du Barry, would be present in the royal party. 'It seems inconceivable,' he wrote to Maria Theresa, 'that the King should choose this moment to accord an honour which has so far always been refused.' To the applause of a vast multitude, the procession of carriages made its way – without the King however, whose unpopularity might have evoked a less enthusiastic reception. Arrived at La Muette the Dauphine met her brothers-in-law, the Counts of Provence and Artois, the future Louis xviii and Charles x, boys of fourteen and thirteen. And among the Court ladies stood, glittering with diamonds, the Du Barry, all smiles. At the dinner the King asked Marie Antoinette what she thought of the lovely black-eyed blonde at the end of the table. 'Charming' was the answer, and turning to Madame de Noailles the Dauphine asked what was the lady's function at the Court. 'To amuse the King,' she was told. 'In that case,' she replied, 'I shall make myself her rival.' An innocent response; in a few weeks it could no longer have been made.

Certainly this woman, powerful as she undoubtedly was, must have awaited the arrival of the Dauphine with some misgiving. A new face at Court, young, beautiful and highly born, what would this mean for her? She must by all means make her position as secure as possible, all the more as her protector the Duc de Richelieu had sent her this letter:

Take great care, my adorable Comtesse not to follow the idea which M. de Noailles has put into your head, to go to the Waters at Darrèges so that you will not be there when Madame la Dauphine arrives, under the pretext that you would not have an important position in the fêtes which are being organized ... The Comte, who has given you this advice, cannot be a friend of yours for he owes his post to Choiseul, who would profit by your absence to rob you of your ascendance over the King. You are his divinity, do not leave him for a moment. Young and beautiful as you are, you ignore the dangers of absence ... age feebles desire if it is not constantly excited. I will not say more, my divine Comtesse.

She received the same advice from the Duc d'Aiguillon and it seems likely that with all this in mind she set herself to wrest from the King, by alternate cajolery and sulks, permission which he had always so far refused. He gave in unwillingly, from a mixture of indolence and love of a quiet life, and her end achieved, the Comtesse could ignore the disgust of her adversaries.

On 16 May came the departure for Versailles, where the Dauphine was dressed in her wedding gown of silver brocade while the Dauphin was persuaded to put on his costume of cloth of gold sewn with diamonds, while in the antechambers the assistants at the semi-private nuptials fought their last battles of relationship and precedence. The vast palace with its five thousand inhabitants seethed with life; in the courtyard there was an incessant flow of carriages bearing the invited guests, while the uninvited crowds surged up and down in their anxiety to miss none of the show. At one o'clock precisely the master of ceremonies led the royal couple hand in hand into the Gallery of Mirrors. Slowly they advanced, Marie Antoinette with her swimming gait and her delicately poised head, her young beauty all the more enchanting by comparison with her shambling groom, in his sumptuous costume which had cost more than twelve thousand good French livres. In the chapel, blazing with lights and crammed to suffocation with the high nobility of France, squeezed together in their magnificent dresses, the Archbishop of Rheims blessed the rings, and the thirteen pieces of gold, symbolic price of the woman; the King, having advanced, bowed his head in assent, and the ring was placed on the bride's fourth finger. The Prelate blessed the two children kneeling before him and the deed was done. The Curé of Versailles brought the registers to be signed, the King signed, the Dauphin signed, and Marie Antoinette affixed her name with a hand that trembled so much that a tiny ink spot stands there beside it. During the reception which followed a terrible storm broke over the château, one of those natural disasters which accompanied Marie Antoinette throughout her life, after which the royalties supped at a table for twenty-two with the King at its head. Marie Antoinette had little appetite; the Dauphin on the contrary set to with a will – he was a gross feeder. 'Do not overload your stomach on such a night,' advised that connoisseur, his grandfather, to which he replied: 'I always sleep better when I have eaten well.' It was on another occasion that the King had observed that Louis August was not a man like any other: watching the alluring Marie Antoinette he may have hoped that here was the cure for the boy's dullness.

After the fireworks, nothing remained but to put the couple to bed, and here the Court crushed in to see the Archbishop of Rheims bless the couch, the King offer the nightgown to the Dauphin and the Duchesse de Chartres offer her nightwear to the embarrassed bride. Everyone had remarked on the Dauphin's boredom, and next morning under the date 17 May he wrote his famous 'Rien' – Nothing. And the Abbé Vermond reported to Vienna, 'When I was with her this morning, the Dauphin came in. "Have you slept" he asked. "Yes" was the answer. He went out without a word and the Dauphine amused herself with her little dog.'

On 19 May a masked ball was opened by the Dauphin and his wife dancing a minuet, and terminated by a firework display, the greatest ever seen in France. Pyramids of fire alternated with cascades and alleys lit by the thousands of roman candles. The public danced the night through, but Marie Antoinette was already in bed with her insufficient husband. Perhaps it was all to the good, wrote her mother, 'you are still so young and for your health it may be better to wait awhile'. This sounds wise, but what of the neglected child, the object of all the rumours and scandal of a Court like a whispering gallery? Her days and evenings were filled with opera and theatre performances, but night after night she came back to a young man who not only failed in his duty, but in whom manners and consideration were entirely lacking. Mercy wrote to the Empress: 'The Dauphin does not show his wife the least sign of taste or admiration,' and the Abbé Vermond commented: 'My heart is broken.' It was the more distressing because by this time Marie Antoinette had captivated the King and the whole Court by her beauty. It was the carriage of her head, her way of walking which delighted all who saw her. Horace Walpole later summed her up when he wrote: 'When she moves it is grace in person. They say she does not dance in time, then it is the measure which is wrong.' Her brother Joseph was more severe, he too judged her amiable but too easily carried away by unimportant pleasures. 'She is a madcap,' he said.

She enjoyed every moment of the fêtes which were to terminate by a day's offering by the city of Paris. The King had decreed it, and in spite of the general misery the bourgeois had planned a magnificent welcome. On the Place Louis xv – today the Place de la Concorde – a Corinthian temple had been erected, crowned with the portraits of the Dauphin and Marie Antoinette and their arms; it was planned to set off from thence the fireworks which would end the festivities. The banks of the Seine had been inundated with perfume since the morning; and at five o'clock the fountains of wine began to run. The Dauphine, accompanied by Madame Adélaïde and her suite, had set off from Versailles, and the young girl was doubtless, and forgivably, longing to see the effect of her charm on the inhabitants of the great town. Arrived at the Sèvres bridge they could see the sky lit with the first salvo of fire in their honour. Suddenly at the Cours la Reine their carriage with its six horses was halted by a terrible noise and the sound of running feet, and a frantic multitude of three hundred thousand people met her frightened eyes. The crowd had decided, after the way of crowds, to rush towards the rue Royale where the fair was situated. There they were met by another human flood coming from the quays, and within the space of minutes the whole mob, men, women and children suffocating in the semi-darkness, panic-stricken and helpless, were engulfed in a sea of horror. Carriages were overturned, the horses died under foot, the police were helpless, six thousand dead, said the official records, to say nothing of the wounded. The carriage of the Dauphine had been turned quickly, and half senseless with fright she regained Versailles.

Next morning the Dauphin wrote to the Hôtel de Ville. 'I have received news of the disaster that has overtaken the rejoicing which was offered to me. I am deeply affected by it. They have brought me the money which the King gives me each month for my pleasures, it is all I have. Use it for the most unfortunate.' Marie Antoinette followed his example, and we may remember the story of her as a little child, bringing to her mother her savings for the relief of a poor family.

On the same morning one hundred and thirty corpses were marked and laid in the cemetery of the Madeleine, in the same plot where thirty years later her decapitated body would be thrown. It would be hard not to see, in the disasters which so far accompanied her short life, a sinister augury for her future.

2

The Dauphine

Now that the rejoicings were over, the Court returned to its habitual round and left Versailles for Marly, and Mercy commenced his long series of reports to Maria Theresa. Realizing the importance of her daughter's marriage for the policies of Austria, the Empress had taken the precaution, not only of providing her with advice but of making sure that she herself would be kept informed. Mercy was commanded to note the most intimate details of the Dauphine's life; apart from his official letters, secret reports would be sent, so that between his own observations and those of the Abbé Vermond neither Marie Antoinette nor her spouse could so much as speak a word without its being known. They were surrounded by spies, benevolent it is true, but still spies.

It must have been at Marly that the Dauphine finally succeeded, through a mixture of sweetness and persistence, in breaking through her husband's reserve. At first the Dauphin kept his accustomed way, he slept soundly all night so as to be ready at the break of daylight to join the hunt, from which he returned exhausted, and without uttering a word tumbled into bed again. It was during this time that Marie Antoinette began to come under the influence of her aunts, and particularly that of Madame Adélaïde, who had apparently forgotten her opposition to the marriage, and welcomed her young niece on all occasions. And to whom else could the poor child turn? Had not her mother recommended her to make a friend of this virtuous lady? The Empress was to regret her advice as the months wore on. At last at the beginning of May the patience of the Dauphine was rewarded, and she was able to have a conversation with her husband. She had taken to heart her mother's counsel, 'the wife ought always to be submissive to her husband, her chief interest should be to please him and do what he wishes. Everything depends on the wife, if she is pleasant, sweet and amusing.' Marie Antoinette had seen that her mother in spite of being Queen-Empress had known how to be all these things to a husband whom she adored, and her home had been happy in consequence.

Little by little the sulky boy had grown accustomed to this gay pretty companion, his nervousness was vanishing, and in a long talk he admitted to his wife, 'I know very well what the marriage state demands. From the beginning I made a rule for myself which I intended to keep. Now the time I have fixed is here. You will see that at Compiègne I shall live with you in all the intimacy which you can desire.' And on the 9th the Dauphine wrote to her mother, 'My dear husband is much changed, and to his advantage. He shows much liking for me and even some confidence. He does not like the Duc de Vauguyon [his tutor] he is afraid of him.' With some justice, for they had found him listening at the door to their conversation.

But it is understandable that Vauguyon, fearing the decline of his influence over his pupil's life, should be doing his best to keep control of it. The Abbé Moreau had lost no time in visiting Vermond who had received him coldly, and the Duc was trying by every imaginable means to get rid of Vermond, without success, for Marie Antoinette was devoted to him. She had been at Court too short a time to understand the underground intrigues which prevailed there, and it was unfortunate that the head of one of the two principal parties should be that very man who had engineered her marriage, the Duc de Choiseul. The other party was that of the so-called 'Dévots', its leaders were the Chancellor Maupeau, the Governess of the Children of France, Madame de Marsan, a member of the powerful Rohan family, the Duc d'Aiguillon, a favourite of Madame Du Barry, and Vauguyon. Du Barry hated Choiseul, and Madame Adélaïde had inclined to this party in her opposition to the Dauphin's marriage. At least Mercy, the Austrian Ambassador, realized what this web of intrigue could mean in the life of the young Dauphine, and now his reports to the Empress were supported by the comments of her daughter, who wrote:

The King is full of goodness for me and I love him tenderly, but it is pitiable, the weakness he has for Madame Du Barry, who is the stupidest and most impertinent creature imaginable. She played with us every evening at Marly, she was twice beside me but she did not speak to me and I did not try to enter into conversation with her, but when it was necessary I spoke to her.

And she concluded: 'I forgot to tell you that yesterday I wrote to the King for the first time, I was very afraid because I know that Madame Du Barry reads all the letters, but you may be sure, my very dear Mother, that I will do nothing either for or against her.'

The Dauphine's reaction to the favourite is very understandable, it is prejudice, but the prejudice of an innocent and virtuous young girl suddenly transplanted into a world which she had never even imagined. Madame Du Barry, the former Jeanne Bécu, preserved her hold over the worn-out roué by a variety of tricks not always in the best taste, though witty; she had begun her life as little better than a prostitute without education or manners, but going through what she herself called the 'Seminary of debauch' in the most famous brothels in Paris. They were, however, frequented by the highest nobility, and since she was quick to learn she picked up enough from their conversation to be able to entertain them, and of her beauty there was never any question. From lover to lover she rose through the interest of a rich Farmer-General to the notice of a certain profligate Comte du Barry, who offered her a residence. In persuading her he wrote, 'not only will you meet in my house, where you will be the mistress, Marquises, Dukes, but even Princes who will be honoured to know you.' Here she installed herself and soon she was writing to the Treasurer of the Marine and offering herself to him. In June 1768 the Queen, Marie Leczynska, died after a long agony and Louis xv, who had cast his eye already on Mademoiselle Vaubernier, the present name of Jeanne Bécu, needed only make a decent pause before taking the beauty for his mistress 'en titre'. But first she must be married, and a complaisant husband was found in the brother of the man who had been the architect of her fortune, the Comte du Barry. She was married in July 1768 and her future seemed secure; one thing only remained to make it completely so, she must be presented at Court to the King and the royal family, a ceremony which Court etiquette demanded before a lady could enjoy all the rights of royal favour. This took place in April 1769 and her late lover wrote to her: 'There you are, my dear sister, at the most elevated point to which you could aspire, but to retain it you must exercise the greatest circumspection, particularly with the King. Always be gay and in high spirits, but in public show reserve, the tone of the Court ... Show politeness, and affability, especially with the women.'

Wise words, but on her way up Madame Du Barry had made two most dangerous enemies, the Duc de Choiseul and the French public: one she was to ruin, the other would ruin her.

This was the woman who had so enchanted the King that when Marie Antoinette arrived at Versailles she was in a position to choose ministers of State, to see the Princes of the Blood at her feet, and to be the power behind the throne through whom all advancement lay. It must be said in her favour that she had closed the infamous Parc aux Cerfs, the King's private brothel, which Madame de Pompadour had opened, and since she was not a bad natured woman, she was generous as such women often are and very anxious to please, so that the King could say to the remonstrances of his Minister Choiseul *'Elle me contente, c'est tout'* (She pleases me, that is enough).

On 12 July the Dauphine wrote to her mother, who had evidently wished to know how she spent her days, 'Madame, my dearest Mother, as to what you ask about my devotions, I have communicated only once', and she gives the reason:

I will tell you what I do. I get up at 10 or half past nine, and having dressed I say my morning prayers, then I breakfast and then I go generally to my Aunts where I find the King. This all lasts till half past ten. At 11 I go to have my hair dressed. At midday the Court is called and there the whole world has the right to enter, at least, not the common people. I put on my rouge and wash my hands in front of everybody, then the gentlemen go out and I dress before the ladies. At midday is the Mass, if the King is at Versailles I go with him and my husband, if he is not I go with the Dauphin, but always at the same time. After the Mass we dine before all the Court, but it is always finished at half past one because we both eat very fast. From there I go to the Dauphin if he is free, if not I go to my own apartments. I read, or I work. I am making a waistcoat for the King and with God's grace it may be finished in some years. At three I go to my Aunts, sometimes the King is there; at four the Abbé [Vermond] comes to me; at five the music master till six. At half past six again to my Aunts or to take a walk. From seven o'clock we play (at cards or other games) till 9, then we sup, and when the King is not there the Aunts come to us, but when he is we sup with them where we wait for him. He comes generally at half past ten, but I am allowed to lie down on a big couch and sleep till his arrival. If he does not come we go to bed at eleven o'clock. This is all our day. I entreat you my dear Mother to forgive me if this letter is too long. My only pleasure is to talk with you. And please forgive me if it is dirty, I had to write it as I was dressing two days running, I had no other time . . . I must finish now for it is time for the King's Mass.

This account of her day is more remarkable for what it does not say than for what it does. In the short time she had been at Court the Dauphine was gathering a good insight into what went on there, particularly the life of the King. Although Louis xv had deteriorated in his private life he had never ceased to take a commanding place in the pursuit of his government. He attended the meetings of the Council, he worked with his ministers and he kept in touch through the Duc de Broglie with his secret agents in Europe. Unfortunately he was becoming more and more influenced by the favourite and her entourage. He had installed her in her own apartment above his own, while awaiting the perfectioning of the suite which we know today as hers. Here he could visit her at any hour, waiting for him in the négligés which she was so fond of, the flowing white diaphanous robes which set off by their purity her voluptuous and obscene beauty. Here he could forget that his empire overseas was crumbling, that his navy needed reorganizing, that there was no money, and that the Parlements resisted all attempts to change the methods of taxation. And when he was reminded of these trying facts by Du Barry and her friends, the Chancellor Maupeou, the Controller of Finance Terray and his mistress, he could leave it to them to find a solution.

One may read many things into this letter of the Dauphine, a sense of loneliness, of futility, a faithful child not wishing to complain, but showing that she is doing her best to follow instructions, that she misses her freedom, that she had no company, that all her days are constrained into a rigid pattern. What did she receive from her mother in return? One long sermon after another; she must have suspected that she was spied upon – for the best reasons admittedly – from Maria Theresa's intimate knowledge of her behaviour. Her mother praised her docility and sweetness but told her not to glorify herself, it was the gift of God. The Empress analysed what she considered the chief faults of the French royal family very acutely, their society was too restricted, and thus they became surrounded by discontented people, a prey to every sort of jealousy and intrigue. Where the Court is freer, she said, and when contact exists with the world outside, it may be more demanding but then these disadvantages are avoided. 'I beg you as your friend and as your loving Mother do not let yourself go. It is for you to set the tone at the Court, do not be negligent either of your appearance or your behaviour, if you are you will regret it.'

It was a pity that the young Dauphine could not have known something of the social life of Paris, so different from the inane excesses of the Court. In the city the salons, where the famous hostesses held court, intellect and wit were prized and women like Madame du Deffand, the friend of Horace Walpole, old now, but once a beauty and Madame Geoffrin who gave two dinners a month, one for artists and one for men of letters, set the tone. The art of conversation, so French, of which one half consists in listening, was perfected in France. There were love-affairs, liaisons, it is true, but conducted with elegance, politics were not forgotten and later in the reign the influence of the women was enormous and could not be discounted. But for the Dauphine all this was unknown ground, she had to be content with the intrigues and etiquette of Versailles.

Meanwhile she awaited the promised date at Compiègne with impatience, but alas when it arrived, to her dismay, nothing happened. Rien. The Court knew this very well, and, so Mercy informed the Empress, the aunts were the best informed and disturbed the Dauphine with their comments, particularly the spinster, Madame Adélaïde, always the chief trouble-maker. The King too, stimulated by the ill-natured comments of Madame Du Barry, intimated his surprise to his grandson, who again promised to fulfil his duty in September. 'I love my wife,' he replied to the

King's remonstrances, 'but I must have time to overcome my timidity.' One must imagine the Dauphine's state of mind, disappointed in her hopes of a successful marriage, frustrated in her desire to fulfil what she knew to be her duty, to produce an heir to the throne, outraged in her thoughts by the very people she ought to respect, she could hardly be blamed if she threw herself into whatever distraction she could find. During the boring meals, while her husband shovelled in his food she diverted herself by laughing with her young ladies-in-waiting at the expense of the silent crowd watching her eat with greedy eyes, and Mercy reported to the Empress. 'Madame the Dauphine makes fun of people whom she finds ridiculous, and since she is witty it gives the more offence.' Soon she was corrected by Madame de Noailles whom she had christened Madame Etiquette, and this lady too became the target for her sallies. Her mother disapproved of her riding, it was bad for her complexion and her figure and, what was more important, for her hopes of an heir. So the young people took to donkey riding, and one day the Dauphine was thrown. 'Run quick,' she exclaimed, 'and ask Madame de Noailles what is the correct attitude for the Dauphine of France when she is thrown by an ass.'

And this brought the Abbé Moreau once more upon the scene. He had never given up his hopes of preferment; and when as a result of the King's pleasure in seeing the ardent and lovely young creature riding at his hunting parties she took to her horse in spite of her mother's gloomy predictions, the Abbé composed a joke in which the discarded donkeys presented their 'humble and very respectful remonstrances by the donkeys lately in her service'. This was enough for Marie Antoinette; in the *Gazette d'Utrecht* is the story how she assembled eighty of the beasts in the forest at Compiègne and accompanied the cavalcade to the Château to the accompaniment of flutes and possibly the braying of the donkeys.

The Empress scolded away, prompted by Mercy; her daughter ate too many sweets, and Madame Windischgrätz returning from Versailles to Vienna had reported that she did not clean her teeth, and what about her corset, the Windischgrätz had found that her waist was bigger. 'If you will send me your measurements I will have corsets made here for you, they say those of Paris are too stiff.'

'What do you read?' shouts Maria Theresa; reading her letters one has really the impression of a storm. 'You have not sent me the list. Since you can neither play nor sing and do not dance well, you should occupy your mind with good books.' 'My Princess was annoyed,' wrote the Ambassador, and with good reason it seems; no worse method could be found to influence a headstrong girl. 'I will be treated like a child till I am thirty,' lamented the Dauphine, and we imagine her flouncing out of the room. But in fact her conduct did conflict with the rigid principles of etiquette at the Court of France, where, says Madame Campan, the custom of having young ladies wear hoops of three ells in circumference was certainly invented to entrench young princesses so respectably that the malicious gaiety of the French, their proneness to insinuations and too often to calumny, should not by any possibility find an opportunity for attack.

The Dauphine was to find that she had gone too far; the King sent for Madame de Noailles, and indicated his displeasure to her. 'I do not mind if the Dauphine, in the intimacy of her household, gives free course to her gaiety, but in public she must practise more reserve,' he said. And there is no doubt that all Maria Theresa's preaching shows her anxiety lest the alliance should in any way be disturbed. 'Remember always that you are a good German,' she recommended her daughter.

Mercy's strictures were however tempered by praise and in this the Abbé Vermond concurred. 'The Dauphine is acquiring a judgment and insight so far in advance of her years that I am often surprised. To these qualities she adds something more important still, a frankness and truthfulness which even in the smallest matter has never failed.' And Marie Antoinette had the disarming habit of acknowledging her faults, and always hoping and promising to do better. She was lovable and lovely and in Paris where the affairs of Versailles were all known and talked about the verdict was the same. 'There is but one opinion,' wrote Madame du Deffand to Horace Walpole. 'She is becoming more and more beautiful, she is charming.'

Her mother, however, found that her looks had gone off. She had asked for a portrait, and had sent her favourite artist, the painter Liotard, to Paris expressly for this purpose, but not, she says, in négligé or in man's dress. It must be in a costume befitting her position. Later she wrote:

I await your portrait with impatience. I am afraid it has been delayed through your riding and the Carnival. I would like to know whether you dance better than you did when you were here, especially the contre-danse. I hear of an infinite number of Balls, and above all that you are without the Dauphin, and they say that you are changed, this means that you are happy. I begin to be worried that you are not yet Dauphine [she means a real wife]. I am afraid that the Comtesse de Provence will be before you, they tell me great things of her, that she is sweet and of excellent character, and with a very good figure.

But on 24 December 1770 the world was startled by the news of the exiling of the Duc de Choiseul, which agitated the Empress in a particularly personal way. This affair, which was triggered off in a rather ridiculous manner, was in fact the culmination of the enmity between the Duc and Madame Du Barry. He had been the most vigorous opponent of the King's choice and had made no secret of his disdain of the favourite's clique; he was their sworn enemy. The immediate cause of the quarrel was this. One evening at Choisy a play was being given and Madame Du Barry with two of her friends arrived late. All the seats in the front row were occupied by the Court ladies who showed by their looks and still more by their open mockery that they had no intention of moving. The most audacious was the Comtesse de Grammont, the sister-in-law of Madame de Choiseul, and the favourite was forced to seat herself towards the back of the hall. On the following morning the Comtesse received a *lettre de cachet*★ forbidding her to come within fifteen miles of the Court; the whole clan of the Choiseul were up in arms and hurried off for help to the Dauphine. She was furious, but Mercy succeeded in calming her and advised her to apply to the King on the only indisputable point, that a lady attached to her household had been exiled without consulting her. This she did, the embarrassed King made some excuse, but Madame Du Barry was watching and her royal lover did not dare to contradict her. The Duc de Noailles was called in and wrote an obsequious letter to the favourite, who replied that in spite of the insults Madame de Grammont had heaped on her she would not bear rancour, 'only let her stay away from the Court and I will remain indifferent to her'.

★ The *lettre de cachet* was the way by which the King could get rid of unacceptable people without condemning them to death. It sent a man or woman to an indeterminate imprisonment in a Bastille, of which there were thirty in France, that of Paris being the chief. Here they could spend a living death forgotten by all.

But the affair did not stop there, for now Choiseul became implicated. He differed from the King in an argument with England over the possession of an island to which Spain laid claim. Choiseul was ready to support Spain even to the extent of war with England, while the King, who preferred peace at any cost and was constantly whipped up by his mistress against the Duc, finally capitulated and exiled him.

The Empress wrote in haste to her daughter:

I will not deny that I am very disturbed, I have never seen anything in their [the Choiseuls'] behaviour but honesty and humanity, and they were sincerely attached to our alliance. I cannot know the reasons which the King has had for his action, and you even less [the Dauphine, on the contrary, knew very well]. You will need even more now the advice of Mercy and the Abbé, who I am afraid will be much upset by this stroke, but do not allow yourself to adhere to any faction, remain neutral, behave well, please the King and obey your husband.

In these words Maria Theresa shows her ignorance of the habits of the French Court, which was riddled with intrigue. She continued however with some percipience, 'Be more than ever reserved with everyone, I dislike having to say it, even with your aunts; I esteem them, but make no confidences. I know what I am talking about, perhaps better even than Mercy.' At times her fifteen-year-old daughter must have felt that she was doomed to pick her way through a quagmire.

Everyone at Versailles knew that the disgrace of Choiseul was the work of Du Barry, and her associate the Duc d'Aguillon was almost immediately taken by the King as his Foreign Minister. As for the Duc himself, he retired with dignity to his possession at Chanteloupe where he set up a kind of opposition Court, frequented by multitudes of his admirers and sympathizers in opposition to the Royal Court.

What interested Versailles to the exclusion of all other topics was the conduct of the Dauphine. Her affection for Choiseul as the author of her marriage and the Austrian alliance was known and it was expected that she would show disappointment at least, and perhaps resentment. But Mercy was ready with wise advice, she might seem to regret his departure, but no word of displeasure must escape her, she must sorrow for the King's displeasure but not seek to justify her friend nor must she seem to acknowledge his enemies. As usual she obeyed, her behaviour was so circumspect that not even the most avid scandalmonger could find matter for gossip. However, in spite of herself she began to be regarded as the head of the party of revenge, they need only wait, their turn would come, and before too long. Her greatest danger lay in her aunts. By every means in their power they added fuel to her resentment. They reported every word that was said against her; d'Aiguillon spoke of her as a coquette, and Du Barry called her the little redhead. What had been at first only a vague dislike and distrust ripened into a real hatred which was to last her lifetime, and which prompted her to repay d'Aiguillon in kind. It was from the disgrace of Choiseul and his exile that the Dauphine hardened in her treatment of the favourite.

It was at this time that the Comtesse moved into the apartments prepared for her directly above those of the King. Into these rooms, nearer to His Majesty than had been those even of the Pompadour, she transported the most exquisite of her treasures, her Sèvres porcelain painted after Watteau, her wonderful furniture, her pictures, her tapestries, it was a nest fit for a queen, the apartments of the Dauphine could show nothing like it. Here the King visited her by a secret passage and the besotted monarch even transacted business in her apartments. Here all the plans for Court amusements and the engagement of the players were decided, here the Crown Prince of Sweden and other equally important personages were received. Artists, painters, all who hoped for royal favour besieged her antechamber, and Madame du Deffand could declare 'Madame Du Barry is more powerful than her predecessor, or even the Cardinal de Fleury. It is frightful, no one knows where it will finish.' It finished indeed by a '*lit de Justice*', called for 13 April, which was held in the great hall of the Guards in the Château of Versailles. Here the last of the Choiseul party were obliterated, and even the Princes of the Blood, who had refused to attend, were exiled. The Dauphine, who in her innocence hardly understood what was happening, wrote to her mother:

There is a good deal of excitement here. Last Saturday there was a *lit de Justice* to affirm the ending of the old Parlement, and to form a new one. The Princes of the Blood refused to attend and protested against the decision of the King; they wrote a very impertinent letter, and all signed it, except the Comte de la Marche, who behaved very well on this occasion.

Library of
Davidson College

She did not realize what a victory this was for the favourite and d'Aiguillon.

At the end of six months of intrigue and political pressure, d'Aiguillon in fact took the place of Choiseul, and the triumphant Du Barry made every effort to extort at least politeness from her adversary: she complained to d'Aiguillon, to Mercy and finally to the King himself. And now was enacted a pretty little comedy. Mercy found himself one day in the course of his duty in the apartments of the Comtesse who, paying little attention to her other guests, set herself to charm him. Of course Marie Antoinette was informed in no time, and the next day she reproached the Ambassador, who replied 'Madame, today something even more remarkable will take place. I am ordered to meet the King himself in the apartment of Madame Du Barry.' This meeting did in fact take place and in the course of a conversation when the Comtesse had left them alone together, His Majesty urged Mercy to use all his influence with the Dauphine. 'One word will be enough.' This he did, but all the answer he got was that the Dauphine acted as she did for fear of displeasing her aunts. It was a poor excuse, but one must imagine the state of mind of this girl, disappointed in her dreams of a Versailles which would be paradise after the gloomy Court of Vienna. The visions of herself, young, lovely, winning all hearts, the beloved child of the King and the happy wife of a young husband, all these were faded; what remained was the dreary daily intrigue, the poisonous gossip of her aunts, the fear of losing the King's affection, and an unfulfilled marriage.

On hearing that the Dauphine was afraid of displeasing her aunts, Madame Du Barry offered to persuade the King to allow her to be absent from the Court on occasions when his daughters would be present. In fact she was ready to make any concession if only the Dauphine would consent to acknowledge her by a word. Finally the Ambassador, having tried every argument, pointed out to the Dauphine that she was faced with two alternatives. Either she could stand on her dignity and refuse to acknowledge Madame Du Barry, thereby showing that she knew the true status of a woman whom she despised, or she could pretend to ignore the character of the favourite, and treat her like any other lady who had been presented at Court and who appeared there with the approbation of the King and his family.

But still Marie Antoinette remained firm in her determination to disregard the existence of the 'creature'.

Then Mercy played his last card. He represented to the Dauphine the danger which might threaten the Franco-Austrian alliance if she persisted in thus affronting the King's desire. Her loyalty to the creator of this alliance, Choiseul, might destroy his work, and bring her mother's cherished policy to disaster. This last argument seems to have been successful, the Dauphine capitulated and consented to speak at least a word to the Du Barry, but in the presence of Mercy. It was arranged that the Ambassador should bring the Comtesse to the Dauphine's 'Circle' on a Sunday night and the 'word' would be spoken as it were, by chance. On the night arranged all was set, the Dauphine began her round, a word to this one and to that. As she approached the Comtesse, Madame Adélaïde suddenly called, 'It is late, let us go, we will wait for the King in the apartment of my sister Victoire.' Marie Antoinette turned. All was over; she had imprudently told her aunts about the arrangement, and they had with malice ruined the whole plan.

When the Empress heard from Mercy that the plan had failed her anger knew no bounds, in a letter she trounced her daughter.

What, just a word, a remark about a dress or some such thing costs you so much. I am afraid you are too much influenced by your Aunts. If you will only read what I have written you on this subject you will see what I mean. You are afraid to talk to the King, you will not speak to others to whom it is your duty to speak. You should see the Du Barry as a lady admitted to the Court and to the Society of the King.

She goes on and on and then adds that all this is not for the sake of grumbling, but because she loves her daughter so much that she wishes to help her. How many mothers have done the same and how many daughters have become tired of it. Maria Theresa and her confidants seem to have overlooked the fact which Marie Antoinette insists upon, that she was nearer to the problem than they were. This admirable woman, sitting in her little study in the Hofburg and writing, writing, writing, had no real insight into the world of Versailles. With a mixture of intuition and a wisdom beyond her years Marie Antoinette had judged Madame Du Barry from the first, and her revulsion against the sort of woman she saw was so strong that she could not force herself to enter into any contact with her. It was this, more than the constant pressure of the aunts, which made her inflexible against Du Barry and her creature d'Aiguillon. At this point Kaunitz entered the lists; he dictated a speech which he advised the Dauphine to make to the King: 'My dear Papa, the Duke d'Aiguillon has remarked to the Comte de Mercy that you have observed in me a too strong aversion towards some of those who form your society. Do me the favour to say exactly what you wish me to do and deign to believe that you will be exactly obeyed.' A great deal of this insistence sprang from a political anxiety; for the Empress and her Ambassador it was imperative that the King's friendship for Austria should be preserved. She wrote to Mercy, 'My daughter must keep in the favour of the King, she must treat the Favourite properly and consider the benefit it will be to both our courts and perhaps even to the alliance.' And Mercy in reply, 'It is necessary that Mme the Dauphine acts favourably towards Mme Du Barry so that I may be able to make use of the Comtesse.' But the sixteen-year-old girl was not to be moved. 'If you were near enough, as I am, to see everything which happens here, you would know that this woman and her clique will never be satisfied with a single word, they will always go further and demand more.'

But now Mercy, in his capacity of experienced diplomat and amateur of the young ladies of the Opera, and believing that all that was necessary was to detach the Dauphine from her aunts' influence, set himself by every means to do this, aided by letters from the Empress. Even Kaunitz, who saw the whole affair in the terms of the Franco-Austrian Alliance, entered into the battle with a long dissertation on the power of Madame Du Barry and the pernicious exhortations of Madame Adélaïde. For the question of the partition of Poland was the object of the Austrian Chancellor's deepest preoccupations; the Emperor Joseph was only too eager to add to his possessions by a part of the booty, though his mother was equally against Frederick and the Tsarina's plan to dismember the unfortunate country. In order that their policy might succeed it was necessary to have the tacit consent of France, and Louis xv, the son-in-law of the late King Stanislas, might very easily be persuaded to cast his weight on the other side if Marie Antoinette continued to offend his beloved mistress. So the whole affair was high politics. The Empress wrote:

You follow nobody but your Aunts. I esteem them, but they have never understood how to make themselves esteemed either by the public or by their family, and you wish to take the same road . . . Their influence is the cause of all your mistakes . . . Is my advice, my tenderness, of less value to you than theirs? I must admit, such a reflection wounds my heart.

To which her daughter replied that such a thing could never be, but she did not add that she would change her conduct. Now the affair had reached a point where Mercy really feared that the Dauphine might be laying up serious trouble not only for herself but for the alliance. In a letter of 19 December 1771 to the Empress he wrote:

Having regard to the character of the people who govern the King one cannot too much suspect the possible effects of their bad faith. The King, not old by the number of his years but by the sort of life he leads, becomes always weaker, he may disappear in a short time. The dominant party cannot contemplate this event without trembling, above all when they attribute to the Dauphine a hatred and spirit of vengeance which they judge by their own manner of thinking and acting. They see too that Madame acquires more and more power over the Dauphin, and thus affairs will one day rest in her hands in consequence. These reflections, occasioned by the fear which a bad conscience always induces, might produce some very strange results on the part of these atrocious people, who will see no other means of saving themselves, and who will stop at nothing.

What Mercy feared above all was that to get rid of a Dauphine who had after all not produced an heir to the throne might be considered in the light of events which had been known to occur at the Court of France, or simply of an abdication. However on New Year's Day 1772, she finally gave in and, one must believe for the sake of a little peace, condescended to say to Madame Du Barry at the King's reception: 'There are a great many people at Versailles today.' It was the event of the day, all Versailles talked of it, in the Paris salons it was discussed, the Du Barry was in raptures, and the King heaped compliments on his granddaughter. To her husband the Archduchess said, 'I have spoken this one time, but I have made up my mind to stop at that, this woman will never again hear my voice.' And to her mother she wrote:

Madame, my beloved Mother, I do not doubt that Mercy had informed you of my conduct on New Year's Day, and I hope that you are satisfied with it. You must believe that I will always sacrifice my prejudices and repugnances as long as I am not asked to do anything contrary to my honour. It would break my heart if there were any quarrel between my two families. It is very hard to do my duty here.

This affair has a great significance for any study of Marie Antoinette's life and character. She proved over and over again her inability to compromise, she could neither trust persons of whose character she disapproved, nor come to terms with them. One may admire this uncompromising attitude, but it can also be extremely dangerous in political life. Her husband, on the contrary, has been depicted as a vacillating uncertain character, but we shall see how in his defence of the monarchy, which was after all his reason for living, he was willing to come to terms with conditions which *au fond* he detested, but by which he might achieve his aim. One cannot call Marie Antoinette simply obstinate, it was an affair of character, stronger than herself, and if she was finally obliged to give in, she did it with regret and a bad grace. Poor young thing, the dull life in a rigid etiquette-ridden Court, the constant preaching of her mother, with no friend who could enter into her difficulties other than her husband, who shared her antipathies but did not contribute to her happiness, one must feel deep pity for her. And admiration too for her constant good humour, the gentleness of her replies, an admiration which Mercy conveyed to the Empress on more than one occasion.

The year 1772 took on a somewhat happier hue. She wrote to Maria Theresa that her dear husband showed great affection for her, and apparently had more confidence in her. She could tease him about his slovenly dress and his greediness, and even try to dissuade him from his inordinate love of building and carpentry. In this she was rather less successful, and nothing would keep him away from the workmen around the palace, from whom he always returned covered in plaster. However when his brother Provence married the Princess Marie Josèphe of Savoy the Dauphin did not refuse to make one of an agreeable quartet. The four young people got on very well together, and were joined by the Dukes of Chartres and Bourbon and their wives, and amused themselves by secretly acting small plays and comedies, a habit which Marie Antoinette had grown up with in her own home, when the Court poet Metastasio had written for her brothers and sisters plays which Christoph Willibald von Gluck set to music.

Her brother-in-law Provence insisted that he was very well pleased with his plain wife and indeed he might well be, for Marie Josèphe lost no time in becoming pregnant. 'Is it true?' asked the Dauphine. 'Certainly, Madame,' replied the proud father, 'there is no day when it may not be true.' 'We are very happy together,' she wrote her mother, 'and I hope it will always be so. My sister is very sweet, very easy and very gay ... I was afraid that she would be absorbed into the party of M. de Vauguyon and Madame Du Barry but she spoke very reasonably about them to me.'

She added that she would not comment on the appointment of Monsieur d'Aiguillon as Foreign Minister since she did not meddle with politics, but she warned her mother about the Coadjutor Prince Louis de Rohan who had been named as the next ambassador to Vienna. He came from a great family, she said, but his life was undesirable, and resembled more that of a soldier than a prelate. To which Maria Theresa replied as always that her duty was to respect the King's choice. Here again we are confronted by an affair small in itself which would have enormous consequences in the life of Marie Antoinette. She had found at the Court of Versailles besides her husband's brothers his two sisters, Mesdames Clothilde and Elisabeth, whose education was in the hands of Madame de Marsan. Madame Clothilde was the less attractive of the two, being so excessively fat that she was always known as *la grosse Madame*. Madame Elisabeth was a very pious gentle girl and the Dauphine soon struck up a friendship with her; this annoyed the governess, for she was sorry for the ugly sister, and always tried to bring her forward. She revenged herself by commenting unfavourably on the education which Maria Theresa had given her youngest daughter and this brought the Abbé Vermond into the fray; he riposted by criticizing Madame de Marsan and of course all that he said was faithfully reported to that lady, whose salon became the centre of gossip and intrigue against the Dauphine. They criticized her gaiety, her wit, her love of fun, and all this was retailed in Vienna by the new Ambassador de Rohan, his excuse to the Empress being his concern for her daughter's reputation. Maria Theresa at last became suspicious, and sent her private secretary, the Baron de Neni, to Versailles, to report to her on Rohan's accusations. This he did, and, says Madame Campan, 'the Empress detected under the calumnies proofs of the enmity of a party which had never approved of the alliance of the House of Bourbon with her own.' All this was known to the Dauphine and was added to her continuing dislike of Rohan.

The truth was that the Dauphine had never been so popular, so admired, and she was to have proof of this very shortly, for at last the King had consented to the Entry of his heirs to their City of Paris. It was three years since the first lamentable arrival there and the Dauphine had long wished that the traditional Entry might be permitted. Since the wars of the Fronde the Bourbons had avoided Paris, latterly Louis xv had deserted the city alto-gether and neither his queen nor his daughters had ever seen it. But when at last Marie Antoinette summoned up her courage and frankly asked the King's consent, he could hardly refuse it. The Entry was fixed for 18 June, and the citizens threw themselves into preparation for the great event.

The unwisdom of the isolation of the Court at Versailles was to show itself only in the tragic happenings of later years; in Paris admiration of the Dauphine's stand against the hated favourite reached from the common people to the salons, the country felt dispirited and ashamed, decent folks kept away from the Court and only intriguing adventurers remained. The writings of Jean-Jacques Rousseau and the Encyclopedists had disseminated new ideas, and all the King's burnings of books on the Place de Grève were not enough to stifle them. Admiration for the English Constitution, which Voltaire had brought back from his stay in the island, excited the young philosophers and added fuel to their disgust with the monarchy, which resorted to every means for filling its empty treasury. The Abbé Terray had no resource but to redouble the taxes, edicts which the Parlement refused to register flowed from his office and in the country his agents found themselves faced with a misery so great that it resulted in sporadic risings, brutally suppressed. Through all this the people, who had lost all love and respect for their King, saw in the persons of the young Dauphin and his wife their only hope, and the wave of enthusiasm which greeted their visit to the capital city was its expression.

When the day arrived the Governor, Marshal de Brissac, set off at eight in the morning with his cortège to meet the two royalties arriving from Versailles at the Gate of the Conference, and at eleven the cannon from the Invalides began to thunder. The bands played and soon the people, massed on either side of the gate saw the procession of the Dauphin and Dauphine escorted by the household guard of His Majesty. They were accompanied by the old Marshal de Richelieu, whom neither of them loved very much for his support of Du Barry. But he was the First Gentleman of the Chamber and as such had the right to accompany the royal guests. The whole of Paris was in the streets and the crowds could not find sufficient means of manifesting their joy. But let Marie Antoinette describe it all herself. She wrote to her mother:

I had last Tuesday a day which I shall remember all my life. We made our entrée into Paris. We have received all the honours which one can imagine but it was not they which touched me the most though it was good, but the tenderness and kindness of this poor people, who in spite of the heavy taxes they bear, were in transports of joy at the sight of us. When we went to walk in the Tuileries there was such an enormous crowd that we could not move for three-quarters of an hour. The Dauphin and I repeatedly told the guard not to strike anyone, which had a very good effect, but there was such orderliness during the day that in spite of the crowds which followed us everywhere no one was hurt. How fortunate we are in our state to gain the love of the people for so little. Tomorrow we will go to the opera in Paris and I think on two other days to the Comédie Française and the Comédie Italienne. I realize every day more and more what my dear Mama has done for me. I was the youngest and you have treated me as the eldest; my heart is filled with tender gratitude.

This touching recognition of the generosity and good humour of the ordinary people was matched by the Dauphine's own tact. On reaching Versailles her first words to the King were: 'Sire, your Majesty must be well loved by the people of Paris, for they have given us such a welcome.' Nothing could be more calculated to disarm any jealousy which Louis might have felt. In fact this visit set a crown on the popularity of Marie Antoinette, she had reached a point which she was never after to attain. The people, so little spoiled by their monarchs, who for the last two reigns had kept aloof and unknown in their palaces, opened their hearts to the vision of youth and beauty, and even the Dauphin, usually so awkward, was moved to a more friendly attitude as he walked with his radiant wife on his arm. In the words of an observer: 'The Dauphine has persuaded her husband to adopt a very good habit. A Prince who wishes to be the Father of his people cannot show himself too often in the company of his family.' And Mercy wrote to the Empress that volumes could be written on the praise of the Dauphine which could be heard on every side from the people in the gutters to the elegants in the salons.

Marie Antoinette's letters breathe love and tenderness at this time; her patience and submissiveness to her mother's constant criticism are exemplary. She applauds the Dauphin, his behaviour during the entrée could not have been better, at the Comédie Italienne she was in tears when the public cried, with all the actors, *'Vive le Roi'* and one of them added 'and his dear children'. She compares it to the time when her mother had announced the birth of her first grandson, and adds:

Although I was only a child I felt how greatly all hearts were touched by the happiness of my tender mother. The Dauphin was wonderful all the time he was in Paris and if I dare to say it, he has gained immensely through the air of friendship which showed between us. Perhaps it is this which put about the rumour that he kissed me publicly, though this is not true; but my dear Maman is deceived if she thinks that he has not done so since my arrival here. On the contrary, everyone remarks on his attention to me.

But when Mercy wrote to the Empress he received the same cold douche as always.

Three years of life at the French Court had taught the Dauphine many lessons, not the least of which was that few people were to be trusted, and her good sense told her that her aunts were not among these few. She was later to say to Mercy, 'When I arrived in this country I was too young and too lacking in experience. I gave myself entirely to my aunts, who led me into many mistakes. I know better now how to exercise my judgment.' But in freeing herself from this doubtful influence she left herself open to spite and revenge. She knew it and said so, she and the Dauphin kept their own counsel and laid themselves open to as little slander as possible. At the presentation of Madame Du Barry's niece she had been icily polite, having heard that the King had

not addressed a word to either of the ladies. Everyone had seemed
content with her behaviour. Not her mother, who immediately
replied from Esterhazy, where she had gone on a pleasure tour,
although she had not wanted to, being too old for such amusements and trailing over the dusty roads. It is to be hoped that the
Mass which Haydn wrote for the occasion consoled her somewhat.
In this sour humour she wrote to her daughter:

I do not agree with you about your treatment of the young Du
Barry. What you tell me about the King's good humour does not
reassure me. One of these days you will find yourself alone in this
wrong behaviour; you have already felt the change in your Aunt
[Adélaïde] so now, no false pride in reversing your ways, the goodness
of the King well merits this attention and indulgence on your part.

It is remarkable that Marie Antoinette put up for so long with
her mother's criticism, and perhaps the reason was that she knew
only too well that a great deal of it was true. She defended herself but always promised to do better. She was after all very
young; if she played with the children of her attendants or with
their dogs, it was from a childish longing for games which the
well-meaning but rigid etiquette of her chief lady-in-waiting,
the Comtesse de Noailles, could not tolerate. All this was balanced by her excellent qualities. She meant so well, but the frivolity of her nature was more easily noticeable than her modesty,
her compassion, her humanity. Mercy and Vermond insisted
on all these in their letters, but nothing would convince the
Empress. 'I am persuaded,' wrote Vermond, 'that if Your Majesty
would sympathize with the weakness of youth and accustom her
daughter to regard her as a friend, she will have great satisfaction.' He had noted, no doubt, that the Dauphine was beginning
to think that her mother no longer loved her, and Kaunitz in
his brusque way advised the Empress 'not to lose her time in
preaching to her daughter for it did no good and might annoy
her. Just use her for the good of the Empire and that will be
enough.'
As a result the Confessor and the Ambassador embarked on
a course of political instruction, greatly to the distress of their
pupil, who had little taste for such matters. For her, politics were
mainly the affair of personalities, and this can be understood if
one remembers that apart from her journey from Vienna, she

had never seen – and would never see – any of the country or the people whose Queen she would one day be. She was moved by the 'good people' of Paris; what did she know of their lives, their hopes or fears? But she tried to understand, she hoped her brother would not meet the King of Prussia, she was interested in the affairs of Parma, but she soon fell into her old distaste, hoping only that one day perhaps she would finish by understanding politics.

However, at the end of the year 1773 she could feel some satis-faction, she was admired at Court, adored by the people, and best of all she had completely changed her husband, who was now devoted to her. He said she always gave him good advice, she amused him and above all she was tolerant of his infirmity. For after three years of marriage it was evident that something was radically wrong with Louis August. The excuse of youth and dormant sensuality could no longer be valid, all the more since he was now in love with his wife, and both made every effort towards a normal life together. But the deformation of the organ, which might have been set right with little trouble in early child-hood now gave him so much pain at certain moments, that no result could ever be reached. The doctors spoke to him of the small operation which would, they said, put everything right, but even a small operation in those days of no anaesthetics could be agonizing, and the mere sight of the instruments discouraged the Dauphin. So the unfortunate couple kept on, hoping always that nature and a more violent desire would put matters right. Mercy, who knew everything, speaks of the Dauphine's tears, and her husband's sad question, 'Do you love me?' 'Yes,' was the reply, 'you must not doubt it. I love you truly, and I esteem you even more.' The young prince appeared much moved, he caressed his wife tenderly and promised her that when they returned to Versailles he would recommence his régime and there he hoped that all would be well. But Mercy reported in December that hope appeared to be as far off as ever.

In the midst of this disappointing and humiliating life Marie Antoinette took what amusements offered themselves. She went to masked balls in Paris just as her mother had done in Vienna, and like her was agreeably stimulated when she could flirt with a stranger under cover of her domino. On one night she arrived late and noticed a young man who had recently been presented

An engraving on the occasion of the marriage of Marie Antoinette's brother, Joseph, to Princess Josepha of Bavaria in 1765

Madame Du Barry by Richard Cosway

Car ayant dormie 12 heure
et demie toute desuite
il ses trouve tresbien
portant et en état de
partire nous somme
donc de peris hier ici
ou on est prié 1 heure
ou l'on dine jusqu'a
1 heure du soir sans
rentrer chez soi se que
me déplait fort car après
le diné l'on joue jusqu'à
5 heure que l'on vat au
spectacle qui dure
jusqu'a 9 heures et demie
et en suite le soupe de
la encore jeu jusqu'a
... heure et meme la demie
quelquefois mais le Roi

Madame très chere Mere
Je ne peu vous exprimer
combien j'etoit touchée
bonté que Votre Majesté
marque et je lui jure que
je n'ai pas encore recu
de ses chers Lettres sans avo
les larmes aux yeux de
... d'être d'une aussi tendre
bonne Mere et quoique
suis tres bien icy je So
rai pourtant ardemmen
de revenir voir ma c...
et tres chere famille
moins pour un instan...
Je suis au desespoir
v: M: n'a pas recu m...
j'ai crut quelle yrai...
... le courier ma...
Mercy a jugé appr...

The first letter written
by Marie Antoinette from
Paris, to her mother

Madame Adélaïde

to her; he was attractive, tall, handsome, and she enjoyed a conversation with him without revealing her identity. But as the crowd began to gather she was forced to depart. The stranger was Count Axel Fersen, the son of a Field-Marshal in the Swedish Army and he was making the grand tour of Europe. He noted in his *Journal* that he had met the Dauphine – just the note, no more.

Tormented by a husband who awakened her senses without ever satisfying them, she threw herself more and more into a round of distraction, though her pleasures had their serious side too. In the autumn of 1773 Christoph Willibald von Gluck arrived in Paris. What joy, what excitement to welcome her old tutor, someone fresh from her beloved Vienna. This was something different from the visits of stiff Court worthies, and he would bring different music too. He did indeed, but she was soon made aware that his music was not at all to the taste of the French. He had sent his score of the opera *Iphigénie* to the director of the Paris opera, who had returned it affirming that such music was written with the intent to kill all the traditional French opera. In addition he had done his best to prevent Gluck from coming to France, but the Austrian Ambassador, whose mistress was one of the leading operatic stars, was able to exert his influence and the composer duly arrived and presented himself to his former pupil. It seemed like a breath of clear air for Marie Antoinette, someone who knew her, and all her family: together they could reminisce and together plan for success. She wrote to her mother that she was playing again her 'dear harp' and she sang with him – though not always in tune. And then, more important than all, he played for her his opera *Iphigénie*, inspired by the great tragedy of Racine, and bearing all the marks of his own original genius. What did Gluck want to do with opera, and why did his music arouse such varied reactions of love and hate in the public? In his own words:

I wished to avoid all those abuses which had crept into Italian operas through the mistaken vanity of singers and the complicity of composers ... I endeavoured to give to operatic music its proper function, that of seconding poetry by enforcing the expression of the sentiment and the interest of the situations, without interrupting the action or weakening it by superfluous ornament.

The rehearsals began, and enchanted Marie Antoinette, but the interpreters were less enthusiastic. Deprived of the opportunity to display their roulades and graces, the music seemed to them flat and dull, though with time they were forced to acknowledge its grandeur. The scenes and battles at the opera house were calmed by the Dauphine who was determined that her composer should have his triumph, all the more because a strong faction against him had arisen headed by such arbiters of fashion as Marmontel and d'Alembert, the darlings of the salons. They fetched Piccini from Naples and set him up in opposition and the public divided itself into two battalions, the Gluckists and the Piccinists. The date of the first performance had already been fixed, when the principal tenor fell ill. Horror! Could he be replaced? 'No,' said Gluck. What could be done, for the Royal Family had engaged themselves for this first evening. And to the surprise of everyone the impossible happened, the Family changed its date, and on 19 April the curtain went up on *Iphigénie*, the work which revolutionized opera. The audience was brilliant; all were there, except possibly the Comtesse Du Barry, who had headed the opposition; the reception was favourable, the majority of the listeners were moved by this 'German' music, with its simplicity and lofty majesty. 'With this music,' wrote one hearer, 'one might found a religion,' and Jean-Jacques Rousseau exclaimed: 'Since one can have so much pleasure during two hours I imagine that life is worth while after all.'

By the beginning of the year 1774 both the Empress and Mercy were aware that the King was unlikely to last much longer, and more and more they realized that the definitive role in the new reign would be in the hands of Marie Antoinette. 'It is necessary,' Mercy wrote, 'that she should begin to think of the authority which the Dauphin will never be able to handle with sufficient strength.' To which the Empress replied:

I tell you frankly that I cannot wish that my daughter should be too influential in affairs, I know only too well through my own experience what a grievous load government and monarchy can be. Moreover I know the youth and volatility of my daughter, which joined to her lack of taste for application makes me fear for the success of the government of a monarchy as rotten as that of France is at present.

Maria Theresa was not thinking only of her daughter and France; she was a prey at this time to very grave concern for her own country. Since the year 1771 Frederick II of Prussia had been pursuing a policy which would inevitably lead to the partition of Poland; together with Catherine of Russia he had begun by defeating the Turks and continued his success by demands which would have chased them completely from Europe and divided their possessions with Russia and Austria. This the Empress vigorously opposed, though the Emperor Joseph supported it. This refusal infuriated the Empress Catherine and her Cabinet, who knew in addition that their plots were supported by Frederick. The result of Kaunitz's Eastern policy was that Austria was suddenly confronted, as the defender of the Turks, with a war with Prussia and Russia together. Step by step during the years 1771 and 1772 Maria Theresa was led along a path of which she disapproved in her inmost being, until in February 1772 Russia and Prussia signed a treaty partitioning Poland and offering to Austria participation in the neighbouring countries. Kaunitz found himself in a difficult situation. Ought he to follow the Empress in her refusal to profit from the misfortune of Poland, or should he consider only the advantage to Austria of an expansion of her territories? He proposed to the Empress that she should waive her objections if Poland were compensated by the cession of Moldavia and Wallachia, provinces which Turkey would in any case lose.

But now Joseph took a hand. His ideas were totally opposed to those of his mother and he forced Kaunitz to withdraw his proposal. Why should Austria be more idealistic than Russia or Prussia? she should profit by the occasion to enlarge her territories. The Empress was in despair:

I have never been in such anguish in my whole life. When my country was attacked I rested on my rights and on Divine Goodness, but in a case like the present when right is not on my side, nothing is left me but the anxiety of a heart which is unaccustomed to duplicity. Good faith is the most precious jewel which a monarch can possess, and we have lost it forever.

In such complicated circumstances it is easier to understand the Empress's letters to her daughter, and the reiterated advice to her never to alienate the favourite and through her the King. She was haunted night and day by the spectre of Austria's danger and the fear of war with an unassailable enemy. The behaviour of France in this situation is more obscure. The public was surprised and horrified when they learned of the entry of an Austrian Army into Poland and the occupation of Lemberg. Louis xv was less surprised, for he had been kept informed by his secret agents of the intentions of the three powers. Now Mercy and the Empress redoubled their efforts, for they realized how much a Du Barry favourable to Austria could influence political climate. They left no stone unturned, no argument unspoken. Mercy even went so far as to quote the case of the sons of Noah who threw a cloak over their father's nakedness, a way of indicating that Marie Antoinette should veil the weaknesses of the King. At last the troubled young woman seemed to flinch. One day, returning from Mass she said to the Ambassador, 'I have prayed. I said, My God if You will that I should speak, make me speak. I will follow Your inspiration.' Mercy at once replied that perhaps the voice of her august mother might be taken for that of the Almighty, and some moments after, seeing the favourite passing with her friend Madame d'Aiguillon the Dauphine said, with her eyes on Du Barry, 'It is such bad weather, one cannot walk in it.' Taken as Divine inspiration it was not much, but it had its effect. It was followed by a series of small incidents in which she relaxed her extreme distaste, she even allowed Du Barry to appear in her circle, which the Comtesse lost no time in recounting to the King. France registered no opposition to the partition of Poland, apart from the public clamour, which was great. Satirical verses, disgusted cartoons flooded the press, but without avail. The deed was done and Frederick could write to d'Alembert, 'The Empress Catherine and I are two brigands; but that Empress Queen, how will she reconcile herself with her confessor?' He was indeed incapable of understanding such a woman as Maria Theresa, who crucified herself for what seemed for the good of her Empire. And her daughter unwittingly had lent herself to political plots of whose far-reaching nature she could have had no clear idea, so involved were they with palace intrigue.

On 27 April 1774, eight days after the successful presentation of Gluck's *Iphigénie*, the King was seized by a sudden chill. He was at Trianon, and was immediately taken to Versailles where his doctors attended him, and decided that although he had a fever his state was not a cause for anxiety. He wished only to see Madame Du Barry. On the next day, when the Dauphine visited him, he seemed worse, he had been bled twice, and was surrounded by a crowd of doctors, surgeons and apothecaries, who had only one subject in mind; should the King be bled a third time? The question was crucial, for a third bleeding was the signal for the reception of the sacraments, and these the King could not receive as long as he kept his mistress. On the third day it was acknowledged that the King had the smallpox, the Dauphin and his wife were confined to their own apartments where only the Counts of Provence and Artois and their wives could be with them. The unfortunate Dauphin, suddenly presented with the unalterable fact of his approaching accession, could only weep and say, 'I feel as if the universe was falling about my ears.' In this sad case Marie Antoinette rose to heights of devotion and kindness, she spent herself in strengthening his failing spirits, to comforting his sense of terror at what lay before him. 'She behaved like an angel,' wrote Mercy and indeed throughout the following days her conduct was irreproachable. The whole château was on tenterhooks; all knew that with the third bleeding would come the confession and the obligation to dismiss his mistress, and that would mean the dismissal of d'Aiguillon. In this crisis the behaviour of the King's daughters surprised everyone. With a singular devotion they refused to leave the sick man. Madame Adélaïde undertook the direction of everything, but she was not able to forbid the King to see his mistress, who arrived when Mesdames had retired and stayed the night with him, holding his hand and wiping his forehead with her handkerchief. Unfortunately no one believed that it was from love that these women undertook this revolting task, for the Court was far less interested in the condition of the King than in the political changes which might result from it. As for the public of Paris, there was no sign of regret or pity. Nobody remembered the days of his youthful glory, only his excesses, the heaviness of his taxations, the failure of his policies. Prayers were offered in the empty churches, the reliquary of the Patron Saint Geneviève was opened without a person to bow before it. All hoped for only one thing, his death, and the opening of a new and more hopeful régime.

Of the young people, Marie Antoinette was the only one who had been inoculated, following the new fashion imported into Vienna from Turkey, and she offered to stay with Mesdames beside the King. This was however not allowed. At last, on 7 May, the King consented to make his confession and to receive the Communion after thirty-eight years of abstinence. But first he took leave of Madame Du Barry, who departed, taking with her d'Aiguillon who would naturally be involved in her fall.

In the early morning of 7 May all had been prepared for the

solemn act which would prepare the dying King for his long rest. The Regiment of Guards and the Swiss formed a path along which proceeded the clergy of the Parish, the bishops and the Cardinal de La Roche Aymon, the grand Almoner of France, bearing the sacred vessels. Followed by the Dauphin and his two brothers, the Princes and Princesses of the Blood, the high officers of the Crown, the ministers of State, all bearing lighted candles, they reached the top of the staircase leading to the royal apartment, where Mesdames awaited them. Marie Antoinette with the Comtesse de Provence knelt in the Council Room, and through the open door she could see for the last time King Louis xv. What she saw was frightful, his face was unrecognizable, covered with suppurating sores, the mouth open in agony. In spite of all the open windows the stench was almost insupportable, but in his swollen hands he held the crucifix which his daughter Madame Louise had sent from her convent.

The low tones of the ceremony reached her terrified ears, and she longed for the ordeal to be over, but hardly had La Roche Aymon said the last words than the King's confessor, who was also her own, the Abbé Maudoux, spoke in his ear. The King wished to make a public confession, it was the price which the good Abbé had exacted in return for the absolution. The Cardinal Almoner was forced to agree, and advancing to the door he spoke to the royal pair and to the assembled Court. 'Sirs, the King commands me to say to you that he asks God's pardon for the scandal and offence which he has caused Him and his people; if God grants his recovery he will show his penitence, support religion, and comfort his peoples.' The words fell into a silence as of a tomb, it was the repudiation of all the ignoble elements which had surrounded him.

But the unhappy sufferer was not dead yet, still he lingered; the Dauphin had given orders for the immediate departure of the Court to Choisy; in the courtyards the carriages stood ready, through the open windows came the horrible odours of the death chamber which no fumigation could dispel. All waited for the agreed signal, a lighted candle placed in a window which would be extinguished the moment the monarch expired. At a quarter past three on 10 May the light went out and at the door of the Oeil de Bœuf the Duc de Bouillon, the Grand Chamberlain, announced 'The King is dead, long live the King!'

The Dauphin and his wife were in their apartment awaiting the terrifying news. It might come at any moment now, and suddenly they were struck by an extraordinary noise, like distant thunder, an explosion of sound. It came from the immense crowd of the Court who had been watching for the signal of the King's death. Through the Palace they raced, along the Gallery of Mirrors till they were halted by the door to the royal apartment. It was opened, as was her right, by Madame de Noailles, and they saw their King and Queen on their knees. Weeping, they embraced each other, crying, 'Oh God protect us, we are too young to reign.'

This touching anecdote, reported by Madame Campan, may be true, it has been accepted as such by generations of biographers, but it seems to us that though the King's death was shocking, the young people could not have refrained from speculating upon its imminence for some time. Marie Antoinette, as she wrote her mother, had been reading history – the *Mémoires de l'Estoile*, an account of the reigns of Charles IX, Henri III and Henri IV. 'One sees day by day how everything happened in those days, the good and the bad, the laws and the customs. I find the names and sometimes the origins of the people who are at our Court.' And later she says that she is reading Hume's history of England, doubtless in her husband's translation. She has been so constantly represented as too frivolous to read or to think about anything but pleasure, that it is justifiable to see in these chance statements another Marie Antoinette. She had been married four years and during this time she and her husband had come to understand each other better than it has been thought. His influence on her can be seen from time to time in her letters and she was too innately decent, too kind-hearted not to sympathize with him in his physical disability.

And what Louis XVI thought about his grandfather and his own accession can be seen through his first acts. He was a good student of history, and as such he must have been well aware that the last two Kings of France had died execrated by their subjects. Louis XIV, after raising France to a peak of glory, succeeded in making himself as hated as he had formerly been beloved. His body was accompanied to the tomb by a populace screaming insults or gloating over the verses written by the pamphleteers of the day:

Que je vous plains pauvres Français,
Soumis à cet empire
Faites comme l'ont fait les Anglais
C'est assez vous en dire.*

The deficit was 78 millions, the public debt two and a half milliards, only the poorest classes were taxed, the aristocracy and the Church going off scot-free.

And now Louis xv, 'the Well-Beloved' whom his people had idolized had left them in even worse case. The libertine who said *'Après moi le déluge'* had made an edifying end, but his people were not much impressed, as the following demonstrate:

Louis a rempli sa carrière
Et fini ses tristes destins
Tremblez voleurs, fuyez putains,
Vous avez perdu votre père. †

or

Ci gît qui nous a donne le système en naissant, la guerre en grandis-
sant, famine en vieillissant, et la peste en mourant. ††

No wonder the new King and Queen were overwhelmed by the obligations of the task before them.

---

*I pity you poor Frenchmen / Subject to this rule / Do as did the English / With that enough is said.'

† Louis has ended his career
  And attained his sad destiny
  Tremble you thieves, take flight you whores
  For you have lost your father.

†† Here lies the one who gave us the system at birth, war in manhood, famine in old age, and the pest in dying.

3

The Young Queen

WITHOUT loss of time the Court transferred itself to Choisy, while the remains of the late King were hustled off by night to the royal tomb in St Denis. Louis xv was the only King of France whose heart was buried with him, for when according to custom the first Surgeon, Monsieur Andouille, was ordered to open the body he refused. It would be his death, he assured the Duc de Villequier; however, if the Duke would hold the head he would operate. The Duke promptly disappeared and the stinking corpse was hastily dropped into a coffin filled with spirits of wine. It arrived by night in Paris to be met by exultant crowds crying 'tally-ho' in imitation of the King encouraging his hounds. Such was the lamentable end of Louis the Well-Beloved.

Only one person wept for him, Madame Du Barry. As State prisoner she was escorted to the Abbey of Pont aux Dames. D'Aiguillon left with her. The Court mourning, however, was all embracing and magnificent, millions of livres were spent on black for the Princes, purple for the King and Queen, 322,000 livres for their carriages alone. All the lackeys had new clothes, all the furniture was draped in sombre stuffs, and the uniforms of the grooms of the stables and officers cost a fortune. For a country on the brink of bankruptcy this seems excessive, but the show must go on.

In Paris the scene was completely different: tears were shed it is true, says a biographer, but they were the sentimental tears of tender feeling for the young pair. But, says Madame Campan, the anti-Austrian party let no opportunity slip to cast some malicious comment on the young Queen, and very soon Marie Antoinette's unfortunate spirit of mockery betrayed her. At La Muette gathered all the ladies who had the right and the honour to present themselves in homage and condolence to the new Queen. Young and old they gathered; there were pretty young women in the latest modes, and aged grandmothers up from their country estates perhaps, in clothes which might be heirlooms. The ceremony was long and one of the ladies-in-waiting, the Marquise de Clermont-Tonnerre, exhausted, took the opportunity of resting on the floor hidden behind the wide panniers of the other ladies' robes. There she amused herself in a very stupid way, pulling at their gowns, making droll faces and was so funny that the Queen, in spite of the solemnity of the occasion could not help smiling behind her fan. It was noticed, and the noble old ladies decided audibly that the Queen made fun of those who had troubled themselves to do her honour, that she cared only for the young, and that never again would they be seen at Court. The story spread to Paris and next day as usual ribald verses celebrated the Queen's folly.

Four days after the accession Marie Antoinette wrote her mother, who had already formed her own opinion of the event. The King and Queen were too young, if only they could have had a few more years. 'I find nothing which calms me, my daughter has never known how to apply herself, and this will be a great obstacle for her.' This was also the opinion of Prince Xavier of Saxony. 'It remains to be seen,' said he, 'whether the Queen will have an influence in affairs. If she has it augurs badly, for she is inconsequent, and completely Austrian. She is so flighty and so childish that she will never follow a system.' In Marie Antoinette, her double nature fought; the good solid German girl, well brought up, pious, obedient and well meaning was counteracted by the Lorraine, easygoing, pleasure and beauty loving, seeking amusement and friends, affectionate and faithful to those she cared for. Neither of these characteristics was French; the caustic wit which she possessed was her undoing. This was seized upon by her enemies, who were not a few, and brought to the public notice.

But for the moment she was happy, she saw only the brilliant future, the glorious present. Her next letter to her mother shows it: 'The new King seems to possess his People's heart, he works ceaselessly, and replies with his own hand to all his ministers whom he cannot see. He has a taste for economy and the greatest desire to see his people happy.' And she continues, 'I cannot help but feel gratitude to Providence, which has chosen me, the last of your children for the finest realm in Europe. I feel more than ever what I owe to the tenderness of my august mother, who has taken such care to procure for me this fine establishment.' To this letter the King added a postscript, he would have great need for the counsel of the Empress, whom he cannot sufficiently thank for the gift of her daughter. The Queen evidently felt this to be a little cold for she completed the letter: 'You will notice, my dear Mother, that though he has much tenderness for me, he does not spoil me with compliments.'

This young King of nineteen and a half was faced by a terrifying situation; without training or knowledge, without any experience he had to begin the task of governing and only his devotion, his integrity and his application to hard and continued work could help him. He inherited a France rich in resources but without liquid money and with an immense deficit. Moreover, in a Europe torn by dissension, France in order to protect herself needed a good navy with which to face England and a well organized and commanded army to keep Piedmont, Germany and the Low Countries at bay. She had nothing except the deficit. Choiseul had been dismissed by his grandfather and had been replaced by the Abbé Terray, who had indeed reduced the budget but at the price of a discontented populace, particularly the peasants and the lower classes, and a Parlement, defeated it is true, but always boiling inwardly against the power of the Monarch. And since the parliamentary places were bought and sold they were taken up by aristocrats, many from the great hereditary families of France, of whom the Orléans were the most powerful and the richest. Their wealth was indeed fabulous, and had been augmented by the marriage of the Duc de Chartres to the daughter of the Duc de Penthièvre. They had allied themselves with the Parlement and England and they affected to support liberty of thought; Freemasonry was their agency for the establishment of agents all over France. Lastly, they were partisans of the exiled Choiseul.

Finally there was the Church, still apparently powerful but in effect split and shaken by doubt and something like atheism in high places. This could only be absolutely antipathetic to Louis XVI who was by his upbringing and nature, as well as his position as Most Christian King, deeply Christian, a fervent Catholic with a faith which could not ever compromise to the end of his days. The churches were half empty; the people were disgusted by the rapacity and licentiousness of many of the higher clergy such as Rohan and Talleyrand. The *Philosophes* mocked at the pious clergy and their outmoded ideas, and were idolized by the women, always so powerful in Paris, the intellectual blue-stockings.

Opposed to all this we have the young King, who felt himself at home with the people of his country, those who worked with their hands as he could, who were decent and courageous, who suffered but in some way managed to keep themselves going. For them he wished to govern, he wished to be loved and honoured by them and for them he must address himself to the most immediate problem, the choice of ministers.

The Court had been forced, on the fourth day after their arrival at Choisy, to move, for Mesdames were found to have caught the smallpox from the late King, and the fear of further infection was great. The King and Queen therefore took up residence at La Muette, much nearer to Paris, and here every evening the good citizens would delight themselves with the spectacle of their Sovereign walking in the Bois de Boulogne like a simple bourgeois with his wife on his arm, sometimes with his family, sometimes admiring the Queen as she amused herself driving one of the new carriages with two wheels called a cabriolet. Sometimes too, when the weather was fine, they could be seen enjoying a picnic of strawberries and cream and milk. And the Duc de Croy recounts a scene which is typical of Marie Antoinette. Riding in the park she met the King walking alone, having dismissed his guards. Lightly she sprang to the ground, ran to him and he, taking her in his arms, gave her a hearty kiss. The watching crowds were in ecstasy, cries of *Vive le Roi* and clapping of hands filled the Bois, it was an idyllic moment.

Such charming gestures were accompanied by others more important. She refused to accept the customary gift of the 'girdle of the Queen', offered at each accession, which entailed the levying of a heavy tax. The King too had directed the priests of Paris to distribute 300,000 francs to the poor, saying that if they had not sufficient funds for this charity they should apply to the Abbé Terray for money from his own and the Queen's purse. One of his first acts was to suppress the 'corvées' or forced work on the roads, the *lettres de cachet* and the permission to torture. All this made him immensely popular and the French people, with their customary facile enthusiasm and indeed their optimism, loudly applauded him on every possible occasion.

His family life too was exemplary; in continuance of her taste for simplicity the Queen had substituted for the royal suppers, where only men were present, intimate meals with a few friends and attended by the King. She had always detested the custom, hallowed by long usage at the Court, of taking dinner in public. As long as she was Dauphine she had observed it, and one can imagine how little appetite she can have had when every bit was noted by a crowd of strangers, for anyone in proper dress was admitted to stare. Usage had also decreed that the Queen should only be served by women, in fact only appear surrounded by women: she was followed in the palace of Versailles either by her lady-in-waiting, or by two of her women in Court dress. Now she would be simply accompanied by the chief valet, and two footmen. All this scandalized the older courtiers who were frozen in their conservatism, and was also seized upon by the scurrilous pamphleteers of the day. Worse was to follow. Marie Antoinette had long wished for the innocent pleasure of seeing a sunrise, and this seemed a perfect moment when she could enjoy it. With the King's permission she arranged that, accompanied by a numerous company in order to disarm criticism, she would go to a height near Marly where she could enjoy the sight. A few days later this harmless pleasure was seized upon by her enemies and a disgusting libel appeared in Paris entitled *Le Lever de l'Aurore* (the Rise of Aurora). It was also during this stay at Marly that the jeweller Boehmer was introduced to the Queen; he brought with him six pear-shaped diamonds, earrings which had been destined for the Du Barry, and hoped that Marie Antoinette would buy them. She already had magnificent jewels, some brought with her from Vienna and some belonging to the gifts of the last King, but these were unique and she greatly desired to buy them. The price was high, but was reduced by the substitution of two of her own stones for two of the others. She could then pay for them from her own money and this she did over the next four or five years. And this record is important for the light it throws on the later affair of the Necklace and indeed on the accusations made in her trial.

The etiquette which regulated every moment, and almost every movement of the Monarch and his Court had never been acceptable to Marie Antoinette, and was indeed absurd and out of date. But much of it had been prescribed by Louis xiv, who ruled in a glacial absolutism supported by an obsequious Court utterly dependent upon his goodwill. Now came a young woman, who for the first years of her life at Versailles had been forced to conform; at last she was free, her mother might scold, Vermond might preach, Mercy might advise, but she was Queen. It is worth while to look at the code which prescribed the manner by which she would be allowed to dress. When she awoke her chocolate was served, but she could not drink it in peace although it was, with the croissants, a memory of her Viennese days, almost the only food she enjoyed. The so-called '*petites entrées*' began. Her doctor, her surgeon and her reader, the Abbé Vermond, the four first valets of the King, and his chief surgeons and doctors entered her bedchamber. Then came her bath, which she took, since she was extremely modest, enveloped in a long gown of light flannel closed to the neck; when she emerged four of her women held up a huge sheet behind which she put on a négligé. She then lay down again until at about eleven o'clock she rose to be dressed. This is how Madame Campan describes the ceremony:

It was a masterpiece of etiquette: everything went by rule. The Lady of the Wardrobe and the lady-in-waiting, both of them if they were there, helped by the chief lady's maid and the two ordinary lady's maids played an important role, the lady-in-waiting passed the petticoat while the Lady of Honour poured the water for washing the hands and passed the chemise. If a princess of the family happened to be present the Lady of Honour relinquished the latter function to her, but not directly to the Princesses of the Blood. In this case it was passed to the first lady's maid, who passed it to the Princess of the Blood. Each of these ladies scrupulously observed these usages as their right. One day in the winter it happened that the Queen, already quite undressed, was in the act of receiving her chemise from my hands when the Lady of Honour entered, and hastily taking off her gloves took the chemise. At that moment someone scratched at the door, it was the Duchesse of

Chartres; her gloves were off as she advanced to take the chemise, but the Lady of Honour could not give it to her, she passed it to me, I gave it to the Princess, when again someone scratched at the door. It was the Countess of Provence. The Duchess of Chartres presented her with the chemise. The Queen held her arms crossed on her breast, and appeared to be cold. Madame (the Duchess of Provence) saw her uncomfortable attitude and throwing aside her handkerchief but keeping her gloves she passed the chemise, but in doing so disarranged the Queen's hair, who bursting into laughter to disguise her impatience remarked 'It is odious, what a nuisance.'

As Madame Campan rightly remarks, in all courts there are rules of etiquette for special and ceremonial occasions. Only at the Court of France were the royal personages pursued into the most intimate moments by prying eyes so that even their infirmities were not private. And naturally such a state of affairs gave rise to intrigue, for all the courtiers involved, even the most highly placed, made use of their intimacy with their royal masters to further their own or their friends' advancement.

But this was not the end. Once dressed the Queen proceeded to seat herself before her toilet table, when her hair would be done and her rouge applied. For this the doors were open for the 'grandes entrées', when the gentlemen of the Court might enter and salute her. One after the other they inclined themselves before her while she acknowledged them by a movement of her head and a smile. For the Princesses and Princes of the Blood she simply put her hands on the arms of her chair and made as if to rise but remained seated. It was said of her that she had the gift of saluting half a dozen persons at once so that each thought he was singled out, her manner was gracious, her smile so sweet.

The King, for his part, was going through very much the same sort of ritual in his apartments with the difference that he treated the whole thing as a sort of joke. By the time eleven o'clock, the hour of the *lever* arrived, he had already been up for three hours, had visited his little forge, greeted his locksmith friend, and to amuse himself further had seen the people arriving at the château for his *lever* from one of the roofs. His rather coarse pleasantries enlivened the course of the ceremonial, not, it must be said, much to the taste of the courtiers who were often the objects of his buffoonery. He therefore sustained the Queen in her plans for simplification. She wrote to her mother that the King had allowed her to choose for herself the persons who would compose her establishment, and she had taken the Abbé de Sabran as her First Almoner, a Lorraine, and she also remarked that people (probably Mercy and Vermond) exhorted her to move the King to clemency towards 'any corrupt creatures who had done much harm during the previous reign'. In this context she mentions her favourite Count Esterhazy, who had incurred her mother's displeasure through his dissolute life and indiscretions. She says he is reformed, and evidently has it in her mind to play him off against the Empress's evident anxiety about the treatment of Du Barry.

During these first months of the reign her conduct was impeccable. 'I will try to commit the least faults possible,' she wrote to her mother. 'I wish and hope to correct myself little by little and without ever meddling with intrigue be worthy of the confidence of my dear husband.' He recognized her docility and willingness, he was touched by her affection, good-hearted himself he appreciated it in others, and as a token of this he presented her with the Petit Trianon for her own particular use. With the gift went one of his rare compliments, 'It has always been the residence of the favourites of the Kings, it must therefore be yours.' She returned the compliment by giving an elegant dinner in his honour.

She might well be loved, for she seemed to have gained in graciousness, in beauty. She had the royal gift of an excellent memory for faces and names, she showed her desire to please by the warmth of her smile, and her tact and adroitness in replying to whomever addressed her won general admiration. With all this she preserved the dignity which was hers by nature, it was said by someone that while you might offer another lady a chair you would never think of offering her anything but a throne. But all these good qualities served little to protect her against the gossip which was already floating around Paris, stimulated by the vicious tongues of her secret enemies, the party out of power. The Queens of France had in the past never come in contact with anyone but courtiers, now the Duchesse de Chartres had brought a dressmaker to the Queen, the famous Rose Bertin, and Marie Antoinette, the preliminaries of her toilette over, would retire to her boudoir and there confer with her on 'les Modes'. Naturally this woman and her assistants took back with them every bit of scandal they could collect, and the same was true of the coiffeur whom the Queen chose for the erection of the complicated hair styles of the day. From such small tittle-tattle whole fables were compiled to suit the Parisian love of flippant chatter. Madame Campan comments, 'Her wish to substitute successively the simplicity of Viennese Court life for the usages of Versailles was more harmful for her than one could imagine.'

The King meanwhile had been busy choosing the various ministers for his government. 'How must I act?' he had asked at his accession. 'I should like to be loved.' Louis XVI was fundamentally a good man and like all such he seems to have believed in the innate goodness of human nature. He wished to reform the nation without changing too much of its ancient customs. The liberties and privileges of the three orders should be preserved but with a new life infused into them. But he was far from understanding the spirit of the nation which he was called upon to rule. During the century a new philosophy had been emerging, and it saw too the birth of a new class, the well-to-do bourgeoisie.

Louis XIII had had his Richelieu, Louis XIV his Mazarin, and particularly the latter had been taken from an early age by the Minister and the Regent his mother on their frequent journeys throughout the realm. Louis XVI had no one. As a phlegmatic but docile boy he had watched with disgust the final years of a decrepit and discredited monarch. He had learned one thing at least. 'No one has taught me anything,' he said, 'but I have read history and I have noticed that the thing which has always reduced the State has been the influence of women, legitimate or mistresses.' In a much later letter to her brother the Emperor, Marie Antoinette commented on this determination with regard to the conduct of foreign affairs. She deplored her lack of influence, and continued: 'When I learn a part of an affair, I have to manage to extract the other part from the ministers by letting them believe that the King has told me all. When I reproach the King for not having spoken frankly to me, he is not annoyed, he seems to be somewhat embarrassed, and often he says that he had not thought of it.' But she speaks too of what she calls the 'dissimulation of the King', whose natural suspicion had been strengthened by his governor: 'Since before our marriage M. de Vauguyon had warned him about the influence which his wife might have on him, and his sinister design was to frighten him with stories invented against the House of Austria.'

But nevertheless Louis displayed percipience in his choice of ministers. One of his first actions on arriving at Choisy had been to write to M. de Maurepas, a man of seventy-three who had been retired for many years, thanks to a dispute he had had with Louis xv over funds for the navy and a quarrel with the Pompadour. He had great experience, and had been appreciated by Louis xvi's father, all of which decided Louis to ask his advice. It was wise; he said in effect that he would consent to be the King's adviser, to have frequent conferences with him but not with whatever ministers he might choose, he would not interfere with them nor for them. He also insisted that the King should not act precipitately in selecting his ministers and all this prudent advice accorded so closely with what Louis wanted that it was agreed upon to the satisfaction of the public who hailed the reappearance of Maurepas, less so to the courtiers, who did not happen to belong to his following, nor to the Queen who disliked his wife, the aunt of her *bête noire* d'Aiguillon.

The ministers chosen finally were, for Foreign Affairs, Vergennes, a man of consummate tact and finesse, former Ambassador at Constantinople and Stockholm and who had only one enemy, Choiseul; as Minister for War, the Comte de St Germain; as Minister of the King's Household, Malesherbes, universally respected, but curiously enough an Encyclopedist and liberal. Most important of all, for the Treasury, Turgot. This appointment had been the longest and most anxiously debated. It meant the retirement of Maupeou and Terray, who were detested by the public but able administrators. Turgot was especially prized as an honest man and a technician. He agreed with the science of the production of wealth, and he applied his conception of the natural laws of Property, Security and Liberty to the ills which France was suffering from. He saw in the scarcity of grain, for instance, the restrictions imposed on the farmers who were not free to sell, so did not produce. He was the hope of the liberals and when he met the King for the first time he said, 'It is not to the King I give my devotion, but to the man of honour.' 'You will not be deceived in him,' replied the King with feeling; they were both honest, well-meaning men, and the news of their meeting and Turgot's intentions spread in France and the European world, which watched with anxiety and interest.

Marie Antoinette, however, from almost the first moment of the accession was the object of changed policy in her mother.

Until now the Empress had confined herself and the advisers Mercy and Vermond to guarded allusions to the Alliance and the Dauphine's participation in politics. Already in her second letter she began to give advice, to insist that the interests of France and Austria were intimately linked, and with a total lack of tact she commented on the choice of Maurepas which she attributed to the influence of the aunts, and further remarked, 'above all no Aunts'. This letter so disturbed Mercy that he recommended the Queen not to show it to Louis and explained to Maria Theresa that her daughter had shut the letter away, and would finally burn it.

The three years which followed the accession were to seal the fate of Marie Antoinette: they were the years of the follies, often serious, sometimes trifling, which destroyed her in the public estimation. Her virtues so often went unnoticed, while every mistake, either political or personal, was seized upon and magnified. If she had at this time enjoyed the steadying happiness of a family, for which her decent Austrian heart yearned, how different her life would have been. But she was still childless, and married to a man who spent most of his spare time either in his forge or carpenter's shop or in the hunting which he adored, and from which he returned to her tired and dirty, and with little of interest to talk about.

It is small wonder that she turned to the company of amusing men like the Comte de Besenval who regaled her with the latest titbits of gossip and witty stories, and to her dressmaker and modiste who flattered her into setting the exaggerated fashions for which she has been blamed for centuries. She had done away with much of the Court ceremonial; she loved to tell the story of how one of the Dukes of Lorraine, the ancestor of her father, had been used to raise his taxes. Going to the Mass, once the Office was finished he rose, and lifting his hat he announced how much money he needed, and this was immediately supplied by his faithful and loving subjects. Nothing of this kind would be acceptable to the French who were accustomed to regard their Kings with a respect bordering on awe, and their Queens as women who passed their time either in providing heirs to the throne, or in their oratories praying for the souls of their husbands or the good of the dynasty. A contemporary writes: 'The French people, in spite of the inconsequence for which they are reproached, and perhaps because of this inconsequence. quickly ceases to respect the authority which governs them from the moment when it loses a certain gravity. They need a gravity which sets an obstacle to familiarity.'

The Queen, although she had in an earlier letter to her mother commented on this inconsequence, was not aware of the dangers to herself that arose from the same inconsequence in her own character. But her letters to her mother do show much common sense, and a desire to amend her ways. The letters between the two women in these first months of the reign show a greater intimacy and a much happier tone than before. Both had been shaken by the recent events, and both were happier in themselves through the public approbation. The Empress speculated on the amount left by the late King, which her daughter tells her is considerably less than hoped for, and retails the gossip running in Vienna apropos of the King's generosity in giving the exiled d'Aiguillon 500,000 livres as a *douceur*. The news that the King and his two brothers and the Comtesse d'Artois had all been inoculated put the Empress in a corresponding fever of anxiety, only appeased when she heard of their recovery with little disfiguration except to Louis' nose. The Queen assured her Chère Maman that she would not run into exaggerated expenditure, but rejoiced in the increased allowance which Louis had conferred on her. She also assured the Empress that her 'Aunts' had no influence on her, that it was true that d'Artois was lively and hair-brained but that she knew how to manage him, and as for Monsieur and Madame (the Provences) she would take very good care not to trust them. She also reported that during the journey from Compiègne to Fontainebleau she suffered so much from the movement of the carriage that she vomited several times, the heat being unbearable; this was most favourably remarked by the public but her dear Maman would be disappointed to hear that it meant nothing, for in a couple of days she was as well as ever. The King hunted with more caution than before, he showed the greatest complaisance to everybody and was more attentive to the ladies than he had ever been. In short, everything was in rose colour, until she sadly reported that the Comtesse d'Artois was eight days late with her period, a fact known to the whole Court and an evidence of the sort of publicity which the royal family had to put up with, and on 17 December 1774 she wrote:

My dear Mother will have less pleasure in hearing that the Comtesse d'Artois is pregnant; she has passed the first two months. I admit that I am disturbed that she should become a mother before myself but I feel all the more obliged to pay her attention. The King a week ago had a long conversation with my doctor; I am pleased with his advice, and I have a good hope that I will soon follow the example of my sister.

But Mercy wrote to the Empress: 'Something which I have always suspected and feared has happened; it is that the Queen, struck by this event, and reflecting on her own condition, finds with reason a very grave subject for pain, and I see with apprehension that her Majesty is inwardly affected in a most agonizing fashion.'

The King during all these months had been working hard with his ministers. He had been inundated with petitions from the towns and provinces, all of which he insisted on reading himself, and he had found a secret instructor, Jaques Masson, Marquis de Pezay who kept him informed on military matters. There had been a great funeral service for the late King in Paris to which the Orléans had refused to come, since they would not acknowledge the new Parlement constituted by that monarch. For this impertinence Louis xv had exiled them to their property at Villars Cotterets and their enmity was given a new impetus. The old Parlement had been hostile to royal authority and it was for this reason that the King had disbanded them. Now Orléans, egged on by his son, the Duc de Chartres, took advantage of the general disorder, and even fomented it. On leaving Marly he had appeared on the streets of Paris during the funeral service wearing his Cordon Bleu, an act of disrespect and a clear sign of what his future policy would be throughout the reign. Maurepas, fearing that such open provocation might breed revolt, lost no time in going to the King, and after considerable discussion prevailed on him to recall the Parlement exiled by Louis xv in 1771. On 10 November 1774 the members of both the old and the new were convoked to the King's *lit de Justice* and on the 12th Louis, having left La Muette at half past seven and heard Mass in the Sainte Chapelle, appeared in the great Hall to meet them all. Endless discussions and speeches began, too long to be reported here: the result was satisfactory to all but the King himself, who doubted the good faith of the reconstituted Parlement, but the Princes of the Blood were recalled from exile, to the delight of Marie Antoinette, who only wished for peace in her family, as she wrote her mother.

She found plenty of distractions with which she could occupy herself and enjoy her new-found popularity. The Carnival of 1775 was the most brilliant ever seen and she danced twice a week, on Mondays and Wednesdays. Court mourning was over and the entire royal family and the Court joined in the display; the ladies wore white taffetas with flowing tulle, and the men blue velvet with a white waistcoat embroidered with blue. Sometimes they all wore costumes of the style of Henri Quatre, the most admired of all French Kings, and on 23 January the King himself opened the ball. It is true he went home before half past three which was the time when the Queen left the opera, but the spectators were enchanted, all Paris talked of it, and the statue of the admired King Henri IV was embellished by an anonymous hand with the placard 'Resurrexit'.

Marie Antoinette was also enjoying the freedom to choose her own friends. She had a disposition which demanded a confidant, someone to whom she could open her heart, especially since in this respect her husband was so wanting. Until now her friend-ships had been of a transitory order, with women who had caught her fancy or shared her pleasures. Now she was growing older and looked for a more solid and durable relationship. The Comte de Provence says that friendship was a necessity for her; in the midst of the horror of the Revolution she wrote to one of her faithful friends: 'They have taken everything from me except my heart; it is the only unhappiness which I could not support.'

The first of these more lasting relationships was with the Princesse de Lamballe, the daughter of the good Duc de Pen-thièvre, and widow at the age of twenty-one of the Prince de Lamballe. No one could be more to the taste of the Dauphine than this ravishing beauty, blonde with deep blue eyes, graceful, elegant, and the personification of innocence and youth. With it all she was gay and witty, pleasure-loving, entering into all the Court amusements. Having first met during the Carnival of 1771, the two young women quickly became inseparable and while the Court mourning for Louis XV lasted the Princess was one of the intimate circle around the royal family. 'I am glad that Madame de Lamballe does not leave you: you love her very much,' commented Louis XVI. 'Ah, Sire, her friendship is the joy of my life,' replied the Queen. The relationship reached its peak in 1775 when her project for creating the Princess Superintendent of her household was realized. The office had been suppressed because of its cost to the Treasury and the opportunity it gave for disputes with ministers. Turgot was particularly opposed to its re-creation but the Queen, determined to give pleasure to her preferred friend, obstinately refused to give in and finally won. Her resentment against the Minister's opposition continued, however, and was to bring disastrous results.

Unfortunately what Turgot had feared came to pass, and the new Superintendent, urged on by her relations, many of them enemies of the Queen, lent herself to intrigues which distressed and annoyed her patroness. Marie Antoinette sought not only a confidant, a sincere friend, but surrounded herself with a flock of young people of both sexes who sustained her by their admiration or flattery in her ambition to be the leader of fashion and manners. The Court was gradually being deserted by the older generation of nobility, the 'centuries' as the Queen laughingly called them, who found themselves out of place and denigrated at the new Versailles, where the rules of etiquette no longer put everyone in his proper place. It was taken over by young men of a different type, headed by the Duc d'Artois, who considered himself the mould of fashion.

By this time Marie Antoinette had become thoroughly under the influence of Rose Bertin; daily conferences took place in which ever more elaborate confections were designed. One day when the Queen was in the process of deciding on the tint of a dress which her dressmaker had christened 'Honest Composition', the King entered. What should she choose, this discreet brown taffeta perhaps? 'It is flea colour,' said her husband. Immediately 'puce' became the rage, and every smart woman in Paris burned to have a dress of puce silk. But it was in the dressing of hair that the most outrageous nonsense existed, so much so that Maria Theresa expostulated with her daughter, and the *Gazettes* were full of comment. 'They say you wear your hair dressed thirty-six inches high and with all the ribbons and feathers that go with it. You know that I have always been of the opinion that one should follow the fashion within reason but never to be outrée. A pretty Queen, full of "charm" has no need of all these follies.' This advice fell on deaf ears, though the Queen with considerable disingenuity seeks to calm her mother's fears: 'It is true that I think a good deal about my dress and as regards the feathers every one wears them, it would seem extraordinary not to do so. The height is lessened since the end of the carnival balls.'

The fashions of Versailles were aped and exaggerated by Paris, and in turn the frivolities of the capital were introduced at Court by d'Artois. Everything English was *à la mode*, including the races, which until now had been confined to Newmarket. The Duke had his racing stable, where one of the grooms was a miserable undersized little man named Marat. The Queen drove with d'Artois in the Bois and even condescended to present the prizes at the first race meeting. In pouring rain she assisted at the spectacle and crowned the victor, one of her friends, the Duc de Lauzun. The winter of 1774 was long, the snow lay for six weeks around Versailles, and prompted the young people to disinter the old sleighs which were in the stables. From then on there were continual sleigh parties, which gradually appeared even in the Champs Elysées. Nothing could appear more innocent, but the Parisians saw in this exercise an attempt to introduce the life of the Viennese Court and they added to this the rumour that the Queen intended to re-baptize the Petit Trianon, 'Little Schönbrunn'. It was the beginning of the suspicion that she wished to submit French politics to the interests of Austria.

She had now her 'Coterie', her Society. There was the Comte d'Adhémar who could sing to his own harp accompaniment; or the Comte de Vaudreuil, an exquisite and highly cultivated man, or Esterhazy the Hungarian for whom Marie Antoinette had always had a weakness. He was the subject of a quarrel with the Minister for War. The Comte wished to command a regiment and was sent to Montmédy, too far from Paris for his satisfaction. 'It is enough, Monsieur,' she said to St Germain, 'that you should persecute one of my friends. Why do you send the regiment of Esterhazy to Montmédy, which is a bad garrison? Look for a nearer place and content Monsieur Esterhazy. And come and tell me what you have found.' Another foreigner was the Prince de Ligne, more than half Austrian, who possessed a splendid château at Beloeil, but adored Versailles. He however was a true friend, it was only his Austrian influence that rendered him suspect to rumour. One of the closest of her intimates was, however, the

Baron de Besenval, a Swiss who had the position of Lieutenant of the Swiss Guards. He was older than most of the others and prided himself on his place as her counsellor. He amused the Queen with his scurrilous wit, and his risqué stories, he brought her all the chit-chat of the Salons and at the same time he used his ascendancy to further the causes of his friends, of whom the chief was the still absent Choiseul. He hated d'Aiguillon as much as she did. But the closest of all was the Duc de Lauzun; Mercy warned her against him in vain.

André Castelot recounts an example of the wit which lightened the ennui which is the curse of courts. One day Marie Antoinette, turning to an old Field-Marshal who spoke of nothing but his two war-horses, asked, 'Monsieur, to which of these horses do you give the preference?' 'Madame,' he replied with comic gravity, 'If it was a day of battle, and I was mounted on my piebald I would not dismount to mount my bay, and if I were mounted on my bay I would not dismount to mount my piebald.' A moment afterwards they were speaking of the prettiest women at Court, 'Monsieur,' asked the Queen, turning to one of her familiars, 'Whom do you prefer?' 'Madame,' replied the gentleman questioned, with the same gravity as the Field-Marshal, 'If on a day of battle I were mounted . . .' 'Enough, Enough,' cried the Queen bursting into laughter. It seems harmless enough, a pretty woman laughing at a slightly risky joke, but this was the Queen of France, who should know that every word and action was watched and reported, and should never allow herself the slightest descent from the position she occupied.

Sometimes the King penetrated to these intimate reunions, but he had the habit of retiring at eleven o'clock. His disappearance was awaited with impatience, and one day someone had the idea of advancing the clock, and he disappeared, leaving the company to indulge in more improper joking. Next day all Versailles knew of the trick, which was naturally most severely commented on. But the Queen paid no attention, for her all that mattered was to amuse herself. The sinister misgivings of her mother were only too justified at this time. She was not helped by the visit of her younger brother Maximilian, travelling incognito with the title of Count of Burgau, and accompanied by the Count of Rosenberg, a man who had enjoyed the trust of Maria Theresa for forty years.

The arrival of the Archduke was awaited with excitement by Marie Antoinette, he would be the first of her family to be seen since her departure, and she longed to welcome him. Unfortunately the young man showed a serious lack of tact, and very little interest during his stay. In the first place he refused to pay the duty calls on the Princes of the Blood which etiquette demanded, insisting that as he was incognito this was not necessary. This was taken in very bad part by the public, always attached to the House of Orléans. He showed his ignorance of France in various ways. Madame Campan writes that visiting the Botanic Garden of the King he was presented by M. de Buffon the celebrated naturalist with a copy of his works, to which the Archduke replied, refusing the book, 'I would be sorry to deprive you of it.' The Parisians gurgled with malicious joy over this response. In her letter to the Empress, the Queen comments:

I am very sad over my brother's departure, it is cruel to think that we will probably never meet again. He won commendation here for his politeness and attention for everyone. He did not succeed so well with what he was shown, because he was always very indifferent. I think that later on he will be more in a state to profit from such a journey.

But she was aware that his rudeness inspired accusations against her on the part of the Princes. They were forbidden by the King to appear at Court for a week or ten days.

Since his arrival in the intimate circle of the Queen the Baron de Besenval had gained more and more influence over her. He was not only a courtier but a brave and successful soldier, well known to generals in the field for his intelligence and valour, and meriting his rank of Lieutenant-Colonel of the Swiss Guards. His fortunes had been intimately linked with the Duc de Choiseul, and he had asked for permission to follow the Duc in his retreat to Chanteloup. With the death of Louis xv de Besenval was free to return to Court, where he struck up a close friendship with the Comte d'Artois, and, as we have seen, with the Queen. Thus he was somewhat different from many of her entourage, having experience and besides the capacity to please, a courage and tenacity in support of those whom he esteemed. Being a supporter of Choiseul it followed that he hated the architect of that minister's downfall, d'Aiguillon, who now lived in Paris, devoting himself to circulating all the defamatory rumours against the Queen. He was protected not so much by the Minister Maurepas as by his wife, whose nephew he was.

Besenval set himself to persuade the Queen that d'Aiguillon's presence so near to the Palace was not tolerable; he should be sent, not to Veretz which the King had suggested, but to Aiguillon on the borders of the Garonne. In this he was supported by Mercy, and the Queen approached the King who as usual half consented and then, advised by Maurepas, retracted. Besenval admits frankly in his memoirs that he was determined to achieve the return of his patron Choiseul and with this end in view he so worked on the Queen that she was in favour of stronger measures. They only needed a pretext for the exile of d'Aiguillon and this was found in the affair of the Duc de Guines. Ambassador to the English Court, Guines spent most of his time in Versailles. However he had been suspected and finally caught smuggling; at first he attempted with screams of offended pride to throw the blame on his secretary Tort, but convicted of the offence he declared it was all a plot of d'Aiguillon.

It was not hard to convince Marie Antoinette that she should support the Duc de Guines, since she disliked Maurepas and Guines was one of her favourites. It is impossible to fight with a Queen, remarked Maurepas sadly. She at last prevailed on the King to acquit Guines, who retained the post of Ambassador, while d'Aiguillon departed from Versailles and Paris and came to rest in his half-ruined château at Aiguillon. The Queen had thus got rid of her fiercest opponent and could continue her dissipated life without the constant criticism emanating from him and his friends in Paris. But the letters from the Empress continued; the journals in Vienna and the accounts of her spies kept Maria Theresa well informed on the activities of her daughter. She was even more disturbed by the rumours of discontent in the provinces of their two realms – in her own it was the constant recruiting for the army, the corvées, in France the price of bread. She saw in it the sickness of the time. There was a restlessness, a loosening of old custom, religious belief was shaken and in the case of the courts a lack of dignity which she feared would lead to a lack of respect. But Marie Antoinette seemed to be possessed by a sort of madness, she turned the night into day in search for distraction, and what was more important she appeared more and more in public without the King. Her excuse was that the King much preferred to go to bed early and snore away the night in peace, and moreover he was well informed on all her movements. But her mother touched on a far more acute point, 'All the letters from Paris,' she wrote on 2 June 1775, 'say that you are separated from the bed of the King and that you enjoy very little of his confidence.' She continued that not only did this augur badly for the succession, but she predicted nothing but unhappiness and sorrows for them both, in spite of the brilliant position which Rosenberg had foreseen during his visit with the Archduke. Marie Antoinette should devote herself to the King, should be his constant companion, and so behave that he would find in her company the greatest pleasure and the most faithful cooperation. The truth was that the King worked hard and long with his ministers and his main relaxation – hunting – was as much for his health as for his pleasure.

Maria Theresa's sermon was inspired by Mercy, who had written in great agitation, imploring the Empress to insist on this theme. The Queen did not reply until after the ceremony of the Coronation which took place on 11 June. She had at first been unwilling to attend this most important function, unwilling to interrupt her amusements for a long and wearisome ritual, sanctified by ancient custom though it was. But the insistence of the Abbé Vermond, commissioned by Mercy, finally persuaded her. It would be, although she could not know it then, almost the last time that she would appear before the French people in a favourable light.

And in truth she was much moved by the whole historic ritual; at the great moment when she saw her husband holding the sceptre and invested with the crown of Charlemagne, when she saw the massive doors of the Cathedral open and heard the crowds chanting *Vive le Roi, Noël, Noël*, she had not been able to contain her tears. When the King regained his place after showing himself to his people, the whole edifice resounded to the cheers and clapping of hands, and through the rest of the long and trying ceremony she sat as if in a trance, while often the King gazed at her with adoring love. There followed a great banquet, and in the evening the royal pair, arm in arm and without guards, walked in the garden of the Archbishopric surrounded by the crowd half out of their minds with excitement and wonder. On the day after, following the immemorial custom, he rode on his charger, The Victor, decked with a caparison of silver, preceded by trumpets and the great nobles, to St Rémy, there to touch for the King's Evil, the scrofula. Two thousand four hundred sufferers heard the words, 'God cure you, the King touches you', while he placed his hands on their heads.

And on 22 June Marie Antoinette wrote to her mother:

The Coronation was in every way perfect, it seems that everyone was pleased with the King; he should be the same with his subjects, great and small all have shown the greatest interest, the ceremony in the Cathedral was interrupted at the moment of the coronation with the most touching acclamations. I could not control myself. I did my best during the whole time to respond to the feeling of the people and though it was very hot and very great crowds, I do not regret my fatigue. It is a very surprising thing and at the same time very happy, to have been so well received two months after the uprising, in spite of the dearness of bread, which unfortunately still continues. It is a prodigious thing in the French character that they let themselves be transported by bad advice and then forget it in a moment and return to good. It is certain that seeing people who in their misery treat us so well, we are the more obliged to work for their benefit. The King seems convinced of this truth. For myself I will never in my life – should it last a hundred years – forget the day of the Coronation.

She continued her letter by assuring her mother that the separation of their beds was only temporary, and because of a persistent cold she had suffered from. And further that their apartments were most inconveniently placed, to visit each other they were forced to go through the Oeil de Bœuf, the meeting place for everybody. They were therefore having a small communicating passage made – vestiges of it exist today.

But how could she describe in a letter, even to her mother, her real state of mind, the hidden reason for the life she was leading, frantically drugging herself with superficial pleasures which helped her to forget the frustration and disappointment of her private situation? If she stayed late at the opera balls it was to put off the return to a husband who wearied her. For the King now loved her and he too suffered from the fact that he could never give her the satisfaction which every normal woman needs in marriage. For psychologists now know – what most women have known for a very long time – that sexual satisfaction is a stabilizing force, but that continual teasing without this satisfaction can be disastrous. With Marie Antoinette, years of an unfulfilled marriage were made more hateful by her deep longing for children; she has been accused of indifference, but this she denied. 'The indifference is certainly not on my side,' she wrote, 'but you may judge if my position is not embarrassing', and by now the King too was feeling this embarrassment. At the end of 1774 he had a serious conversation with his doctor, who advised him to have the small operation which would release the impediment to complete union, but when after consenting he saw the instruments spread out, his courage failed him and he put it off again. So at this point his unhappy wife gave up hope and threw herself into a mad whirl of hectic gaiety, and the friendships with women which fulfilled to some extent her longing for love and understanding.

She continued her letter to the Empress by assuring her that on the days when she rode in the Bois with the Comte d'Artois the King was hunting and she could not be with him. She informed her about the progress of the Comtesse d'Artois' pregnancy and later, on 14 July, she wrote 'I feel suffocated by the joy of Monsieur and Madame', who had also produced a child. 'It is not that I do not feel it to be natural, I approve of it so much that I have hidden my tears in order not to disturb their joy. They have gone to spend two weeks in the strictest incognito at Chambéry. It is frightful that I cannot hope for the same happiness.' She also said that they were economizing except for the State baptism of the two royal babies Artois and Provence. This was essential as an example for the people; fortunately the harvest promised well, and the great shortage would be surmounted.

But on her way back to Paris, from the Coronation, driving in her great coach over the splendid roads, did she notice the men whose labour maintained them? Did she see their hands raised imploringly and hear their cries for bread, or care for the miserable women and children, old before their time? She drove through the enormous forests where the great lords hunted their game and where no peasant could destroy so much as a hare for his starving family. If she could have listened she might have realized that there was a faint hope stirring in the people that with the coming of the new reign they might be remembered in their hovels and misery, and she might have reflected that starvation can reach a point where death and life meet, and life must protest.

How much of this she saw one cannot tell. Her emotions were always fleeting, and what stirred her one moment was forgotten the next. She had, it is true, referred to the revolt of 2 May when an army of peasants had appeared at the gates of Versailles demanding a hearing; ragged and pinched with hunger they were not voiceless, they presented their Petition of Rights and the King had come out on a balcony and spoken to them. They were very different from the well-to-do bourgeois of the rich town of Rheims, who had watched her with her husband and applauded them both. She thought it was part of the French character to be easily roused to impatience and as quickly to forget it. But in common with all the Court and the nobility she was blind to the urgency of reform. Turgot with his new laws might have the answer to the need.

Her letter did not please the Empress. She felt it to be disingenuous, and said so to Mercy, and the following two letters are of immense importance. They were discovered by Stefan Zweig in the course of his researches. It will be remembered that the Archduke Maximilian had been accompanied on his tour by the Count Rosenberg, an old and valued friend of the family, who had known the Archduchess all her life. On 17 April after his departure from Versailles she had written to him, no doubt to prolong the pleasure she had felt in seeing and talking to him. She felt in other words she could 'let herself go' with him:

The pleasure which I had in talking with you, Monsieur, was equalled by that which your letter has given me. I will never be disturbed by the tales which are told in Vienna as long as you are there to contradict them, you know Paris and Versailles, you have seen and judged. If I had need of an apologist I would confide myself to you; in good faith I would concede more than you say; for example, my tastes are not those of the King who cares for nothing but hunting and mechanical work. You will agree that I would be somewhat out of place in a forge, I would never be Vulcan, and the role of Venus would displease him much more than my tastes, which he does not disapprove of.

It is possible that this letter remained private, but a second missive on 13 July in which Marie Antoinette went much further and spoke of her husband in most egregious terms decided the

Count to show them to the Empress. In the interim between the two letters she had been involved in an intrigue which had as its object the return of the Duc de Choiseul to Court. The author of the plot was the Baron de Besenval, who, encouraged by his success in the exile of d'Aiguillon, lost no opportunity for congratulating the Queen on her venture into the field of politics. He persuaded her that it was necessary for her to make sure that ministers should be chosen who would be favourable to her wishes. He reminded her of the devotion which Choiseul had always shown for the House of Habsburg, and so worked on her feelings that she consented to give the Duke, then at Rheims for the Coronation, a private audience. The only difficulty was to get the King to authorize this meeting. The Queen promised to exert every art of which she was capable, to be alternately coaxing and demanding, and most important of all to catch her husband when he was in the good humour induced by the moving events of the last few days. She insinuated with pretended innocence how glad she would be to talk with her old friend Choiseul, but she did not know when it could take place seeing that every moment was fully occupied at Rheims. Would the King suggest a time? And Louis XVI, unsuspecting did indeed suggest the time, the afternoon of two days following. The audience was given, it occupied an hour and aroused a whirlwind of curiosity in the European chancelleries, where every rumour, every scandal, was discussed. Choiseul behaved with great discretion, insisting only on his devotion to the Queen, but the airs which the plotters Besenval and d'Artois gave themselves aroused the suspicions of the King, who thinking himself made a fool of, showed his resentment to Choiseul. On 14 July at the Queen's reception, Choiseul was announced, and to the amazement of all, the King suddenly rose and departed. And on the following day when all those invited to the Coronation came to pay their call of leave-taking, Choiseul, advancing to kiss the King's hand, was left gasping as Louis snatched his hand away, with a grimace. The Duke understood and left the same day for Chanteloup.

But Marie Antoinette in her childish glee, paid no attention, her small personal success was more to her than the King's displeasure and on 13 July she had written the following letter to the Count Rosenberg. We will give it in full for it is decisive in the career of the unfortunate Queen:

Bust of the Comte de
Provence (later Louis
XVIII, King of France)

Bust of the Comtesse de
Provence

The Duc d'Artois (later
Charles x, King of
France)

The composer Gluck hands his opera *Iphigénie* to Marie Antoinette

I was not satisfied, Monsieur, with my last letter because I was in a hurry to catch the post. I must refer to the departure of M. d'Aiguillon in order to give you a just account of my conduct. This departure was absolutely my work. The measure was full; this wretched man conducted every sort of espionage and wicked scandal. He endeavoured to brave me out in the affair of M. Guines; immediately after the lawsuit I demanded his exile from the King. It is true that I did not wish for a *lettre de cachet*; but nothing was lost for instead of remaining in Touraine as he wished to do he was requested to continue his journey to Aiguillon which is in Gascony. You will perhaps have heard of the audience which I gave to the Duc de Choiseul at Rheims. It has been so much talked about that I guess that old Maurepas was frightened to go to bed in his house. You will understand that I did not give it without consulting the King but you can have no idea how adroit I was in not giving the impression that I was asking permission. I simply said that I would like to see M. de Choiseul, the only difficulty was to find the day. *J'ai si bien fait que le pauvre homme m'a arrangé lui-même l'heure la plus commode ou je pouvai.**

When the Empress saw this letter she was in the greatest consternation. What a style, what language. 'The poor man' – where was her daughter's respect? So might a Pompadour, a Du Barry talk, not a princess of the House of Habsburg-Lorraine. She also disapproved of the elevation of the Princesse de Lamballe. With two sisters-in-law Piedmontaises, why another Piedmontaise? They would only care for the interests of their own nation. And she went back to her old sermon, it is the Queen's love of dissipation which is at the root of all the mistakes. As for the Emperor, he was even more horrified than his mother. He wrote a terrible letter which he fortunately showed to the Empress, who prevented him from sending it. The original is lost, but from his letter to Mercy we have his thought: 'What a style, what a manner of thinking. This only confirms all my inquietude. She is running to her ruin, she will be too fortunate if she can keep, in losing herself, the virtues of her position. Rosenberg has put me in a cruel state of embarrassment in letting the Queen know that he has shown me her letter.' Marie Antoinette must have been shattered when she received her mother's condemnation, but she replied with great dignity and restraint:

---

* I did it so well that the poor man himself arranged the most convenient time for me.

Madame, my dearest mother, I would not dare write to my august mother if I believed myself as guilty as she believes me. To be compared to the Pompadours, the Du Barrys, to be covered with the most frightful epithets does not become your daughter. I wrote to a worthy man who has your confidence, and to whom I believed myself able to give my own. Since he has visited this country and knows the value set on certain phrases [she evidently means the 'poor man'] I did not need to be afraid of any misunderstanding. My dear mother judges differently, it is for me to bow my head and to hope that in other circumstances she will judge me more favourably, and if I dare say so as I merit . . . My dear mother will, I hope, be pleased to accept the respect and tenderness of her daughter who is desolated to have displeased her.

In the opinion of this writer a slightly different tone is beginning to show in this and other letters to the Empress from that of earlier letters from the Dauphine. Marie Antoinette was now the Queen, and of a state as great as Austria. It is true that she always remembered that she had been an Archduchess, but she felt that in becoming the wife of Louis xvi she had been honoured, but not ennobled. The style of her replies struck her, on reflection, as more than cold, especially that to her brother. She said to Mercy that her mother saw events from a distance, she judged too harshly, 'but she is my mother who loves me, and when she speaks I can only bow my head.' She was happily reassured by the Empress's next missive and peace seemed to be established between them. For the moment, but unfortunately not for long.

Following her return to Versailles she plunged once more into the round of dissipation, and still worse, having once tasted power she let herself be tempted into interfering with the creation of ministers. Prompted by Besenval she supported his intrigues. La Vrillière, whom he disliked, had been replaced by M. d'Ennery, another member of the coterie, now it was the question of getting rid of the Controller, M. Turgot. She had not disliked this 'honest man' on his appointment, but since he had violently opposed her designs for the Princesse de Lamballe on the grounds of unwarranted expense her wrath had been aroused. Now came the appointment of the Minister for War; Turgot and Maurepas chose for this important post M. de St Germain, whom Besenval found totally inadequate. He called him a mocker, mischievous and fundamentally suspicious, and states in his memoirs that Maurepas only supported him because he preferred nonentities for ministers. But when he endeavoured to dissuade the Prime Minister, he found himself butting against a closed door. M. de St Germain was appointed, and Marie Antoinette, equally annoyed, asked her friend what she should do now. Make a friend of Maurepas was the reply, send for him, seek to convince him that you wish your past enmity forgotten, that you esteem his ability to serve the King, and that you wish for nothing better than a firm understanding with him.

In the autumn the Court moved to Fontainebleau, and since this palace was further removed from Paris and its pleasures, it was all the more imperative that amusement should be provided there. The season was rainy and the Queen remained for most of the time indoors. Surrounded by her coterie she was the prey of her own ennui and their intrigues. Already her friendship for Madame de Lamballe was on the wane, her heart had been caught by another beauty, the Countess Jules de Polignac, for whom she would conceive a more lasting attachment. They met for the first time in the salon of the Princesse de Lamballe, and in the course of a long conversation the Queen was attracted by the moderation of her remarks. She showed such common sense, such a sympathetic approach to every subject, combined with a gentle gaiety that Marie Antoinette, already a little out of love with her favourite Lamballe, was enchanted. The Countess was not a regular beauty, but what was much more winning, had an exquisite voice, low and melodious; her blue eyes and raven hair, her manner of walking, her ease and simplicity, made her the perfect foil for the Queen's vivacious blonde loveliness. She was utterly without guile or ambition for herself, but unfortunately for the Queen she was surrounded, and much influenced, by a horde of relations and friends among the courtiers, who would use her constantly to further their intrigues.

Marie Antoinette felt a great need for friendship at this time, for her immediate relations were either hostile, like the aunts, now removed to the palace of Bellevue, or suspiciously untrustworthy like the Comte de Provence and his wife. The Comte d'Artois was her favourite it is true, but he was only too apt to lead her in exactly the wrong direction. Here then was a friend exactly to her measure, one who could show and receive tenderness and warmth, and she threw herself into the relationship with her customary impetuous exaggeration. She saw the Comtesse every day, sometimes many times a day, making excursions with her to Trianon, caring for her when she was ill, and even, when the Comtesse was brought to bed, installing the whole of her Court at La Muette in order to be near her. In return the Comtesse really loved her royal friend, asking nothing for herself. No one could reproach her for obtaining extravagant favours. It was the intimacy which infuriated the enemies of the Queen, as she became more and more involved in the Comtesse's set, which included men and women like the Comtesse Diane, sister of M. de Polignac, or M. de Guines. Laughter with a feeling of bells in the air, perfume, seem to haunt the apartments still at Fontainebleau, for this bubbling gaiety needed a more unconstrained atmosphere than the great salons of Versailles. The rooms which Marie Antoinette chose at Fontainebleau show her taste. Gone were the pomposity of the Grand Monarch, the overdecorated fussiness of Louis xv. The new style was more delicately intimate, with its clear colours and refined simplicity of form which suited her distinguished bearing and beauty.

Her enemies felt, however, that this unconventional society, with its ridiculous games and its freedom was very little suited to a Queen of France. 'I have seen her,' wrote a contemporary, 'sitting on a couch, and everybody else freely standing, or walking about in groups in the salon. There was a gaming table, a piano, a billiard table, and each person occupied himself as he thought best.' It seemed that only there the Queen could breathe freely. I am myself, she said. This is how she passed a great part of her days. The result of this conduct was to hasten the exodus of all who had constituted the Court. The Queen of France in public estimation passed for the 'prisoner of a coterie'.

Indeed if her immediate circle had stopped at being merely entertaining even the calumny of her enemies would have been unavailing, but unfortunately all these creatures were employed in furthering their own intrigues. The intimate friend of de Vaudreuil, the Comte Adhémar, rich through his marriage with a widow, was already Minister of France at Brussels, but he coveted the post of Ambassador at Constantinople, or at Vienna. This was opposed by Maria Theresa, and the Queen was forced to give in, but his vaulting ambition aimed then at the Ministry of War.

In spite of the pleading of Madame de Polignac, Marie Antoinette was again forced to refuse, without however withdrawing her friendship from Adhémar who was consoled later with the Embassy to London.

There was about the Court at this time a young man less favoured but destined to play a far greater part in the life of the Queen than she could dream of. He was little formed to be a courtier, poor but of noble family, an Auvergnat, with the somewhat rustic qualities of that rugged country, awkward, bad at games and dancing, he was nevertheless possessed with a secret passion for glory, and determination to win it, though he could not quite see how. His name? Marie Joseph Gilbert, Marquis de La Fayette. He was attached to the great family of the Noailles, and married to the daughter of the Duc d'Ayen. Since both wished to help him they succeeded in obtaining a post for him in the Court of the Comte de Provence, but La Fayette, seeing little future there, refused it and was summarily sent as punishment to the army at Metz. This garrison was commanded by the Duc de Broglie, and when he joined it had a guest, the Duke of Gloucester, son of George III, who enlivened the officers' mess with accounts of the war in America. At a dinner in his honour La Fayette listened as the Duke pointed out how dangerous it might be for the English cause if the American rebels had any allies or aid, little thinking that the youngest officer there was already inflamed with the desire to give them exactly that. Since the Anglo-French Treaty of Paris, so disgraceful for France, there had arisen a considerable sympathy for the insurgents – public opinion considered that they were resisting oppression – but the attitude of the government was ambiguous, and no real aid had been forthcoming.

La Fayette felt that his moment had arrived. Deputies from the American Congress were in France; together with the young Comte de Noailles he sought them out. And now filled with ardour and devotion he began one of the most picaresque adventures in history. This is not the place to tell his story which terminated with his triumphal return to France, having been the hero of the Republican Army, the friend of Washington and one of the victors in the decisive battle against the English. This man was something different from the courtiers so beloved by the Queen, but she had only noticed him to give him one of her laughing nicknames, Monsieur Blondinet.

87

And yet there is evidence that she was not so feather-brained as the world believed her, only too much at the mercy of her heart and her affections. In a letter to the Empress on 15 December 1775 she speaks about her brother-in-law Monsieur. 'I have never forgotten what my dear mother said to me about the Piedmontais character, and in this respect he is not ill married.' She did not know what he had in mind at that moment. He loved writing letters and she had been shown one ostensibly addressed to a man in his court but in reality for her eye. It contained so much that was base and false, that though they seemed to be friends she could never feel any sincerity in him. She says 'I am convinced that if I had had to choose a husband from the three brothers, I would prefer the one I have; although he is awkward he is sincere, and he is full of attention and kindness for me.' More important still in the eyes of her mother is her news about her married state, there has again been talk of the operation, the King cannot make up his mind to have it, and his doctors and hers do not agree. She would never lose sight of the importance of this essential part of her duty. But Paris was full of satirical songs, and the worst were those against the King's condition, which was known to all. She was not spared either, and was accused of all the sins, including Lesbianism. Such rubbish could be left to the public, she wrote, she would not take notice of it nor would anyone with good taste. Here she was wrong, led astray by her pride; such vile accusations would haunt her path, the cause lay deeper than she knew.

For the times were sick and the King might have said with Hamlet: 'Oh cursed spite that ever I was born to set them right.' Even in the last days of the seventeenth century thought had been changing, becoming freer. Faith was challenged by reason and the eyes of Frenchmen had been turned beyond the seas. Nearest to them was England, where a peaceful and successful revolution had been accomplished. But in France how could such a thing be done? Turgot, the philosophic Controller General had his plan. An honest man, he proposed to achieve some kind of reform of the poverty-stricken state by taxing the clergy, the nobles, and the Parlement itself, all of them hitherto exempt. The outcry was prodigious, and within a few short months he found himself dismissed.

And within the palace, isolated from the stormy approbation in

Paris of the successful insurgents beyond the ocean, the paltry internecine strife around the Queen continued. The two favourites, the displaced and the triumphant, were at each other's throats. Mercy regularly informed the Empress that they quarrelled without ceasing. What was much more important was that the Queen was again interfering with the appointment of ministers. On 5 May 1776 she wrote a very disingenuous letter to her mother in which she announced the retirement of Turgot, but disclaimed any hand in the matter. M. de Malesherbes had left the ministry two days before, and was replaced by M. Amelot. M. Turgot was sent away the same day and M. de Clugny replaced him. 'I admit to my dear mother than I am not displeased by these retirements, but I had no hand in them.' On the contrary, as Mercy knew and reported, she had been actively engaged in the intrigue against Turgot, who was hostile to her protégé the Comte de Guines, and even spared no arguments in favour of his being sent to the Bastille. Mercy wrote:

All this was the result brought about by the people surrounding the Queen who were all united in supporting the Comte de Guines. Her Majesty was obsessed; they succeeded in irritating her *amour propre*, in blackening all those who in endeavouring to support the good things resisted her will; and all this took place during races or promenades, or during the conversations in the salon of the Princesse de Guémenée. In fact they are so successful in confusing the Queen, in dulling her with dissipations that, joined to the extreme willingness of the King to give in to her, there seemed no way of bringing her to see reason.

And yet, when one considers the strains to which the Queen was subjected, it seems that one can do nothing but pity her. Every now and then in her correspondence with her mother a sentence, a remark shows the real feeling which lay behind so much that appears reprehensible. On 14 January 1776, when the Court was back in Versailles, she said, speaking of the Empress's projected visit to Flanders:

Nothing could be happier or more useful for me. When I left Vienna I was still a child; my heart was certainly torn at parting with my dear Mother, but my need and my spirit were far from realizing that never again would I find such tenderness and such good counsel. If I have the happiness to relive these moments they would be very precious, and would influence the rest of my life.

And Mercy reported that she had been extraordinarily moved by the news that her mother might come. Such small comments show another side to her nature. Was the real woman the one whose stricken unsatisfied heart reached out to the only comforting love she had known, or the frivolous, painted, dressed up doll who has so often been presented to posterity for the last two hundred years?

It is true that her extravagance was increasing, her purchases of jewels at this time were outrageous. Like most women she adored the pretty sparkling stones and she was continually tempted by the merchants who besieged her *lever*, during the final stages of her toilette. She bought a magnificent pair of diamond ornaments costing ten thousand pounds and shortly afterwards a magnificent pair of bracelets. With every letter from Mercy the Empress's concern grew. Now it was the enormous extravagance of the man whom Marie Antoinette had installed as Controller of her Stables, the husband of her beloved friend, the Comte Jules de Polignac. He had doubled the number of the horses in the Queen's stables, and created a service of his own, footmen, coachmen, grooms, postilions, all paid with the King's money and fed and housed in the Royal Mews. He submitted the bills to the Chief Groom of Stables whose complaints against this demand grew and grew, until it seemed that a duel between the two men was imminent. But Monsieur Tessé was persuaded to swallow his wrath, and depart for a vacation in Italy. The Parisian public was, of course, perfectly aware of all this through the indefatigable efforts of the press and correspondents; so was the country. All was laid to the Queen's door. These were *her* friends, intent on feathering their nests at the expense of the State. And the King, who might have put some kind of a stop to it, in his uxoriousness paid her debts, and tolerated her extravagance. In June 1776 the Court was forced to move to Marly because of the illness of the Comte d'Artois – he had the measles. He was indeed gravely affected and there was fear for the Comtesse who was pregnant again and near her time. They kept her husband's danger from her, and her lymphatic nature prevented her from worrying; and the Queen in writing to her mother again gives an indication of her bitter thoughts and regrets when she points out that if she had children like the Comtesse d'Artois her whole life might be different and it was not her fault that she had none.

It is obvious that she knew very well who sent the adverse reports which her mother received and her pride refused to allow her to be disturbed at the gossip circulating in Vienna. In all the correspondence with the Empress there is hardly a word of approbation or praise from the mother who after all had condemned her to this fate, and in most of the immense volume of literature which has dealt with her career we find little compassion for this woman of twenty-one, living in an isolated society but at the mercy of a public hardly less foolish and extravagant than herself. The whole air was impregnated with change. Montgolfier was venturing into the air with his balloons, to be welcomed after his victorious ascent in the Tuileries garden by the Duchesse de Polignac and half the nobility of France. And Mesmer was exercising his feats of what seemed like legerdemain, while again Parisian society sat open-mouthed in wondering circles around him. His claim to be a legitimate medical practitioner, which was recognized by the French Academy of Sciences, counted for much less than the mumbo jumbo of his séances with their clouds of incense, cabalistic robes, and skilful manipulation of his patients' limbs. Even the Queen signalled her interest and approbation. In fine, it was a world which lived on sensation, a disintegrating world avid for the moment, blind to the writing on the wall.

But in October of that year Mercy had even graver excesses to report. The famous horse races organized by the Comte d'Artois and the Duc de Chartres at Fontainebleau were attended by the Queen and her Court and the horrified Mercy wrote that she was seated in a sort of Pavilion improvised for the occasion, which hardly separated her from the crowds. The excitement as on any racecourse passed all bounds of decorum, and the Comte d'Artois, never very self-contained, and hysterical in his desire to win, rushed about urging on his jockeys and insulting them when they lost. Mercy was forced to recognize however that the Queen 'kept her air of grace and grandeur'. She managed to persuade the King to join the party in November, but His Majesty, little attracted by the spectacle, risked a very small sum of money. 'When you bet,' he said to those who played the high game, 'you bet with your own money. As for me I play with the money of others.'

He permitted, however, that a gaming-table should be opened

at the palace for the game of Pharoah, but on condition that it should be for only one sitting. The Court played all night and into the morning, though the Queen left the room at 4 a.m. having lost. The game continued and picked up again on the following night and this time the Queen stayed till three o'clock. The King reproached her on the following day. 'You said we could play without saying how long the sitting could last,' she told him, 'is it our fault if it went on for thirty-six hours?' Her husband laughed at her, and said no more.

If the Queen was reproached by her mother and her advisers Mercy and Vermond, she might very well have replied that at her age, the Empress, now so censorious, was no less gay and pleasure-loving. Had she not gone to the Redouten Balls in Vienna, had she not had her favourite friends and had she not loved magnificent jewels and beautiful clothes? And with less reason, for she was happily married to a husband whom she adored and who satisfied every need of her ardent nature. The answer might have been that Maria Theresa was monarch in a very different society from her daughter, and her mother might have added that in these years times had changed, and were now changing still more rapidly.

It is pleasant to think of Marie Antoinette in a more happy and less feverish mood, in her creation of the small palace which the King had bestowed on her, the little Trianon. Here she could indulge her love of an open-air life such as she had enjoyed in her childhood at Schönbrunn and the hunting-lodge of Laxenburg, and add to them all the charm of her own taste. Versailles was too large, Marly too austere, Fontainebleau too far away, Trianon was perfect for her designs. It had already served this purpose for Louis xv, a place where he could relax, easy of access from the great palace, yet far enough away to be quiet; now she could be at home there. The building was small but placed in the midst of a garden already embellished by order of the late King with a collection of rare and exotic trees and bushes and with parterres laid out following the formal designs of the classic French garden of Le Nôtre. But Marie Antoinette, after the dinner given in honour of her generous husband, was thinking of a pleasure-ground more in keeping with the taste of the time and her own. English gardens were all the fashion, with their natural development of the terrain, their lawns opening on to the vista of fields, their groups of trees skilfully disposed, their flowers growing as if more by chance than by design. And with it all the pseudo classic temple or arch crowning a vista, and offering a perfect site for a meal in the open air.

Horace Walpole in England, or her friend the Duc de Ligne in Belgium, had gardens and she was determined to have the same at Trianon. She added to the park, brought water from Marly to form a stream, and a waterfall and lake, built ruins, undulating hills, and everywhere she planted flowering shrubs and trees, imported from as far away as Lebanon, from Corsica, Italy and Crete. It became a paradise, and matched the exquisite interior of the palace with its delicate carvings echoing the flowers and fruit outdoors. In the dining-room was the famous table made for Louis xv which mounted through the floor and did away with the necessity for servants. In the salon the walls were ornamented with carvings of little Cupids playing with lilies and garlands of laurels, the handles of the doors forged by Louis xvi himself, but the chief jewel was the boudoir of the Queen herself, as we can see it today, the panels carved with the fleur-de-lys entwined with the initials M.A., and the delicious pale blue of the coverings on chairs and couches echoed in the satin scarves holding back the curtains of the lace-covered bed. On the chimneypiece is a clock with the arms of Austria and on the walls were two pictures, now in the Palace of Versailles, one of the little Archduchess dancing a ballet at the wedding of her brother Leopold, the other of her sisters in a scene from an opera. Maria Theresa had sent these paintings by Wertmüller to her daughter as a gift for her new toy.

The library of this Queen who has been pictured as never reading anything comprised 2,930 volumes, and though it was on the light and amusing side, for this was a country house, a place for relaxation and pleasure, there were 1,158 volumes on the sciences and arts, and 1,328 of belles lettres, and judging from the state in which the surviving volumes are today, they were read, together with 536 novels and 408 plays.

In this small domain the Queen could at last be herself; surrounded by the few friends dearest to her heart she could indulge her longing for naturalness; her dress was without the ornament necessary for life at Versailles, muslin, and the blue ribbons she loved, hair *en négligé*, large straw hat which went so well with her blonde beauty. Later she would build the Hamlet with its rustic farm, its cows and sheep, she could give fêtes for the village children, and even, at the end of 1776, adopt one of them, so great was her maternal desire. For it must be remembered that we are considering the life of a woman, not simply an historical figure, a creature of flesh and blood, warm-hearted, vulnerable, who enjoyed at this moment for the first time since coming to France a friendship with a woman whom she trusted, as young and beautiful as herself, on whom she could lavish all the adoration of her generous nature.

She was so foolishly loving, she could not see that when she limited the company at Trianon to the few friends, she offended all the courtiers who considered that they were slighted, that her 'simple' palace cost millions of livres, and was watched by the disapproving eyes of the French public. She was full of sympathy for the misery of the peasants when by chance she saw them, but she did not relate their wants to her own extravagance. It was the business of the Minister of Finance to see to their demands. Only her mother and Mercy, more alert to the comments of the mass, could reiterate their warnings, she simply did not listen. And her husband who might, if he had been a stronger character, have refused to sanction her spending, was either too indolent, or too concerned with affairs of State or what is more probable, too conscious of his own shortcomings as a husband to interfere; he loved her now and she must indeed have been enchanting.

Unfortunately, at Trianon as in Versailles, the Queen was surrounded by her coterie, and more and more intimately associated with Madame de Polignac. This gentle violet-eyed beauty was to cost the State through her family and friends half a million livres a year. The Queen could deny her nothing. She later became governess of the royal children, and her husband received the title of Duke. Worst of all, the Queen constantly showed her affection, she walked arm-in-arm in the gardens of Versailles; when parted for a day long letters were exchanged. Madame de Polignac now had her own salon in a large hall in the palace facing the Orangerie. Here she received three days in the week. 'Does she receive the whole of France?' wrote the Prince de Ligne to the Prince de Lille, who replied:

Yes, on Tuesday, Wednesday and Thursday from morning till night.

During these seventy hours there is a general ballet, anyone can enter anyone can sup. It is astonishing how this rabble of courtiers abounds. During these three days the hothouse is also occupied, made into a gallery, it contains a billiard table. On the four other days the doors are open to us, the others, the favourites.

The favourites were all those who had found the way to minister to the Queen's insatiable thirst for diversion; as a reward for amusing her they demanded favours, either in appointments which cost money, or in a familiarity which was even more costly to the Queen's reputation.

During the Carnival of 1775 the Queen's appetite for pleasure reached its climax. By now she must have been pretty well without hope of a normal sexual life with her husband, she was subject to sudden bursts of irritation, of excitability, commonly called in those days the vapours, and these could only be assuaged by an immoderate round of gaiety. She burned the candle at both ends, was never home before dawn, and most perilous for a woman in her position, she conducted herself with a freedom which allowed a corresponding licence in the behaviour of those surrounding her. Mercy was in despair, he wrote that she was incapable of refusing any demand made upon her, and was only happy in the company of those who provided her with distractions. When he and the Abbé Vermond tried to reason with her, she listened to them with the utmost patience, she admitted all their criticisms, for her native intelligence told her that their strictures were just. But they could not make her see the real necessity for restraint.

Sometime her courtiers went too far, however, hence the scene which became so famous and which had such disastrous results. The Duc de Lauzun appeared one day in the salon of Madame de Guémenée wearing a magnificent heron's plume in his hat. The Queen admired it, and he offered it to her by the hand of Madame de Guémenée. Since he had worn it, the Queen had never imagined that he could offer it to her, and was most embarrassed and at a loss what to do; she accepted it, and hesitated whether to give him a present in return. Afraid that if she did, it might be either too much or too little, she compromised by wearing the feather once. The Duc, too flattered by the honour done him, some time later asked for an audience which she granted, as she would have done to any noble of her Court. It is Madame Campan who tells the story, for she was in an adjoining room. Some minutes after his arrival, the Queen opened the door, and said in an angry voice, 'Leave me, Monsieur.' Monsieur de Lauzun bowed profoundly and disappeared, very agitated. The Queen said, 'This man shall never appear before me again.' Some years after, when by the death of his uncle he became Duc de Biron he wished for the important post of Colonel of the French Guards. Marie Antoinette gave it to the Duc de Châtelet. His bitter hatred was thus assured, she had made an enemy. But one may see in this account another side; it was the equivocal behaviour of the Queen which raised false hopes in the dandies surrounding her, the whole atmosphere of her Court was taking on a colour which gave some basis to the spiteful comments of the Parisian press, to her two mentors and through them to the Empress.

Another disquieting evidence of the Queen's state of mind was her growing passion for gaming. Every night, when she was not at the opera balls which she attended under the fragile disguise of a mask, she sat late at the card-table, winning or losing, most frequently the latter. Her expenses grew into debts which, added to the expenses of her Court, had reached a terrifying total. At Trianon she was not content with beautifying her property, she must have her theatre there and her troup of players. It is true that very frequently she herself with her friends were the actors, but this was another grievance for the French public who were not accustomed to see their Queen playing the soubrette. It was in her eyes an innocent and cultivated pleasure, but by this time every action of hers was misinterpreted, lampoons proliferated, all viciously abusive. The King too was not spared. His uxoriousness and his notorious defect were sneered at.

In fact Louis had more serious things to think about. In 1776 the American colonies had rebelled against the English and Vergennes, the Minister for War, had to decide whether he should support them or the English, a difficult choice. He chose the colonials, but only to the extent of supplying them with arms through intermediaries, of whom Beaumarchais was one. After the Declaration of Independence, France received as Ambassador Benjamin Franklin. His fame had preceded him. He was a scientist, had discovered, thanks to his remarkable powers of observation, such useful things as the lightning conductor, and was moreover brilliant in conversation and a wit, all of which appealed mightily to the French. He was elected to the Academy of Sciences. Liberty was in the air and the Parisian bourgeoisie formed a very odd idea of the American insurgents, thinking them all rustic idealists and not realizing that in fact the revolution was the protest of an educated middle class against fiscal laws which it refused to tolerate because they were unjustly imposed.

Voltaire too, was in Paris; at the age of eighty-four he had decided to make the journey and go down in a blaze of glory rather than the ten years his doctors promised him if he stayed quietly in Ferney. His wish was fulfilled, Paris and indeed all France was at his feet, every class found something to adore in this old fighter. The intelligentsia thought him the greatest writer and intelligence in Europe, an opinion which Europe echoed. To the reformers he was a prophet, to the philosophers he was the enemy of the Church with his famous cry *'écrasez l'infâme'*. Only Versailles held aloof, and Marie Antoinette refused to receive him. How could she, the pious daughter of a profoundly devout mother? She would have been quite incapable of understanding his books even if she had wanted to, and though she might have been more sympathetic to his real concern for human beings, she could not have approved the means he advocated to procure their betterment. He wanted a limited monarchy, an enlightened aristocracy deprived of its unearned privileges, and the suppression of the power of the Church and a less privileged priesthood. Neither she nor Louis XVI could estimate the influence which this man had had on the thought of his time, nor foresee its results for themselves. Back in 1725 he had been insulted at the Comédie Française by the Chevalier de Rohan, and made an impertinent reply. Two or three days later he was dining with the Duc de Sully when a message was sent in that someone wished to speak to him and on his going down was set on outside the door by valets of the Chevalier, who stood on one side and encouraged them. Furious, Voltaire challenged Rohan to a duel, an unthinkable occurrence for an aristocrat, and the result was imprisonment in the Bastille. But fifteen days later he was released on condition that he left France, and in a few weeks he was in the house of his friend Lord Bolingbroke in London. The French Court, the *ancien régime*, had made a dangerous enemy. They were more vulnerable than they thought: 'I have no sceptre,' he said, 'but I have a pen.'

In 1776 Turgot had fallen, his reforming zeal had not been able to withstand the palace intrigues against him; Marie Antoinette and her coterie were jubilant, Artois in particular was hysterical in his triumph. The Queen was somewhat more restrained and the Empress warned her that since she was no longer so popular, she should endeavour not to offend the public. Once more she had let her personal feelings rule her public behaviour. It was the first important political mistake she made.

Turgot was replaced by Necker, the Swiss financier and millionaire, an extraordinary man who was much more than a mere money-maker. From the age of fifteen when he entered the bank of Isaac Vernet in Geneva, his rise had been quiet but uninterrupted and at the end of the Seven Years' War he had emerged with a fortune, some said millions. He was already in Paris and now he needed a wife, one who could sway the salons as he would sway finance. For in the Parisian world women were all-powerful, they vied with each other in attracting the famous travellers or the prominent writers or politicians of the time.

He found what he wanted in Mademoiselle Susanne Curchod, the daughter of a Swiss pastor and like himself rigidly educated in Swiss Protestantism. She was beautiful, intelligent, musical and ambitious. Having failed to marry Edward Gibbon, to whom she had been engaged, she found herself in Paris, a governess, and on the look-out for a match. They married and by the time Necker was created Director of Finances in 1777 her drawing-room had become the most famous in Paris. She had worked for four years to make it so. It was frequented by Grimm, the most prolific correspondent of the time, Marmontel and Diderot. Fortified by such famous names she aimed higher still; at a dinner in her house a gathering of *Philosophes*, so reported Grimm, 'having eaten a copious dinner and talked nonsense on a number of subjects resolved by unanimous vote to erect a statue to Monsieur Voltaire'. The sage was conquered, he called her Hypatia, wrote verses to her and corresponded with her regularly till the day of his death.

It seems a strange choice for Louis XVI to make, a Swiss banker, a Protestant and a liberal, but the times demanded stringent measures. Necker had the confidence of the English banks, he was an economist, a writer and a man of strict moral life, which recommended him to the Queen. He had learned on his way up how to manipulate and conciliate people. Mercy commented in his dispatches on the happy way in which the Minister managed never to offend the Queen by a formal refusal, instead he reasoned with her and patiently showed her how difficulties could be surmounted without conceding essential principles. He went further; 'Of all the King's ministers M. Necker is the one of whom the Queen has the most favourable opinion and whom she considers most.' Even when, after reducing the King's Court he proposed to make economies in hers, she submitted with not too bad grace and wrote to the Empress, 'If the reform is executed, it will be a very good thing not only as an economy, but also in regard to public opinion.' She authorized Mercy to convey her approbation to the Neckers, and to say that she always read with interest about his financial operations.

This was enough, of course, for her coterie, who had at first approved of Necker, to turn against him, and to do all in their power to damage him in her eyes. Without success, however, for once she stood firm.

One may comment very fairly on the discrepancy between Marie Antoinette's approbation for Necker's 'moral life' and her toleration of the immorality of various members of her Court, particularly of Madame de Polignac's lover, M. de Vaudreuil. It cannot be denied that she was inconsistent in this as in much else. If one seeks for an explanation one might say that this had been the attitude of the Court of Versailles for centuries and that she, like Louis XIV's mistress, La Vallière, accepted it while personally preferring a good life, and appreciating rectitude and probity in others, particularly Ministers of the Crown.

It is impossible to exaggerate the pressure which these people put upon the Queen, they besieged her night and day and through her love for Madame de Polignac they could attack her where she was weakest. In turn, bewildered by their persistence, and without the political experience which would have helped her to withstand them, she worked upon the King. Louis was throughout his life incapable of reaching a decision without hesitation; and besides this, as we have already pointed out, he was in a position of some difficulty in his relations with his wife. She had a much firmer will than his own, his inadequacy now made him feel guilty, and finally he felt a warmth of affection which made him desire to please her even at the expense of his better judgment.

At the beginning of the year 1777 it seemed that at last the Queen was to have the pleasure of her brother's visit. The Empress had decided that it could be put off no longer, in the interest of their two States and far more in the interest of their families, by which she meant the succession. The Emperor would come but in the strictest incognito, and without any official reception, and his mother wrote that she hoped that her daughter would speak to him with complete confidence and sincerity, believing in his discretion and trusting in the advice he could give her.

His visit was delayed because of the political situation at home, where the Turks and the Russians, the Portuguese and the Spanish were all causing trouble, and the Empress was all the more agitated because she felt that the slightest false step, besides bringing a malevolent pleasure to her 'bad neighbour' might be followed by worse consequences. She wrote on 3 February 1777 that in his rage at the opposition he had sustained from Austria he lost no opportunity in vilifying its rulers and policy, and she deeply regretted that her daughter would not see her brother. The pleasure which the King of Prussia showed at the postponement proved quite clearly how important the meeting was. And she again implored Marie Antoinette to moderate her public behaviour, to stay more with the King, so that the insinuations against her in the courts of Berlin, Saxony, Poland and elsewhere should be groundless. Distrust of the King of Prussia was the mainspring of all her political thought.

The Queen answered: 'Although I have very little experience I cannot help feeling great disquiet about all that is happening in Europe. It would be terrible if the Turks and the Russians recommenced the war. At least in this country there is a great wish to preserve the peace.' Mercy commented:

If ever I can flatter myself that I have made an impression it is in this instance. I saw the Queen frightened by the picture which I presented to her, of the possibility of the risks of war, of the influence which Her Majesty might have in cooperating on many issues, of the personal interest, on the credit which would come to her from such influence, as against the discredit towards which she moves [through her pursuit of amusement].

In March her mother still feared for peace, and she also commented on the appointment of the Prince de Rohan to the office of Grand Almoner, for which he was so unfitted. He would be

an enemy of her daughter, who very well knew this; his licentious
life ill fitted him to be a priest. He had done much harm in
Vienna – and was later to do much more in Paris – and mother
and daughter agreed that his position near the throne was dis-
tasteful, to say the least of it. From this time on the diplomacy of
Mercy and the pressure of the Empress all contributed to the
increasing subservience of the Queen to the Austrian necessities,
a subservience which would cost her much more in public esteem
than all her frivolity put together. The '*Autrichienne*' would be
the name by which she was called, and the hatred of the 'foreigner'
would finally sign her death warrant.

But now the great event was to be the visit of her brother the
Emperor Joseph II; she hoped so much from it, first the pleasure
of seeing someone from Vienna, her beloved home, then, the
possibility of his influencing the King in the matter of the desired
operation, and further in the consolidation of the Austro-French
Alliance. We have seen that the Emperor was a man of very
decided opinions, and this was immediately apparent in his
insistence on strict incognito. He would travel as Count
Frankenstein, and decided on occupying a lodging-house instead
of the apartments which his sister had arranged for him in
Versailles. This put the Princes of the Blood in a turmoil; how
were they to receive him if he condescended to visit them?
Would he sit on an armchair, and they, would they sit on a bench
or on a chair with a back? Should they conduct him to the door
of the salon, or to the entry in the antechamber? They need not
have worried; from his arrival Joseph criticized the strict etiquette
of the Court of Versailles and flouted it whenever possible. His
first interview with Marie Antoinette passed off in great affability.
'If you were not my sister,' said the Emperor, 'I might even
think of remarrying if I could find so charming a companion.' If
only this happy state of affairs could have continued; alas Joseph
soon began to criticize not only the Court but the King. He
seemed to have assumed that he would find in Louis XVI a sim-
pleton, easily influenced to follow the policy which was nearest
to Austria's present design – the annexation of Bavaria. He found,
however, a young monarch by no means as stupid as he expected,
and moreover advised by an exceedingly able Minister, Vergennes, who regarded Austrian demands with a sceptical eye.
This being so the Emperor was all the more convinced that only

the growing ascendancy which the Queen enjoyed over her husband could influence French policy in the desired direction.

On her side the Queen did all she could to render her brother's stay agreeable, but his passion for effacement made her task difficult. His first public appearance was at the Opera, where Gluck's *Iphigénie* was given. Joseph at first hid at the back of the royal box, but the Queen insisted on drawing him forward to the great satisfaction of the public, who when the choir sang 'celebrate our Queen' on the entrance of Clytemnestra applauded vigorously. A fête in the gardens of Trianon might have been expected to win his approval. The delicious grounds were illuminated, light shone on the temple hidden among the trees and the lake reflected the delicate colours of the dresses and costumes of the men and women. Laughter and music abounded, could anything have been more brilliant, more refined, a more perfect setting for the Queen's beauty and grace? Alas, the festivity evoked general dissatisfaction, first from those courtiers who had not been invited, and then from the public who objected to the expense.

On the other hand, this same public approved strongly of the Emperor. He was frugal, slept on a camp-bed, was served by one servant and criticized the extravagance of Versailles. He was, however, not above visiting Madame Du Barry in the luxurious retreat at Louveciennes, where she had by now been allowed to retire, and where she held Court. But the main object of Joseph's visit was achieved, he had succeeded, after prolonged conversations, in persuading his brother-in-law to agree to the terrifying operation; but this would not be enough, and he lost no time in lecturing his sister on her faults, especially on the separation of their beds. She must be more of a wife, listen less to the claims of the set of vultures who surrounded her, spend less time in the 'Gambling hell' in Madame de Guémenée's apartments, waste less money on clothes and jewels. He was observant, visited institutions in Paris such as the Invalides, attended the sittings of the Parlement and the Academy, and criticized the King for never having done the same. In his two months' stay he learned more of France than its two monarchs had done in all their lives. All this ravished the public, while the Emperor himself knew perfectly well what he was about. First to secure the dynasty, and secondly to arrive at an understanding politically with his brother-in-law and frustrate the misgiving of the 'bad neighbour', Frederick of Prussia.

He stayed two months and left with Marie Antoinette a wordy letter of advice, most of it repetitive, but some of it penetrating. He realized that the Queen had no profound love for her husband but asked:

Do you try to make yourself necessary to him, do you sacrifice any of your own pleasures for his sake, do you keep silent on the subject of his failings and mistakes, and do you refuse to allow others to comment on them? Do you conduct yourself with the dignity befitting your station, or do you leave your King alone, night after night in Versailles while you rub shoulders with all and sundry in Paris?

None of this was much different from the reiterated warnings of her mother, but he finished his long letter with words which should have struck cold to her heart: 'Truly I tremble for your happiness, because in the long run things cannot go on like this. The revolution will be a cruel one, perhaps of your own making.' Like all prophecies it was too simplified, but for this one woman's life it was true.

In spite of his brusqueness, his satire and his criticism, the Queen was heartbroken when he left and she honestly meant to follow his advice. All her letters to the Empress were full of the pleasure she felt at the success of her brother's visit in the eyes of the nation and her resolve to heed him, and on 30 August 1777 she could write:

I am in a state of the most profound happiness. Eight days ago my marriage was perfectly consummated, the trial was reiterated and more completely than the first time. I wanted to send the news to my dear mother at once, but I was afraid it might be premature. And I wanted to be absolutely convinced. I do not think that I am already pregnant, but at least I have the hope that I may be at any moment. What will be my dear mother's joy, I know it will be as great as my own.

The Empress's reply was true to type, no explosion of joy, instead a long sermon which would have done justice to a mid-wife: 'Never refuse yourself to your husband, no more late nights nor nocturnal parties, you can play billiards or a quiet game of commerce, no more high play, you lose too much, which after all the State must pay. Listen to the experience of a mother.' To which her daughter replied that the King did not like to share a room – possibly because he was an early riser, in order to visit his forge or carpenter's shop. But he passed some of his nights with her, and visited her every morning, his tenderness and love increasing all the time. Indeed he had confessed to his aunts that he experienced an entirely new pleasure in the changed circumstances, and was sorry that he had waited so long.

He had plenty of other things to think about and none of them could be called pleasureable. Necker, who had been installed as Director-General of Finance, was endeavouring to rescue the depleted treasury by means of loans, the provinces were in a state of turbulence, ministers such as Turgot were made or dismissed according to the whim of the Queen egged on by her coterie, and above all, the Emperor had not succeeded completely in disguising the real motive for his visit. When asked his opinion on the American rebellion, he had refused to comment saying, 'Sir, I am silent, my business is royalist', a proof that in spite of his desire for reform, he was not prepared to renounce his legitimate position. On his way home he had stopped at Brest and Toulon, which he had pronounced the finest harbours in Europe, but had been distinctly pessimistic on the condition of the French Navy.

Following her first outburst of satisfaction the Queen set herself to wait month by month for the hoped-for pregnancy. And month by month she was forced to write her mother that nothing had changed in her condition. Poor woman, not only had she to bear her own anxiety, but the eyes of Europe were upon her; was she really barren, was it after all not the fault of the King that he had no heir to his throne? Not least apprehensive was Monsieur, until now the heir-apparent. This devious man had his private hate, nourished in secret and subterranean plotting. If the Queen bore a son, a Dauphin, goodbye to his hopes. And of all the foolish conduct which she might have chosen, the Queen chose the most unwise. Forgotten were the good resolutions, gambling began again for ever higher stakes and by the end of the year she was deeply in debt. With horror Mercy watched the figures mount. He remonstrated in vain; with the Director-General forbidding gambling, what could the public think of this flouting of the law at Court? She did not care, she would not be bored. D'Artois, as mad as she, bet her that he could construct a château in the Bois de Boulogne during the six weeks while the Court was at Fontainebleau. She accepted, the stakes were a hundred thousand francs. This was the château of Bagatelle a 'little nothing', and to build it nine hundred workmen toiled day and night. And Mercy recounted that since this was not enough, the patrols of the Swiss Guards were sent on to all the roads to find wood and whatever other materials they could commandeer on wagons coming into Paris. They paid for what they took it was true, but since the materials had already been sold, the people watched with disgust, and blamed the King for what they considered his stupid toleration of the Queen's excesses. Louis admitted to Mercy that he was far from approving his graceless brother, but he had no means of stopping him. Only the Queen could have deterred him, and she herself was an offender.

At the end of 1777 Louis XVI recognized the Independence of the United States and signed a treaty of alliance. This meant war with England, a war which nobody wanted and which could bring no good to France, for which Necker was forced to increase his borrowing, principally for the Navy. And in the beginning of the year 1778 the letters from the Empress were showing signs of a much deeper anxiety. The Elector of Bavaria had died on 30 December. In the expectation of this demise Joseph had already negotiated with his heir, the Elector Palatine, the cession to Austria of some districts of Bavaria to which he pretended to have the right. This was vigorously opposed by the Empress who feared, and rightly, that Frederick of Prussia would adopt a bellicose attitude towards Austria. In fact Prussian troops were immediately sent to the frontier where they were joined by those of the Elector of Saxony. The vital question was, what would be the reaction of France, and Maria Theresa from the beginning of the year in her own letters and through Mercy sought the influence of her daughter, not only on the King but on his ministers.

Her mother wrote, 'I ask you to listen to Mercy with attention. It is the peace of Europe which is in question, the friendship of the King which is doubly dear to me because of the tie which unites our political interests which should be forever indissoluble.' The Queen replied, on the advice of Mercy, that she was convinced that an object so essential to the understanding of their two States should continue in peace. Her mother insisted in succeeding letters that the danger was that the King of Prussia should achieve an understanding with France, 'which would cause my death', a remark which made the Queen blench, as it was doubtless meant to do. In letter after letter she reminded the Queen of her duty to her family and her '*patrie*' and in interview after interview Marie Antoinette sought to bend the King to her will. But on this one point Louis XVI remained intractable; secretly fortified by the wise counsel of his Minister Vergennes, he refused to allow France to be drawn in more than was necessary to make Frederick think twice about commencing a war. And to his wife he was explicit: 'It is the ambition of your relations which will upset everything,' he said. 'They began with Poland, now we have the second edition in Bavaria; I am annoyed for your sake.' The Queen reminded him that he had been informed about the Bavarian affair. 'I was so little in agreement with it, that we gave orders to the French ministers to let it be known in the Courts where they were appointed that the dismemberment of Bavaria did not meet with Our approval,' was his reply.

At the same time, the beginning of the Carnival, an affair exploded at the opera ball of which Marie Antoinette sent an expurgated version to her mother, knowing very well that the story would be circulated with delight by the scandalmongers of Vienna. During the masked ball the Comte d'Artois, promenading with the dismissed lady-in-waiting of the Duchesse de Bourbon, was assailed by the latter in no measured terms. 'Nobody could speak like that but Monsieur d'Artois or a scamp,' cried the enraged Duchesse, and she tore the mask from d'Artois' face. The scandal grew when next day d'Artois boasted that he had slapped the Duchesse's face in return. At this the husband took a hand in the affair, and challenged his cousin to a duel. They were to meet in the Bois, and the Prince de Condé prepared relays of horses on the route to Belgium in case his son Bourbon killed the King's brother. All the efforts of Marie Antoinette, Besenval and Vaudreuil were unsuccessful in preventing this incredible affair. The adversaries met and after a few moments Artois lightly wounded his opponent and the combatants confessed themselves satisfied. But the mischief was done, the public blamed the Duc de Chartres, Bourbon's brother, for treating it too lightly, and inevitably Marie Antoinette for not preventing it, and taking d'Artois' part. She was unwise enough to appear next night at the Comédie Française and while Condé and the Duc and Duchesse de Bourbon were warmly applauded, only a few cool handclaps greeted her. Still worse, during the opera ball she was assailed by women in the crowd who reproached her for not being at the side of her 'snoring husband', and all her response was laughter. But she told the Empress that the King came to her bed two or three nights in the week and she was filled with hope. It was high time that something should save her from herself.

In March 1778 the Queen, beset daily by the demands of her mother and the insistence of Mercy, called in Maurepas and Vergennes, for by this time she had a shrewd idea who was strengthening the resistance of the King. It is true that she herself had been half-hearted in her support of the Austrian demands, her real country as she reminded the Empress was France, and too she must have been aware that Joseph's policy of aggrandizement had not his mother's full support. The two ministers listened to what she had to say and appeared in favour of the alliance, 'but they are so afraid of a land war that when I had pushed them to the limit of the King of Prussia commencing hostilities they were ambiguous in their replies'. At the end of the month the King of Prussia protested officially against the Habsburg demands, and insisted on the withdrawal of the Austrian troops from Bavaria. Maria Theresa was beside herself with anxiety, and she insisted that the Queen should support Mercy when he demanded that France should reaffirm the treaty of 1756, which stated that in case of aggression France would supply 24,000 men, or money. But she also reproached her daughter with a lack of firmness, she was too occupied in dissipation to pay sufficient attention to important matters.

On 19 April, however, Marie Antoinette had other news to impart, news which took precedence over everything else. She was at least practically certain that she was pregnant. She knew that her mother would share her joy, and she assured her that since the hope was aroused in her she took the greatest care to avoid anything which might imperil the happy event. She admitted that she was worried over the military situation and in fact she had seen Maurepas and Vergennes again, and had spoken with more heat – and she could show heat when she was excited – but the response of the ministers was still the same, the treaty did not guarantee the Austrian empire in its new appropriation of territories. And she concluded with the wish that she could be spared all this terror at a time when it was essential that she should remain calm. What to her was Poland, what Bavaria. Nothing could take precedence over France, her *'vraie patrie'*. And this *was* France, within her.

Mercy and the Empress only saw in the Queen's condition an augmented power over her husband and redoubled their demands, without success. Louis XVI remained firm. Maria Theresa represented to her daughter the danger which a Prussia, master of Europe, would be to France. 'It is he,' she wrote, 'who wishes to make himself dictator over the whole of Germany; for the last seventeen years he has brought misery to Europe by his despotism and violence.' Marie Antoinette raged against the manner in which she was treated by the Ministers; she only heard of decisions through Mercy, she was unable to get anything out of the King. Finally in a great scene, urged on by the Ambassador, she confronted her husband, reproached him with his lack of care for those nearest to her, and worked herself up into a storm of tears and arguments. His silence desolated her heart, she was ashamed that her mother should see how little she meant to him. One can imagine the troubled King; he loved her now, she carried his child, his hope for the succession, what could he say? His good sense warned him and he said, 'You see that I am wrong in everything, there is nothing I can say to you.' She was disarmed.

She threw all the blame for her husband's intransigence on his Minister in her letters, and on her side Maria Theresa employed every argument which could appeal to either the Queen's real love for the country of her birth, or her dawning sense of France's danger. Both of them had a horror of war: as women they thought not only of politics but of the immense misery which it brings. The Empress knew exactly how to touch her daughter's feelings, gone were the grumblings, the constant criticisms, instead she wrote tenderly of her daughter's health, her love for her brothers, and appealed always to the deep affection which they had for each other. Frederick had his invaluable ambassador and his spies in Paris, and in St Petersburg a tacit ally who was as suspect for the Empress as the King himself. At this juncture the political acumen of the Empress found another argument. What would happen to France if the Emperor, despairing of help, were to turn in another direction, if some sort of union was effected between Austria and England? Versailles was already preoccupied with the danger of a maritime war. At this moment Frederick, certain that the Low Countries were guaranteed by France, turned his back on them, and marching East entered Nachod in Bohemia, and the war, so feared by the Empress, broke out. She wrote to Mercy that she was frantic with worry, and he, less considerate of Marie Antoinette's condition than she, showed the letter to the Queen, on whom it had a disastrous effect. She countermanded a fête arranged for the Trianon and, bathed in tears, rushed to her husband, and with his approval once more convened Maurepas. This time she did not spare the Minister. Over and over again she had spoken to him, always with the same evasive answer. Only the non-interference of France had encouraged the King of Prussia. Maurepas was at a loss what to answer except to excuse himself; his policy remained the same.

Now the Empress was ready to sacrifice anything. She sent an envoy to Frederick offering to renounce all pretension to Bavaria if Prussia would on his side renounce the succession to Bayreuth and Anspach. She met with refusal and her son angrily disagreed with her; the war continued and he was forced to retire. Cries of indignation and despair! 'Save your House and your brother,' she wrote. 'I will never ask more of the King that may involve him in this unhappy war, only that he should make a show of assembling generals and troops as if to help us.' Again the Queen went to the King, at that very moment in conference with Maurepas and Vergennes. What she asked seemed so reasonable, simply a mediation which could do no harm to France, and this time she seemed to convince the ministers. During the whole summer the matter hung in the balance and one must pity the Queen torn in two directions, between the love of her mother and family and her loyalty to her second home.

Her letters were interspersed with all the personal details of a daughter expecting her first child; the two women were united at least in this. Her health was good, she was in a trance of joy, at times she said she could hardly believe it was true. In June she had moved to Marly where the air was better than at Versailles. She did not drive much, or only rather slowly and she walked a little each day. And she measured herself, she had put on four and a half inches. She had all sorts of ideas as to how her baby should be nursed and brought up, it would not be swaddled, but put in a sort of cradle which would leave it much more free. The public too seemed better disposed towards her. When the good news was announced a *Te Deum* had been sung, and to share her happiness with the people she had sent twelve thousand livres to Paris and four thousand to Versailles to be spent on people unable to pay for nurses in childbirth, a gesture which was warmly welcomed. The King was in the seventh heaven of contentment. He felt himself as a father at last, he loaded his wife with attentions. She noted the first movement of the child, and played one of her favourite tricks on her husband. Entering his apartment, she said: 'I come Sire, to complain of one of your subjects who has been so audacious as to give me a blow on my stomach.' Louis laughed with his great horse laugh and embraced her tenderly.

Not everybody was equally pleased. The aunts were cool in their felicitations, the sisters-in-law cooler still, while Monsieur wrote to the King of Sweden that though he had managed to suppress his feelings outwardly, his friend could imagine what he felt within himself. And the ministers, sensing that with the birth of a Dauphin the Queen's position and influence would be even more assured than it had been, lost no opportunity for circulating insinuations against her on the score of her excessive interest in a foreign country. The courtiers who had not been invited to Marly, too small to accommodate the whole of the Queen's Court, felt left out and resented all the more that the favourite Madame de Polignac had been sent for in haste by the King to comfort the Queen. The Comtesse de Marsan, whose apartments had always been a centre of intrigue, gave an eager ear to the scandals by Rohan's secretary, Georgel. The writers of the libellous verses circulating in Paris drew on these sources of scandal.

The summer of 1778 was extremely hot, and Marie Antoinette, who suffered from the stuffy air of her apartments, took pleasure in walking on the terrace in the cool of the evening. It was the Comte d'Artois who brought the musicians of the Chapel Royal to add to the pleasure of the balmy nights; the Queen, lightly dressed in simple percale with a big straw hat veiled with muslin, leaned on the arm of her sister-in-law, sat on a bench, or slowly paced up and down the terrace. The effect was charming and it was not long before the citizens of Versailles discovered that they might enjoy it too. One of them, a young officer pretending not to recognize the Queen, or perhaps really not knowing at first that it was she, spoke to her, and since he was amusing she took pleasure in joking with him. After a few minutes the ladies rose and the young man having by this time realized to whom he had been speaking, was sufficiently stupid, or tactless, to boast of it. The same thing happened on another occasion, but this time the Queen was offended and spoke of the matter at her toilet to Madame Campan, who recounts the episode, which she says was afterwards told with the most scurrilous comment by the Queen's biographers. It has not escaped repetition to this day. Madame Campan even tried to point out to her royal mistress the disastrous effect which might follow such imprudent behaviour, but the Queen merely laughed at her. These concerts did in fact give rise to the most disgusting imputations, so disrespectful that they were a disgrace to the society which gave them credence. It was even implied that the father of her child was the only member of the royal family who had been capable of a numerous offspring. A few days before her *accouchement* a manuscript was thrown through the Oeil de Bœuf, a whole volume of songs and scribbles about her and other well-known women. It was taken at once to the King, who felt the dishonour shown to his wife. He had himself been present at the promenades and had seen no harm in them. Perhaps he asked himself if his own conduct in leaving her so much alone had not contributed to her unpopularity. Even her mother seems to have had a moment of responsibility towards her, to have put on one side the purely Austrian considerations which obsessed her and thought of her daughter first. She wrote to Mercy that she feared that Marie Antoinette had perhaps been pushed too far, and the effect might have been to render her too importunate to the King, suspect to his ministers and odious to the nation. It was a pity that she had not considered this earlier. Now it was too late. Nothing that the Queen could do would ever eradicate from French minds the deep belief that she was suspect and to be hated as a foreigner caring nothing for France and guilty of partiality to the country of her birth.

As the time drew near for her *accouchement* she thought more and more of what lay before her. She had the natural pleasure of all mothers in preparing for her baby, the nurse was chosen, though she expressed the wish to nourish the child herself. She amused herself with the layette, above all she realized that all France was watching her, and beyond the frontiers, all Europe. Would it be a Dauphin? This was her hope and that of the King. Even M. de Maurepas seized the opportunity to represent to her how much more dear ought to be the interests of France, to which she replied that she appreciated the justice of what he said, and that she would play no further part in the affairs of the Austrian war. She kept her word.*

It is certain that she had never advocated an armed intervention, and for this we cite the evidence of a man who could not be accused of partiality, the Prussian Ambassador, von der Goltz. Writing to his master he said that Maurepas admitted in justice that the Queen listened to reason when he represented to her that the child which she carried cried without ceasing to her that she was before all Queen of France; and that she, much moved, thanked him for reminding her of her real duty, and that in effect she had, during the later course of the affair, never intervened.

The negotiations for peace were finally concluded on 13 May at Teschen. The Empress was thankful, Joseph humiliated in his pride and discontented with France, a country which he said was allied and which posed as friend. He was forced to renounce his pretension to Bavaria, but the Empress wrote on 1 May 1779 expressing her gratitude to the King for his good offices and Marie Antoinette replied that she desired before all the understanding between her two peoples. But the French public did not forget that a huge subsidy in cash – fifteen millions of livres – had been sent to Joseph. They had seen the lorries loaded with gold leaving Paris, and had put it down to the account of '*l'Autrichienne*'.

* See the correspondence of Mirabeau with the Comte de la Marck.

4

The Necklace

As the time for the Queen's *accouchement* drew near even the French public seemed inclined to forget its malicious and mean thoughts and the whole nation prayed for her safe delivery and, of course, for a Dauphin. Her mother was more sensible; from the experience of a woman who had produced sixteen children she knew that, as she said, boys could follow girls, but she too, with all the population of Vienna implored Heaven and the Saints for a safe outcome. The French Court was more occupied with intrigues, antiquated custom demanded that a numerous assembly should be present at the actual birth of a royal infant, doubtless to assure its legitimacy. Hundreds of people from Paris invaded Versailles, not a bed or a lodging was to be had, and the price of food mounted daily.

On 18 December the Queen went to bed as usual, but at half past one the pains began, and Madame de Lamballe and the chief ladies-in-waiting entered her bedchamber. At three o'clock M. de Chimay fetched the King and this was the signal for all the princes and princesses who were in the town to rush to the palace, while pages tore off to Paris and St Cloud. The royal family, the Princes of the Blood and their wives seated themselves around the bed. The Court of the King and that of the Queen crowded in the apartments adjoining. When the Doctor Vermond cried '*La Reine va accoucher*', the enormous waiting multitude precipitated itself into all the rooms. The unfortunate Queen's

bed was only protected by a fragile golden balustrade but the
King had taken care to tie up with strong cords the curtains which
surrounded it, otherwise they might have fallen down on the
struggling body of the agonized woman. It was impossible to
move in the room, and men even climbed on to the furniture the
better to see the spectacle of a Queen of France reduced to the
common lot of any woman in childbirth. At half past eleven in
the morning the child was born, a girl. It was carried immediately
into the next apartment to be cared for and handed to Madame
de Guémenée; the King, beaming with excitement followed. Suddenly a cry was heard, 'Air, air and hot water!' The lack of
air, the noise, and her natural exhaustion had gone to the Queen's
head, she was suffocating; horror struck the Court, Lamballe
fainted, only the surgeon kept his head, and since there was no
hot water he bled the Queen's foot, which had the immediate and
happy effect of bringing the blood from her head. She opened
her eyes, she was saved, but it had been a near thing. Everyone
rejoiced, laughter and tears, felicitations, a wave of jubilant
congratulations swept over the throng. Couriers departed for
Madrid and Vienna, the Marquis de Béon prepared to ride for
Paris there to acquaint the dignitaries of the town and all its
inhabitants with the splendid news. Meanwhile the Cardinal de
Rohan, the Grand Almoner, prepared to baptize the infant.
Monsieur represented the King of Spain, godfather, and Madame
and the Empress, godmothers. A solemn *Te Deum* was sung in
the Chapel and in the evening there were fireworks. Not only
Versailles, all France was drunk with rejoicing. Prisoners
incarcerated for debts owed to nurses were liberated, all the
principal houses of the towns were illuminated. The baby was
named Marie Theresa Charlotte; it was a pretty little thing but
it was not a Dauphin. When, after all the ceremony, it was finally
handed to its mother she pressed it to her heart. 'Poor little one,'
she murmured, 'you were not wanted. But for me you will be
all the more dear. A boy would have belonged to the State. You
will be mine, you will have all my care, you will share my
happiness and you will lessen my pain.'

The King was beside himself with pleasure, he felt a new
dignity in his role of father. He could not see enough of his little
daughter, he even gave up his usual riding, visited her cot in the
early morning and returned to spend most of the afternoons

Portrait of the
young Queen

Madame de
Polignac, the
Queen's favourite by
Madame Vigée Lebrun

Comte Axel de Fersen, aged twenty-eight years

beside her. The day when the baby first gripped his finger was a wonder to him. The Queen quickly regained her strength and on 8 February, accompanied by the King, Monsieur and Madame, and the Comte and Comtesse d'Artois, she went to Paris, there to give thanks at Notre Dame for her happy delivery. She wished to signalize it in her usual generous way, one hundred young people were to be married, each of whom received a considerable dowry, and alms were given to the priests in many parishes. Fireworks accompanied the visit, and performances at the Comédie Française were open to the public free, the King's box being occupied by the charcoal burners and the Queen's by the fishwives. This was in accordance with ancient custom.

Marie Antoinette herself did not take part in these rejoicings; she had the common sense to make her visit a purely religious one. After the Masses at Notre Dame and St Geneviève she returned quietly to Versailles. And for a considerable time it seemed indeed that the old order of constant amusement had given place to a much more discreet and rational life. She was an impeccable mother, she followed every development of the baby's growth with the maternal care of a bourgeoise. There was to be no sending away of her child to strange nurses, no lack of love and comfort for infant troubles. The Carnival passed quietly. Mercy reported to his mistress that gaming had been much more restrained, in short it seemed that with the birth of this child, the frustrations of Marie Antoinette's life which had driven her in a sort of despair to ever extended excesses was over. She was truly a wife, her husband adored her, she had every hope of more children, she was indeed a woman and a Queen.

Unfortunately in March she was attacked by measles, and this forced her to retire to Trianon in order that the King should not run the risk of infection. And still more disastrous was her choice of companions to lighten her boredom in convalescence. She picked the Ducs de Coigny and de Guines, the Comte Esterhazy and the Baron de Besenval. There were of course her favourite ladies also; her sister-in-law was there and the Princesse de Lamballe and Madame Elizabeth, now grown into a charming girl and a great favourite with Marie Antoinette. But the Court gloated over the choice, all the scandalmongers were in high glee. Mercy was as usual horrified, but his advice had been disregarded, and now the four gentlemen were named the Queen's nurses, who, said gossip, did not leave her even at night. It was also amusing to speculate as to who would be the four 'nurses' chosen to attend the King should he fall ill? One may say that the stars in their courses worked against Marie Antoinette. If only she had not had the measles, such a simple thing, if she had remained at Versailles, the change in her behaviour which had been accomplished by her maternity might have continued. With her baby to absorb her time and interest and a warmer affection for her husband, together with the real desire to follow her mother's admonition and her brother's serious advice, the Court might insensibly have been restricted in its malign influence. History is full of these 'ifs' and there never was an 'if' more full of ill omen for the future.

For when she returned to Versailles she found that the King, having got over his exuberant joy at finding himself a father at last, had returned to his habitual way of life. He liked the place, here he was at home, and he had arranged his apartments to suit himself; here he had his library with all his family papers and his Salle de Géographie with his maps, his globe, and all his instruments. In the rooms above he had his forge and carpenter's shop and, above all, the observatory where he could use his telescope, and forget his short sight. Here it was that he saw his two trusted ministers Maurepas and Malesherbes, and could confer with them in secret, for he was a secretive man, who denied any confidence to his wife. He knew her indiscretion, her constant correspondence with her mother and above all he distrusted her Reader the Abbé Vermond, devoted to Choiseul and Loménie de Brienne, to whom Louis XVI did not speak one word during all his years at Versailles. Under his eyes hung the portrait of Charles I of England by Van Dyck which Madame Du Barry had bought for Louis XV, he studied it, and learned its lesson.*

So when the Queen returned to Versailles she found herself as deserted by her husband as she had ever been. True he visited her bed, for they both realized that more children were expected, he showered her with presents, but of companionship there was none, he wanted peace and to pursue his ordered life without feminine interference. He must have been a very poor lover. But he was busy enough with the affairs of State. During the year 1778 Louis XVI after signing the agreement with the American

* It hangs today in the Louvre.

insurgents, had entered half-heartedly into a maritime war with England. For a good many months the French Fleet did not move out of Brest, but it was useful as a threat. However, on 27 July, the ships did venture out; apart from some desultory cannonading nothing decisive occurred. A second squadron sailed from Toulon but after encountering a terrible storm put back to refit. The war in America was already costing France considerable sums, and the last thing which Louis XVI wished was for further expense in the present state of the country and the deficit which all Necker's borrowing had done little to revise. Then the combined fleets of France and Spain, sixty-eight battleships, met the English fleet of thirty-eight. The English first took shelter in the harbour of Plymouth, then came out inviting attack, but sailed away unharmed. It was the vacillating policy at Versailles which was responsible for the French half-heartedness. The King, who in his heart did not desire the war, was supported by Vergennes and Maurepas but still under attack from his wife. And Necker, up to his neck in borrowing, feared any further demands on the French economy already sick unto death.

As for the Queen, once more in Versailles, and happily re-united with her daughter, a few months after her return she was again pregnant, a proof that she had returned to her interrupted life with her husband. Unfortunately an accident brought on a miscarriage. The King, says Madame Campan, could not have been more solicitous during this trial, he spent hours beside her bed and mingled his tears with hers. The mishap was kept a secret from her mother and the family, and Maria Theresa ceaselessly – and doubtless irritatingly – continued to press for the signs of a new pregnancy and a possible Dauphin. She felt her end approaching, worn out by the anxiety of an Eastern policy which she did not approve. She insisted more and more that the Queen should consider above all the consolidation of the Franco-Austrian Alliance and the Queen replied in kind. May 1779: 'Certainly my greatest care will be in future to sustain the union between my two countries. I have felt the need only too acutely and the disquiet and the unhappiness which I have suffered during the past year cannot be expressed.' For she was against the American involvement and felt instinctively the danger to all monarchy if one was assailed. In this she was perhaps wiser than Louis, whose indecision led him to give in when he should have been firm.

The Emperor had committed the imprudence of creating the Archduke Maximilian Elector of Cologne, a step which France considered unfriendly: it saw its frontiers vulnerable either to attack or to the necessity in the case of defence of establishing a considerable force to uphold neutrality. Frederick of Prussia was equally disturbed by the French permitting this installation so close to his borders, even more because Maximilian had lost no time in proclaiming himself Bishop of Münster, Grand Master of the Teutonic Order, etc. However, following Frederick's protests he desisted from further aggrandizement. But the ill-feeling aroused in the Prussian and French public persisted, and in the case of the latter the blame was of course laid at Marie Antoinette's door.

During the summer of 1778 an old acquaintance had reappeared at the Court of Versailles, the young Count Axel Fersen, who had pleased the Queen on his former short stay. She welcomed him with so much pleasure that he wrote to his father: 'The Queen, who is the loveliest and most amiable princess that can be imagined has had the goodness to inquire more than once about me.' She had received him at her Sunday receptions and at her card-table, and he remarked that her pregnancy was far advanced and very noticeable, which would indicate that both were enjoying an agreeable friendship and nothing more. But her interest grew, and soon she expressed a wish to see him in his Swedish officer's uniform and admired him in it. None of this escaped the notice of the Court. Always quick to suspect the worst, they were sure that Fersen was in love with the Queen, which may very well have been true, given her beauty and allure, but also that she was more than half in love with him. Contrary to all notions, the Polignac faction were not against such a possibility; a foreigner was safer than a French noble, who would be surrounded by a gaggle of relations all avid for favours. The conduct of the Count was irreproachable and soon he decided that retreat was the better part and applied for permission to join the next expedition to America. After some delay, it was decided that he should join Rochambeau, and he came to take his leave of Marie Antoinette. 'The Queen,' wrote the Swedish Ambassador to King Gustav III, 'could not take her eyes off him, and sometimes they were filled with tears.' The Ambassador continued with the famous response made by Fersen to the Duchesse de Fitz James, 'What,' said she, 'Monsieur, you are leaving your conquest.' 'If I had made one,' he replied, 'I would not abandon it. I depart in freedom, and unfortunately without leaving any regret behind me.' 'Your Majesty will agree that this response showed a wisdom and prudence in advance of his age.'

With Rochambeau he joined the army reinforcing the American troops. La Fayette commanded an insurgent force, Miroménil another French contingent and together they took part in the victory of Yorktown, where the English were finally defeated.

The year 1780 began with an affectionate exchange of letters between the Queen and her mother. Maria Theresa feared the English even more than the King of Prussia, but she passed lightly over the necessity for the alliance to continue durable and firm and the two ladies chatted amicably about their health and the obvious devotion of Louis XVI for his Queen. But by February the tone was somewhat changed. The Empress guided by Mercy referred to the influences at Court which abused the Queen's goodness. Was it true that the Comtesse de Polignac had demanded a Duchy, and that Marie Antoinette had bestowed millions of good French livres on her friend? Everybody commented most unfavourably upon such frantic extravagance at a time when France was at war and the economy pushed to its extreme limit. The English Navy was becoming stronger every month, Rodney's fleet struck terror into her heart. To which the Queen replied with her usual ambiguity, the reports were exaggerated, it was the King who bestowed the gifts on her friend, not only from the goodness of his heart but from the desire to make his wife happy. Charming, but deceitful, for by the month of May Marie Antoinette and all her Court had moved to La Muette in order to be near the Comtesse, who was about to be brought to bed. They were together every day and nearly all day, and in June the Comtesse was in fact created a Duchess. She had married her daughter to the Duc de Guiche, and had received from the King 800,000 livres as a dowry – the usual dowry in such cases being 6,000 livres. The Duchesse herself received with her title 400,000 livres and the promise of estates to the value of 35,000 livres of income.

The Empress had asked whether it was true that a certain Monsieur de Vaudreuil – she did not mention that he was the lover of the new Duchess – had received a present of 30,000 livres for no apparent reason but simply on the request of the Queen. To which her daughter replied that M. de Vaudreuil was a gentleman of position who had suffered in his property by reason of the war. He was beloved by the King and the Comte d'Artois. Here is another instance of the Queen's inconsistency; not only did she bestow favours on Madame de Polignac and her husband but she could so far forget her dislike of immorality as to favour the lover too. All her mother's remonstrances could not bring home to her the danger of her conduct. Perhaps her daughter knew quite well that the Empress had forced herself to tolerate her husband's mistress at her Court. It was the fashion of the day. She made no answer to her mother's insistence that such excessive generosity to favourites was most out of place at a time when Necker was proposing drastic economies in the royal households. These put people out of work and created unnecessary jealousy and dissatisfaction was created in depleted regiments and services when they were compared. 'If I do not tell you, who will? I cannot be silent when I see you giving in to the avidity of pretended friends.'

The libellous pamphlets circulating in Paris and about Versailles were not so restrained. Madame de Polignac's child, was it the Queen's or M. de Vaudreuil's they asked, because M. de Polignac had been in the country for the last year!

These coarse jokes left the Queen unmoved; her pride would not allow her to notice them and indeed she was far too occupied during this summer with her little girl, who was beginning to walk and to recognize her parents, and with the enjoyment of her domain of Trianon. Her gardens were approaching their perfection, her apartments were finished and the theatre was ready for the plays which she intended to give before a specially selected audience. For the actors were her friends, her 'coterie', herself and her young sister-in-law, Madame Elisabeth. She had invited Madame, who refused to take part, regarding it as beneath her. 'But why?' asked Marie Antoinette. 'You are not a Queen.' 'No, but I am the wood of which they are made,' was the cutting response. They chose light operas, comedies; some of the little company were really good actors, more were mediocre, among them possibly the Queen, but they enjoyed themselves, and only the royal family were admitted to see them. Surely there was no harm in all this. She loved to act and, besides, acting had been the fashion at the Court of France. Had not the exquisite Pompadour and the young Duc de Chartres delighted Louis xv? But this was different. La Pompadour was not the Queen of France, so when Marie Antoinette exclaimed in the broadest accents as the servant Gotte, 'Nous les domestiques' and Louis xvi laughed with his 'gros rire' they were not wise enough to see that they were injuring their own prestige. Similarly, the vast palace and the etiquette which Louis xiv had devised to imprison his nobles and render them absolutely dependent had become a Court where the monarchs were at the mercy of a scheming band of mainly dissolute, idle, pampered good-for-nothings, who had not a purpose in life but to flatter them and suck them dry.

In September Necker began to put into action his proposed economies for the palaces and Courts, and this immediately encountered violent opposition from the establishment, who saw their comfortable lodging disappearing. About sixteen hundred 'lazy bones' were dismissed. 'I will put some order into my house,' declared the King. Even Marie Antoinette economized that year, she only ordered ninety-three dresses, very simple, in muslin, forty-one important toilettes and very few feathers. Unaffectedness was the fashion, but the courtiers who had been excluded from Trianon grumbled, and their complaints were repeated in Paris.

In October more serious intrigues were afoot. Vaudreuil wished to get rid of the Minister for War, Montbarrey. The Prince was a man of elegant dissipation whose mistress, an actress at the Opera, Mademoiselle Renard, used her influence over her lover to line her purse with the bribes from aspirants to places in the Department of War. Even the Queen had found that her choice had been rejected in favour of the Demoiselle's friend. Besenval now took a hand. He wished to further the cause of Marshal de Ségur, and arranged with the Duchesse de Polignac that she should begin to insinuate to the Queen the necessity for change at the Ministry. But unfortunately for their plot it had gradually become clear to Maurepas that Montbarrey was not the ideal man for his job, and he had settled on another candidate, Monsieur de Puységur. By this time the Queen, convinced by

Madame de Polignac, had gone to the King; she spoke of the worthless Montbarrey, and praised Ségur, giving him the highest recommendation. Louis as always reported this conversation to Maurepas, who, taken by surprise, neither disagreed nor accepted the Queen's recommendation, while resolving within himself to do all in his power to contravene it.

He was served in this emergency by the arrival at Versailles of Ségur, who turned out to be an oldish man, having lost one arm in battle, and riddled with gout. Maurepas immediately pointed out to the King the stupidity of such an appointment, and put the blame on the Duchesse de Polignac who abused, he said, the Queen's friendship, and he put forward the name of his own candidate, Puységur. The King, annoyed that his wife should be made use of in this way, hurried to her apartment, and found her for once of his own opinion; in turn she called Madame de Polignac. A terrible scene followed. The Duchess first denied the accusations of the Queen, but then raising her voice she said, since the Queen imputed to her such base calculations, it would be far better that she should withdraw from the Court. She would give up her appointments and retire. The Queen, horrified at the prospect of losing her friend, burst into tears; she reasoned, she implored, then seeing that the Duchess remained firm, she threw herself on her knees, embracing her friend in a fit of real despair. Madame de Polignac on her side, truly moved by pity and love – for she was equally the catspaw in the affair – mingled her sobs with Marie Antoinette, lifted her to her feet, and the two women held each other warmly embraced. After such a scene, as generally happens, the friendship was even more firmly established, and the Queen promised to demand Montbarrey's resignation and to support Ségur. On 17 December 1780 Montbarrey resigned.

The next days saw frenzied activity on the part of both sides. The coterie, Polignac, Necker and the Queen held firmly to Ségur, but Maurepas remained equally firm in his support of Puységur. Finally, on the 24th, in the apartments of the King, Marie Antoinette took Madame de Polignac on one side and whispered to her that they had lost, and Maurepas had won. At nearly midnight the Duchess surged into the Queen's apartments; she described the Court in a ferment, the public watching the battle between the Queen of France and a minister, she painted

the affront to her dignity if she were defeated. She so worked
on the Queen that at seven o'clock next morning the King was
forced to send for Maurepas who was surprised when the Queen,
speaking in a most reasonable tone, asked for what reason he so
opposed the appointment of Ségur. He stammered something
and the King then said, 'Well, Monsieur, act as if you were me,
decide.' The Minister, still uncertain, replied that he dared not
decide in such company; when the King muttered something
which might have signified his favourable opinion of Ségur,
immediately the Queen seized on it, and saying 'Monsieur, you
have heard the will of the King, send at once to M. de Ségur
and acquaint him with it.' As Maurepas left the room, the King
took him by the hand and whispered 'Do not abandon me.'

In fact Maurepas seriously considered resigning; only the
King's insistence kept him at his post, but the significance of
Marie Antoinette's success was lost on no one. The Court, and
the public too, believed that the sceptre had passed into her
hands, and Mercy wrote that 'she has the power if she will use it
to govern the nation.' Eight months later he was to lament that
she used this power so little and was so tired and bored by politics
that she limited herself to bestowing favours on her friends. Maria
Theresa knew nothing of all this, her letters were principally
intended to insist as ever on the importance at all costs to preserve
the alliance in face of Frederick II and the English, and to produce
a Dauphin. Her last message was written on 3 November 1780,
it was exceptionally tender in tone. She had been thinking of all
the past times, the happy times, and was content to know of
her daughter's pleasure in her little child and with her husband,
though she was still sad that they occupied separate beds. She was
of those who believe that successful marriages are made in a
double bed. She said too how glad she was that Marie Antoinette
had returned to Versailles with her Court. 'I know the boredom
and the emptiness [of Court life] but believe me, if there is none
the mischance which can result may be much greater than the
small annoyances which are part of it. Especially in your case
with such a lively nation.'

The Queen had in fact promised to occupy her apartments at
least three days in the week, but it was too late; she had succeeded
in alienating all who had suffered from her satire or her disdain;
in some cases they simply stayed away, in others had she only

known it she had made implacable enemies. Such was the Duc de Chartres, Philippe d'Orléans, self-dubbed Equality of the Revolutionary period. She had been friendly with him as Dauphine, when he as the Duc de Chartres was a young and handsome man, but as time went on she disliked him more and more. After the battle of Ushant where he was reputed to have hidden himself below decks, she wrote advising him to leave the Army and return to Paris, thus making a bitter enemy. The world of action was closed to him and he fell back on mediocrity, and a life of pleasure. Gout and apoplexy plagued him and his interests were divided between debauchery and indescribable orgies and an intellectual and false liberalism which he could not really feel, but which served to mask his implacable cabal against his King and Marie Antoinette, and his passionate love of money. He added to his already immense fortune by building the colonnades and shops around the garden of the Palais Royal and made it into a centre for gambling and prostitution. He was the richest nobleman in France and the least noble. He had a printing-press in his palace where the lampoons were concocted which he sent out all over France through his agencies, the Freemasons, of whom he was the Grand Master, and the secret or open clubs which would proliferate under the Revolution.

At the end of November, Maria Theresa, the last of the House of Habsburg, died. She had been ailing for some time with a sort of catarrh which made breathing difficult. In addition her rheumatism troubled her more and more. On 25 November she was much worse and the doctors advised her to take the last Sacraments; on the 28th it was the Extreme Unction. She confessed and afterwards, along with the Emperor, she blessed through him all her children, and gave him her instructions for her subjects and the administration of the Empire. She passed a terrible night, but she would not sleep. 'I will not be surprised,' she said, 'I wish to see death approaching.' She sent her daughters away, fearing that the sight might be too much for them. Alone with her son, suddenly she rose from her chair, and then collapsed. 'You are ill,' said he. 'Well enough to die,' was the reply. 'Light the death candle and close my eyes,' she told the doctor, 'that would be too much for the Emperor.' He knelt beside her – she was gone. She died as she had lived, open-eyed and courageously, she was a great monarch. But she had made one mistake. Her ruling idea was for her Empire, with it she identified the House of Habsburg. To it she was prepared to sacrifice everything, and she did indeed sacrifice her daughters. One of them paid the price for all, Marie Antoinette. How could she have imagined, knowing the child's character and temperament as she did, that a mingled course of advice and admonition could make of the good-hearted, inconsequent, harum-scarum tomboy a responsible monarch? She knew the mixture of obstinacy and impulse, of light-heartedness and principle which distinguished Marie Antoinette throughout her life, and knowing it she threw her into one of the most depraved Courts in Europe and was then surprised that her daughter steadfastly refused to have any truck with one of its leading powers. The Empress was herself the architect of her daughter's tragedy.

In 1781 Marie Antoinette would be twenty-six years old, her beauty had ripened, her health was good, her *joie de vivre* at its full. She had fulfilled her wish, her small apartments both in the Palace of Versailles and in the Petit Trianon, where her chaste and impeccable taste had directed the craftsmen and artists to produce a miracle of refinement, were a joy to her. And to crown all, she was again pregnant. This time everyone assured her, and she was herself convinced it would be a Dauphin. But she was still the slave of the Polignac circle, still unable to free herself from her chains. She still bestowed favours lightly on unworthy objects, still tolerated men whom she did not even like, such as Vaudreuil, because the Duchesse insisted on them. In July she received a second short visit from her brother and gave a fête for him at Trianon, an evening of great gaiety and complete lack of etiquette, for the gardens were arranged to form a sort of village market, where the Court ladies, disguised as peasants behind their stalls, sold favours and tickets for a lottery in which everyone gained a prize.

According to the memoirs of the Prince de Ligne, the Emperor was astonished that considering the 'surroundings of the Queen and the air of licence which reigned at the Court, she had preserved her virtue. Her tact impressed him as much as her majesty. It was as impossible to forget it as to forget himself. In her presence too much freedom could not be risked, nor too naughty a story be told.' And she declared that she would not receive ladies who lived separated from their husbands. This on the occasion of a visit of the Princess of Monaco. So much had the happy birth of her child changed her and so faithfully did she try to amend her ways; if only the public could have known it.

The news was good. Vergennes had manipulated a European peace, the Americans were victorious at Yorktown. France's now magnificent fleet disputed England's claim to be mistress of the seas, and Necker published his *Compte Rendu* (Account Rendered) in which he proclaimed an excess of receipts over expenditure amounting to six million livres. It was inaccurate: there was instead a deficit of fifty millions. But it was the book of the year; everyone read it and was reassured. It was true that France had gained little from all the money spent; however she retained the right to fortify Dunkirk, the territory of Senegal, and influence in Annam (Vietnam). And a firm friendship had been cemented between her and the new American State.

On 22 October 1781 the Queen was brought to bed. In one of his entries in his diary the King describes the event: 'The Queen had passed the night of 21–22 October very comfortably. When she woke she felt some slight pain but took a bath after which the pains continued slight. I gave no orders for the shoot which I had intended at Sacle. Around midday the pains grew worse, she entered the labour bed, and exactly at a quarter past one by my watch she was delivered of a boy.' It had been decided that this time only a few ladies would be in the room; the King's establishment was in the Salon de la Paix adjoining and the King noted the names. A much more lively account was given to the King of Sweden by M. de Stedingk:

There was a great silence in the room as the child was born and the Queen remarking this thought that it was another girl. Mastering her disappointment she said: 'You see how reasonable I am, I am saying nothing.' The baby was taken away by Madame de Guémenée and when in the antechamber the truth was known, it was a scene of joy past all description. People laughed and cried, embraced and congratulated each other. The King, with tears streaming down his face, shook hands with everybody indiscriminately and took every opportunity for pronouncing the words 'My son'. When the child was ready he was baptized, and only then did Louis XVI, followed by Madame de Guémenée bearing the infant, enter the Queen's chamber with the words '*Monsieur le Dauphin demande d'entrer*'. The Queen's joy was touching to see, husband and wife were locked in each other's arms, and when she held her son Marie Antoinette felt that at last all her years of uncertainty and despair were forgotten. Giving him back to Madame de Guémenée she said, 'Take him, he belongs to the State, but I have my daughter.'

Paris rejoiced equally, the people went mad, the streets were full, men and women congratulated each other as if they were one huge family. Money was distributed to the poor, free food and drink stood in the buffets while the various guilds produced gifts.

Out to Versailles they all streamed, with flags flying and music at the head of each deputation. The chimney sweeps brought a huge chimney-piece, with a little chimney sweep perched on top, the butchers had a fat steer, the pastry cooks some special bread for the Queen, the masons, the shoemakers, the tailors, all were there and the locksmith had fashioned a lock for the King which had a trick, and which he tried in vain to open. He stood on the balcony overlooking the great courtyard, beaming with happiness and pride. The market women had special deputations to the Queen as was their custom. There were fifty of them, well dressed in black silk, and Madame Campan says that some even wore diamonds. They were received at the Queen's door by the Princesse de Chimay, and three were introduced to her Majesty, who received them with her usual smiling grace. She liked the fishwives less, they were loud and insolent in bearing, though on this occasion the three obligatory speeches were specially complimentary. They had even produced a poem of some verses, of which the following was the most elegant:

> *Ne craignez pas cher Papa*
> *De voire augmenter vot' famille*
> *Le bon Dieu s'y Pourvoira*
> *Fait's en qu' Versaille fourmille*
> *Eut-il cent Bourbons chez nous*
> *'Y a du pain, du laurier pour tous.**

* Don't be afraid, dear Papa
  To see your family grow larger
  The good God is providing it
  Act so that Versailles swarms
  If there were a hundred Bourbons here
  There is bread, and laurels for all.

And the future regicide, Collot d'Herbois, was so unfarseeing that he wrote:

> Conserve, o ciel protector
> Les jours d'Antoinette.

On the 26th The Messieurs (merchants of the town) heard a grand *Te Deum* in Notre Dame in the present of the King and two days later they journeyed to Versailles in order with the King's permission to see the Dauphin. His Majesty graciously permitted this, first instructing them to address the baby as Monseigneur. The Provost had the honour of delivering a short address in the name of the town of Paris, and the baby's nurse, named appropriately Madame Poitrine,* smiled throughout. On the 31st the town returned to felicitate the Queen, and inquire after her health, which she declared to be as well as anyone could expect.

It appeared that Paris thought that this would see the end of the ceremonies. They had incurred considerable expense in the last year, no less than seven princesses and princes, relations of the royal family, had died and each one had necessitated mourning. In addition the town had been obliged to arrange a solemn funeral service for the Empress Maria Theresa. This had meant special coats for the heralds, purple velvet with her arms embroidered on the breast; other dignitaries had equally magnificent mourning robes and the whole church was hung with black. Monsieur Caumartin, Provost of the merchants, groaned when he thought of the cost and hoped that rejoicing for the Dauphin's birth could be put off, at least until the end of the winter, which promised to be hard. Bread was dear, and fêtes in the bad weather would mean huge fires in the streets; where was the wood to come from? But Marie Antoinette, not to be deprived of her pleasure, laughingly asked if they must wait till Monseigneur would be old enough to dance at the ball, so the merchants were forced to give in, and it was fixed for 23 January.

And now the Provost and his men had enough to think about, first it would be necessary to erect buffets in various quarters of the town so that the poorer people would not mass themselves together, for they were hungry and would certainly avail themselves of any food that was going free. At the Hôtel de Ville, from whence the King with the Queen would see the firework

* Madame Breast.

display, a special room was decorated in her favourite colour, a tender blue, here she would return after her 'churching' at Notre Dame. The usual muddles over protocol arose, poor M. de Caumartin was in despair. The Princes of the Blood, having been invited only after the supper, declared to the King that since there would be no use in their coming to an occasion where they would be mixed up with '*tout le monde*' they preferred to stay at home, while the Dukes were in a bad temper because their invitation was the same as that sent to the '*haute noblesse*'. The Provost felt that if it had been the other way round the result would have been the same.

However, on 23 January all was in readiness. Fortunately the weather was fine, all the mud had been swept from the streets, the sidewalks, where there were any, were clean and the people had prepared to illuminate their houses when the evening came. Six thousand big cages for bonfires had been placed and 3,141 lamps hung, and everyone looked forward to the show. The Queen left La Muette with her procession at nine o'clock, with her were Madame Elisabeth, Madame Adélaïde and her ladies. She was received at the Conference Gate by the Governor, and her reception by the crowd was sufficiently cordial. After all, she had provided the realm with an heir. She proceeded to Notre Dame where she prayed, then to St Geneviève, the patron saint of Paris, and then to the Hôtel de Ville where she awaited the King. He arrived with pomp, accompanied by his two brothers, the Prince de Lambesc, and the Duc de Coigny and the Captain of the Guard the Duc d'Ayen. A banquet was offered in great splendour, only the Duc de Provence and Artois sat with the King and Queen, the rest of the Court were seated on raised benches around the chamber protected by balustrades from the populace which defiled during the three hours the ceremony lasted, feasting their eyes on the royalties, the brilliant dresses and jewels, and snatching whenever they could something of the dainties the servants carried to and fro. For there was a certain amount of disorder in the kitchens, and it was said that the Dukes came off very badly – by the time the royal repast was over they were still with the hors d'œuvres.

But it seemed that there must always be something to cloud Marie Antoinette's pleasures. The King was in a bad humour that day, and refused to stay for the evening, returning alone to La

Muette, and in addition to this an infamous pamphlet had been affixed that morning to the doors of the cathedral itself, so menacing that an attack was feared and the poor Queen passed the day in a state of terror. At the end of it her party returned to La Muette and on the way she stopped her coach at the Hôtel de Noailles to greet M. de La Fayette, the hero of the hour.

Two days later came the masked ball, a magnificent affair. Thirteen thousand people were invited and thousands more invited themselves. The Queen, who was not expected, arrived and stayed until two o'clock in the morning, and next day the labours of M. de Caumartin were rewarded, for when he appeared at Versailles to pay his respects to the King and Queen, the King gave him 30,000 livres which would somewhat lighten the load of expense.

The last of the festivities was a ball offered to the Queen by the corps of guards which took place in the opera house of the Château. Here she appeared dazzlingly magnificent, and opened the dancing with M. de Moret, the eldest of the bodyguards at five o'clock in the afternoon. At six o'clock a supper was offered to the public and later when they had all departed with cries of 'Vive le Roi', 'Vive la Reine' and all the family, there was a masked ball. Even the King came and stayed some hours but Marie Antoinette in the highest spirits remained for most of the night.

The festivities over, the life of the Court took up its usual round. But with a slight difference: the Queen now had her two children to occupy her thoughts and time. Like her mother she gave precise instructions to those who had charge of them and was constantly with them. She adored them, she wished that they should be brought up without the excessive etiquette which had so bored her on arrival at the Court. But Mercy reminded her of the advice of her mother, who had written:

I do not think that all etiquette should be expunged from the lives of royal children, only they should have no excessive luxury or ease of living. It is the fashion now, following Rousseau, to make them into peasants, completely free; this does not please me. Without nourishing their pride, they must be accustomed from babyhood to a certain bearing, without which inevitable difficulties will ensue to the sovereign and his family if they do not distinguish between themselves and others.

Wise woman, she knew, as someone has said, that every monarchy needs a nimbus. But she was perhaps less aware of the ferment which was going on in France, thanks to the mania for everything English or American. Her daughter, nearer to it, might have had some inkling of the danger. The American declaration proclaiming as a self-evident fact that 'all men are created equal, and that they have inalienable right to life, liberty and the pursuit of happiness' was a death knell to privilege, and was completely incomprehensible to the King, who for all his simplicity was convinced of his royal individuality. The wily Franklin with his air of bonhomie, his fur cap and backwoodsman manners, which captivated Paris society, did not impress Louis XVI. He had seen the medallions made at Sèvres with the American's portrait and the legend: *Eripuit coelo, fulmen sceptrumque tyrannis*; with his rough sense of humour he ordered from the same factory a chamber-pot at the bottom of which was placed the same medallion and device, and sent it to Madame Diane de Polignac, who had brought the original to his notice.

But to return to the Queen. Marie Antoinette was now in the full radiance of her beauty according to her painter, Madame Vigée le Brun, who certainly had every opportunity for seeing her during the hours of sittings. She was fairly tall, well made, with magnificent shoulders, arms and hands, small and perfect feet. Her manner of walking was very personal, either fairly fast, or with an undulating motion, most graceful. No one could bow as she did, including all around her in the smiling inclination of her head. But, above all, it was the brilliance of her colouring which was distinctive. Madame Vigée le Brun wrote: 'I have never seen such brilliance, and brilliance is the word; for her skin was so transparent that it had no shadows. I could never render the effect as I would have liked, the colours were lacking with which to paint this freshness, these fine tones which belonged to this charming face alone, and which I have never found in any other woman.' And her kindness and sympathy were also recorded by the artist at the moment when, pregnant herself, she had the commission to paint the Queen. Then too we have the testimony of her brother Joseph when, on his second visit he had occasion to comment on the 'licence' of the Court. She was equally discriminating in her choice of plays to be rendered in her theatre; in fact she was insensibly changing her manner of living. She was less seen in the circle of the Duchesse de Polignac, though her affection for the favourite remained as strong as ever. This was a crucial moment in the life of Marie Antoinette. If she had had a firmer husband, a King capable of ruling with the decision which the times required, she might very well have become the model mother and spouse which one side of her nature designed her to be. She was especially proud of the home which was her own, the Petit Trianon, where she stayed longer and longer, leaving Versailles to the King. Her small apartments there were – and are – a dream. The fastidiousness of her taste was equalled by the genius of her artists; colours, design and workmanship all combine to give us the impression of refined and delicate feeling which no ordinary or common woman would have wished for. It is her personality which speaks to us there.

She delighted in doing the honours of her small domain. When the Princes of Hesse-Darmstadt with their wives who had been brought up with her arrived in 1780 on a visit, she took them to the opera, drove with them in the woods of Marly and even went shopping with them. Above all she showed them Trianon, with its intimate salon, the piano and her favourite harp. She advised the ladies on what they should wear for her exquisite theatre, not too many diamonds nor too much paint, and for the drives not too big hats, and simple dresses; in fact she made them feel so happy that a friendship began which lasted till the very end. She had decided not to dance any more, she was 'too old' she said, but when the Grand Duke Paul of Russia and his wife, a princess of Württemberg, travelling incognito under the title of Count and Countess of the North came to Versailles, the occasion was slightly different in tone. For these were rulers of a great country, Prince Paul would one day be Tsar, and both the King and Queen were somewhat ill at ease on the first encounter, Louis XVI because he was always more or less ill at ease, and Marie Antoinette because, as she confessed, she felt that the role of Queen was more difficult in the presence of other sovereigns, or princes made to become so, than with courtiers. But the ice was soon broken, no one could for long withstand the Queen's natural charm especially when she set out to please. The fête given at Trianon was all her inspiration. *Zémire et Azor*, the charming *opéra comique* by Grétry, was played, and the ballet *Jean Fracasse* by Gardet. The ravishing theatre presented a glittering array of beauties, and the supper afterwards was followed by the illumination of the gardens, a fairy spectacle. Then the Queen did dance to the delight of all. Fête succeeded fête, Versailles in its greatest splendour at the King's command, and finally at Chantilly, where the Prince de Condé eclipsed all others in magnificence. Even the Grand Duke was dazzled. 'We are a very long way away from each other,' said the Prince to him as they parted, 'but if Your Highness permits and the King approves, I could one day go to St Petersburg to repay the visit which you have graciously condescended to make.' 'We will receive you with enthusiasm Monsieur,' replied the Grand Duke, 'and the Empress will only be too happy to see you in our savage country.' Could Condé imagine, asks a commentator, that fifteen years later he would indeed visit Russia as a refugee, and that his Chantilly would be no more than a ruin?

But Mercy, observing that power was becoming more and more concentrated in the hands of the Queen, also saw that the empire of Madame de Polignac was in no way diminished. Maurepas had been behind most of the plots against Necker, who was hated for his *Compte Rendu*, and for the efforts he made to curtail the power of the nobility and their privileges, and in May 1781 the Minister had been forced to hand in his resignation. The Queen, who had esteemed and supported him, spent the day in tears, the nation and all those of the Court who had any probity were equally alarmed; they saw in him the financial genius who, even if they did not approve of all he did, was more capable than any other restoring the ruined economy. Marie Antoinette made haste to write her brother that she had had no hand in his fall, and that she deplored it. Another matter equally dismayed the watchful Mercy. At the end of 1782 the Prince de Guémenée had become a bankrupt, and for an enormous sum, thirty-three million livres – which obliged his wife to resign her post as governess of the royal children. Now came the question of her successor. The Queen thought of the pious Princesse de Chimay, or Madame de Duras, but here Besenval put in his word. Why not her best friend the Duchesse de Polignac? The Queen objected at first, she thought the Duchesse would not care for such an onerous post. On the contrary, said the Baron, if you do not give it to her everyone will think that your Majesty is not capable of pleasing her best friend. The appointment was made, and the public knowing very well that this would mean another increase in the already over-generous revenues of the Polignacs, did not hesitate to demonstrate its displeasure. The Queen's excuse was that she would thus have more opportunity to be with her children; and indeed she was a devoted mother. They were always around her, and Mercy writing to Joseph II complained that Madame Royale interrupted her mother with her little games when she should have been paying attention to more serious matters. 'I see myself in even more difficulties than before,' grumbled the Ambassador.

Maurepas died a few months after his victory over Necker. Only Louis XVI regretted him, he was flippant, intriguing, and was suspected of having encouraged the King to allow full rein to the Queen's dissipation in order that she should not take an interest in nor disturb his policies. He was not replaced. Vergennes, equally trusted by his master and a more reliable person than Maurepas had ever been, became chief minister without the title. Necker had been succeeded by Joly de Fleury, who in turn was displaced by d'Ormesson. The latter was supported by Marie Antoinette who appreciated his somewhat brusque honesty. Not so the Polignac clique who immediately began their intrigues against him. He resigned and their candidate was given the post, M. de Calonne. Neither the King or the Queen liked or trusted him, he was brilliant, smooth and charming. A contemporary writes:

M. de Calonne had all the qualities of a man of the world, but very few of those of a Statesman, and even less of those necessary for a financier. His genius was eminently dangerous because he was persuasive but his decisions stemmed from false bases. His imagination gave birth to and his eloquence forced the adoption of measures which neither good sense nor reason could admit.

He was deeply in debt and he had been after this post for a long time, using every bit of influence or intrigue he could find to obtain it. Artois, Polignac, Vaudreuil and all their clique were for him and Madame de Polignac sent the Baron de Breteuil to the Queen to plead his case. She resisted for a long time but finally she gave in and persuaded the King to appoint Calonne.

Her repentance was not slow in coming: she resented the pressure Madame de Polignac had put upon her and even remarked in that lady's presence that French finance passed alternately from the hands of an honest man without talent into the hands of a clever man without honesty. The Duchesse must have seen signs of her diminishing influence, and indeed Marie Antoinette had a new friend, the Comtesse d'Ossun, who was her lady-in-waiting, and the Mistress of her Wardrobe. She was paid a minute sum in comparison with the immense revenues of the Polignacs. Her responsibility was enormous, no account was paid without her signature, and the figures terrified her. Marie Antoinette had generally for the winter, says Madame Campan, twelve '*grands habits*', twelve simple dresses called fantasies, twelve splendid dresses with panniers and trains, these were for the evening in the State apartments where cards were played. The same number for the summer, and of course all were renewed for each season. Rose Bertin, who took her creations straight to the Queen instead of to the wardrobe, sent in unconscionable bills, six thousand livres for a dress for New Year's Eve. She had to wait for her money, however, for the treasury was empty and it was only in the beginning of 1784 that the new Finance Minister, whose motto was, 'spend freely in order to appear rich', found the money.

The people of Paris grumbled, the men because their wives tried to follow the fashions set up by the Court, the merchants because they never knew what stock they must lay in. And because they knew that the King had most simple tastes they threw all the blame on Marie Antoinette. But when she dressed more simply they were equally critical, she could please no one. A portrait by Madame Vigée le Brun showing the Queen dressed *à la Créole*, in a plain muslin dress, was exhibited in the salon of 1783, and all the world flocked to see her dressed 'like a lady's maid'. And the merchants shouted that she wanted to ruin the silk trade of France in favour of the Belgian muslin makers, her brother's subjects. '*L'Autrichienne*'. A name was given to the picture, 'France masquerading as Austria reduced to covering herself with a shawl'. In spite of her enormous expenditure – the figures rose each year – their real resentment was for the stranger whom they suspected always of subjecting the interests of France to the demands of a foreign power. They were shortly to have their fears accelerated.

The treaties of 1715 had shut the mouth of the Scheldt and

given the care of it to Holland, an arrangement which continually annoyed the Emperor, because it hindered the free trading of the Low Countries to his Empire and particularly that of the port of Antwerp. Before the American War he had made representations to France, but consented to shelve the subject till the war should be over. Now he brought it up again, demanding the free passage on the river mouth, the States General refused, and he ordered one of his ships to force the passage; the Dutch cannonaded the ship and took it. Immediately an Austrian Army appeared on the scene and the States General asked France for aid. The response was to be foreseen; in Paris and Versailles everyone was on the side of the Dutch, even the ministers most supposed to be favourites of Marie Antoinette, Ségur, Castries, Minister of the Navy, and the Baron de Breteuil, once Ambassador to Vienna.

The Emperor lost no time in drawing his sister into the fray. He demanded her aid, insisting that he had supported France, especially in her attitude to the American War although his sympathies were with England. The Queen refused to intervene between the King and his ministers. To her he said that all he wanted was reparation for the insult to his flag, to the King he insisted on the cession of Maastricht and the territory surrounding. He even in a note to Mercy suggested the one desire of the Queen was to avert the threat of war, which advanced daily. He sent an ultimatum to the States General; the reply was to place two army corps, one on the banks of the Rhine, the other on the Flanders frontier, under the orders of the Prince de Condé. The Queen was torn both ways – on one side she saw the rupture of an alliance which she had sealed with her own person, on the other the French, her people. The King was watching all this with interest. She noted that her husband when she was alone with him spoke quite differently from when he had conferred with the Minister; she pressed both of them and the Emperor too, not to insist on the difficulties of the situation, to bend all their efforts towards understanding, but much as she wished to help her brother, the interests of France were paramount. So one day, during a private audience with the Ambassador of Sweden she insisted, 'You can be certain that when each side has taken up its stand I shall not meddle in anything, and in any case I never forget, in spite of my affection for the Emperor, that I am Queen of France and mother of the Dauphin.' Admirable sentiment, and a pity that the public could not hear it.

Thanks to negotiations, suitable propositions were formulated; the Emperor renounced his claim for the opening of the Scheldt, the Dutch offered a reparation for the insult to the Austrian flag and made the token gesture of the cession of Maastricht which the Emperor immediately handed back, for it was a necessary frontier against Germany. Both sides haggled over the indemnity. 9,500,000 florins, said Joseph. 5,000,000, replied the Dutch. The Queen was on tenterhooks, would the talks break down? Finally France agreed to pay part of the sum and in return peace was signed, followed by a treaty between France and Holland which made the sacrifice worth while. But the public, seeing only the disadvantages of money leaving the country, ascribed this new prodigality to the inevitable – Marie Antoinette.

In June 1783 Marie Antoinette received a friend returned from America, the Count Axel Fersen, much changed in appearance by his three years of war; he was thinner, older, was he still as attractive? Possibly so, but the Count wished, as he wrote to his father, to establish himself in a solid position, and for this he felt that marriage would be necessary. He had seen in England before leaving for the war a young lady who would be distinctly suitable, and had in fact written to her during his absence, but without a reply. Failing her he thought the daughter of M. Necker would be a good match. After a month, however, he wrote to his sister a remarkable letter, that he was glad to have heard that Miss Leyel was married and that he would not think of another wife for he knew that 'since he could not belong to the only person he would wish for, he did not wish to belong to anyone else.' This month had sealed his fate and that of Marie Antoinette; there is no other record but one can surmise that they loved but knew that it was an impossible love, and resigned themselves.

Of one thing he was determined, he must stay in France; he must at least be able to see her, and he set himself to find a way. The proprietor of the Royal Swedish Regiment, the Count Alexandre de Sparre, wished to sell, and Axel wrote to his father asking if he would help to find the one hundred thousand livres demanded. Papa Fersen replied laconically that he saw no harm in the transaction if either he or his son had had the funds necessary. Here the King Gustavus III intervened and asked Louis

XVI to give an appointment to 'an officer who has served in Your Majesty's armies in America with distinction'. The King immediately complied, doubtless persuaded by his wife who wrote to her cousin that she would do all she could to support his wishes. Two days after Louis XVI named the Comte de Fersen '*Mestre de camp, propriétaire du Royal Suédois*', and Axel paid the Comte de Sparre the hundred thousand livres he had borrowed. Since the King gave him a retainer of the same sum he was not out of pocket when he repaid his debt.

The lovers' wishes were fulfilled, Fersen would spend a good part of the year at Versailles; for the moment he left to join his King who was travelling in Europe incognito under the name of the Count de Haga.

The winter set in cold and bitter, the poor suffered and Marie Antoinette who was at heart a compassionate woman, though like that of many people her charity was inconsistent and without method, gave from her savings to the priests in some of the hardest hit parishes of Paris and Versailles. Calonne, who knew very well that the Queen disliked him, seeking to gain her favour came and offered to give her a million from the three millions apportioned for the public relief work so that she could distribute it at her pleasure. She refused, saying that this money must be used solely in the name of the King, and that she would provide her own charity. Madame Campan records that, entering her private rooms the Queen said to her, 'Compliment me, my dear, I have succeeded in avoiding a trap which might have brought me into great trouble. This man will succeed in ruining the finances of France. They say that it is I who have placed him, the people believe that I am wasteful; I have never wished that any money from the Royal Treasury, even for the most reputable purpose, should pass through my hands.' She had, through this refusal, made an enemy. Following her mother's example, she began to teach her children to be charitable; she explained to them that they must not count on many toys for that Christmas for the money was needed for the poor. If only she had been more steady, if she had ever been able to relate her private expenditure to that of the public sector, she would not almost immediately afterwards have embarked on an expensive project which was again to lower her in the esteem of French society. She persuaded the King to buy the property of St Cloud, which belonged to the Duc d'Orléans. The reason given was a valid one. Versailles was urgently in need of repair; the architect of Trianon, Monsieur Micque, had been called in and gave his opinion that the work could be finished in six years if the Royal Treasury would furnish the required money in prompt payments. The King asked how long it would take if the payments were not prompt? Ten years was the reply. The King then recalled that the Regent in a somewhat similar case had taken the Court of Louis xv to the Tuileries, and it was this idea of moving the Court which gave rise to the purchase of St Cloud, also the Queen had fallen in love with it one day when she was driving through. The first proposal was that in the interests of economy an exchange should be made, St Cloud against Choisy and La Muette and a forest, this would provide the equivalent of the sum asked by the Duc. But then it was realized that by this method all those employed in the two properties would be put out of work; this was inadmissible and finally some millions were paid. The Queen then suggested that St Cloud should be her property instead of needing a Governor and all the staff, thus saving expense. The King consented and St Cloud became hers. It was set up as at Trianon, the servants wore her livery, and orders were issued 'By order of the Queen'. This all gave great offence, especially to the better classes who saw in it an attack on the monarchy and its laws, and when the royal family moved out there it became the fashion for the people to drive out there on Sundays to see the fountains and '*l'Autrichienne*' walking in the park with her children.

The dice were all loaded against Marie Antoinette; now came a further unfortunate throw. It was not a political matter in the beginning but seemed simply an affair of the Queen's amusement and good or bad taste; the political repercussions were however immense. Beaumarchais had sent a play, *The Marriage of Figaro*, to the Théâtre Français towards the end of 1781, but the censor had refused his authorization. This infuriated Beaumarchais, a man who was used to getting his own way by fair or foul means. He was already well known in the Parisian salons and now he began a campaign for the public performance of his work. He read it himself in all the smartest literary circles, it became the rage; to have the author reading was fought for by the very people whom he pilloried. It was a curious sight, these French aristocrats laughing at themselves, the sport of the man who held them up to derision and censorship. It became so notorious that the King finally consented to its being read to him in the presence of the Queen. Madame Campan describes the scene, when she arrived in the private cabinet of the Queen she found a chair and a little table placed for Her Majesty and the King, who said that she should read it to them both although it would be difficult because of the scratchings out and foldings up, the result of frequent journeys. She must not talk about the interview, it was private. In the course of the reading, the King, who was far from being stupid, exclaimed with astonishment several times, but particularly where Figaro speaks of the State prisons and the Administration he jumped and protested vigorously. 'It is detestable, this shall never be played: only if the Bastille were destroyed would this piece be anything but a dangerous piece of inconsequence. This man makes fun of everything which in the Government should be respected.' In saying this the King proved that he had far better judgment than the majority of his courtiers; his native common sense triumphed over their futility and self-destruction. 'So it must not be played,' said the Queen. 'Certainly not,' was the reply. Incredible as it may seem, neither Beaumarchais nor the nobility had the slightest intention of obeying their King's orders. Secretly the actors and actresses were told to study their parts, tickets were issued for a performance at the Théâtre Français, the carriages were rolling up when at the last moment a messenger arrived with a *lettre de cachet* from Louis XVI written and signed in his own hand forbidding the representation.

The public was furious, words like tyranny, oppression were bandied about and Beaumarchais was out of his mind with rage. 'Well,' he is reputed to have said, 'he doesn't want it shown here, but I swear, I, that it shall be played, perhaps even in the cathedral of Notre Dame.' Terrible and prophetic words, if true. In any case he had not finished with the King. A devious and unprincipled man, he was accustomed to use every means to gain his aims. He knew that the only person to approach would be the Queen, and through her weakness for Madame de Polignac. So Vaudreuil was only too glad to promise a performance in his château, and Beaumarchais let it be known that all the compromising references had been cut out. At least, this was what the Queen believed, and when the Comte d'Artois and she assured the King of this, he at least consented to the performance of the expurgated version.

The scene at the Théâtre Français on the first night of one of the world's, most famous comedies was indescribable. Everyone who was anyone in Paris was there, and an immense crowd of nobodies as well. The audience was half suffocated, but it stayed, for everyone must be able to boast next day that they had seen it. 'What do you think will be the verdict, success or not?' asked the King of M. de Montesquiou as he was leaving for the theatre. 'Sire, I hope it will be a failure.' 'And I too,' said the King. 'Yes,' said the actress Sophie Arnould when she heard this, 'it is the sort of play which fails fifty nights in succession.' And she was right; from top to bottom the house applauded all the cynical attacks on the established order, the real wit of the work persuaded this corrupt and blasé nobility that laughter is not dangerous, and in their guarded box Beaumarchais, the Abbé Sabatier and the Abbé Calonne, his friends, enjoyed the success of the first open attack on the monarchy.

Monsieur, who had gone in the expectation of a failure or at least less of a success, was annoyed. He was not far from the throne himself and might justly suspect any aspersions on it. The Queen, says Madame Campan, was very disgusted with the persons who had made use of her to persuade the King. But the sad fact is that she proceeded to prepare a private performance of a play by the very man who had so outrageously insulted the monarchy. *The Marriage of Figaro* offered a character which she felt was made for her, 'Rosine', the prettiest little woman in the world, gentle, tender, lively, fresh, appetizing, nimble of foot, slender waisted, with rounded arms, and such hands, such feet, such teeth, such eyes. Who else at Court could boast of all these charms? Gone were her good resolutions, not to dance any more, to be dignified, the Mother of the Dauphin. It was too tempting; it seems incomprehensible, but after all d'Artois was to play Figaro, and it would be in the strictest privacy; only the family would be there and her chosen few friends. It was a success, says Grimm, but the news soon leaked out and the public was astonished to hear of a Prince of the Blood speaking the cynical lines of a Figaro.

But the attention of the Queen during the last few days of rehearsals had been drawn to something of far greater moment than the temporary excitement of a play. Without any warning she was plunged into the scandalous affair of the Necklace.

With the exception of her love-affair with Fersen this is the episode in the Queen's life which has most attracted attention, both on the part of her biographers and the public. It has indeed all the attraction of a *roman scandaleux*, of the most lurid whodunnit. And it brought the most terrible consequences in its train.

Ever since the accession of Louis XVI there had existed hotbeds of hatred and calumny where the reputation of the Queen was besmirched. The three aunts, relegated to their dull residence in Bellevue, revenged themselves for their diminished importance by circulating every bit of real or imagined scandal. Their palace was the chosen rendezvous for everyone who had a grievance; those who were no longer invited to the Court, the old and forgotten nobility, bitter in their resentment, the people to whom she had forgotten to say a word, or whom she had wounded by her comments, they all were there. And in the town at the Palais Royal the Duc d'Orléans whom she had mortally offended openly encouraged the writers of lampoons, of insulting verses, and even had, it was said, his own private printing press for circulating them. So that when, on 24 May 1785, she made an entry into Paris to render thanks at Notre Dame for the birth of her second son, the Duc de Normandie, the reception by the watching public was glacial. Fersen, who was in Paris, wrote his King, 'The Queen was received very coldly, there was absolutely no applause, only a complete silence. It was a frightful shock for her.' She at last fully realized the dreadful gulf which existed between her and her people and breaking down she sobbed in the arms of her husband, 'What have I ever done to them, what have I done?'

She was soon to find out. It was another of the turning points in her life where a choice was presented to her and where to us with hindsight it seems she chose wrongly. It is possible that if she had consented, as the King and Breteuil advised, to let the whole thing peter out without the publicity of a trial the shock to the monarchy might have been avoided. But who can tell; to us the Revolution seems inevitable, only Marie Antoinette herself might have been saved the concluding horror of her death, and perhaps the monarchy in some limited form might have been preserved. The actors in this drama were three, the Prince Louis de Rohan, Grand Almoner of France, the Comtesse de La Motte-Valois, with her confidant Retaux de Villette, and the real victim, Marie Antoinette. Who were these people? The Grand Almoner we have met before, it was he who met the little Archduchess on her way to France, and in conducting the Mass made such an unfortunate impression on her that it coloured her attitude to him forever. Louis René Edouard, Prince de Rohan, came from one of the greatest families of France. Unfortunately his way of life did not conform to the nobility of his rank. When – thanks to the influence of his uncle the Prince de Soubise, and his aunt the Comtesse de Marsan, added to that of Madame Du Barry – he was appointed Ambassador to Vienna, it will be remembered that Marie Antoinette, young as she was, commented most unfavourably upon it, and in this she was supported by her mother. The Empress deplored his influence on the young ladies at her Court, who were all mad about him. He was licentious and splendid, magnificent and profligate and took them in by his lavish expenditure, and extravagance, and above all by the air of grandeur and nobility, which only masked a depraved mind, and after two months she summed him up and detested him as a man worthy neither of his ecclesiastical rank nor his position as ambassador.

However, Joseph II and his Minister Kaunitz were not so bitterly opposed to Rohan, the one because the Ambassador's pranks amused him, and the other because his 'lack of capacity' placed him at his mercy. And Aiguillon looked upon him as a useful spy at the Vienna Court. With the accession of Louis XVI he was recalled to France, but the young King would not receive Rohan on his return and Marie Antoinette refused to speak to him. He was not exactly in disgrace, for he received a sum of fifty thousand livres to pay his debts, but he was not acceptable at Court. The Rohans, however, were not disconcerted. They were immensely powerful, and they succeeded in procuring for him the Cardinal's Hat through the King of Poland, 'Worthy protector of a worthy protégé,' wrote Maria Theresa cynically. The Sorbonne named him their *proviseur*, though he was rather weak on doctrine, and Louis XVI had been worried into promising him the reversion of the office of Grand Almoner. Marie Antoinette had been bitterly opposed to this, but on the morning after the death of La Roche Aymon the Comtesse de Marsan was at the King's bedside when he woke up and drove him into acquiescence. So we see Rohan with all these titles and in addition Member of the Académie Française, a Commander of the Order of the Holy Spirit and the possessor of eight hundred thousand livres of income.

But the Cardinal, not satisfied with all this, felt the irritation of a man who was wounded in his vanity and obstructed in his ambition by the Queen's coldness, and made every effort to be acceptable to his sovereign without the slightest change in her manner towards him. Madame Campan tells how on a previous occasion he had insinuated himself disguised into the grounds of the Petit Trianon during a fête given by the Queen. It was hopeless; though she pardoned the concierge who had let him in she never gave him so much as a look, and he, on the other hand, could not give up his determination to be in her good graces, to soften her inflexible conduct. In her pride she regarded her position as impregnable, she had shown the same intractable obstinacy with Madame Du Barry, both cases show an invincible distaste of a certain sort of person, a man or woman of openly irregular life. She was too fastidious to make any concessions or to compromise. If she had accepted the constant overtures of Rohan, who, like the favourite, only asked for a token recognition, how much sorrow she might have been saved. But she could not. It is this characteristic which must be remembered in her affair with Fersen.

At this stage Rohan came into contact with a certain Madame de la Motte. Who was she? She claimed to be, and in fact was, descended from the Valois through the Baron de St Rémy, a natural son of Henri II. Poor and an orphan, the priest of her parish had recommended her to the Bishop of Langres and to a charitable lady, the Marquise de Boulainvilliers, who put her in a Hospice in Passy near Paris where she stayed six years, after which she went as apprentice to a dressmaker. The King was persuaded to award her a pension, and she passed a further two years in the Abbey of Longchamps; it was hoped that she would embrace the religious life. This was not at all to the taste of Mademoiselle and she and her sister repaid their benefactress by running away to the village of Bar-sur-Aube where they arrived with six francs in their pocket and managed to awake the pity of yet another kindly lady. Jeanne was by this time a very attractive young woman; without being exactly beautiful she had great charm and was in addition a consummate actress. By nature bold and enterprising, she could pretend timidity and gentleness or any other quality calculated to please. She was no-ticed by a nephew of her benefactress, and by June 1780 they were married. He was the Comte de la Motte, an officer in the Gendarmerie, already deeply in debt, but being quite unscru-pulous and very enterprising the couple saw no reason why they should not do well. Her husband rejoined his regiment and soon they were in trouble again. Once more they turned to Madame de Boulainvilliers, who forgivingly presented the Comtesse de la Motte to the Grand Almoner of France, the Cardinal de Rohan, who was on his way to Strasbourg.

This was the beginning. Soon the pair were in Paris, where they lived precariously from one stratagem to another until the wife obtained for M. de la Motte a commission in the Bodyguard of M. d'Artois, and this in turn led to an audience with M. de Richelieu. From this came their transition to Versailles where Jeanne, standing in the crowd waiting for the passage of the Queen, pretended to faint, obviously in the hope that either Her Majesty or some other princess would notice the poor young creature. Unfortunately the ruse did not work so she then pro-ceeded to faint in the apartment of the Comtesse d'Artois. Again unsuccessful, she played the same trick at Madame Elisabeth's *lever*, and this time it succeeded. The gentle and kindly princess gave her 1,500 livres and an appointment at the Court, minor it was true, but still in the right place to pursue her intrigues. Life was still precarious, however, poverty was always near and in 1782 in the month of June, as a last resource, she obtained an audience with the Cardinal de Rohan to whom she had been presented years before. She pleased him, her sad tale touched his heart, she came back over and over again and through flattery, to which he was always vulnerable, charm and persistence, she succeeded in attaching herself firmly to him.

Now the drama could begin. From 1783 her contact with the Cardinal became ever more intimate, he received her at Strasbourg, helped her with money and with the petitions she directed at the King, and listened to her confidences and presumably confided in her. With the result that in 1784 she came to him with the following story: she had succeeded in arousing the interest of the Queen, who was determined to see that the last of the Valois should have a more secure future. Also she was, so she said, honoured by the friendship of Marie Antoinette and was in a position to aid her benefactor the Cardinal. Not a word was true, as was later proved by the Queen herself, but strange to say Rohan swallowed the whole fabrication, he was caught. He could have checked on the veracity of the tale, but he was so dominated by Madame de la Motte that he did nothing. Soon Jeanne was bringing him letters, all forged, in which the Queen called her, 'My dear Comtesse, my dear heart'. They were written on blue paper and were all the work of the third party in the plot, Retaux de Villette, a slippery customer who called himself the 'Countess's' secretary.

On one thing the prelate insisted, would it not be possible for the Queen to accord him an audience be it ever so short? The Comtesse put off replying until at last forced to invent something, she said that the Queen of course could not so suddenly alter her public conduct towards him, but she would meet him one evening in the gardens of Versailles. This should have warned him, but unfortunately public gossip had so often accused Marie Antoinette of meeting her lovers by stealth in the groves of the gardens that he saw no trap. Not only that, but the charlatan Cagliostro, by whom he was completely dominated, had predicted that a very high influence would bring him to the summit of all his desires. He was delirious with joy, he could hardly contain himself, and every evening disguised in a long robe with a wide hat he walked in the gardens, waiting and hoping for the improbable moment – improbable that is to all but a man made mad by his own vanity and ambition.

On 24 July Madame de la Motte rushed up to him as he waited 'Come quickly,' she whispered, 'the Queen permits you to approach.' He rushed after her, saw a woman dressed in white with a big hat who pressed a rose into his hand and murmured 'You know what this means.' On the instant a man dashed up, 'Here are the Comte and Madame d'Artois coming.' 'Make haste, make haste,' cried Madame de la Motte softly, and the Cardinal took to flight, convinced however that Marie Antoinette had spoken to him, that his future was assured. What was the explanation of so remarkable an encounter? Very simple: Madame de la Motte had found in the Palais Royal, home of the 'girls of the street', a young girl who closely resembled Marie Antoinette and had brought her to Versailles telling her that she could do something which would be of great use to the Queen, and promising her fifteen thousand francs if she obeyed orders. For that sum of money, the young woman would have done anything. She wanted to know what was the mysterious 'something'. 'You will see when the time comes,' replied the Comtesse. When the day came she was dressed in a white gown with a mantle of white, and a hat of the same kind as worn by the Queen. 'I will take you,' said her mentor, 'to a place in the park; a very great lord will approach you, you will give him this letter, and this rose, and say softly, "You know what this means." That is all you have to do.' When the critical moment came, however, the girl was so frightened that in her trembling she forgot to give the letter. Rohan paid no attention to that, he was beyond reckoning, his gratitude to Madame de la Motte knew no bounds, he was her slave. And now the intriguing creature could begin to reap the fruit of her cunning. First it was a letter, forged by Retaux which asked for sixty thousand livres which the Queen needed for people in whom she was interested; then four thousand for another purpose and on and on, he paid, and Jeanne de la Motte harvested. Her manner of living had now completely changed, she had a house, horses, magnificent furniture, dresses, jewels and she and her husband went to Bar-sur-Aube to show themselves off to their quondam friends and be admired. She did not even mind if she was talked about at Versailles, where all gossip finally ended up, and now begins the second act of the drama.

Two of the Queen's jewellers, Boehmer and Bassange had some time before assembled a magnificent diamond necklace, 593 perfect stones put together with much care. It was a royal jewel, and at the time of the birth of his first child they offered it to the King who, they hoped, would present it to his wife. He was indeed overwhelmed by the splendour of the necklace and took it to the Queen, who however refused it. 'We need ships more than diamonds,' she is reported to have said. Now what were the jewellers to do, where would they find a customer for so valuable a jewel? It was offered here and there, no sovereign would buy it, and finally Boehmer, in despair, requested an interview with the Queen. Throwing himself on his knees he stammered, 'Madame, I will be ruined if you do not buy my necklace, there is nothing left for me but to throw myself into the river.' Marie Antoinette regarded him coldly. 'Rise, Monsieur,' said she, 'I did not order this jewel, and I have already refused it. Do not speak to me again. Try to divide it and to sell it and do not drown yourself. I am very displeased that you make such a scene before my daughter. Retire.' She thought the affair was done with. But in December 1784 Bassange heard someone speaking about the influential Madame de la Motte. He instantly saw the possibility of a further attempt, went to the Comtesse and implored her to use her influence with the Queen. She said neither yes nor no and two days later they brought the necklace for her to inspect. The adventuress hesitated, but on thinking the matter over she invented an ingenious plot.

For three weeks the jewellers waited with ever-increasing anxiety, then Madame de la Motte sent for them and told them that the Queen had decided to take the necklace but could not do so directly. She therefore commissioned 'a very great person' to negotiate the affair for her and three days later in the presence of the Comte and Comtesse this personage appeared. It was, of course, none other than the Prince de Rohan. He saw the jewel, asked the price and made his conditions. The price was set at sixteen hundred thousand francs, the payment should be in four six-monthly instalments, to start on 1 August. The necklace should be delivered on 1 February. The agreement was entirely written by Rohan and the jewellers signed it.

On 1 February they arrived at the Hôtel de Strasbourg, and on this occasion the Cardinal confessed to them that the necklace was designed to go to the Queen and even showed them a letter in her hand which said, 'I am not used to treat in this way with my jewellers, you will keep this paper and arrange everything in a way which you deem acceptable.' And for fuller confirmation they saw the act of acquisition with all the items undersigned 'approved' and her signature – Marie Antoinette de France

The whole thing was a forgery, Retaux's masterpiece, but since the jewellers had never seen the Queen's handwriting nor her signature they were completely taken in and retired satisfied that they would soon see their wonderful necklace upon the royal neck for which it had been designed. The final act in the comedy was to come. On the same evening the Cardinal left for Versailles with the precious packet, he went at once to Madame de la Motte's lodgings in the Hôtel de la Belle Image. Hardly had he arrived than a man entered with a letter for the Comtesse; she took it and when they were alone again read it. Concealing it in her hand, she said that it was from the Queen and that the bearer was from Her Majesty's Chamber, his name was Desclaux. When the man re-entered Rohan concealed himself behind the hangings and he saw Madame de la Motte give the package containing the necklace to him. It was of course Retaux, and Rohan was later to identify him as the individual who had come to the rendezvous in the thicket at Versailles.

The next day was a feast day, and Bassange and the Cardinal were in the gallery at Versailles, eager to see the jewel upon the neck of the Queen, but to their astonishment she was wearing only her usual diamonds; they consoled themselves with the thought that she was doubtless waiting for a favourable opportunity to tell the King of her purchase. But as the weeks wore on and the diamonds did not appear Madame de la Motte was at some pains to quiet the misgivings of the indignant Cardinal. More of the little notes on the pale blue paper had to be written, while her husband made haste to London, there to cut up the necklace and sell the pieces; when he returned he paid one hundred and twenty thousand livres into the bank of Pergeaux, a very nice fat sum, the pickings from this incredible piece of chicanery.

Now the moment for the first payment was approaching and the Comtesse, to gain time, fabricated another letter from the Queen, in which she intimated her opinion that the price had been too high and that she insisted on a reduction of 200,000 francs. The Cardinal agreed to tell the jewellers who were at first much disturbed, but finally agreed. They wrote a letter to Her Majesty, which they took themselves to Versailles, for they had a commission to deliver there. They waited until Marie Antoinette returned from Mass, and handed the missive to Madame Campan who took it to her mistress, who read it quickly. In it they spoke of the pleasure they enjoyed in serving her, and in knowing that she would possess the most magnificent parure of diamonds in the world, and that it would adorn the neck of the greatest and best of Queens. Bewildered, the Queen asked her lady what it could possibly mean, it was incomprehensible to her, and having a candle at hand with which she had been sealing letters, she held the fatal paper in the flame, saying it was not worth keeping.

On 1 August Madame Campan left Versailles for a short rest in her country home, where she received a visit from the jeweller

Boehmer, in a state of violent excitement. At the end of July the Comtesse had produced a letter from the Queen stating that she could not pay until October; they and the Cardinal too were beginning to distrust the authenticity of these letters, but for some reason Rohan would not push an inquiry; he had become so involved with La Motte, that he dared not risk any explanation. To keep him quiet she brought him thirty thousand francs, ostensibly for Boehmer, but so little did not satisfy the jeweller and, on 2 or 3 August, he insisted to the Comtesse that they would wait no longer. With cool effrontery, she declared that it had all been a plot, that the Queen's signature was false, and that if they wanted their money they should go to the Cardinal 'who was rich enough to content them himself'. Half distracted, Boehmer had made his way straight to Madame Campan, who made it clear to him that not only did the Queen not own his necklace but that she had repeatedly declared that she would not buy any more diamonds. 'If I have money to spare,' she had said, 'I will spend it on my property at St Cloud.' Boehmer then asked when her Majesty would reply to their letter, and on his explaining what letter, Madame Campan replied that the Queen had burned it, without giving it a thought. The unfortunate man insisted that he was owed an enormous sum, and was reminded that his accounts had long ago been settled and that as for the necklace the Queen had refused it when offered it by the King. Then it all came out, that she had bought it through an intermediary, the Cardinal de Rohan. 'What!' shrieked Madame Campan. 'A man to whom the Queen has not spoken since she came from Vienna eight years ago?' In vain Boehmer reiterated that this was only pretence, that the Cardinal stood very well with her Majesty, that they had seen letters. 'You have been robbed, my poor man,' replied Madame Campan and she advised Boehmer to go at once to Versailles and to see the Baron de Breteuil, laying the case before him.

The jeweller set off but unwisely tried once more to achieve an audience with the Queen, who was however involved in the rehearsals for the Trianon performance of *The Marriage of Figaro*, and refused to receive him, being bored to death no doubt with these trumpery solicitations. A few days later, however, when Madame Campan returned to Versailles she called him to Trianon, and there he revealed to the Queen the whole unbelievable story. At the end

of it, when he had gone, she was in a terrible state; to think that
a man like the Cardinal could imagine that she would employ
him in such an intimate matter, or in any matter, was unbearable.
And who was this Madame de la Motte? On being told that she
claimed to be the last of the Valois, the Queen exclaimed that
there were no Valois, she must be an impostor. She could not
imagine how everyone could have been so taken in, she felt her
entire innocence, and feeling this, wished that the whole affair
could be taken into the open – thoroughly investigated. On 15
August there was a conference in the King's study between the
Baron de Breteuil, Minister of the King's Household, M. de
Miroménil, Keeper of the Seal, and Marie Antoinette. On
hearing the facts they all agreed that it was flagrant fraud, and
the crux of the whole affair was that the Cardinal had affirmed
solemnly to Boehmer and Bassange that he was treating directly
with the Queen, for after their interview with Madame Campan
in their desperation they had visited the Cardinal and suggested
to him that his intermediary might be deceiving him. He would
not hear of it, though by this time his confidence was beginning
to waver; he was too deeply involved to admit any suspicion.

On 15 August, Rohan, wearing his pontifical robes, was on his
way to the Royal Chapel when he was stopped by the chief valet
with the message that the King wished to see him in his study.
The Queen was there with the Minister of the Seal, and M. de
Breteuil. The King immediately asked him if he had bought any
diamonds from Boehmer. He answered yes and that he believed
that they were given to the Queen. 'Who could have given you
this commission?' asked His Majesty. The Cardinal replied that
it was the Comtesse de la Motte-Valois who had given him a
letter from the Queen and he had believed that he was doing
Her Majesty a favour. Marie Antoinette now intervened to ask
him how he could believe that he, to whom she had not addressed
a word in eight years, could think such a thing, and Rohan
admitted that he had been woefully deceived but that he would
pay for the necklace and all would be settled. And he drew from
his pocket the letter written by the Queen to Madame de la
Motte, and signed by her. The King taking it from him exclaimed
indignantly, 'This is neither the handwriting of the Queen nor
her signature. How could a Prince of the House of Rohan, how
could the Grand Almoner, believe that the Queen could sign

herself Marie Antoinette de France. Everybody knows that the
Queens of France sign only with their baptismal name.' And he
ordered the Cardinal to go into the adjoining room and there to
write what he considered his justification. He returned after a
quarter of an hour, embarrassed, and with reason; he begged his
King to spare him and even some of the ministers did the same,
but Louis XVI was adamant.

The drama which was unfolding must be considered in the
light of what we already know of the characters of the protag-
onists. Marie Antoinette we have seen since childhood obsessed
by the dislike of a man whom she was by nature incapable of
understanding. Once before she had obstinately refused to recognize a person whom she considered inferior in morals and in
position. The pious daughter of a deeply religious mother, she
considered that he disgraced the purple which he wore, he
offended both God and man, and nothing, absolutely nothing
could induce her to tolerate him. Rohan was equally obsessed.
Rich, well-born, holding some of the first positions in the land,
only one person eluded him, Marie Antoinette. For years he had
endeavoured to make himself acceptable to her, without ever
effacing the effect of his slanderous gossip about her life as
Dauphine when he was in Vienna. Not only was she unapproach-
able, she was inaccessible. Her antipathy was so deep-rooted that
all efforts over the years had not served to change in one iota
her attitude. His wounded vanity, his arrogant assumptions had
blinded him to the patent absurdity of this latest intrigue. Between
them stood the King, that good-natured ordinary man, whose
common sense warned him of the dangers inherent in an open
inquest which would bring the whole House of Rohan into the
arena. He stood between his ministers and the Queen; on one
hand those persons who with him were responsible for the
good name of France, and on the other his adored wife, in tears,
outraged in her dignity as a Queen and a Habsburg, and as a
woman, insulted by the intrigue of a man she detested. Could he
hesitate? He did not. He gave the order to arrest the Cardinal.
'I cannot do other,' said he to the protest of the ministers, 'neither
as King nor as husband.'

The doors were opened into the Salon de Pendule, and the
Cardinal left the King's Cabinet. The whole Court, assembled in
the gallery of the Grandes Entrées watched in a stunned silence

while he passed through the Council Chamber followed by a young lieutenant of the guard who had been ordered to accompany him to his Hôtel. It has been recorded that Rohan was as pale as death and hardly able to stand, but he was sufficiently cool to be able, taking advantage of the momentary lapse by the guard, to scribble a note to his private secretary, and to pass it to one of his people. It was the order to burn immediately the red dispatch case and the papers in it. And this the Abbé Georgel did, thus destroying all the evidence contained in the forged letters of the Queen.

Three days afterwards, on 18 August, Madame de la Motte was arrested in her house in Bar-sur-Aube, returning from a fête in the Château of the Duc de Penthièvre where she had been received with all the honours of a wealthy member of the highest society. She was taken to the Bastille where the Cardinal had preceded her and on 5 September the King instituted a Parliamentary inquiry into the whole affair.

The scandal was outrageous, the public response immediate. That a Rohan, the Grand Almoner of France, should be arrested in the full light of day in the Palace was unheard of, but tragically the opinion was not that he must be guilty but that the King had made a mistake. Even the Parlement, designed by its essence to uphold the State, reacted against the King's demand for an inquiry; the President, at the instigation of d'Epremenil, declaimed against the 'carrying off' of Rohan, the clergy resented the insult to the Church, and the nobility were up in arms at the affront to their order. The ladies of the Royal Family, only too pleased to have a rod to beat the Queen with, supported the Cardinal, while the whole clan of the Rohans, Soubises, Guémenées, Condés, disregarding any friendship they might have had for her, condemned her unheard. Every person or party which was against the monarchy, all the disappointed, the mean, the petty, combined to swell the chorus of vilification. Long before the trial was even begun, the affair had begun to take on a political aspect, and the Rohans were employing every means of corruption in order to secure a favourable verdict for the Cardinal. The man himself showed his political flair; he had been used to dress in civilian clothes before the affair, now he never appeared but in his full clerical robes; he affected a humble and ingratiating manner, presenting a picture of the good and contrite priest unjustly accused, while the ladies of his House and party wore full mourning on every occasion in public. The Queen had written to her brother, 'Thank God we have seen the last of this horrible affair.' She was wrong, she had not, and never would see the last of it. She thought, as always, that by ignoring it she could prove that she was innocent of any part in it, her attitude only served to inflame the public against her. She could not yet realize that the Cardinal, by the mere fact that *she* had condemned him, became a hero in the eyes of Paris and all France, so unpopular had she become. The women were the worst, writes Madame Campan, they wore hats '*au Cardinal*', they sported ribbons with the family colours and they sang in the streets:

> *Notre Saint Père l'a rougi*
> *Le Roi, La Reine, l'a noirci*
> *Le Parlement le blanchira*
> *Alléluia.**

His defence was that he had been the victim of a plot, that he had been deceived throughout, and when at last he appeared before the Parlement on 30 May 1786 he was received with the greatest honours, he was given a seat; he was treated not like an accused but as a Prince, said a witness. As for Madame de la Motte, she denied everything, and accused Cagliostro of being the evil genius who had brought the Cardinal to the theft of the necklace. But there was too much evidence against her; where did she get the money for her extravagant manner of living, horses, carriages, servants, to say nothing of the fêtes, dinners, and receptions at Bar-sur-Aube? And the diamonds which her husband, still in London, had sold there, where did they come from? Certainly, replied the Comtesse, they were diamonds which the Cardinal had given her to defray all the expense. And, moreover, if she had been guilty, would she have stayed in France to be taken to the Bastille? As for the Cardinal, he wrote a letter to the King asking that if the arguments before the Court proved that he had been guilty of nothing more than having been himself deceived, he might be sentenced 'as the King would pronounce according to his justice and mercy'.

* Our Holy Father has reddened him
  The King, the Queen, have blackened him
  The Parliament will whiten him
      Alleluia.

On 22 May 1786 the Parlement assembled, there were sixty-four judges who listened during six days to the various pieces of evidence, and on the seventh the Prosecutor General rose to speak. He demanded that the document signed Marie Antoinette de France be declared a forgery, that the Cardinal should appear before the High Court there to declare that he had believed in the affair of the meeting in the thicket, that he had contributed to the deception of the jewellers, in allowing them to believe that the Queen knew about the sale of the jewels, that he should admit his repentance and ask pardon of the King and Queen, resign from his appointments, give alms to the poor and remain for the rest of his life remote from the Royal residences, and return to prison until the sentence should be terminated. He concluded, 'The Cardinal alleges that the rendezvous in the garden favoured his illusions. But could he possibly believe in such a meeting, by night and in Versailles, and in so believing did he not commit the gravest offence against his Queen?' Well yes, unfortunately he could, for the public had during the past years been persuaded that this was exactly how Marie Antoinette met her supposed lovers. And the hatred they bore her burst out while his last words were still echoing round the hall. The Advocate-General sprang to his feet and shouted, 'The Cardinal ought to be acquitted, and you,' turning to Joly de Fleury, 'you with one foot in the grave, you wish to cover your ashes with ignominy?' To which the Prosecutor replied with calm, 'Your anger does not surprise me, Sir. A man devoted to libertinage like yourself must of course defend the Cardinal.' Amid laughter Séguier replied, 'It is true that I sometimes visit prostitutes, and that I even leave my carriage in front of their doors. It is a private affair. But nobody has yet seen me sell my opinion for success.'

The interrogations followed. Retaux de Villette came well out of them. Madame de la Motte declared that she had seen two hundred letters from the Queen to the Cardinal and that she called him '*tu*'. This evoked a hurricane, it was too much even for those who wished to believe the worst. Rohan appeared calm, pale and dignified; he told with sadness his story, making himself appear even more gullible than he was in fact, and left the hall, saluting the assembled judges, who rose and returned his salutation. The young Oliva, heroine of the 'thicket' was late in appearing, she had to give the breast to her baby born in the Bastille, which touched the hearts of the Judges. Cagliostro also appeared, giving as his title 'a noble stranger' and addressing the Court in a mixture of Latin, Italian, Greek and Arabic.

On 31 August came the verdict. After eighteen hours of deliberation, by twenty-six votes against twenty-two, the Cardinal was declared entirely innocent. Cagliostro also, and the little Oliva was freed from all accusations. Retaux was banished from the country, and Jeanne de la Motte was condemned to be branded on both shoulders and confined for life, a ferocious sentence.

Paris went mad, ten thousand persons shouting for the Cardinal surrounded the Bastille, whither he had been taken for safety. Next day he went to the Hôtel de Soubise surrounded by applauding men and women. The Hôtel was brilliantly illuminated, 'as if', says Madame de Sabran in a letter to the Chevalier de Boufflers, 'he would illuminate his shame by the light of day'. The fishwives were there to congratulate him and to brand the Queen and through her the monarchy as the principal offenders. As Goethe remarked, 'The event filled me with apprehension, as if I saw a Medusa's head.'

The King did not hesitate to exercise the justice which Rohan had asked for; he was relieved of all his offices and exiled to his abbey at Chaise Dieu; his friend and evil genius Cagliostro was ordered to leave Paris and the kingdom within three weeks. Marie Antoinette was aghast, the verdict was incomprehensible to her. She broke down completely and Madame Campan found her weeping in her boudoir. 'Congratulate me,' she sobbed, 'the plotter who wished to destroy me has been acquitted, you can be sorry for your outraged Queen.' And she added, 'But I for my part can be sorry for you French. If I have been judged unjustly, what may happen to any of you if you have a case which touches your honour or your position?'

While she rehearsed *The Marriage of Figaro* did she ever reflect, one wonders, on the words of Don Basilio on the vicious strength of calumny? She was judged on the foolishness of her childish years as Dauphine, on her political ineptness as a Queen, on the rumours spread by her enemies, and the terrible state of the country whose Queen she was. She and the monarchy and all the French nobility, if they could only have realized it, were caught up in an upheaval for which they were utterly unprepared, a moment of crisis which would engulf them all. The hungry and miserable peasants, the wretched townsfolk looked at those who ruled them, and they did not like what they saw, and they used whatever stick they could find with which to chastise. In this case it was the Cardinal. Shortly it would be worse.

5
Maturity

THE ending of the affair of the necklace had left Marie Antoinette in a state bordering on despair. Not only had she been subjected to a frightful experience on the part of the public but she had a strong suspicion that her most intimate friends had not been entirely loyal to her. She had made a mistake and she determined to make no more. It is true that she sent for the Duchesse de Polignac to come and comfort her, but in other days she would have rushed herself to her friend's arms; she began to appear much less frequently in the Duchesse's salon, sending before her arrival to know what other guests were there, a clear sign that she disapproved of some of the habitués. As the Comte de Provence wrote, 'The Queen wished for a judgment [in the affair] which would publish the truth. She was wrong, because in such affairs it is always better to let them die quietly of themselves. The Queen, however, only listened to her offended heart.' Perhaps now she had learned this lesson.

In any case she tended in the last months of 1786 to retire more and more into privacy. In July she was delivered of her last child, the princess Sophie. She had spent the month of June by herself, for the King had gone on a tour of Normandy from whence he sent daily accounts of his success. It was an extended tour and was something for which Louis XVI was just the right sort of King. It took him first to Cherbourg where he could examine in great detail the immense works which would create the military port, he saw the citadel, inspected the troops, and enchanted all by his simplicity, good humour and frank interest. At Caen, where he was presented with the keys of the town, he called the crowds 'my children', walked about among them and there and in Le Havre and Honfleur he was hailed with cries of *Vive le Roi*, to which he replied *Vive mon Peuple*. His daily letters to his wife said that she would have been satisfied with him for he had never been bad-tempered or 'shown his surly voice'. It was reminiscent of the times when the Kings of France felt it their duty to see and be seen by their people, before Versailles had laid its freezing hand on their freedom. When he returned to Versailles he picked up his second son, the Duc de Normandie, saying, 'Come here, my big Norman, your name brings good luck.'

During his absence Marie Antoinette had been occupied with the finishing touches on her little hamlet at Trianon. In the lovely summer weather it was a pleasure for her to drive there and in installing the farmer and his wife, with all the inhabitants of the farm, cows, chickens, sheep, to forget the trial and its horror. The place seems to us a toy and so it was, but there was enough reality for her to enjoy her own butter, eggs and fruit, and to rest in her little house, only a stone's throw from the exquisite Little Trianon. In November they were at Fontainebleau and here some of the success of Normandy still remained. Madame de Staël, writing to the King of Sweden, remarked on the crowd which surrounded the Queen wherever she went, all seeking to be noticed by her. She was still beautiful, though she had lost some of the gaiety and insouciance of her youth; she had put on some weight, and her manners, though they had lost nothing of their charm, were more restrained. During the winter at Versailles the balls she gave in the Princes' Courtyard were as brilliant as ever: it was as if by some clairvoyance the Court felt that it was the last flowering of an epoch. The ballroom was arranged like a fairy palace, representing the garden of the Trianon with its thickets, its fountains and its statues. The billiard-room was illuminated and was separated from the gaming-room by a mirrored wall. But high play was forbidden – the Queen no longer gambled, she played trictrac, no more serious betting, and her personal expenses, though still high, were all curtailed. It would be too much to suppose that the figures of her expenditure on clothes to the rather eclipsed Rose Bertin should have gone to nothing, but in comparison with what was spent by the aged Madame Adélaïde or demanded by the Duc de Provence or the Comte d'Artois they were low. And the Minister Calonne was always there to supply every demand. It is again Madame de Staël who summed up what all the memoirs of the time tell us, 'It is, I believe, impossible to put more of grace and affability in politeness; she has a sort of graciousness which never permits you to forget that she is Queen though she herself seems to forget it.'

And she was at the same time supremely mother. Her children were ever in her thoughts, wherever she was one or all of them were with her. She watched over their cradles, played with them and like her mother before her gave most exact directions as to their upbringing to those in charge of them. So much so that Mercy, like Kaunitz before him, complained bitterly that when he had an audience with the Queen one or other of the babies was always under foot. We have her instructions to Madame de Tourzel, the Governess who replaced Madame de Polignac. 'I give to the care of Virtue that which had been confided to Friendship,' she wrote charmingly, and a long note dissects for Tourzel's guide the character of the Dauphin:

He is like all the children who are well and strong, very violent in his rages, but he is a good child, loving and even thoughtful when his prankishness does not carry him away. Since his babyhood he has been unable to ask for pardon, he will do whatever you wish if he has been naughty, but he cannot bring himself to ask for pardon. But he has no idea of rank in his head and I do not wish that he should; our children will learn soon enough who they are.

This is the speech of a mother who has studied her child long and tenderly; in it and in all her behaviour at this time one can see those qualities of humanity and goodness which were so fundamental a part of Marie Antoinette's nature, and which her youth and inconsistencies had obscured. Her tragedy was – and we cannot insist on it too often – that she was placed in a position which she was too young to handle, in a sick society which she had no means of evaluating, a world already shaken by revolutionary ideas. She was almost alone in seeing the danger inherent in the American revolution and was against the aid given to the insurgents by the French and even by the King. As her brother Joseph II had said, her first reactions were almost always right, she lacked only the consistency to sustain them. As the Prince de Ligne wrote in his memoirs, 'Only wicked people could say anything bad about her, and only stupid ones could believe them.' Unfortunately there were plenty of both surrounding her.

One day Madame Campan found her on her couch weeping sadly with letters strewn around her. 'Ah,' she exclaimed, 'the wicked ones, the monsters. What have I ever done to them? Ah if I could only die.' Doubtless the letters contained some of the abominable insults which more and more were hurled at her. Wherever she turned they appeared, nailed to the gates of the Palace, slipped into her rooms, who knew by what hand. The time was past when she could take them lightly, could laugh at them. The pamphlets bore such names as 'Aurora Arises', 'The love-affairs of our Queen', 'The Coquette and the Impotent Husband', and now 'The Essays on the Life of Marie Antoinette', and from Madame de la Motte in London the infamous *Mémoires*. They emanated not only from the pamphleteers of Paris, but from the circle nearest to her; she was credited with dozens of lovers, every gentleman to whom she had shown a liking was accused of having found his way into her bed; she was called Messaline, Frédégonde, and all this poisonous innuendo would be cited against her by Fouquier-Tinville in the proceedings of the Tribunal which condemned her to death.

In 1787 this unfortunate woman suffered the loss of her little daughter Sophie. Profoundly unhappy she shut herself up at Trianon alone with the King and Madame Elisabeth, to whom she wrote, 'Come to me, we will lament together for the death of my little angel. I need all your love to console my unhappy heart.' And when they attempted to comfort her by saying that after all the little girl had only been a baby, she replied, 'Yes, but she would have become a friend.' Like her mother she began to seek consolation in religion, but she was unable to absent herself from the world around her and found that more and more her advice was needed in the realm of politics.

In the beginning of 1787 it was apparent that Calonne so far from having reduced the deficit had only succeeded in adding to it. He suggested to the King that Parlement should be called in order to sanction a tax on land. The idea appealed neither to the King nor to the Parlement and it was decided to call instead the Assembly of Notables. These were persons, as the name implies, from every province who by their position were competent to advise. Unfortunately nine days before the opening of the Assembly Vergennes died and the King lost his wisest guide, and still more unfortunately the opening which had been set for 29 January was postponed until 22 February. The Notables were obliged to kick their heels in Paris and were assailed by the chorus of criticism and hatred which filled the capital, and besieged by everyone who had an excuse for discontent. Following the custom of mocking everything it was announced that the Great Troop of M. de Calonne would give its famous representation of the piece 'False Appearances of Debts and Mistakes'.

The Assembly opened and listened to a speech from Calonne in which he exposed with justice and vigour his plans for political and financial reform. Unfortunately, not content with this he attacked Necker who, he said, for all his banking experience and undoubted genius, had not been able to stabilize the finances and who in his *Compte Rendu* had been guilty of falsehood. Stung to the quick Necker retorted in a *Mémoire Justificatif*, which he sent to Versailles; the King forbade him to print it, he disobeyed and was exiled. Madame de Staël tells how the news was brought to his family as they sat with friends in their salon and how bewildered she was, knowing her father to be 'noble and disinterested in all his feelings'. She rushed to Versailles to implore the help of Marie Antoinette, but in spite of her liking for the financier the Queen refused to act. On 8 April Calonne fell; he was exiled to his estates in Lorraine and together with the public he attributed his disgrace to Marie Antoinette. Having escaped to England later on he was suspected of collaborating with Madame de la Motte in her *Mémoires*.

Louis XVI now had to find another Comptroller-General. The choice lay between two men, Necker and the Archbishop of Toulouse. The King disliked them both, but it would be impossible to recall Necker at this juncture, and Loménie de Brienne enjoyed a general reputation for competence and sagacity. He had worked for fifteen years in anticipation of this moment, was the intimate friend of the Director of Marie Antoinette, the Abbé Vermond, and had done all in his power to ingratiate himself with the Court. But Louis distrusted him and disliked his worldliness and his sympathy with the *Philosophes*. 'At least the Archbishop of Paris ought to believe in God,' said he. But his wife carried the day, she was not alone in her appreciation of the ecclesiastic, most of France shared it. On 17 May 1787 the Archbishop therefore became the Minister of Finance. In one thing the King agreed with him, they both believed that an absolute monarchy was necessary for France, and they both hesitated to call the Estates General. Both procrastinated before sending to Parlement the edicts which decreed the reforms, and when they did act they met the determined resistance of that body. It went so far as to state that 'the Nation represented by the Estates General has the sole right to permit to the King those subsidies which the situation demands'. This was open opposition, fomented by all those 'liberals' who looked with admiration at the English limited monarchy. The Salons fulminated against the King and with complete lack of judgment took the side of those nobles who would suffer most under such a change. Necker's daughter, Madame de Staël, led among the nobles, financiers, journalists and *Philosophes* who thronged her drawing-room, in pointing out how much they would all profit under 'liberty'.

On 6 August the King held a *lit de Justice* at Versailles when he ordered Parlement to register the edicts he had sent to them. They refused and were promptly exiled to Troyes. Paris went mad; nobles, clergy and citizens joined in their opposition to Louis XVI and he, unfortunate man, unable to sustain his determined attitude, was forced to recall them. They were welcomed by the Parisians, at their head the Duc d'Orléans, who had identified himself with the opposition to Versailles. The King already regretted what he had done and had, in order to assist Brienne in his efforts to reduce the deficit, made enormous reductions in the establishments of himself and the Queen. This was a further affront to the clergy and the nobles, who saw themselves without the support which had always subsidized their indolence. As for the Queen, she had little taste for balls and extravagance, for as if the death of her little girl were not enough for her to bear, the Dauphin showed signs of being unwell.

The situation worsened from day to day. In desperation the King called a second *lit de Justice*, where he ordered that an edict permitting him to issue a 420 millions loan should be registered. Pandemonium ensued. Deputies sprang up on the benches and roared their dissent; for the first time the words 'Tyrant, Despot' were heard. And now Orléans rose and spoke: 'If the King is holding a sitting of Parlement, the votes should be collected and counted, if this is a *lit de Justice* he should command silence.' And he added, 'This register is illegal.' It was true that the King, to appease the magistrates, had omitted the words 'by my express command' in his address. The situation was thus ambiguous, but nothing could excuse the insolence of Orléans to his King, who, taken aback, stammered 'Yes, it is legal, legal because I say so.'

One can imagine in what a state Louis returned to Versailles and the anger of the Queen when she heard of all this. It is difficult to know precisely what part she played in the repressive measures which followed, the exiling of d'Empremesnil and Monsabert, and even the Duc d'Orléans, but Mirabeau was later to write, 'The King has only one man beside him – the Queen', and Fersen, in a letter to his father said:

The King is always weak and suspicious, he has confidence only in the Queen and it seems it is she who does everything, the ministers go to her and inform her on every subject. It is said that the King has begun to drink and that the Queen encourages this passion so that she can get him to sign anything she wishes; nothing could be more untrue; he has no taste for drink, and this vice would be too dangerous, for anyone else could get his signature as easily as the Queen.

It may also be said that Fersen was in a position to know, for according to St Priest, he was two or three times a week at Versailles, riding in the park. The Queen did the same, alone, and these rendezvous caused a public scandal, in spite of the modest behaviour and dress of the favourite, who never showed anything in his public life and was, of all the Queen's friends, the most discreet. May it not be conjectured that because he really loved the woman, not the Queen, he was careful of her and satisfied to be with her and to help her if he could? Shortly afterwards when he was recalled to Sweden, for Gustave III was at war with Russia, both Marie Antoinette and her husband felt the loss of a sincere friend.

On 5 November 1787, Marie Antoinette received a long letter from the Emperor her brother, explaining his reason for entering the war which had broken out; by the Three Power Treaty between himself, Turkey and Russia, he was bound, three months after having been appealed to, to declare war on whichever of the two powers had attacked. Russia was responsible under the same conditions. In the same letter he reminds her how sitting in the park at Trianon he had warned her against her coterie, whom he suspected of using her only to further their own designs and had recommended her to refuse their requests from time to time. Then she would soon see who were her real friends and those who, to use his own phrase, 'only set their sails to every good wind, uncertain and even careless of how long it may last, if they can only procure for their friends or relations all that they can.' Very wise words, but unnecessary, for Marie Antoinette had already begun to concentrate on her family, her husband and her duties. With the Comtesse d'Ossun, who was also a close friend of Fersen, she shared the quiet life at St Cloud, where simplicity was the order of the day. Gone were the exaggerated modes, gone too was Rose Bertin, the balls and high gaming parties were over. Music, walking and playing with her children, these were the pleasures which compensated somewhat for the dislike she had for politics and affairs of State. It was all no use, the public was not to be won, they had made up their mind that she was the cause of all their troubles, and they stuck on the gates of Versailles such lampoons as the following.

Louis seize interdit, Antoinette au couvent
D'Artois à Saint-Lazare, et Provence Régent.*

For Provence in his devious way, working quietly underground, never forgot for a moment his frustrated ambition.

She had a new cause for anxiety and one much nearer to her heart, her eldest son, the Dauphin, was showing alarming signs of weakness. As she wrote to Joseph II, though he had never been strong he had seemed to be making progress; now he had one hip out of place as well as his back; he was feverish and had trouble with his teeth. She remembered that the air of Meudon had been of help to the King, who had also been a sickly boy, they were therefore sending the Dauphin there in the hope that he too would profit. She compared him with his brother, who was, she said, as strong as a peasant. With some humour she says that she is accused of being pregnant again; if she had been pregnant every time the public suspected it, she would have as many children as the Grand Duchess. It was the same this time as the others, there was not the slightest sign of it. She added that she hoped that the war would not be a long one and that she understood the necessity

* Louis Sixteenth shut up, Antoinette in a convent D'Artois in St Lazare, and Provence Regent.

for Joseph's entry into it. The tone of her letters is always the same, warm, intimate and confidential.

Nothing could be further from the political scene. Brienne was a failure, of all his measures for economy only one was popular, the diminution of the Royal establishments. In these economies the Queen led the way for, as she said, if she had known the true condition of the Treasury she would never have made the purchases she did, she would have been the first to institute reforms in her household; but she had been unable to form an idea of the extent of the trouble since whenever she asked for a sum she was sent double the amount. From the beginning of the Assembly of the Notables she had given up her evening card-playing and released the three young men who directed it. She continued her economies in the month of August, suspended the work in progress at St Cloud, and asked the Duc de Polignac for his resignation from the post of Controller of her Stables. The King, for his part, gave up a great part of his hunting establishment, his falconry, and decided to sell La Muette and Choisy. It might be thought that all this would make the monarchs more popular; on the contrary it gave great umbrage to all those who lost by it. Polignac was furious, for he lost fifty thousand livres of revenue, and Vaudreuil his position as Chief Falconer, while the Duc de Coigny – who later would be one of their truest friends – so far lost his head as to make a scene with the King. As for Besenval, he declared that if one was never going to know where one stood financially from one day to another, one might as well be in Turkey.

On 8 May, the King held another *lit de Justice*, where he ordered the registration of new edicts, one of which modified considerably the jurisdiction of the Parlements throughout the country; the other took from them the registration of laws and bestowed the right on a plenary Court. Unfortunately Brienne was far from making such sacrifices, he had used his power to enrich himself in the most flagrant way; he had named himself Prime Minister and when the Marshals de Ségur and de Castries refused to accept this, he deposed them and gave their offices to second-rate relations of his own. More, when the Archbishop of Sens died he named himself for the post, a vastly more lucrative one than Toulouse. All this inflamed public opinion and naturally the blame for his appointment fell on the usual person, Marie

Antoinette. It was she, they said, who had recommended Brienne at the prompting of her mentor Vermond; he had brought her into the Council of State and here she had been forced to decide what would be her role. Seeing the provocative attitude of Parlement and the unrest in the provinces it had been thought essential to limit their power, and plans were laid in secret for the edicts which were in fact proposed at the *lit de Justice* in May. She deplored the necessity for making these changes but they were essential if the King's authority was to be maintained. But the natural goodness of her heart betrayed her once more and when Brienne fell she was imprudent enough to send him presents – to soften the blow – and here we are reminded of her mother who did precisely the same thing over and over again.

She had the comforting feeling that the Dauphin's health was improving: the air of Meudon did him good, he had no more fever, his teeth were coming through, all would be well. Her other children were happy and healthy and they were all going to St Cloud for Whitsun. She herself was as well as she could expect with so much to disquiet her, but she was becoming a real matriarch, for the King needed all her energy to keep him going. He hunted three times a week, and returning indulged in enormous repasts, after which he went to sleep. Heavy and phlegmatic, this good-natured man seemed to have no idea what was happening nor any premonition that his royal power was waning.

Parisians had rejoiced at the fall of Brienne. His effigy had been burned outside his palace, everyone behaved as if with the calling of the Estates General the millennium would come, and as a sign of the times the Comte de Mirabeau joined the Third Estate. This extraordinary man with his enormous head of hair and his stentorian voice was at the same time by his very grossness imposing. In the country brigandage was spreading, for if starving people in their hopelessness crowd together in little groups, larger ones will grow. On 27 April the Quarter of St Antoine had risen and Besenval had ordered thirty Gardes Françaises to quell the riot, with orders to hold their fire if possible. But St Antoine would not yield until faced by the Swiss Guard and two cannon: the Quarter shrank back but did not cease to plot. No one seemed to understand that hunger and misery can make men reckless even of life itself. The assembling of the Estates General was a rallying point for the whole nation. At last its voice would be heard. Louis XIV had said '*L'état, c'est moi*', now France said '*L'état, c'est nous.*'

It was sad that this increased power gave Marie Antoinette nothing but alarm, she had no training for political affairs, and as we have seen almost the only decisive action in the King's life with her had been to keep her away from politics and above all from foreign affairs. She had, it is true, more than once interfered with the appointment of ministers, but it was always due to the sinister influence of the people she loved, who had done more towards her destruction than any enemies. Now she was face to face with a crisis; from all over the country one cry went up, the Estates General should be convened. As if there were some magic in the name the insurgents in Brittany, in Dauphiné, reiterated the demand. In Paris the Cour des Aides took it up, the Assembly of the Clergy even went so far as to say to the King 'Your Majesty's glory is not to be King of France but King, of the French people.' Such language had never been heard before; it was convincing.

At the beginning of July frightful hailstorms had ruined the coming harvest. For sixty leagues round Paris total destruction of the farms brought the threat of winter famine in a dreadful certainty. Faced with all this, the King and Brienne resisted no longer, the convocation of the Estates General was fixed for 1 May 1789.

The Queen wrote to her brother: 'Your war, which threatens the peace of Europe, our troubles, make this an unhappy year; God grant that the next will be better. Farewell, my dear brother, I embrace you a thousand, thousand times with all my heart.' It was the last time she would ever write to him. Joseph was spared the agony of seeing his sister's tragic end, the end which he had always feared and his mother had predicted.

On 26 August 1788 Loménie de Brienne fell, and the King consented to send for Necker. It was Mercy who served as go-between, and the financier at first refused the place which was offered him to collaborate with Brienne, the Queen having suggested this solution. 'I tremble,' she wrote to Mercy, 'at the thought that it is I who summon him. *It is my fate to bring bad luck.* And if infernal machinations lead to his failure or if he diminishes the authority of the King, I will be even more detested.' She was face to face with reality at last, gone were the days when she could laugh at the scurrilous verses, the gossip and the scandal, knowing herself innocent of designs unworthy of her. Gone was the hauteur of the Habsburg Archduchess. If she could have the courage to say 'I bring bad luck' she had come a long way towards the development of that heroic side of her character which would bear her up to the end.

Now both she and the King gave in and she invited Necker to attend her in her cabinet, and when he came she painted such a picture of the troubled nation, the King's distress, and her own anxiety that he accepted, not too unwillingly since he would be given plenary power. His daughter Madame de Staël was in raptures, now she foresaw the time when all liberal thought and plans would come to fruition, a new France would be born. Her father was less enthusiastic, he found the King's Treasury almost empty. On the other hand, the news of his arrival had a phenomenal effect on the European Stock Exchanges, the funds rose on the first day by thirty per cent. He saw very clearly all the dangers and the explosive situation; but the Queen was right, he was a financier but no statesman, or even a politician. 'Ah, if I had only had the fifteen months of the Archbishop,' he cried to his daughter, but even if they had been his it is doubtful whether the crisis could have been averted, for now it was imperative that the composition of the Estates General should be decided upon. Since 1614 it had never been called. The convocation of the Estates General, wrote Michelet, is the true era of the birth of the people. It called the whole nation to the exercise of their rights. It was composed of three orders, the Clergy, the Nobility and the Third Estate or Commons, and since Necker was a businessman called upon to restore the shattered credit of nation, he determined that the businessmen should be heavily represented, the growing middle class in fact. The basis of taxation must be broadened, and who but they would understand this? He therefore supported the proposal that as the population of France had certainly increased since 1614, the Commons should be doubled. This announcement let loose a flood of essays, leaflets, pamphlets; every journalist, every historian, and the popular press hurried to give their opinion, their theories for the reconstitution of France, as if, wrote one commentator, the country was a country without tradition or customs, a New Found Land. To stem the tide of discussion the King called the

Notables to decide; considering more what they stood to lose than the public good, they reacted strongly against any such increase, and this inflamed Parlement, which took shelter behind the King, so lately the object of their execration, declaring that the matter was to be decided by him alone. Louis, at a sitting of the Privy Council at which the Queen was present for the first time, ordained that the Commons be doubled. In this the Queen supported him, but the credit went to Necker.

Early in 1789 the representatives were elected amid general disturbance. Mirabeau demanded the fusion of the three orders into one Parlement while the Abbé Sieyes insisted that the Third Estate, from having been unconsidered in France, ought to be made supreme. Fersen wrote to a friend:

The fermentation of thought is general, no one talks of anything but a constitution. The women of the salons are the worst and you know as well as I do the influence they have. All consider themselves administrators and speak of progress; in the waiting-room the lackeys read the brochures which appear all the time, I do not know how the printers cope with them; it is the fashion at this moment, and you well know what a power this is.

It was necessary for the Minister to form some sort of agenda for the Estates to consider, and in the first place to decide where they were to meet. The Queen hoped that it would be in some town sufficiently removed from Paris – Orléans or Tours or perhaps Rheims; they would be less at the mercy of popular outcry, and the deputies freer. The King decided on Versailles; Necker and he were too strong for her.

Another decision, of the utmost importance, whether the voting was to be by individuals or by Orders, was unfortunately left to the Estates themselves; they were also allowed to direct their own work. This could only lead to confusion and was an instance of Necker's incapacity to take a strong and consistent line. Of course the Queen was blamed for any and everything which displeased. The nobility in particular took offence at her support for the increase in the number of the Third Estate; they addressed a memoir which was handed to her by the Comte d'Artois, and since it did not meet with an immediate response, the Comte was offended and a coolness between them began. The Polignacs supported Artois, and the Queen suffered from a growing isolation. Added to her participation in politics was the increasing fear for her little son the Dauphin, who was failing from day to day. Nothing can be more pathetic than a very sick child, whose patience and sweetness wring the heart. Thus the Comtesse de Laage and the Princesse de Lamballe have left a touching picture of the boy, once so lively and cheerful. He was lying on a mattress spread on a billiard table when they entered his room, reading a history book, and he answered their questions with great intelligence. His principal wish was to be with his mother, it broke her heart to see him so ill, and when she dined in his room she wept more than she ate. She remembered how much he had enjoyed, sitting on his father's knee, a rehearsal at Trianon and started to act her scene for him. In the middle she stopped, she had forgotten the words. Campan, who was acting as prompter, tried to find the place but his enormous spectacles made this difficult. Suddenly the childish voice of the Dauphin was heard, 'Monsieur Campan, take off your big spectacles, Maman cannot hear you.' On 4 May 1775 he was taken to a balcony at Versailles to see the procession of the Estates General which marched from the Church of Notre Dame to the Church of St Louis.

The winter had been frightful, the rivers frozen over, the roads impassable with snow; the windmills could not grind grain, everywhere the people froze and hungered, and even when the spring came it was little better. Add to this a good-natured but weak King, a Queen execrated by the public and vilified by the nobility, and a government totally unfit to deal with the crisis of debt, disorder and disaffection. The procession was, however, most imposing and if anyone present had been endowed with the gift of clairvoyance, surprising.

Here walked the last Kings of France, all unknowing. Louis XVI, Louis XVIII, Charles X, and the Duc de Chartres, who one day would be Louis Philippe. More than this, here was the Duc d'Orléans who would help to send Louis XVI to the guillotine, and on the other hand still unknown here were the men who would conduct the Terror, and Robespierre who would be himself its victim. And too the erstwhile stable-boy of the Comte d'Artois, Monsieur Marat, the Friend of the People.

It was the greatest of great occasions, and began with Mass at the Church of Notre Dame heard by the twelve hundred deputies, the King and Queen and the whole Court. Next came the procession through the bedecked town of Versailles, with every window occupied and the balconies hung with costly tapestries: all Paris was there, and beneath them in the streets were the people, whose Day it was. From all over France they had come, with hope in their hearts, but also with determination: they watched the passing of the procession; first the five hundred and fifty deputies of the Third Estate, lawyers, advocates, magistrates, welcomed with prolonged applause; then the deputies of the nobility, a strong contrast in their splendid clothes, laced with gold, not so many of them, but greeted in silence. Then the clergy, the great Prelates first in their purple and lawn, followed by the humble curates, in contrasting shabby black.

At last came the King and Queen, he in his robes of State surrounded by the high officers of the Crown, she for the last time in her most resplendent garments, sprinkled with diamonds, her beautiful head, with its still blonde hair, held high, her gait graceful and majestic, a Queen to love and admire. Alas, as she passed beneath the balcony where her little ailing child was watching, a cry was heard in the bitter silence which had greeted her, '*Vive le Duc d'Orléans.*' It struck home, the insult was too much, she reeled and would have fallen, but her indomitable courage came to her aid, she straightened herself and without a glance and with the murmured words: 'It is nothing, nothing', passed on.

On the following day the first sitting was held in the vast hall of the Menus Plaisirs which held comfortably the eleven hundred deputies and four thousand spectators. The Queen, on the right hand of the King, had arrived a little late and Madame de Staël commented that she was very much moved and the colour of her complexion changed, pale but composed. She scanned the assembly and particularly the Third Estate, who for their part returned her gaze with curiosity, for most of them had never seen her before. When the King spoke she rose and remained standing until he had finished, and she exercised the greatest self-control during the three hours' speech of Necker, who declared the deficit to be only fifty million, which could be covered, for example, by a tax on tobacco in Brittany. The deputies listened stupefied, and when Marie Antoinette rose to leave they actually applauded her. Taken by surprise, and charmed, she responded by one of those delicious smiles of which she had the secret, and a curtsey which as always included all the onlookers. At the end of his speech Louis XVI replaced his hat on his head, upon which, according to old established custom, the nobles covered themselves. And now took place a symbolic scene which may be regarded as the beginning of the French Revolution. The Third Estate, which in old days had been obliged to listen on their knees to the monarch speaking, asserted themselves, and put on their hats. In the amazed silence some cries were heard of 'Hats off' from the audience and some of the nobles, and confusion seemed imminent. With royal tact Louis took off his hat again and all were forced to imitate him.

On leaving the hall the royal pair hurried off to Meudon where the Dauphin lay dying. His mother after this hardly left his bedside while his father joined her as soon as he could free himself from business. But on 2 June, arriving in haste, the Queen fell weeping into his arms, the Dauphin had died that night at one o'clock and the parents, overwhelmed in their suffering, shut themselves away and would see no one. On the next day some members of the Third Estate forced their way into the apartment to discuss their views with the King; they muttered a few cold words of regret. 'Are there no fathers in the assembly?' remarked the King sadly.

After six weeks of discussion the Third Estate, which now called itself the *Communes*, had put the fear of God into the nobility and the clergy, who looked to the King's authority to save them. This in turn affected Necker, who by a skilful campaign of underground innuendo, at which his daughter was expert, managed to discredit the monarch. At Marly, whither the Court had moved – the last visit Marie Antoinette would make – on 19 June, Louis received his Council. Two days previously the Third Estate had constituted itself the National Assembly and had appointed a Committee of Subsistences with pledges to appoint four other standing Committees to settle the national debt and annual taxation. On 18 June some of the clergy and a good number of the more liberal nobility joined them, and under the guidance of Mayor Bailly they put their case. Marie Antoinette, annoyed because Bailly on an earlier visit had saluted her improperly, treated him on this occasion with coldness; it was her misfortune to be at the mercy of the impressions of the moment, she showed dislike for those who displeased her, and occurrences like this, apparently unimportant, were distinctly harmful to the King's cause.

Necker arriving at Marly added his voice to those of the deputies, whose plan was that the King should consent to the union of the Three Orders and that they should be authorized to modify the constitution with a guarantee to create two Chambers. After two hours of discussion the King, it was said influenced by his wife, refused. Louis XVI, seeing in this National Assembly what he rightly called 'a dangerous scission', closed the Salle des Menus Plaisirs where the Estates had been meeting. When the Commons presented themselves there on 20 June they were turned away by the soldiers guarding it, and a certain Doctor Guillotin suggested that they should repair to the tennis court. Here they took an oath not to separate until they had given – either with or without the King's approval – a constitution to France; a direct defiance to the Crown. In fact, wrote Arthur Young, travelling in France, it meant that the Commons arrogated to themselves complete authority over the entire realm, and contravened all tradition, all laws, and even the constitutional principles of the Estates General. A 'fatal oath' indeed. But Necker and his 'liberals' were in ecstasies and he lost no time in hurrying to the King and advising him to submit. The alternative was to go on attempting to govern, and strange to say Louis XVI chose just this.

On 23 June the Three Orders were summoned to attend a meeting with the King which took the now outdated form of *lit de Justice*. According to the deputy Malouet there would still have been time, with energy and persistence, to obstruct the Third Estate, which might have felt that it had gone too far. But, alas, Necker was as hesitant as the King himself and when Louis did speak it was in the imperative, which irritated the Third Estate, joined by 149 members of the clergy and Orléans. The text of his discourse had been modified by a meeting at which Monsieur and the Comte d'Artois were present. This annoyed Necker, and in revenge he absented himself from the royal séance; he considered his own popularity more than his allegiance to the government of which he was still a member. The King with unwonted firmness declared the proceedings of the last few days illegal and then announced his reforms – the ending of privilege in taxation, the publication each year of the state of finance, the suppression of interior customs duties, the abolition of the Taille and the corvées. But he retained the Three Estates sitting separately and said nothing about the new constitution, and made it clear that if the Estates could not agree either together or with him, he would carry on these reforms alone. 'All defiance on your part would be most unjust. It is I who up to now have done most for the happiness of my people, and it is rare perhaps for a King to ask simply of his subjects that they should agree among themselves in order to accept the benefits he offers them.'

Thus saying he left the hall accompanied by the nobility and clergy. The Commons remained grimly seated with their hats on. Mirabeau sprang to his feet and shouted, 'Sirs, I admit that what you have just heard could be the salvation of the nation, but despotism is always on the watch.' With these words he effaced the favourable impression created by the King, and when the Marquis de Brézés entered to reiterate the orders of the monarch he replied, 'We are here by the will of the nation and only force can remove us.' And the Assembly on hearing this refused to budge and declared itself inviolable.

That evening Necker tendered his resignation, and as the news spread in Versailles the streets were filled with crowds shouting his name. The Queen received him: it was she who had placed him in the ministry in the first place, now she entreated him to stay. The King joined his authority to her request and Necker accepted. It was a triumph for him. His daughter wrote that returning from the audience he was carried shoulder-high by the populace; she was ecstatic, all the illusions of youth and hope seemed to fuse in this moment. Her father was more realistic. When almost all the Assembly crowded into his house he advised them not to push their demands too far. He described for them the present state of France and showed them the good they could accomplish; several wept and promised to heed his advice.

But shouting and weeping would not give the people bread. In the provinces they were living on grass and husks, in Paris the bakers were besieged, insurrection was in the air, a sort of distant unexpressed rumbling of danger was felt in the streets, with their changing groups of arguing people, and in the palace too where the same unease spread through the corridors and rooms. Looking back one deplores the vacillating policy of Louis xvi and the equally uncertain advice of Marie Antoinette, but one must remember that what they felt was the anxiety for France, for their authority. It had not yet occurred to them that their own safety was menaced, they were still reigning, still monarchs, the old régime was not yet quite dead. Not quite, it had about three weeks more to live.

But now Louis XVI felt that the time had come to call in the troops. Talleyrand, Bishop of Autun, had already suggested it but he had resisted; at last he brought them in under the command of the veteran Marshal de Broglie. Unfortunately most of the regiments were foreign soldiers, their loyalty was questionable and the populace feared them. When Paris heard this news the town was in an uproar. The crowds assembled at the Palais Royal, the headquarters of Orléans, and a young man, by name Camille Desmoulins, leaping on a table seized the branch of a nearby tree, made himself a *cocarde* and thundered against the enemies of the country. The mob carried the busts of Necker and the Duc d'Orléans and screamed insults at the names of Artois and Marie Antoinette. They threw stones at the soldiers on the Place Louis XV (today Place de la Concorde) and when the Prince de Lambesc moved a handful of troops into the Tuileries they fled in great disorder, filling the streets and streaming to the Hôtel de Ville. There they demanded the tocsin and arms; the Gardes Françaises threw themselves into the commotion, marching against the Royal Guards whose commander de Besenval had no orders and retreated towards Versailles. On the next day the disorder was even greater, barricades were put up, houses were pillaged, and the mob surging back and forth in the streets added to the general alarm. On 14 July early in the morning they surrounded the hospital of the Invalides. They had come to find arms; the Governor tried to shut the gates, but the old soldiers themselves took the guns and delivered them to the crowds. Thus armed they precipitated themselves towards the Bastille. After a short siege the fortress which only *seemed* to be well defended, but was in reality defenceless, capitulated; the maddened multitude surged forward; pressed by those behind they lost their heads completely. Within a space of minutes they had murdered the principal officers and the Governor de Launay himself, whose head stuck on a pike served them as a standard as they rushed to the Hôtel de Ville where they killed the Provost of the Merchants, Flesselles. The Terror had begun.

Louis XVI had gone to bed peacefully and was doubtless snoring when the Duc de La Rochefoucauld-Liancourt burst into his room. 'The Bastille is taken, the Governor is murdered, they are carrying his head around the town.' The King woke up. 'But,' he stammered, 'is it a revolt?' 'No, Sire, it is a Revolution!'

Quickly the Queen was aroused. What should be done, should the Court leave for Metz? The Queen was in favour of this, but the Marshal de Broglie, who knew the garrison there, disagreed. The King decided on abdication, a terrible decision to make, but as Mercy writing to Leopold admitted, there was now what he realized was a frenzy of feeling against the Queen. 'It goes so far,' he said, 'that they have exposed her head with that of the Comte d'Artois in the garden of the Palais Royal', for this was Orléans' headquarters which issued a flood of defamatory hatred. On 8 June Mercy had written a letter to the Queen which was so important for her future conduct that we reproduce it partly here. After saying that he could go further verbally if the Queen would give him an audience, he proceeds:

It is of the highest importance that the Queen should burn all the letters addressed to her but it is also essential that she should keep a copy of some matters which may be written. These copies should be in an unknown but sure hand, in a form which in all circumstances cannot provide a proof either of what is written nor of the person from whom it comes. This will not be difficult, in adding a precaution equally easy for the conservation of such writings . . . it may be of the greatest use in certain cases.

He also presses the Queen to keep her own counsel in the following days and advises her what to do about her banknotes which will be changed very soon into assignats, thus losing the interest.

It is obvious that he was a prey to the gravest doubts, that he feared that anything might happen. His fears were reciprocated, for four days later the Queen replied. Speaking of Mirabeau she said that in his opinion the only weapon which they could employ was the one which was used against them – money. But where to get it? She examines the possibilities of a loan from the sovereigns of Spain, Naples or Sardinia. They must be dead secret and she had not much hope because no minister was to be trusted, they all served their own interest rather than that of the King. Mercy's other idea was to induce Prussia and Austria not to intervene with troops or a counter-revolution, but as the guarantors of all treaties between them and France, and to insist on their disapprobation at the treatment of the King. They could speak with the voice of those who are strong. She asks his advice and continues, 'I cannot but tremble when I think of the days to come, they hold for us all that is cruel and hurtful and we must live through them. One needs a supernatural courage at this moment. Everything goes from bad to worse. I despair.'

She looked at her husband, for whom she had sympathy and affection; he was first and foremost her King. She saw her son, in her eyes the future King of France. What could the future bring him; how could she help to preserve his throne for him? And she saw the danger of her friends; on 16 July she sent for the Duchesse de Polignac and received her weeping. She implored her to leave, the King entered and joined her entreaties. 'In the name of Friendship leave,' said the Queen, 'I am afraid for all of us.' That same night the Duchesse left, accompanied by her sister-in-law: at the last moment Marie Antoinette, generous as ever, sent her a letter and 500 louis, with the words, 'Adieu, sweetest of friends, the word is terrible but it must be said, I have only strength to embrace you for the last time.' This was the signal for a general panic, one after the other the nobles left, and Fersen, who was still at Valenciennes with his regiment, saw passing through to Coblenz the Duc de Bourbon, the Duc d'Enghien, Vaudreuil, the Polignacs, Coigny, Calonne, Lambesc, Luxembourg, the Castries, Breteuil and even – the Abbé Vermond! All had profited in one way or another from the friendship and generosity of Marie Antoinette, all deserted her in the hour of trial. One friend stood firm, Fersen, who decided to return to Paris. He knew, as he wrote his father, that 'In this country there are no laws, no order, no justice nor discipline nor religion, and how are they to be re-established? I do not know, but these are the effects of Anglomania and philosophy, and they have ruined France.' He returned to be near and help the woman he loved and admired, he was to be almost her sole comfort during the dark days of fear and uncertainty.

For it was still no more than uncertain; something might still be saved. On 15 July the King went himself on foot without escort to announce the retreat of the troops. He could not have made a more popular gesture; at his return he was hailed with cheers. He had said, 'I trust myself to you, I wish to be at one with

Marquis de Vaudreuil, lover of Madame de Polignac, by Alexander Roshin

Marie Antoinette on horseback, by Brun

The Baron de Besenval

Dagoty painting a
portrait of Marie
Antoinette playing the
harp

my people and counting on the love and faith of my subjects I have ordered the troops to leave Paris.' On his return to Versailles the courtyards were filled with an immense concourse which demanded the King, the Queen and the children. They appeared on a balcony. Marie Antoinette held the little Dauphin on her arm and her daughter by the hand. Louis sent for the children of the Comte d'Artois and the two princes kissed the hand of the Queen and then their cousin the little Madame; this picture of the blonde heads mingling their caresses should have moved the hearts of stone beneath them, but among the few cries of pleasure grumblings were heard, particularly against d'Artois and the Queen. The King still possessed in some way the love of the crowd, who seemed to regard him as a good stupid man dominated by infernal intriguers.

Now Marie Antoinette was alone and as she wrote to Madame de Polignac, her children were her only source of happiness. The letter she wrote to their governess, Madame de Tourzel, deserves comment:

My son is four years and four months old, his health has always been good but even in his cradle we saw that his nerves were very sensitive, he could not stand the least noise; something to which he was not accustomed frightened him, for example he is afraid of dogs because they bark near him. I have never forced him to have them because I think with the increase in his reason, his fears will pass; he is like all healthy children venturesome, and violent in his venturesomeness, but he is a good child, tender and loving when his wilfulness does not carry him away. He has a sense of pride in himself which may lead him to his advantage if it is properly controlled, and when he is at ease with anyone he can control his tempers in order to be sweet and amiable. He is truly faithful when he has promised something but he is very indiscreet, he repeats what he has heard said and sometimes without meaning to he adds what his imagination prompts him to, it is his greatest fault and something which must be corrected. For the rest he is a good child, though he dislikes having to ask pardon, he does it only with tears.

There is more of this letter, but we have quoted it at some length because it shows not only the Dauphin, the child who was handed over in the Temple to his jailers, but also the mother who brought him up so carefully, watching every characteristic, and who might have given France one of its best Kings if Fate had so willed.

The insults hurled at the Comte d'Artois convinced the King of the necessity for his brother's safety and he and his children left for the frontier. Several days later the remnants of the Court were shaken by the news of the horrible assassination of Foullon and Berthier, which confirmed all their fears. It was now that they regretted not having followed the King's desire and gone to Metz, but the Duc de Broglie and above all Monsieur had dissuaded them. Monsieur – Provence – had his own reasons: disingenuous and false, he emphasized the danger of civil war if the King joined his garrison, and without ceasing to dissemble he kept his brother and his family in the position most disastrous for them.

The Queen, more realistic, had burnt her papers and made her plans. Now she said to Madame Campan to whom she had given her written order, 'When I wrote it, I hoped that it would be useful, but Fate has decided against me, I am afraid that it will be for the loss of us all.'

The King refused to give up hope and, on 17 June, he decided to go once more to Paris. Marie Antoinette attempted in vain to dissuade him, and indeed he was himself prey to the most painful apprehensions. Before leaving he had heard Mass and communicated, and had given to his brother Provence an act creating him lieutenant-general of the Realm in the case of an assassination. The Queen, too, spent the night in a crisis of desperation, she felt herself surrounded by spies, watched every minute. Whom could she trust? The King left at nine o'clock in the morning with a very small escort; arriving in Paris he found the Garde Nationale of the town commanded by La Fayette on horseback and an immense crowd at every window, at every crossing. The streets were lined with armed soldiers and thronged by youths carrying weapons. The fishwives were there in droves, their arms full of bouquets, singing the song 'Where is one better than in the arms of one's family?' And everywhere the *cocarde* with the colours of Paris, red and blue.

He was met at the barrier by the Mayor Bailly, who said 'Sire, I bring to your Majesty the keys of your good city of Paris, they are the same which were presented to Henri IV. He had reconquered his people, now it is the people who have reconquered their King.' It was a bon mot, but not much appreciated by the monarch as he progressed slowly towards the

Hôtel de Ville, escorted by some hundreds of the Assembly, 'very sad and agitated' for on all sides the cry *'Vive la Nation'* had replaced the old welcome cry *'Vive le Roi'*. At the entry of the Town Hall Bailly presented the new *cocarde* which replaced the ancient *cocarde* of the royal house; the monarch took it, put it in his hat and stood on the balcony. What were the thoughts of the last Capet, as he stood there dishonoured, defeated, alone? The shouts of *'Vive la Nation'* could not comfort his sad heart, nor promise any security for him and his. Too worn out even to weep he took the road for home. There the Queen awaited him after a ghastly day. She had gone on her knees and beseeched him with tears not to go, really fearing that she would never see him again. As the long slow hours dragged on, the château became as still as death, she prayed, she saw her children – her 'only comfort' – and with her accustomed energy she prepared as best she could for what might happen. The carriages were kept ready, for if the King were imprisoned she was determined to go to Paris, to his side, whatever might befall, for as she had written to Leopold, 'The King and I are one.' And she had even written a declaration, 'Messieurs, I remit to your hands the wife and the family of your sovereign; do not allow that which has been joined in Heaven to be separated on earth.' Poor woman, she could not imagine what she had to deal with, nor the human beasts who would disregard anything she might write, for hunger and misery had robbed them of the possibility of comprehension. Had not the women seen their children dying like flies and the men suffering cold, starvation, homelessness and fear? But at six o'clock the King arrived, broken with fatigue but thankful that no blood had been shed; she rushed to meet him and in an instant he was surrounded by his children, his sister, and the faithful Campan and his wife. Crying, laughing they heard his story, and though Marie Antoinette was disgusted at the sight of the *cocarde* she was optimistic enough to believe that better days might set in. Alas, the news of the ghastly deaths of Foullon and Berthier was now confirmed. Arrested beyond the capital, they were carried there and then dragged through the streets, tortured and murdered barbarously, their heads placed on pikes and shown through the city, and the bloody heart of Berthier carried through the hall where the deputies could see it. The provinces too were aflame and swarmed with brigands;

châteaux were being demolished, convents plundered, nobles who were suspected of disloyalty to the Revolution murdered. The Assembly which might be expected to take some action against all this did nothing but talk. And the young Barnave, commenting, spoke the words by which history remembers him and which he would later regret, 'The blood that flows, is it then so pure?'

On the 23rd Necker returned; his road from Bâle had looked like a royal progress; in every town the horses had been taken from his carriage, and when he drove into Paris the whole population was at the windows. He received the homage of the newly formed Commune of Paris; his daughter was again in a trance of joy, but Governeur Morris, the American, made a sarcastic comment. 'He has the look and manner of the counting-house, and being dressed in embroidered velvet contrasts strongly with his habiliments. His bow, his address, say "I am the man". If he is really a great man I am deceived.' Madame de Staël's salon was filled with the men of the future, Talleyrand, Clermont Tonnerre, Lally Tollendal, the two brothers Lameth whom the Queen had protected, all sworn to support Necker in his plan for a constitution à l'anglaise, with them in the House of Lords and himself at the head of the House of Commons. All hated the deputies of the right who might oppose them, but most of all they hated that aristocrat, that fiery rascal, that voice and will of iron, Mirabeau, who said openly that he was more for the monarchy than against it and demanded to see the King and be heard at the palace.

The King and Queen both disliked him, his rough manners, his bad reputation, and they were at this time lulled into false security. They had sent the royal silver and treasures to the Mint and the Queen wrote that they were discovering friends whose existence they had forgotten. A charming instance of this is recounted by the nephew of the popular composer André Grétry, who was a great favourite at Court and who had in 1784 produced his most successful opera, *Richard Cœur de Lion*, which contained the air 'Oh Richard, Oh mon roi' later to be famous. He had brought his young daughter to salute the Queen who was her godmother and they were admitted to the Private Apartments where soon Her Majesty joined them, coming from Mass. 'On entering she freed herself from a head-covering and also from an ample black

lace mantle which covered her stately figure and ravishing neck.'
She exclaimed when she saw Bouilly, Grétry's future son-in-law,
that it was not the first time she had seen him, to which he replied
that indeed it was not, for he was the forward young man who
had seated himself beside her on the terrace at Versailles. She
laughed and complimented Grétry on the loyal chevalier he had
chosen for his daughter. Then her attention turned to her god-
child. She asked her age and admired her beauty, saying that she
had everything which could appeal to a good husband, all this
with such grace and friendliness, such courtesy that the young
people were head over heels in love with her. When Grétry
went to take leave he kissed the royal hand and she extended it
as well to young Bouilly, who was completely overcome.

In these summer days she could also dream away the hours
in her Little Trianon, could watch the hay being made, the cows
being milked, could play with her delightful children and pretend
that danger was still far away. And by September Fersen was again
in Paris. Between June and his return he had written two letters
to the unknown 'Joséphine', the first time he had employed this
ruse; evidently he had been warned or had surmised the danger
she was in from spying. He was frequently in Versailles and kept
horses here and in Paris. It seemed he held himself in readiness for
whatever might happen.

All might yet be well in spite of the unrest in the provinces and
the determined efforts of the Assembly to transfer the Royal
Family to Paris, a design firmly resisted by the King. In September
Desmoulins had proclaimed that they ought to send fifteen
thousand men to Versailles to fetch him, and he added horrible
threats against the Queen. Even Mirabeau told a friend that he
feared for Versailles, though he believed that honest men need
fear nothing. The French Guards boasted openly of their plan to
take Versailles by force if necessary, and La Fayette under the
pretext of pacification thought it his duty to warn M. de St Priest.
The Court was alarmed, they made contact with d'Estaing and
reinforcements were brought in, the Régiment de Flandres, who
were well disciplined under their colonel the Marquis de Lusignan,
one of the left wing party in the Assembly and a reassuring
appointment for the patriots who feared counter-revolution.

They were welcomed in Versailles with great ceremony,
blessed in the Cathedral by the Archbishop of Paris and invited

to a banquet where they toasted the King, the Queen and all
the royal family. But the next day when they were entertained
by the resident regiment trouble broke out. The King allowed
them to use the great hall of the opera where two hundred
places were laid; it was lavishly decorated and at three o'clock
in the afternoon the guests assembled at the gate of the château,
were conducted to the hall and began the repast. The orchestra
played, the wine went round, and everyone prepared for a
sumptuous feast. When the second course was served the Duc de
Villeroi, captain of the First Company of the Guards, invited all
the grenadiers and the Swiss who were drinking in the parterre to
come up on the stage and drink toasts to the King and the Queen.
The Queen had at first refused to be present but later, thinking
that the spectacle would amuse the Dauphin, she gave in. The
King, who arrived from hunting, accompanied them. On seeing
them loyal cries of 'Vive le Roi' were raised, and touched by this
they descended among the crowd. The Dauphin was carried
round the hall by a Swiss officer, the orchestra played 'Where
is one happier than with one's family?' and then the air which the
Queen loved from Grétry's opera.

> Oh Richard, oh mon roi
> L'univers t'abandonne
> Sur la terre il n'est donc que moi
> Qui m'intéresse à ta personne.*

The applause was great, everyone was laughing, drinking,
officers clapped each other on the shoulder and swore brotherhood, and among them all, the most gracious, the most lovely,
smiling, greeting, moved the Queen. A light seemed to shine
from her, she was happy, Queen, wife and mother all in one.
Poor woman, it was for the very last time.

The family soon retired and were escorted by many of the
soldiers who went with them through the chapel to their apartments. Then the whole crowd rushed into the Marble Court,
many of the Versaillois were there listening and looking on, the
orchestra played beneath the King's windows, they danced and
sang and the noise must have been frightful. But that was all,

---

* Oh Richard, oh my king
  The universe abandons you
  On the earth there is only myself
  Who cares about you.

no *cacardes* were tampled under foot, no insults offered to the Nation. It was true, said the Queen later, that some white *cocardes* were worn but that was natural, all the army at that time wore them, only the King and the National Guard wore the Tricolour. On 3 October the Queen received a deputation of the National Guard to whom she had presented colours on 30 September. On this occasion she said, 'I am very happy to have given the colours to the National Guard of Versailles. I am enchanted by what happened on Thursday: the nation and the army should be attached to the King as We ourselves are also.'

On the next day there was another banquet, where a good deal more wine was drunk, everything and everybody was toasted and after the manner of very young army officers some of them lost their heads. They sang, they roistered, bottles were broken, but not so many that four hundred were not left, and a very good time was had by all. On 4 October it was the turn of the Municipality of Versailles to be the hosts. This was more orderly, no doubt they were all tired.

On Sunday the blow fell! A certain lieutenant-colonel, who had not been invited to the fête on 1 October and resented it, persuaded one of his friends, editor of the *Courrier de Versailles* to publish a series of articles describing the 'orgies' which had taken place! While Paris starved the soldiers drank and gorged and the Queen declared herself 'enchanted' with it all. This was the 'Austrian's' way to corrupt the French people. His attack was seized upon with delight by the demagogues in Paris; Desmoulins, Marat and others shrieked that it was a conspiracy, those who had been there denied any such thing but their evidence was disregarded; the pretext was there; the public, inflamed, was ready for anything. They gathered at the Palais Royal: everything had been worked out, provided for by the subterranean plotters. Immense sums of money had been spent by the Orléans faction to corrupt the forces, every means of inflaming the passions of the lowest mobs had been employed, now the time was ripe. There was no bread and they should go to Versailles and ask the King for it. The women taunted the men. Next day, they said, they would take matters into their own hands. The police did nothing, and the next day it was indeed they who gave the signal. Those preparing the riots had judged cleverly that they would be less suspect until the moment came to arouse them;

once aroused they would become Furies. And it was so. In the rain six thousand women took the road; the march on Versailles had begun.

Over the muddy roads they streamed, armed with weapons they had obtained from a raid on the Hôtel de Ville before leaving. Many of them, it appeared later, were men disguised as women, wearing white and with their pockets full of gold. The conspirators considered that as women they would not be fired on and could lead the multitude. At their head was a sinister figure, Maillard the hussar; successful at the Bastille, he would be one of the chief murderers of the Terror. He carried a drum and led them to the Louvre and the Place Louis xv.

Here they were divided into bands. All the houses and shops were barricaded, not a soul was to be seen, and frustrated in their hope of finding food the army took the road to Sèvres, dragging two cannon. There, famished and soaked, they broke open every shop which gave any promise of bread, and finding none, sacked the wine merchants' cellars. Then drunk, howling, cursing and demanding the blood of the Queen they surged towards Versailles. Each of them wished to have a part of the body of the unfortunate woman, one demanded the thigh, another the entrails, they would take her to Paris dead or alive, the bitch! Back in the Hôtel de Ville five or six Grenadiers entered La Fayette's bureau and told him that they were determined to go to Versailles, there to exterminate the Flanders Regiment which had trodden on the National *cocarde*. If the King was too weak to wear his crown, let him put it away! La Fayette tried to appease them; no use, they were determined. He went out to the square and harangued the soldiers, who protested that they knew he was an honest man but remained firm in their decision. He appealed to the Municipals, equally honest and at a loss; the crowd and the tumult grew, goaded by secret agents circulating among them. At last, after the Mayor and La Fayette had been threatened with death, the Municipality capitulated, and ordered the general to proceed to Versailles.

Marie Antoinette was at the Trianon when a messenger sent by St Priest found her in her favourite grotto and warned her; she returned precipitately to the Palace. At the same time M. de Cubières left to fetch the King, whom he found near Meudon, hunting. Opening the note brought, Louis said, 'They are asking for bread, alas I did not know they would come to find it.' As he was mounting his horse another messenger galloped up saying, 'Sire, you are deceived. I come from the Ecole Militaire, there are only some women there asking for bread. I entreat your Majesty to have no fear.' The King stared at him in surprise. 'Fear? but Monsieur, I have never been afraid in my life,' and so saying he galloped at breakneck speed down the deep ravine before him.

Arrived in Versailles where the Assembly was sitting he was met by the President bringing the Declaration of the Rights of Man for the royal assent. It was really an ill-chosen moment, for everybody was asking whether the royal family should fly or remain. In the hubbub of advice and opinions, two things were clear; the Queen absolutely refused to be parted from the King, and His Majesty would accept no plan which promised to shed his subjects' blood. Thus Necker, who had arrived with his wife and daughter, was in favour of the King's staying for he feared for his own popularity if he was left to face the possibility of a counter-revolution, while St Priest had a realistic suggestion but one based on the Queen's leaving for Rambouillet with her children while the Monarch would be guarded by troops well deployed but who might be forced to fire. Both exhausted themselves in argument while the precious hours passed away. Meanwhile, the fishwives, always the most vocal, distributed themselves through the town of Versailles and finally decided to invade the Assembly. Rain was falling in torrents, the women's poor rags were soaked, muddy up to the neck they were a horrible sight. 'Look at us,' they shouted, 'Look how we are clothed, but the bitch will pay for it all.' In the Assembly they stormed over the benches; led by Maillard they reiterated their demand for bread, and were only calmed by the proposal that a deputation should wait upon the King to ask for food and that he should sign the Declaration. This was done and some of the women dispersed after all the bread in Versailles had been collected and given to them, while others stayed on, saying that they had orders.

In the Palace the discussions went on. At three o'clock in the afternoon St Priest had taken what security measures he could, but he doubted the fidelity of any of the regiments, especially the National Guard. In all this there was only one who stood out, the Queen. Her calm, the nobility of her expression impressed all. Amidst the general consternation she alone showed no panic. 'I know that they are coming from Paris to ask for my head; but I have learned from my mother how to die. I will wait with firmness.' The only precautions she took were for her children.

Having told Madame de Tourzel in case of danger to bring them to her, she changed her mind and at eleven o'clock at night ordered that at the approach of danger they were to be taken to the King; this would be the safest place, she thought. And when she was pressed to go to her husband's room herself she refused, saying that she was the chief object of the people's hate and she would not risk their safety.

In these terrible hours Marie Antoinette rose to a grandeur she had not known before, but we who have followed her life through youth and maturity can see that the probability was always there. History is made in a few seconds, in a pinpoint of time, when the individual's entire being is at its height, but it is made on the basis of what the person really is when shorn of the accretion of superficial habit which life brings to us all. It is only a step from one moment to another, a step to heroism or mediocrity: if she had given in, had fled, had considered herself, she would have joined the ranks of those Queens whose names are remembered but nothing more. She lives in history because of those few hours on this one night. Everything that followed was the epilogue.

At midnight La Fayette arrived, having ridden at the head of his soldiers in front of the rioting crowds, alternately exhorting them to restrain themselves and leading them on. As Madame de Staël records, his only love was Liberty with a capital letter, and he was too infatuated to see where liberty would finally land him. He went straight to the King, muddied as he was, and extending his arms in a theatrical gesture said: 'I come, Sire, to offer you my head in order to save that of Your Majesty. If my blood should flow it will be in Your Majesty's service rather than for the ignoble light of the torches of the scaffold.' The King with his down-to-earth common sense replied, 'You cannot doubt, Monsieur de La Fayette, of the pleasure which we always have in seeing you, as well as my good Parisians. Go and inform them of my feelings.' Someone in the throng surrounding them murmured: 'Cromwell.' La Fayette heard and replied, 'Sir,

Cromwell would not have come alone.' The comment of the historian Rivarol is apt: 'The King made certain of a general who was certain of nothing.' He then made his rounds in the château, posted the French Guards before the gates and sent the guards of the château to join his own troops. The Regiment of Flanders had already been quartered in the park and the Body-guard, having been subjected to a hail of stones from the popu-lace, had been ordered to retreat to Trianon or Rambouillet. Persuaded that he had done everything possible and confident in his own popularity, La Fayette retired to rest, and Versailles was wrapped in an uneasy slumber.

Someone has said, only crime never sleeps. One door had been left open, guarded only by a soldier of the Versailles militia. The Marquis de Digoine had observed this: he asked the porter where the key was and was told that he would find it and close the door. He failed to do so, and an officer of the Paris Guard found out the shortest way to the Queen's apartments. At the break of day the hordes began to rouse themselves, groups of men and women armed with guns, swords, pikes and whatever else they could find amassed before the château. Their noise aroused the Queen and two of her terrified women told her that the Palace was invaded. Snatching up a gown and putting on her stockings she rushed to the King; she could already hear the cries of: 'Kill, kill, death to the Queen; where is this damned slut!' One woman was seen sharpening her knife, while another, soaked in the blood of the sentinels who had been slaughtered, screamed still worse insults.

Rushing down the little passage leading to the Oeil de Bœuf, she and the two ladies found the door locked. With beating hearts they hammered on it; would the valets open it? In the general disorder, they did. It was safety, but the King had already left his chamber and was looking for the Queen, narrowly missed by the infuriated mob, who were destroying all that they could find. He returned to his room where Marie Antoinette, already calm and quiet, was comforting her children. The hubbub had, of course, roused La Fayette in the Hôtel de Noailles; flinging on his clothes he appeared in the Salle du Conseil. In the King's chamber the family was assembled, the Comte de Provence and Madame, and the aunts. The Queen and Madame Elisabeth leaned in a window-seat, her little daughter was with her and the Dauphin was playing with his sister's hair. Suddenly he said, 'Maman, I am hungry,' and the Queen answered sadly, 'Have patience, my child, we must be quiet.' The crowd shouted below the window and now those within could distinguish the cries. 'The King, the King, we want the King.' Louis x v I stepped on to the balcony, and was greeted with '*Vive le Roi, Vive la Nation*.' Then came another voice, 'The Queen, the Queen to the balcony.' She hesitated a moment but when La Fayette assured her that it was necessary that she show herself, she said, 'Even if I am going to torture, I will not hesitate, I will go.' She took her children by the hand and went out. 'No children, no children,' yelled the mass, 'The Queen on the balcony alone, alone.' Marie Antoinette hesitated a moment then with a sublime gesture pushed the little ones aside and stepped out, her hands crossed on her breast, a thousand times more beautiful than in her Court clothes, pale, with her hair disordered, majestic in her dignity, her head held high. And with the inconstancy of crowds, the very women who an instant before were yelling for her blood broke into spontaneous cries of '*Vive la Reine*'. She dominated them by her integrity, the purity which shone from her like an enchantment. But she was not deceived. Stepping in, she said to Necker, 'They will force us to go to Paris with the heads of our Bodyguards on pikes carried before us.' She had guessed rightly, for new cries were already being heard: 'The King to Paris.' The decision must be made, and papers were thrown from the windows announcing the departure of the King – his capitulation. When the Queen was asked what she would do she replied, 'My duty is to be with the King and to die at his feet in the arms of my children.'

At one-thirty the cortège set forth. In the first carriage were the monarchs and their children, the Comte and Comtesse de Provence, Madame Elisabeth, and Madame de Tourzel. After half an hour the vast multitude followed, preceded by the heads of two of the faithful Bodyguard carried on pikes, just as Marie Antoinette had predicted. The rain had ceased, the day was fine, nature smiled on the ghastly throng. The women, some wet with the blood of victims, sat astride the cannon singing, shouting, vomiting. 'We shall not need bread now,' they yelled, 'we are bringing the baker, the bakeress and their little brat.'

Behind the main body came the Assembly riding in the royal carriages and then a few lorries carrying corn and flour which had been pillaged from the royal stores. The dreadful journey took seven hours and during it the Queen who preserved her calm throughout often spoke to those surrounding her carriage. 'The King and I,' she said, 'have never wished ill to anyone. People have told you bad things about us, those are they who wish us ill. We love all the French.' And some of those who heard her were actually touched, but only few. What her thoughts were during this long and humiliating journey it is difficult to surmise; it must be quite certain that she could not be as calm as her outer behaviour seemed to show. In the first place she was certainly in a trance of terror for her children: not only did she love them as passionately as any ordinary mother, but with her strong dynastic sense the Dauphin's life was only second in importance to that of the King. She must have surveyed the familiar road and pondered on the many and varied times she had travelled it. She remembered the tragedy of her first visit to Paris; how small it seemed in comparison.

As the cortège drew through Passy she saw on a balcony the Duc d'Orléans, Egalité, with his mistress Madame de Genlis and his children, and realizing how he was gloating over the spectacle she shivered with horror. On the following day she observed to M. Augéard, 'M. le Duc d'Orléans wished to have us assassinated.' It was her only recrimination. Much later during the interrogation of the Châtelet when she was questioned on this remark she said, '*J'ai tout su, tout vu, tout oublié.*'*

It was nine o'clock when they entered Paris. At the barrier of Chaillot they were met by the Mayor Bailly, who had the effrontery to say to the King, 'What a beautiful day, Sire, when the Parisians will possess in their city Your Majesty and his family.' To which the King replied, 'I hope, Monsieur, that my presence will restore peace, concord and obedience to the law.' To the Queen's dismay Bailly insisted that they all go at once to the Hôtel de Ville; worn out with anxiety and fatigue she would have gone to the Tuileries where they were to spend the night. But Moreau de St Merry, when asked if she could be spared this last trial, answered, 'I hope that the Queen will return from the Hôtel de Ville, I cannot be certain that she can go alone to the

* I have known everything, seen everything, and forgotten it all.

Tuileries.' And indeed during their drive the cries of *à la lanterne* were not infrequent.

Louis xvi walked into the hall of the Commune with a firm and decided step. Marie Antoinette followed leading her children. 'I come always with pleasure and confidence to visit my good Parisians,' said the King, and Bailly repeated his words to the people, leaving out the words 'and confidence'. The Queen drew his attention to this and repeated it. Outside, the enormous crowd, composed this time not only of the mob but of many who still hoped for a settlement and were loyal, waited to see the monarchs on the balcony. When they appeared many cries of '*Vive le Roi*', and even '*Vive la Reine*' went up, and in their enthusiasm they added '*Vive nous tous*' – 'Long may we all live.'

With the King's conciliatory determination it seemed that all might still be well. Exhausted, and leading her weary little son and daughter, the Queen arrived at the Tuileries, uninhabited for nearly a hundred years, cold, dark and damp, and almost without furniture, hurriedly set to rights as best they could by a few workmen. It was a depressing sight. The Dauphin wonderingly said, 'Everything is very ugly here, Maman.' His mother answered 'My son, Louis xiv stayed here and found it all right; we must not be more difficult than he' and turning to her ladies she remarked apologetically, 'You know I did not expect to come here.' Somehow they managed to arrange a sort of camping out for the night. The Dauphin's room was open because the door could not be made fast, and his devoted governess Madame de Tourzel spent the hours keeping watch without one moment of sleep. The dreadful day was over, would tomorrow be worse? If Marie Antoinette had known that the Comte de Fersen was in Paris, she might have been comforted by the thought that at least one faithful friend was near, but St Priest, when Axel had wished to enter the Tuileries, had advised him not to do so: 'Your liaison with the Queen is known, even your presence here may endanger her,' he said. Madame Campan, from whom the Queen had taken a touching farewell with the injunction to follow her as soon as possible to Paris, makes a very pertinent remark in her memoirs. She had many occasions to notice that the masses never persevere in their obedience to factions, that they can change quickly when something recalls them to their duty. Thus even the most ardent extremists of the left, when they had the opportunity to see the Queen close to, to speak to her, to hear her voice, were capable of becoming her convinced partisans, and in the Temple some of those who had done the most to drag her there were finally to suffer themselves for trying to release her.

So, on the morning of 7 October, the very women who had insulted her the day before were in the gardens under her windows demanding to see her; they had her there at last, she was a wonderful show for them, this woman whom they believed had been the ruin of France, the Austrian, the stranger, who had spent money like water for her amusements, for her lovers. Perhaps when they looked at her with her children holding her skirts, just as their own did, her eyes swollen with weeping but still exercising that indefinable charm, their hearts were moved, and then they cried '*Vive la Reine*', but when she said that she loved her good people of Paris, an isolated voice called, 'Yes, but on the 14th of July you wanted to besiege the town and have it bombarded, and on the 5th of October you intended to fly to the frontiers.' She wrote to Mercy:

If we forget where we are and how we arrived it would seem there is a movement in the people which should reassure us, especially this morning. I hope that if there could be sufficient bread, things will get better. I speak to the people, the fishwives, the police, all give me their hands and I give mine. One has difficulty in believing what happened yesterday and, on the contrary, it was all less than what we could expect.

She was right in one thing, the price of bread fell almost as soon as the royal family reached Paris, which may have owed something to Necker's connection with the grain trade. Mirabeau accused him: the banker had 'marched to glory on the crutch of famine', he snarled.

For the great Tribune was watching and waiting. While the royal family passed its days receiving deputations and wooing the public his eye scanned the Assembly in the Royal Riding School. There they all were, Necker's party, the people's men, Right, Centre and Left, and far to the Left the extremists, the Mountain. The public gallery was always crowded; there, he thought, sits the real victor with its Commune and Citizens' Guard behind it, the mob, that 'riffraff of Paris' as the Emperor wrote to his brother. Mirabeau's eyes flashed and his lip curled and he wrote to his friend La Marck, 'I have always thought the Monarchy was the State's sheet anchor.'

Meanwhile, the Queen pursued her policy of conciliation. Here she gave the flowers from her headdress to the hands outstretched to take them, there she visited the glass factory and remarked on the goodness of the people when she was received with enthusiasm. Someone spoke to her in German, she answered that she did not understand since she had forgotten her mother-tongue and only spoke French. The whole month was occupied with formal visits, Parlement, the Commune of Paris conducted by Bailly and La Fayette, the University, the Grand Council, and finally the National Assembly who were received by the King with much ceremony and protocol. He sat with his hat on; they however were informally dressed, even the clergy wore short coats. Having saluted the King they desired to see the Queen, at that moment in the middle of her toilette. She saw them, however, seated in an armchair and rose when they entered, which the King had not done. When they asked to see the Dauphin she sent for him and carrying him on her arm went round the room, so that all were satisfied and cried loudly '*Vive le Dauphin*'. The idea of monarchy was so firmly and traditionally rooted in the French that if the Crown had only known how to appeal to it, it could have been its strongest weapon against disaffection. Mirabeau knew this and had already begun his efforts to make some contact with Louis XVI.

As for Marie Antoinette, it is impossible to believe that her whole nature did not react against the conciliation which she practised daily. Calumny is the best way to kill, she had remarked to Madame Campan; would that she had realized this years ago. Now the knives were very near, among the crowds which besieged her windows were still individuals who did not shout '*Vive la Reine*', but the basest insults, filthy words and obscenities; they even, pretending to be deputies, succeeded in penetrating the royal apartments and face to face with the King and Queen blared forth their gibes. It became so frequent that the Ministers proposed to forbid all entry to the Palace, but 'No,' said Louis, 'we can bear all that they have to say to us.' Marie Antoinette was forced now to lose her optimism, she realized with sorrow that all efforts, all compromise was in vain, and acting on this she arranged that her collection of precious objects should be taken to the safe keeping of her jeweller Daguerre, all those exquisite treasures which today delight us in the Louvre. Porcelains, boxes in gold, agate and jasper, lovely and rare, were inventoried and kept by the State.

Another sacrifice was demanded of them. The King believed that it would be wise to dismiss the Bodyguards, they were in danger, he thought, because of their obvious devotion to him and his wife. And he also made a very foolish decision; he allowed the *Moniteur* to publish a book which showed the expenses of the Court. Naturally, the only part of it which interested the public was the expenditure of the Queen, and all over France people were exasperated by the account of the sums extorted from her by the Polignacs and other favourites.

Poor woman, wherever she turned there was difficulty, lack of hope. She wrote to her friend Madame de Polignac:

I wept when I read your letters. You speak of my courage, it needs much less to support the frightful moments which we have passed through than to bear our position, our personal sadness, that of our friends and all who surround us. It is too heavy a burden, and if my heart were not entirely bound up with my husband, my children, and my friends, I would as soon give in. But you others sustain me, I owe so much to your love. But I bring bad luck to all, what you suffer is my fault.

This belief that she brought bad luck not only to herself but wherever she loved had been growing in her for some time. It fought against her natural light-heartedness and optimism; she smiled for her husband and the crowd, her pride held her head high, her breeding sustained her graciousness towards even those who insulted her, but within an increasing fatalism took away the last vestiges of hope. This was perhaps the cause of the cool and curt answers which, as La Fayette noted, she sometimes gave to deputations: her frayed nerves let the truth be seen for a moment. The King, ever more lethargic, gave her no help.

The Queen had really only one comfort: Axel Fersen. He had found a lodging near by, and he saw her almost daily; at the end of 1789 he wrote his sister he had passed a whole day with her. 'You may imagine my joy,' he said. On 9 October he wrote to his father, 'I have been witness of all that passed at Versailles and the arrival of the King and all the Family in Paris. I was in one of the King's carriages. God preserve me from ever seeing again such a sorry spectacle as these two days.' And to his sister, 'The Queen is much applauded as she cannot fail to be when she is known and justice is rendered to her goodness.' Again to his father, 'She is extremely unhappy but most courageous. She is an angel of goodness . . . I do my best to console her. I owe it to her, for me she is perfect. I do not know when I shall rejoin my regiment. I would like to put it off and wait to see if there is anything I can do.' He did, however, rejoin because a mutiny broke out and demanded his presence. But shortly after he returned to Paris and resigned in order to be more free and not distant from the woman he adored. He loved her with devotion, with respect and admiration, but it is difficult to imagine that the woman we know would have found time or opportunity or inclination at this moment of suspense and tragedy to arrange for clandestine love-making. His sister was afraid for his safety but he reassured her 'people like myself who are not important run no risk.' She wrote that the Swedes were becoming more opposed to the Government of Gustave III and he replied, 'I wish the Swedish nobility could see what is happening in France and the deplorable condition of this beautiful Kingdom. That might make them think. It seems that things get worse and worse every day.'

So the unhappy Queen had at least one support. After the first uncomfortable night things had been more or less organized. They had found their apartments and those of their suite. Some furniture was brought from Versailles. The King had the Dauphin near him and Marie Antoinette occupied the rooms below with Madame Royale. She had her library with her, mostly religious or philosophical books with a few classical poets and novels. The rest of the Royal Family were lodged in adjoining apartments, and the Comte and Comtesse de Provence in the Luxembourg. Many of the officers of the Court had returned or had never left. Madame de Lamballe, the faithful friend who had insisted on accompanying the Queen and would be with her almost till the end, was also there. The Queen spent her days very quietly; as she wrote to Madame de Polignac the children were her chief joy and their education her concern. They had always been much with her, now even more of her time was spent with them. When the weather was fine she walked with them in the Tuileries Gardens, which were not open to the public till midday, then came Madame's lessons, carefully watched by her mother, and religious instruction, for she would shortly make her first communion. The King, too, interested himself in his son's education. Already in 1784 he had commissioned a new edition of the history of Télémaque, the story which had influenced his own thinking as a child, and the printer Didot the elder had produced a charming book.

The little boy wished very much to see Paris but it was too unsafe. Instead he had his little garden where he bred rabbits and grew flowers, the best ones being kept for his mother. He also accompanied the Queen when she made charitable visits to the hospitals or to visit the societies which she had founded for the aid of the poor. Here he distributed his own offerings. The place he liked the best was the Foundling Hospital. There he saw other children, and felt them less fortunate than himself, for they were without a *chère maman*. From then on all his savings were for them, he kept them in a pretty box and when accused by his father of being a miser, he flushed, but explained, and 'Oh,' said he, 'if you could only see them, you would pity them too.' His father, overcome with love, held him close, promising to add to his saving. He was bright but lazy, and was not able to read. Seeing that this displeased his mother, he promised to read for her New Year present. Time went on and one day he asked his tutor, 'How long to Christmas?' 'One month,' was the answer. 'Then you must give me two lessons a day,' said the child, and on New Year's Day he burst into the Queen's room: 'I have kept my promise, I can read.' These small stories, so ordinary for any family, are the more touching because they show Marie Antoinette's striving in an exceptional situation to keep up for the sake of the life of these two young creatures the normal development which they needed. And they did need it, for like most children they noticed everything. The Dauphin, one day hearing a lady say to a friend, 'She is as happy as a Queen,' exclaimed, 'Happy as a Queen; you are not talking about Maman for she cries all the time.' She and Madame Elisabeth became friends, although at first the Princess had taken the side of the émigrés, especially her two brothers. At times the arguments within the family became so heated that the Queen could say, 'Our life here is a Hell,' and Madame Elisabeth remarked in a letter to a friend, 'How can I understand her, I am a Bourbon while she is Austrian.' She forgot perhaps that while the Queen was only half Austrian she herself was only half Bourbon. However, they did their needlework together, walked in the garden and in trying to forget for a while the shocking position they were both in came to respect each other and finally to love each other.

Marie Antoinette wrote to her brother:

I cannot speak to you of our actual position, it is heart-breaking and should appal every sovereign in the universe, all the more a good relation like yourself. Nothing but time and patience can return people to their senses, it is a war of opinions and is a long way from being finished yet. Nothing can sustain us but the justice of our cause and our conscience.

A few days after the King's arrival in Paris Necker announced that since Versailles had been eliminated the State would effect considerable savings, but as the budget showed a deficit, a new loan was necessary. He lent a large sum of his own money, but unfortunately failed to rescue the lurching ship of State. At this moment Talleyrand, the Bishop of Autun, suggested that the nation might borrow from the lands belonging to the Church – a third of France. Necker made plans to cash in on this proposal but Mirabeau was before him, and on 30 October he lashed out with one of his great diatribes, evoking the frenzied applause of the Assembly and carrying them with him. Necker, terrified in case Mirabeau might achieve his hope of rescuing the monarchy, put up a young Breton deputy, Lajeunais, to propose that no member of the Assembly should be allowed to become a minister of the King until three years had elapsed from his ceasing to be a member of the Assembly. Necker had won the first round. Mirabeau fumed, he raged, but could do nothing. On 4 November Chénier's play *Charles I Xth* was produced at the Théâtre Français. It had at first been censored by Bailly and then unwisely allowed. It was a clear attack on the throne under the disguise of history, and was received with an enthusiasm which showed, as the Queen had surmised, that under the apparent quiet fires were smouldering. Desmoulins observed that this piece served the purposes of the Revolution better than even the October days and Danton speaking in the Assembly said, 'If *Figaro* killed the nobility, *Charles IXth* will kill the monarchy.'

A Commission set up on 19 December recommended that thirty million livres' worth of Church land should be sold outright to pay the debts, a third of France, that the Government should get a loan of 115,380,000 livres from the Treasury by depositing with the bank assignats, paper based on the Church land to the value of 288,450,000 livres and annuities to the value of 96,125,000 livres. The Commissioners were against the Government paying its debts directly with assignats for they would then become a paper currency. Mirabeau opposed this idea with all the force at his command. It would mean that the soil, the body of France, was to be sacrificed to pay the Government's debts to bankers. Of what use were bankers? What France had was land, good solid workable land. Let that be worked and turned into money and pay with it. But he argued in vain. The Assembly decreed that the Government must give bank assignats as security for the issue of notes and that these must bear interest and be redeemable in five years. And more, the assignats should not be legal tender.

But the French did not like Necker's paper; as always they preferred their good sous in their safe stockings and in no time metal money had disappeared from the land. The paper fell in value, Necker was in despair, the Swiss was defeated; this wretched people would not understand the first rules of banking. In short, by March of 1790, he was forced to admit that some of the assignats must be put into circulation. Mirabeau watched while the crisis drew near; three weeks later the Assembly decided that the bank's notes should be withdrawn and replaced wholly by assignats. And in April Mirabeau's original plan was adopted.

The last months of 1789 brought a pause in the day-to-day horrors which the unfortunate Queen had to face. 'There seems to be a respite,' she said. Fersen, who had been given permission from Gustave III for an undefined absence from his regiment, was continually about the Tuileries; trusted by the King, and intimately necessary to the Queen, he filled the place of amanuensis, go-between and general aide. He was ideally happy, but he did not cease for a moment to consider plans for escape or to endeavour to effect a meeting between the Queen and Mirabeau. Meanwhile, the Assembly had been busy; it had first adjourned the re-entry of Parlement and then suppressed it. The provinces were replaced by departments. But in February the deceptive peace was broken by the revelations of the Favras affair, a plot to take the Royal Family from Paris, of which the Queen was supposed to be aware. The Marquis was tried, condemned and hanged without ever giving a word of evidence which could be held as proof. The Comte de Provence was also implicated and was so frightened that he went to the Hôtel de Ville in order to protest his devotion to the Revolution. The behaviour of the crowd at the execution would have disgraced a band of savages. There were even those who demanded that the unfortunate man should be hanged twice.

One may judge of the Queen's horror at all this; on the Sunday after Favras' death the widow and his little son appeared in mourning at the public dinner of the King and Queen. They were seated near the Queen, who fearing the criticism of the Commander of the Guards, a man named Santerre, was careful not to seem to notice them. When the dinner was over Madame Campan in her room heard a knocking on the door. Opening she found the Queen, who flinging herself into an armchair cried:

We will perish from the attacks of people who have all the talents and are criminals, whereas we are defended by estimable people who have no idea of our position. They have compromised me with both parties, in presenting the widow and son of Favras to me. If I were free to act I could take the child of a man who has just sacrificed himself for us, and place him between the King and myself, but surrounded by the villains who have just done away with his father I did not even dare to look at him. The royalists will blame me for not occupying myself with him, the revolutionaries will be furious when they think that people thought to please me by presenting him!

She sent secretly a sum of money to the unhappy widow.

In October, the bread brought from Versailles had vanished, and the starving St Antoine quarter rose and for no other reason than their condition and their terror hanged an unfortunate baker, Francis, suspected of hoarding, who in any case had not the where-withal to give them food. On this Mayor Bailly hung out a red flag and proclaimed martial law, a poor way of countering misery and want.

The Assembly had become so suspicious that the King and particularly Necker thought it wise to make some step towards affirming his devotion to the new régime. Accordingly it was announced that the King would come over, quite without ceremony, about noon the next day. Great excitement and flurry, the hall must be decorated, but with what? Dr Guillotin advised a velvet carpet, the President's chair to be covered with some velvet – 'of a violet colour sprigged with fleurs de lys', but would His Majesty sit or stand? While they were arguing about this, the King entered and delivered a short address affirming his pleasure with what the Assembly had already achieved. He promised that his son would be brought up to support the new order of things and acknowledged that a wise Constitution would preserve him from the dangers of inexperience and that a true liberty would give a new value to the feelings of love and fidelity of which the French for many centuries had given such touching proofs to its Kings. A storm of applause greeted him and a deputation accompanied him to the Tuileries, where the Queen awaited him at the foot of the steps with the Dauphin. She affirmed all that the King had said, and then flushed with enthusiasm someone shouted that they should all renew the National Oath. In a moment the President and all agreed that everyone should swear; back in the Assembly the gallery even sent down a slip with their oath on it, but at the President's suggestion all stood up and swore again. At the Hôtel de Ville all the municipals swore, and Danton remarked that the public would like to join in this national demonstration of faith. Bailly stepped on the outer staircase, and the multitude to the light of torches all with one voice swore again. This was the famous 4 February. Next day Paris was illuminated and a great *Te Deum* was sung. Each district swore with hands uplifted, the news spread to every village and town, never was seen such a swearing, giving people a fictitious burst of hope, the longing for better times, a touching faith in what were in fact only words, for the Constitution was not yet written, and the men they trusted were indeed fallible. Only the Queen was sceptical. As she said, it would be impossible to please everybody; the nobles were distressed and public enthusiasm would be as always short-lived.

On 27 February she received the news of her brother's death; he had been ill for two years and the anxieties of his country's position had not helped to make his end a peaceable one. He left his successor Leopold a heavy burden, a divided Empire at war with Turkey, and the Low Countries in a state of insurrection owing very largely to his own imprudent reforms. But his sister sincerely regretted him; in spite of his criticisms he had loved her and been a good friend. The new Emperor promised in a touching letter to take his place.

With the approaching spring a concession was made to the royal family; they were allowed for reasons of health to remove to St Cloud. Here they found a small measure of repose, although they thought it necessary to make frequent excursions to Paris in order to keep in touch with events. But for the children it was Heaven, they had the gardens, the forest and the King could even resume the riding so necessary for his health, attended only by one aide de camp chosen by La Fayette. His increasing obesity and all the lethargy which went with it, added to his enormous appetite, did not add to the energy so necessary at the moment. His desire to live his own life was dominant in his day-to-day contacts, though he could be stern in an emergency or when fundamental principles were assailed, such as his religion or his position as a monarch.

Mercy had been working with La Marck to bring about a meeting with Mirabeau, and finally it was arranged. The Queen had been prejudiced against this man, but now she was convinced by Mercy and La Marck. For all his spendthrift licentiousness and turbulent demagogism the Comte de Mirabeau was *au fond* an aristocrat. He believed that in the present chaos only a monarchy could save his country. The Press, which was rampant in Paris, fed the provinces. Everywhere clubs were starting up where endless discussion and debate went on. First the Jacobins, here were the extremists, Barnave, the Lameths, Robespierre, Fouquier-Tinville, all to become famous – or infamous; then the Cordeliers – the Cordwainers – for whom the Jacobins were too cold; and last the Friends of the Monarchy – the Feuillans, with La Fayette their head. These represented property and the respectable patriots.

Therefore when the Comte de Mirabeau wrote to the King on 17 May 1790 promising 'loyalty, zeal, activity, energy and a courage of which perhaps men have little idea. I promise everything, in short, except success, and that never depends upon one man alone', he was believed, for it made an excellent impression and it was clear that agreement might be reached. The King would be a limited constitutional monarch, and he gave La Marck bills for a million livres. This was for the settlement of the Comte's debts, up to 208,000 livres, a salary of 6,000 a month, and a size-able gift when the Assembly should be dissolved. The interview with Marie Antoinette took place on 3 July in a hidden grove at St Cloud. Just like everyone who saw the Queen, Mirabeau was penetrated with her graciousness, her charm. He was con-quered, he kissed her hand on bended knee, his eyes were full of tears, and raising himself he exclaimed, 'Madame, the monarchy is saved.' Considering the times he certainly did not lack assurance.

Edmund Burke was to write after the tragedy:

It is now fifteen or sixteen years since I saw the Queen, then the Dauphiness, at Versailles, and surely never was on this earth, which she hardly seemed to touch, a more delightful being. I saw her just above the horizon, decorating and cheering the elevated sphere she had just began to move in; glittering like the morning star, full of life and splendour and joy. Oh what a revolution, and what a heart must I have to contemplate that elevation and that fall. Little did I dream that when she added titles of veneration to those of enthusiasm and respectful love she would ever be obliged to carry the sharp antidote against disgrace concealed in that bosom. Little did I dream that I should have lived to see such disasters fallen upon her in a nation of gallant men, in a nation of men of honour and of cavaliers. I thought a hundred swords would have leapt from their scabbards to avenge even a look that threatened her with insult. The age of chivalry is gone.

The Queen herself in these days seemed calmer. A deputation of ladies who appeared at her windows, saying 'Have courage, Madame, there are good French who suffer with you, they pray for you and God will hear them', moved her so deeply that she burst into tears. Indeed tears were never far from her eyes these days, but she felt a sort of reassurance, a hope. She needed it, for they were all watched night and day by the Parisian militia, partly composed of the French Guards who had deserted. She remarked, 'How astonished my mother would have been and she would certainly have remarked bitterly if she had seen her daughter, the daughter, wife and mother of Kings, surrounded by such a guard.'

It was one of these guards who, meeting Fersen leaving the château at three o'clock in the morning, was on the point of arresting him. St Priest, who was alerted, stopped him, and it is he who tells the story: 'I thought it right to tell the Queen and observed that the presence of the Comte de Fersen and his visits to the château might be of some danger.' 'Tell him this,' said she, 'if you think it necessary; as for me, I do not care.' And in effect the visits continued as ever. This seems the one evidence – if evidence it is – for the assumption that Marie Antoinette and he were physically lovers. The truth was that she was indifferent at this time either to public opinion or danger.

Although the Queen could enjoy the summer weather and a period of repose, the forces at work against the monarchy were as active as ever. Orléans had been permitted to return from England and Mirabeau, ever on the alert, warned the Court that his agents should be watched. On 6 July he found that bread was being distributed in Paris below the controlled price, and that in one week 67,000 francs had been given to the Régiment de Lorraine, also that some journalists were very flush with money. He suggested that a little counter-undermining might not be amiss, and mentioned the names of certain deputies who might be venal. Also he himself was suspected, and something of his visit to St Cloud had leaked out, but the main thing was to watch Orléans. The nation, however, had other thoughts. All through the winter and spring the towns and districts had been affirming their loyalty to King, Law, and the Constitution. From small villages to towns like Lyons where fifty thousand patriots met with bands blaring to swear Federation, like a forest fire it ran, till at last Paris must also have its Federation ceremony to which deputations from all the provinces would come and the seal be set on the solemn affirmation of liberty. The date would be the anniversary of the taking of the Bastille and the place the Champ de Mars, for here a great symbolic figure and a national altar to world brotherhood would be raised.

But with all the debate and disputes time was short, in fact on 1 July they had only two weeks to prepare for this supreme day. They must hurry, and the whole of Paris turned out to dig. Three hundred thousand square feet had to be levelled, galleries to be built and the huge altar to be erected. The first workmen laboured slowly and were suspect, then came the volunteers, thousands marching, spades on shoulders, old men, young girls; the villages sent men led by their mayors, and the song was heard 'Ça ira' (It will work), never to be forgotten, the song of the Revolution. It must work, and it did. On the eve of the 14th Paris was full of the Federates arriving from east, west, north and south; they all were there. The Champ de Mars was a garden. Through the triumphal arches the crowds were already gathering, four hundred thousand of them. Not all could get into the arena, huge as it was, and the heights of Montmartre and Chaillot were black with spectators. Now came the troops with La Fayette on his white horse at their head, now the Departments with their eighty-three banners waving in the north breeze. The Assembly had not permitted Louis XVI to have his family with him; he was alone on the throne with the President on his left.

Marie Antoinette, with tricolour ribbons in her hair, was seated with the Dauphin and the family at the windows of the Ecole Militaire. The Assembly definitely meant by this action to dis-associate her from the Monarch. Nevertheless, when she looked down upon the throng and felt their enthusiasm, when she held up the little Dauphin for all to see and heard the cry *'Vive le Dauphin'*, and even sometimes *'Vive la Reine'*, she must have felt a hope that her evil star might be averted. Two hundred thousand Frenchmen had worked with their hands to make this day, the vast concourse was animated by one devotion, one hope for a better world, for love not hate. They listened while the Bishop of Autun celebrated Mass and heard the *Te Deum* that followed; then La Fayette mounted the steps to the Altar and swore loyalty to the Nation, the Law and the King. After him the President of the Assembly repeated it and it was taken up by the thousands of throats. The cannon thundered, the bands played, the flags were waved, and the King rose and in a loud voice swore to maintain the Constitution. The Queen held up the Dauphin, saying, 'Here is my son, he joins with me in the same sentiments.' This un-expected movement, says the Marquis de Ferriers, evoked a thunderous cry of *'Vive la Reine'* and *'Vive Monseigneur le Dauphin'*.

But now suddenly the heavens opened and a deluge was let loose ruining the decorations and soaking everybody. It was short-lived, however, and by the afternoon, with their natural ebullience, the masses had forgotten; there was dancing in the streets, jousting on the river, fireworks, a tree of liberty on the ruins of the Bastille with a Phrygian cap on top of it, and during some days the honeymoon continued. The delegates from the country were delighted to see the royal family for the first time and filled the Tuileries gardens. They were especially taken with the Dauphin, who did the honours and picked his flowers for them. 'Come to our province of Dauphiné,' said the Federates from Grenoble, 'we will look after you.' To which the Normans answered, 'No, come to us, did you not once bear the name of Duc de Normandie, you will see how faithful Normans can be.' It was the same when the King reviewed the troops at Chaillot. The Queen drove with the children in an open carriage, she was surrounded by the women, who talked to them, kissed their hands, and even the Queen's arm when she laid it on the window-sill. 'This day,' wrote Madame de Tourzel, 'was really a happy one for the Queen. It was the last she was to know.'

If the King had known how to profit from all this enthusiasm, if he had taken the tide at its full, had mounted his horse and declared that being at the head of the élite of the nation he would henceforth lead them, or if he had at once announced his intention to visit the provinces, he might have succeeded in arresting the course of the Revolution. The Assembly indeed feared this, for Barnave acknowledged later to Madame Elisabeth, 'If the King had known how to take advantage of this moment we would have been lost.'

As it was it was the vacillating King who was lost, and not only he, for during the next weeks two attempts were made to assassinate Marie Antoinette, the second by poisoning. 'Remember,' she remarked sadly to Madame Campan, 'they will not trouble to poison me. They have calumny, which is much more useful for killing people; it is through this that I will perish.' She had waited with terror for whatever might happen on 14 July; as she said herself they needed a supernatural courage to sustain them through such monstrous times. But she also said that true courage was to know how to sacrifice everything if one saw a chance of success but not to fly to other means such as civil war, which she would never tolerate, but which Mirabeau was not against as a last resort. She kept silence when interrogated by the Court of the Châtelet which opened to inquire on the events of the preceding October, but she wrote to her brother that the verdict which absolved the Duc d'Orléans and Mirabeau could only be judged by the whole of Europe and by posterity.

6
The Flight

In August 1790 Mirabeau submitted his plan to the King. He had
written innumerable notes and was becoming discouraged by the
lack of urgency on the part of Louis XVI. 'It is pitiable,' he wrote,
'one might think that the house where they sleep could be reduced
to cinders and they would not even awaken.' The plan briefly was
this; the King should show himself frequently in public, and endeavour by every means to reconquer his popularity, should form
a nucleus of loyal regiments commanded by a trusted general and
finally under their protection leave the Tuileries for a near-by
town, Compiègne or Fontainebleau, and from there treat with
the Assembly. No foreign, but if necessary civil war, which he
regarded as almost certain but unavoidable. He insisted that a firm
line should be agreed on and asked for another interview with the
Queen.

Marie Antoinette was horrified. She wrote to Mercy that the
paper which she was returning to him seemed to her mad from
beginning to end. How could Mirabeau imagine for a moment
that they would do anything to provoke civil war? For the rest
it was out of the question that she should see Mirabeau, he must
not count on it. To which the Count's answer was 'Weak King,
Unfortunate Queen, here is the abyss to which blind confidence
and too exaggerated suspicion have brought you. . . . If I escape
public shipwreck I shall always say with pride, I exposed myself
to disaster in the attempt to save them all, they would not accept

it.' He did not cease his attempts until, weakened by his sense of failure and exhausted by his own fervour, his gigantic power, he died. With him perished the only hope for the monarchy.

Throughout the winter disorders increased in the provinces. In Paris night after night the mean streets and backwaters vomited their shivering half-starved citizens who heard the thunderous voice of Danton in the Cordeliers club demanding action. 'Away with useless kings, give me six hundred noble heads,' screamed Marat. 'To arms citizens, To arms!' And in Nancy the troops revolted, tired of their aristocratic officers and demanding the arrears of their pay. The revolt was put down with a heavy hand but it smouldered dangerously hidden. At Metz the Marquis de Bouillé was in command of the garrison and of all the east and north. He had been appointed one of the four supreme generals by the National Assembly, but was all the same a determined loyalist, a man of principle who refused to take the National Oath till requested to do so by the King himself. He looked with distinct perturbation at the unrest in the armies and perhaps regretted the King's unwisdom when he had decreed that all French officers must show four generations of nobility. And when these noble officers cheated their men of their pay, what could be expected but trouble? In another part of France, in the west, there was an inconspicuous sub-lieutenant, by name Napoleon Bonaparte, who was writing his first letter to his Corsican deputy and noting that after the National Oath a great change had come over the people; before it, had he been ordered in the King's name to fire on the people he would have done so, but now in the nation's name he would not do it.

During the autumn of 1790 the Queen had been more and more convinced that whatever might come, for themselves there was no hope. Her remarks always show long reflection and a deep understanding of their situation, as when in writing to Leopold she notes that the words Liberty and Despotism are so engraved in the minds of the people that they go from one to the other without comprehending either. Until now she had relied on time and patience on the King's part to remedy this; now, although their health continued good and if they could see any improvement around them it would be even better, for themselves things were forever finished. Her one consolation and delight was the friendship with the faithful Fersen, and he had but one idea –

escape. The Queen was beginning to see this as the only salvation for them; as for the King, he observed to Fersen when he was forced to sign the decree for the Civil Oath of the Clergy that he would rather be King of Metz than King of France.

On 19 February Mesdames, the two old aunts, stole away from Bellevue on their way, it was said, to Rome. Their flight had not been unsuspected and though they were armed with passports issued by the Assembly and countersigned by the King, Marat had warned his Patriots what was afoot. Some said they would take treasure with them, others that the Dauphin would be spirited away, leaving a changeling in his place. They were first stopped at Moret, then at Jaulieu and their escort of National Guards showed itself more against them than on their side. At Arnay-le-Duc the populace took a hand and it was necessary for Narbonne to ride to Paris to consult the Assembly, which replied that Mesdames might proceed. By this time Paris was alerted; out poured the crowds from the quarters and it took the determined resistance and persuasion of La Fayette to disperse them. The ladies went on minus their luggage, for the frantic women of Versailles helped by the troops cut the traces of the wagons. Their final grief was that their dear nephew Monsieur, so far from giving them aid, fled to the cellars of his Palace of Luxembourg and remained there trembling till it was all over.

Added to the general confusion was the fact that the émigrés, and in particular d'Artois, were concerting plans for an invasion. The Queen implored her brother to listen to no one, for only she and the King were capable of judging the situation on the spot. The King had even written to the King of Sardinia and to d'Artois saying that if they persisted in their plans he would be forced to disavow them formally. Leopold, on the other hand, who was quite naturally more anxious about Austrian policies than anything else (for as Mercy observed, the great powers never do anything for nothing), still advised patience and waiting for a propitious moment. To which his sister replied that sometimes to do nothing is as bad as to do too much.

What comfort could she get from her lymphatic husband, an introspective man? He could always retire within himself and find a retreat in his books and his religion, but his wife was not the woman to sit down and accept a situation. Her energetic nature looked for a means to circumvent it, or to fight even the inevitable until the last moment. In Axel Fersen she found an answering force; his energy matched her own. She warned Leopold that the peace, not only of France but of Europe, was menaced by the ideas fermenting there, and truly events were going from bad to worse. In Paris on 27 January 1791 the mob attacked and sacked the house of Clermont Tonnerre. At the beginning of February the rumour went round that the Château of Vincennes was being repaired in order that the King could go there by underground passage, and from thence to the frontier. Immediately bands of workmen from the Faubourgs marched to the castle with their tools in their hands to level it. Dispersed by La Fayette and the National Guard they were joined by fresh hordes who attacked a number of armed gentlemen loyal to the King, who had appeared at the Tuileries probably hoping to defend him or even to help him to escape. La Fayette had hardly time to arrive with his Guards, to harangue the 'Chevaliers du Poignard' and to order them to give up their arms, and on their resisting the King was obliged to intervene. As they departed, unarmed, the crowds set upon them with insults and blows.

Now came Easter, and the question was, would the King accept Mass from the hands of a civil priest at St Germain-l'Auxerrois? He compromised by hearing Mass on Palm Sunday under the Cardinal de Montmorency, but did not communicate. On his return from the chapel the grenadiers of the National Guard refused to line the route. At once the town was in disorder, and next day the King decided to leave for St Cloud, He was longing for the fresh air and exercise, and the Queen wished that her children could be away from the troubled atmosphere. La Fayette and the Mayor Bailly had assured them that they could keep order should the people oppose their departure. But they counted without the Cordwainers Club. On 18 April, the King and Queen were about to enter their carriage when they were shocked by an immense clamour, and when they seated themselves with their children the National Guard shut the gates, surrounded the carriages, crossed their bayonets in front of the horses and mad with rage hurled insults at the sovereigns. 'Kill the servants, kill the horses,' they yelled. 'No one can leave Paris until the Revolution is accomplished.' La Fayette shouted at his men in vain while the King remarked sorrowfully to Bailly that it was sad that having given liberty to the nation he should be deprived of it himself.

The bedroom of Marie
Antoinette in Le Petit
Trianon

Portrait of Marie Antoinette, at
Le Petit Trianon

Louis XVI, engraved by
Curtis after the painting by
Boze

An extract from the diary of Louis XVI, during the flight to
Varennes

For two hours they were forced to sit there, subjected to the most revolting insults, 'F . . . aristocrat, great pig', these were the least of the abuses screamed at them. Finally the King decided to descend and immediately the National Guards protested their devotion. 'Be easy,' they said. 'We only want to defend you,' they told the Queen. 'Yes,' she replied, 'but you must admit now that we are not free.' And taking the weeping Dauphin in her arms she re-entered the Château. In the evening the mob went through the place searching everywhere, overturning everything, and when on the following day the King went to the Assembly to protest, the President found nothing better to reply than that 'unquiet agitation was an inseparable part of progress towards liberty'. At last convinced, Louis xvi asked all his faithful entourage to leave him for their own safety. The Grand Almoner Montmorency, Monseigneur de Roquelaure, Monseigneur de Sabran and the priests of his private chapel, and the First Gentlemen of the Chamber left. The Queen did the same for her gentlewomen; on Easter Day they were both forced to hear Mass celebrated by the civil priest who had replaced the old curé.

The Easter days were gloomy, nothing now remained but flight.

Even our lives are not assured. We must give the impression that we will agree to everything, until we are ready to act. . . . But before acting it is essential to know whether you can bring, under any pretext, fifteen thousand men to Arlon and Virton, and the same number to Mons. M. de Bouillé wishes this because it will give him the means to assemble troops and munitions at Montmédy. . . . Our position is frightful. It must be over in the next month. The King desires this even more than I.

So wrote the Queen to Mercy, who had retreated to Brussels. She received a long letter in which the Ambassador enumerated the difficulties which attended a plan at a time when everything was against its success. How could it be in the present state of Europe while the war between Russia and Turkey still went on, before it was certain what London and Berlin had in mind and before one could be sure that there would be no new insurrection in France? Spain, Sardinia and Switzerland had more freedom of movement, but it was reasonable to believe that they would only move if they were sure that England opposed no obstacle, and he insisted on the necessity for directing all attempts for negotiation towards England.

It was the old diplomat speaking and it was a dusty answer to a woman in an extremity. Marie Antoinette received little more encouragement from the Emperor Leopold beyond warm expressions of brotherly love. For he had the same preoccupations as Mercy, and from the point of view of Austrian policy. But on 22 May the Queen wrote him that they had come to a decision: only Bouillé and Breteuil knew the plans and a third person who was charged with all the preparations. She meant of course Fersen, who had been convinced that this was their only recourse and was actively engaged in making their escape possible. He had in fact begun his work before the unhappy events of 17 and 18 April, had collected information through the secret agents of the Powers, had informed Gustave III, and had kept up a correspondence with Mercy. All this had to be done as and when he could, for all communication with the outer world was suspect. He was also responsible for obtaining money and was in constant touch with Bouillé and his friend Taube, urging them to procure the millions needed.

It is time now as an interlude to look at the question which has excited so many commentators for nearly two centuries, the question whether Marie Antoinette and Comte Axel de Fersen were or were not lovers. If it were put in another way, did they love each other, I imagine that the immediate answer would be, yes. And even that it was love at first sight. The other question, were they physically lovers, has been more difficult to answer, partly because of the mystery which has surrounded it and partly because the majority of people cannot imagine a perfect love affair without its physical fulfilment. We know that after their first meeting Fersen renounced his projects for marriage. 'Since I cannot have the only one I would want I will have none other,' he said. During his prolonged absence from Court in Italy he had mistresses to whom he seems to have been sincerely attached; this is also not impossible for a man guarding an unattainable ideal in his heart. When he visited Trianon in the suite of Gustave III Marie Antoinette gave herself the greatest trouble at the fêtes to be attentive to the Swedes present, not sitting down but moving among the tables like a good mistress of a house and talking to everyone. So dissembling she might speak also to the only one she wished to see without singling him out.

During his long journeying Fersen wrote to a mysterious 'Joséphine' and noted many of the dates in his *Intimate Journal*. This journal with many other papers was discovered by the most celebrated writer on this subject, Madame Alma Soderjhelm, in the archives of the Countess Nordenfalk, herself a descendant of Fersen's favourite sister, Sophie. Who was this Joséphine? The assumption has been that she was Marie Antoinette. In November 1784 he wrote for example asking her what should be the name of the dog she had asked him to buy for her, and if there should be a 'mystery about it'. It seems that 'Joséphine' replied that it was not secret. So he wrote to M. de Boye and noted in his *Journal* 'I asked him to send a dog which should not be little like the one belonging to Monsieur Pollett, and say it is for the Queen of France.' So 'Joséphine' must be Marie Antoinette. But Fersen had a close friend, the eccentric Englishman Lord Crawford, and this friend had a mistress, Madame Sullivan. The mistress had a maid who was also named Joséphine and in his *Intimate Journal* Fersen mentions several commissions which had been confided to her, such as forwarding letters to Crawford or ordering articles for him. It is all very confusing, but one thing is clear, that Fersen corresponded constantly with Marie Antoinette, for in the castle of Stafsund in Sweden there were sixty letters from the Queen, which were published in 1878 by the great nephew of Fersen, the Baron Klinckowstrom. They were however incomplete; passages were scratched out, it was believed to have been by Fersen, for the letters were supposed to be sent to the King, Gustave III, in order that he might judge of the state of affairs in France. The explanation given by the Baron was that in order that Gustave should not misinterpret what the Queen wrote Fersen erased passages having political import; but she would hardly have incorporated political comment between affectionate personal words, and this is exactly where the erasures occur. The question today seems academic, for one evening the Baron, ill and feeling death near, called to him an old friend and a faithful servant, and in front of them, in an open fire, he burned the lot.

But research was not satisfied. There was more to be found, and after the discovery by Madame Soderjhelm – who is at some pains in her preface to emphasize the purely scientific purpose of her research, thus distinguishing it from the reams of scandal which have been poured out on the subject – M. Lucien Maury unearthed in the castle of Stafsund a letter in code which M. de Klinckowstrom had overlooked. It is most important and was written after the return from Varennes. Marie Antoinette begins with these words, 'I can tell you that I love you and have hardly the time even for that', and concludes with the words 'let me know to whom I can address whatever I can write to you, for I cannot live without that. Adieu, the most loving and the most lovable of men. I embrace you with all my heart.' These phrases have been taken as unimpeachable evidence that Fersen and Marie Antoinette were lovers, though later writers such as M. Henry Valloton point out that the phrase '*Je vous embrasse*', meaning 'I kiss you', was in current usage at the time, though as M. Castelot also comments, he only cites famous men as using it. But we may also remark it is equally in current use today and among women. Then Madame Soderjhelm cites the entry in his *Journal* which reads '*13 February 1792. Allé chez elle, passé par mon chemin ordinaire; peur des gardes nationales; son logement à merveille, pas vu le Roi.*'* Then come two scratched out words and through the erasure can be faintly read '*Resté là.*'† This entry has been submitted by M. Valloton to expert scrutiny and the Swedish Institute admitted that the words seemed to be '*resté là*', but whether they can constitute a proof of adultery is very questionable. He might have found it impossible to evade the guards again and awaited a favourable moment, or he might have spent the night in conversation, no one can know definitely. Each commentator has his own opinion, and the question is hotly debated even to this day.

What is certain is that either from an old-fashioned sense of chivalry or from a real and devoted love, or simply for the satisfaction of his senses, Fersen was ready to risk his life for Marie Antoinette. He had a curious nature, at once discreet, restrained in his bearing with a certain nobility of manner, and sensual, a bit of a Don Juan, with mistresses in every town he had stayed in, and in fact one living in near proximity to the Tuileries whom he shared with his friend Crawford – Madame Sullivan. He saw her daily, she knew all that he was doing to save the King and his family,

---

* Went to her, by my usual route; afraid of the National Guards; her apartment very fine, did not see the King.
† Stayed there.

she and Crawford left Paris when he did, and were at Mons when he arrived after the flight. As for the Queen, during all the time when she was isolated in the Tuileries, a prey to the most horrible forebodings, convinced in her heart that she at any rate was lost, he was her sole comfort apart from her children. But in such a situation children cannot be all, they cannot listen or advise; her husband leaned on her, not she on him. She was friendless, home-less and hopeless, and with all this she kept up a brave front, corresponded with the Powers, urged, entreated, was diplomatic, insistent and far-seeing. And through it all she had only this one man, who was obsessed with his plans for her survival. Does it matter whether they went to bed together, or whether they found as other lovers have in history that they had gone much deeper and more fully without that? Perhaps when they were both young and impetuous she had used her little secret passages in Versailles about which the dissatisfied, would-be lover Besenval wrote so impertinently. That too is uncertain; for us it is all con-jecture, and we may judge the woman we have been studying each according to our own knowledge of her.

Fersen was prey to intense anxiety on the score of secrecy. Gustave III was well known for a chatterbox, and the émigrés scattered throughout Europe, d'Artois in particular, were without the least discretion and cared far more for their own satisfaction than for the lives of the royal family. Marie Antoinette knew this well when she wrote to Leopold that the least indiscretion would expose them in a frightening manner, although they were supposed to be protected in Paris. They would have no secrets from d'Artois were he not surrounded by people like Calonne and Condé, whom they could never trust. And she implored him once more to promise them eight or ten thousand men whenever the moment was propitious for their plan. Her dream was that when by good fortune they had made their way to Metz or Montmédy they would find at the frontier a large army furnished by the Powers, and that the King, immediately placing himself at its head would from this point of vantage call on all loyal Frenchmen to come to his aid. The Emperor would retire, no foreign troops would enter French soil but Louis XVI would lead his army to Paris, victorious.

Bouillé's first plan was that the King should escape alone and the Queen and her children would follow by another route. This

Marie Antoinette firmly refused to do. Bouillé in his memoirs insinuates that this was because, knowing the hatred of the populace, she feared to become their victim if she was arrested without the King. Everything we know of her character contradicts such a suspicion; she would rather share all the danger which menaced him, and also she knew in her heart that without her he was nothing. Fersen, meanwhile active, had unbelievably ordered on her command a magnificent carriage, painted green and yellow, furnished with everything that the travellers could possibly require, while she set about putting her personal affairs in order. She bespoke in the presence of her entourage a '*nécessaire*' to be given as a present to her sister the Governor of the Low Countries. This was so that she might send her own diamonds in it. It was confided to her coiffeur who left for Brussels with M. de Choiseul. The Crown jewels had already been given to the Commissioner of the Assembly. Madame Campan went from shop to shop in Paris buying six chemises in one, dresses in another, and clothes for the children: they believed that this would escape notice. Fersen was busy arranging for the passports, bringing the dispatches from Bouillé, buying the horses, writing to Gustave recording the flattering expressions of the Queen's enduring friendship for him and visiting the Queen at all hours when he would not be noticed, for it was with her that he must discuss everything. They feared the ineptitude of Bouillé and above all they feared the actual moment of escape from the heavily guarded Palace.

On 26 May he wrote to Bouillé, who had enumerated the detachments of troops who would guard the route to Chalons: 'There are no precautions to be taken as far as Chalons ... everything depends on swiftness and secrecy, if you are not sure of your detachments it would be better to place none until after Varennes in order that they do not arouse suspicion in the countryside.' He insisted on this several times. The departure had been postponed from May in order that the King might receive the two millions due from the Civil List, and Fersen himself contributed every livre which he possessed besides borrowing from all his friends: it is all written in his book of expenses, for he was a meticulous person. All this was supposed to be secret, but how could such a secret be kept when the Tuileries was full to overflowing with servants, guards and attendants on the monarchs and their children and Madame Elisabeth? In fact it was known all over Europe. Now after all the discussion and the delays the final plans were under way. Who was to accompany the fugitives? The man proposed by Bouillé, probably Fersen, was declined, for Madame de Tourzel, the Gouvernante of the Children of France, had the right never to leave them. Then Madame Elisabeth had the right to be with her brother and sister-in-law, but how take six persons in the one carriage with all its unnecessary equipment? And Louis XVI refused to take Fersen, a very foolish decision, for if the Comte had been there many mistakes might have been avoided. However, finally it was agreed that three gentlemen should be charged with the business of paying the postilions and other items of the journey, François Melchior de Moustier, François Florent de Valory and Jean François de Malden. They would also defend the King in case of attack. In addition two ladies' maids were chosen to attend the Queen, which brought the number up to eleven, all this for four people in danger of discovery which might cost them their lives. And in addition it was not noticed that though the three bodyguards were loyal and brave, not one of them knew Paris.

Fersen and Bouillé had finally decided on the arrangements for escort after Chalons had been passed; from Paris to Chalons the party would be relatively safe, for it would not yet be daylight and though there would be the involvement of changing horses twelve times it was hoped that it could be done with speed and without crowds of curious onlookers. From Chalons Bouillé took charge. He stationed at Pont-de-Somme-Vesle a detachment of hussars with the Duc de Choiseul and the Baron de Goguelat, both friends of Marie Antoinette; they would escort the berlin to Sainte Menehould where forty of the Régiment Royal dragoons awaited them. They would form an escort while the troop under Choiseul would bar the road to Verdun and the short-cut leading to Varennes to all travellers. Through Clermont, where one hundred of Monsieur's dragoons and forty horsemen from the Régiment Royal would meet them, they would drive on to Varennes; here would be sixty hussars of Lauzun's regiment and a hundred further on at Dun. So guarded they would finally reach Montmédy where they would instal themselves at the Château of Thonelle.

It all seemed well ordered and sure, but Axel was uneasy, for it required an almost split-second timing, and who could tell what mishaps might arise with so many people involved? He was busy arranging for the passports for the party. The Queen had wished that the children should travel with their aunt, Madame Elisabeth, by the route for Flanders, but the King refused point blank to be separated from his children and a passport was thus needed for the King, the Queen, Madame Elisabeth, the two children and Madame Tourzel. This was procured through a friend of Axels,' the Baronne de Korff, who was on the point of leaving for Russia; she had the same number of people, had approached M. de Montmorin for her passport and willingly agreed to send it back for the King's use. This was thought too dangerous, and she therefore pretended to have lost it and applied for a second one which she got.

Everything was ready for the departure, timed for the 19th at 11 p.m., when it was discovered that one of the ladies' maids – a young woman suspected for her democratic sympathies – would be in service on that night, and the whole plan was put off for twenty-four hours, a delay which as Bouillé says in his memoirs much disturbed him since all his orders had already gone out. Fersen was assiduous in his efforts and his *Journal* notes it all as follows:

Thursday 16th. With the Queen at half past nine. Transported the baggage myself; no one here is suspicious, nor in the town.
Friday. Went to Bondy and to Bourget [to reconnoitre the roads where he would drive].
Saturday 18th. With the Queen at two o'clock till six.

On this day he had the carriage taken to the garages in the rue du Faubourg St Honoré, following the advice of Madame de Korff, and tested it in a short run through Paris; the coachmaker had reported that all was perfect, and he was satisfied. But it may have been remarked, for it was new and splendid, though this in itself might not have created surprise for it would ostensibly have been occupied by a great and wealthy lady. '*Sunday 19th*', continues the diary, 'Took 800 livres and the seals, and stayed at the château from eleven till midnight.' Someone else kept a diary – the King – and when we open it on this day it records as usual 'Nothing'.

The awaited day dawned fairly clear. Fersen, who had been recording the weather with the persistence of a meteorologist, says nothing about it, but since the Dauphin went as usual to work in his garden we may assume that it was not raining. At eleven o'clock the Queen attended Mass, and her prayers must have been deeply felt; she ordered her carriage, took her children driving in the afternoon, and on her return sent for the three men who would be their guards. They had unfortunately spent the afternoon in buying new yellow liveries, the colours of the Duc de Condé which would be recognized everywhere. On entering the apartments they saw the King and Queen for the first time and were acquainted with the work they would perform. The King even said to them 'Our fate is in your hands', and they protested their loyalty and devotion. Malden was then hidden in a sort of cupboard between two doors while the two others and Balthasar, Fersen's coachman, went to the carriage in the rue de Clichy and took it to the end of the Faubourg St Honoré at the beginning of the road for Metz, while Fersen disguised as a cab driver mounted his 'citadine' or hackney carriage and drove off to the Tuileries.

Here he found the Princes' Courtyard full of the carriages belonging to the dignitaries assembled for the King's supper and 'coucher', both invested with a rigorous etiquette; it would have been impossible to change it on this night. 'We are approaching the terrible quarter of an hour,' said the Queen, and indeed one can imagine with what impatience and anxiety they felt the slow minutes passing. The Comte and Comtesse de Provence were there, the future Louis xviii would leave that night by the Route de Flandres and save his life. The Queen was much moved and said to Monsieur, 'Be careful not to upset me, I do not wish anyone to see that I have been crying.' They supped, and at half-past nine the Queen quietly retired and went to her daughter's room. There she told Madame Brunier, who was watching beside the girl, to dress her and take her to the courtyard where they would both be waited for. From there Marie Antoinette passed into the Dauphin's room where Madame de Tourzel, who was in the secret, and Madame de Neuville, who was not, were told to be ready; she knelt by her son's bed – he had been asleep for an hour – and whispered in his ear, 'Wake up, we are going to a place where there will be lots of soldiers.' The little boy, rubbing his eyes looked at her, surprised 'You will command your regiment,' and the child excitedly demanded his boots and his sword. 'Hurry up, let us go,' he exclaimed. While he dressed she told Madame de Neuville that she would accompany the Prince, while the other guardian wept, and threw herself at the Queen's feet, kissing her hands and praying for the success of the enterprise.

Now the children were taken to their mother's room, where they put on their disguises, Madame a simple brown frock and the Dauphin a pretty little girl's dress. By half past ten they were ready and went down to the empty apartment of the Duc de Villequier, of which the Queen had the key. Madame de Tourzel went first with the Dauphin, the others following, and with the Queen silently feeling the way they came to a door leading to the Princes' Courtyard where Fersen had been nervously waiting. The Queen looked out, all was in shadow, she could see no one. Three times she went to the door, then a figure detached itself from the wall and slid inside; it was Fersen. Without a word he took the Dauphin's hand and they went down the steps into the Princes' Court 'lit up as if it were day' full of National Guards, walking about, joking and laughing. With beating hearts they hugged the walls. Once Madame Royale cried out but was quickly hushed when she saw that her mother was behind her; they came to the carriage, mounted it hurriedly, and Fersen on the box urged his horses to a trot, leaving Marie Antoinette looking after them. It was the first time in her life that she had been parted from her children. With a heavy heart she retraced her steps. It was half past eleven.

Within she found the two women, uncertain what they should do. 'You are going to Claye,' she told them, 'Hurry.' Without any preparation or baggage they were taken to a point on the quays where a posting carriage waited for them driven by a man called Pierre Lebas. All this time an 'unknown' had guided them, now he hustled them into the cab and it set off. Within the palace everything followed the appointed routine; the King went to his apartment, Madame Elisabeth to hers, escorted by a captain of the National Guard, while the Queen in her own rooms made her preparations for sleep aided by her waiting women. The windows were shut and bolted and the doors in the corridors as well. At eleven o'clock she was finished. Usually three attendants slept near her: on this night she had dispensed with two of them. The King too was going through the antique parade of his 'coucher'; his first gentleman took his hat and his sword, he and La Fayette reviewed the past evening, he went behind the balustrade of his bed, said his prayers, took off his clothes and sat in an armchair, where one valet took off his right stocking while another took off the left. The Archives tell us that the King seemed preoccupied on this evening and well he might; he went several times to the window and remarked that the night was cloudy. At half past eleven it was done, and his visitors took their leave. He left the ceremonial apartment and went to his private rooms where he went to his bed. Its curtains were drawn, the lights were extinguished and the valet withdrew. This was the moment for which the King waited. Quickly he slipped out through the Dauphin's empty room into the Queen's anteroom where his disguise was waiting for him. Behind him the valet, all unknowing, undressed, put the cord of the bed curtain round his wrist, and quietly, in order not to wake his master, lay down.

During this time Marie Antoinette had regained her apartment and had changed her dress, putting on a grey dress with a black mantle and a large hat with a veil; thus attired she opened the door and crept into the corridor where M. de Malden awaited her. She took his arm and they went down to the courtyard. There they evaded the guards and sought for the road to the rue de l'Echelle, where Fersen would be waiting. They took some time finding it and Fersen became more and more apprehensive, all the more because the carriage of La Fayette going to the 'coucher' had narrowly missed him. He climbed down from his box, walked up and down, talked to another coachman from the numerous fiacre owners who frequented the quarter, and revolved in his troubled brain possible means of restoring the children to the château if by some horrible mistake the King and Queen failed to arrive. Suddenly he perceived a woman alone on a bench near by; it was Madame Elisabeth, brought there by one of her grooms. She entered the carriage and reassured Madame de Tourzel, the King and Queen would soon be there, no one had suspected the flight. And soon they arrived, with M. de Malden. They all embraced joyously.

Once ensconced, the Queen recounted her adventures. They were all so reassured that they failed to take note of the time, midnight – they had lost an hour. But suddenly the King, who knew Paris better than the others, noticed that they were not on the road to the Barrière St Martin where they must pass the customs control; where was Fersen going? He went in fact to rue de Clichy where he jumped down and entered the house of his friend Crawford to inquire if the berlin had left the garage where it had been stored. The concièrge assured him that it had left during the afternoon, and he remounted the box. All this took time. The fugitives were more and more anxious and the Queen could think only of her children straying perhaps through this terrible Paris. The King was calmer, but he too was glad when they perceived the barrier in the distance. Fersen got down again. If Balthasar had followed his orders the berlin should be there. It was half past one in the morning of the shortest day, which was already beginning to break. Fersen disappeared; outside they could hear the cries and laughter from a café. The King, impatient, descended and disappeared in his turn to find the Count. Marie Antoinette was half mad with fear. Two roads led from the barrier, one towards Belgium through Le Bourget, the other to Chalons through Bondy. Could the two guards have made a mistake, and where, oh where was Axel? They had lost an hour and a half of their estimated time.

At last he reappeared, the berlin was a little further on. Quickly they transferred themselves, Fersen mounted the box next the coachman and they departed at a gallop over the plain which stretched wide and deserted before them. The Swede, frantic at the loss of time, constantly urged the driver to push his horses. 'Hardi, Hardi, Balthasar,' he cried, faster, faster. The horses flew and in three quarters of an hour they were in Bondy. The six remounts ordered by Valory were waiting, the grooms too were ready to harness them, and while this was being done Axel advanced, opened the carriage door and bending over Marie Antoinette's hand murmured 'Adieu, Madame de Korff.' No time had been lost here and the King embraced the man to whom he owed so much; doubtless his heart was full of hope and gratitude. There was a brief leavetaking and they were on their way, while Axel stood and watched the woman he loved disappear into the distance.

It was half past two.

Now it was day, and they made good progress to Claye where they found the two ladies de Neuville and Brunier, who had almost given themselves up for lost. When three of the horses were attached to their cabriolet they left following Valory and in advance of the berlin, beside which galloped Malden. Moustier, who was very short-sighted, sat on the box. Now that they were all together their spirits rose, and the sun rose too, on a fine day. They amused themselves by deciding on their names. Madame de Tourzel would be the mistress, the Queen the governess. Her name? Madame Rochet. The King was M. Durand; Madame Elisabeth the Dame de Compagnie; Rosalie and the two children Amélie and Aglaé. Much laughter accompanied all this. More serious was the King's reading of the Declaration which would that morning be read to the Assembly. In it he enumerated the sacrifices he had made for the country's peace. What was his only recompense? The destruction of royalty. And what today his power? The shadow of his royalty, he had not even the liberty of his person.

But nothing could damp their rising spirits for long. They had been wretched for months, poor people, they had suffered so much, now all would be changed. The King declared that when once he was in the saddle again he would be quite different, much wiser, and perhaps even the Queen could forget that she brought bad luck, and believe that it had changed. Now it was six o'clock and they arrived in Meaux. The streets were empty and the horses were quickly changed. Moustier lamented that they were not pushing on fast enough, but the travellers were hungry and paid no heed. They attacked the breakfast thoughtfully provided by Fersen, a real picnic without knives and forks, but it tasted good and the Queen offered some food to Malden saying, 'At this moment M. de La Fayette must be most embarrassed,' a reflection of the King's. It was a glorious day, the road was lined with trees, it was not yet too hot, and the carriage was most luxurious. It was large and wide enough for them all with seats covered with white velvet and green silk curtains over the windows. It contained the Queen's silver travelling coffer and necessary toilet articles, including two silver chamber pots.

After the repast they all made themselves comfortable. Then on their way again. They passed La Ferté-sous-Jouarre at ten o'clock, where the King got out and talked with the onlookers, a most imprudent proceeding it seems. Then at Montmirail he did it again and the Queen trembled so that Moustier shielded her from the gaze of the curious. 'Don't disturb yourself,' her husband said, 'I do not think this precaution necessary. My journey does not appear to me to be at the mercy of an accident.' It was midday. On and on they went, not too unpleasantly. In order to keep the children amused Madame de Tourzel got out and walked and played with them, and after Fromentières the King did the same while Marie Antoinette, more nervous, stayed hidden with Madame Elisabeth in the depths of the berlin. It was midday, and at that moment a rider passed the Barrière St Martin. It was Bayon, sent by La Fayette to catch up with the royal party.

What had happened back in the Tuileries when the flight was discovered? At seven in the morning as usual Lemoine the King's valet had risen and going to the royal bed had said as on every morning, 'Your Majesty, it is seven o'clock.' Receiving no answer he had opened the curtains and to his surprise found the bed empty. He at first thought the King might be with his wife, but after some time he sent another valet to inquire, and then a third rushed in saying 'There is no one in M. le Dauphin's room.' This was enough. They searched everywhere and were joined by the maids of Madame and Madame Elisabeth. Finally they dared to knock at Marie Antoinette's door and receiving no answer, to open it and look in. It was empty, like all the others. Thoroughly alarmed, the group which was growing ever larger alerted the rest of the domestics and the news spread like wildfire through the château and from there into the streets. The King and Queen had fled!

It took only a few minutes for a crowd to gather at the Tuileries; it finally entered the palace and spread through all the rooms. A woman climbed on to the Queen's bed crying her cherries for sale while someone else stuck notices on the walls of the château, 'Dwelling for rent', and 'The citizens are informed that a big man has fled from the Tuileries, anyone finding him should bring him back and will be suitably rewarded.' But it must not be inferred that the feeling of the crowd was humorous, far from it; a growling met the Mayor and La Fayette as they arrived and the General came in for the full force of their reproaches. He had said, 'I will be responsible for the King with my own head,' to which Danton had replied, 'Now we want the King or your head.' But La Fayette, of whom Stendhal wrote that like the Plutarchian hero Epaminondas he lived from day to day doing always whatever thing presented itself, now suggested to Bailly that the King should be followed and arrested. The Mayor agreed but who was to give the fatal order? Who but the hero of the American Revolution, who proceeded to write an announcement which he gave to

Romeuf, his adjutant: 'The enemies of the Revolution have carried off the King, the bearer is ordered to inform all good citizens. They are enjoined in the name of the fatherland in danger to take him from their hands and to bring him back to the Assembly, which will shortly re-assemble. Until then I take upon myself the responsibility for this order.' He added in his own writing, 'This order is extended to include all the royal family.'

It was clever, face-saving, but it was nevertheless a *coup d'état*, and struck at all the respect and prestige which royalty had enjoyed in France. Towards midday the Assembly received the King's Declaration; he protested that only the anarchy which had seized France had forced him to withdraw, he reviewed the sacrifices which he had made since 1789 which had ended in chaos thanks to the revision of the Constitution. He promised amnesty for all offenders against the laws and re-establishment of religion, and he forbade any minister to sign anything in his name. The Assembly listened in silence when this was read and the more moderate felt that the Revolution might perhaps be arrested. Not so the Cordwainers, Jacobins and Orleanists, who gave immediate orders to tear down all signs of royalty, the Fleur de Lys and Royal Arms. Paine and Duchâtelet demanded an edict establishing a republic, Condorcet for the King's destitution, and Laclos prepared for the Regency of the Duc d'Orléans. Meanwhile all the churches sounded the tocsin and inquiries were on foot in all the quarters where the fugitives might have passed. Before long an aide-de-camp brought the postilion who had driven the two ladies to the rendezvous at Claye; he said they were met by a big berlin, he had not seen who was in it but he knew that he had been engaged by Monsieur de Fersen. Fersen, this was the clue. Forthwith Romeuf set off for the Barrière St Martin where he discovered that his comrade Bayon had already passed at midday – an hour ago. Romeuf threw himself on his horse again and galloped away; the travellers had ten hours' advantage over their pursuers.

They arrived at Chaintry at about two o'clock where they found the nine horses already ordered by Valory, but when the master of the posting house came to help, to his amazement he recognized the august travellers. He was overwhelmed, his wife and daughters came running, and Marie Antoinette recognized with a feeling of helplessness that from then on all disguise would be useless. The women could not do enough, the children ran about until the horses were in and everything ready; it was time to start and the Queen with one of those winning gestures which came so naturally to her, took from her *nécessaire* two silver bowls and gave them to Madame de Lagny, the postmaster's wife.

Lagny's son-in-law Vallet leapt to the saddle, determined to conduct them to Chalons, and the party set off. It was obvious that he would pass the word along and the only thing to do now was to speed to the meeting-place with Bouillé's troops. These had arrived at about midday at the inn of Pont-de-Somme-Vesle, the first post *after* Chalons. There were forty hussars of the Royal Allemand commanded by Lieutenant Boudet and accompanied by the Baron de Goguelat, Marie Antoinette's friend. They had dismounted and the officers went in search of Choiseul who had also arrived with his companion the coiffeur Léonard, carrying the case with the Queen's diamonds. He had been completely at sea as to his part in the mystery but now he began to comprehend his role and it overwhelmed him. At about two o'clock the officers betook themselves to a little hill from which they could watch for the first sight of the berlin. It should arrive at any minute, for it was due to leave Chalons at midday. But they watched in vain, nothing appeared. On the contrary an angry sound reached them from the village and they heard the bells of the tocsin ringing. It came from the villagers who had not paid their taxes and who, seeing the troops arrive, had immediately concluded that they were there on their account. So when the impatient officers returned they found a gang of people, some armed with guns, threatening them. Choiseul seeing this was so disturbed that he forgot his orders, which were to *wait for the King* and immediately he appeared to send a speedy messenger to alert the other detachments along the route, then to follow the fugitives to Sainte Menehould and turn them over to the dragoons, after which he would bar the road from Paris and stop anyone coming in pursuit.

Instead of this he decided to retire. It was four o'clock. This was approximately the moment when the two carriages *entered* Chalons, not yet so late that the occupants were grievously agitated, and Marie Antoinette could remember that other time when she had seen this town and had been greeted by bevies of young girls singing:

Princesse, dont l'esprit, les graces, les appas
Viennent embellir nos climats.

Today no singing greeted her, only the afternoon sun blazing down on the crowded carriage, and the steady gallop of the horses' feet over the dusty road as they bore her away from the kingdom which had once seemed so fair.

We return to the royal party who drove on, passing Notre Dame de l'Epine with its lofty spire, where they offered a silent prayer that all might go well. On through the empty countryside, where the road stretched out before them with never a turning, treeless and bare. Suddenly the carriages stopped. Where were they? Leaning from the windows they asked. In Pont-de-Somme-Vesle. But where was the post house and where M. de Choiseul and his hussars? Not here, and M. de Goguelat? No one! The King felt as though the earth had opened beneath his feet and the consternation of the women was unspeakable.

If Choiseul had to go at least he should have had the fore-thought to leave a man behind to inform the King of his intention to take a short-cut by which he could reach the little town of Varennes on the way to Montmédy. All he did was to send the coiffeur Léonard on the agreed route to Sainte Menehould to tell the officers of the detachments there that the King would not pass that way. Later Choiseul denied this, but the note exists. 'It seems that the treasure will not pass this way today. I am leaving to join M. de Bouillé; you will receive new orders tomorrow.'

What were the party to do? They could not go back, the only thing was to proceed as quickly as possible and to find at Sainte Menehould the forty dragoons posted there by M. de Damas. Haste, but no sooner were the horses harnessed than all four of them collapsed. Pulled up with blows they fell again, this time so entangled in their harness that it took all the efforts of the pos-tilions to free them, and one man lost his boots in the struggle. At last they could set off, Valory leading, then the cabriolet, then the berlin escorted by Moustier with Malden on the box.

On, on, they passed the mill of Valmy, the relais of Orbeville, now they were in the Argonne, its mountains on their right, the chalky road before them. They strained their eyes to catch sight of the town and the dragoons. Valory, having arrived before them, had found his way to the post house and to the officer M.

d'Andoins, not without curious examination from the citizens who on this fine summer afternoon were out parading in the streets or sitting contentedly before their shops. The dragoons had already excited their interest, all the more because in the morning forty of Lauzun's hussars had left for Pont-de-Somme-Vesle led by M. de Goguelet. All this movement of troops was somewhat suspect to the Menehouldais, and the troopers, bored with waiting, had distributed themselves among the bars and alleys of the town. At about eight o'clock the master of the posting house at Sainte Menehould, Jean Baptiste Drouet, was on his way home from his fields. As he entered the little town he saw a group of people standing round a large carriage and a cabriolet which was in the process of changing horses. The postilions were in the livery of the Duc de Condé and the rumour went round that it was the Duc himself re-emigrating. As the coach passed some citizens saluted, to which the lady within responded with a negligent but charming bow, in the manner of the noblesse. Drouet later asserted that he had been suspicious; in any case he did recommend the driver not to push his horses too hard over the rough roads of the Argonne. Certain it is that d'Andoins, passing Moustier, muttered under his breath 'Hurry, hurry, you are lost if you delay.' The coach moved off, and hardly had it disappeared than a horseman white with dust galloped up. It was Viet, the post-master from Chalons, bringing a message from the Captain Bayon, La Fayette's officer, which read:

By the order of the National Assembly all good citizens are commanded to stop the coach with six horses in which it is suspected that the King, the Queen, the Dauphin, Madame and Madame Elisabeth are. I have been sent by the City of Paris and the Assembly, but as I am too tired to proceed the recipient of this note is to carry out the orders and if necessary to employ public force.

Immediately d'Andoins tried to draw his men away, but the crowd surrounded them and he was whisked off to the Town Hall while a mad disorder overwhelmed all; drums were beaten, the tocsin sounded madly, barricades were erected, and Drouet and his barman Guillaume saddled their horses and tore off in pursuit. Just outside the town they met the postilions returning from Clermont, where the travellers had changed horses. 'Which way have they gone?' was the hurried question. 'Towards Varennes' was the answer. Without this chance meeting the two

Towards DUN, STENAY and MONTMEDY

Montblainville

Cheppy

Ratantout

Forêt de la
Gruerie

VARENNES
Bois du
Bel Orme

Bois de
Cheppy

Vauquois

Boureuilles

La Biesme

Le four de Paris

L'AIRE

The road followed on horseback by CHOISEUL

Forêt
de Hesse

Lachalade

Neuvilly

le Glaon

Lochères

Orvaux
Bois
Bachin

Route followed by PROUET

Towards
Verdun

les Islettes
les Germeries la Vignette

le Pas
de Vache

Ste Menehould

CLERMONT

la Grange aux Bois

THE ROUTE FROM SAINTE-MENEHOULD TO VARENNES

men would have continued their ride to Verdun and from there to Clermont, and missed the escaping coachload. Instead they took the narrow country road which branches off at Pas de Vache and joins the Montmédy route at Varennes.

It was about half past nine, still light, but the day was drawing in, and through the wooded path the escaping party could see the heights of the Argonne. All seemed quiet, the King studied his maps of their route, the children drowsed and the Queen too relaxed. At Clermont they were reassured by Damas, who had sent his small detachment to a neighbouring village in case they were too noticeable, but he was certain that they had not been recognized, and saw success for the enterprise. Valory mounted and galloped ahead, the driver cracked his whip, and as they left Moustier called out, '*Route de Varennes*.'

Now their worst uncertainty was over; once through Clermont they were reaching the country where M. de Bouillé and M. de Choiseul had established their most reliable troops. They would no longer be alone, but protected. The villages they went through were asleep; they were safe at last. With a feeling of elation Marie Antoinette could rest, with her precious children beside her. A new life might begin; like the King she would learn from experience, all would be well. God help them, behind them at Sainte Menehould the tocsin was ringing, in Clermont hardly had they left than Damas lost all control of his troops, the people were out on the streets, two more horsemen had been sent in pursuit, and on their left, hardly two kilometres away, Drouet and Guillaume were pushing their horses towards Varennes.

And on the heights above them the Duc de Choiseul and the Baron de Goguelat were lost with their forty despairing hussars; for five hours they wandered, seeking the road to Varennes.

All these actors in the ensuing drama were almost within hailing distance of each other; when destiny takes a hand in the fate of human beings the chance is so narrow, the failure or success misses or gains by a hairsbreadth, it is on the toss of a coin. But perhaps destiny was always there, the path was laid down from the beginning and must be followed to the end. The little Archduchess dreaming of happiness and splendour was now this woman tracked like a beast who would have sacrificed everything just for one security, that of her children. The choice was not to be given her.

At about nine o'clock the two officers who had been posted at Varennes to arrange for the relay, M. de Bouillé, son of the General, and Captain de Raigecourt, were surprised by the arrival of a cabriolet with one man in it – the coiffeur Léonard. He leapt out and demanded an immediate relay of fresh horses, those he saw waiting there. They were astonished by his manner and his evident haste, and even more so when he assured them that they need not hide anything from him for he knew all, the King and Queen had left Paris but it appeared that they could not continue their journey. He was commissioned, he said, to take the Queen's jewels to Brussels and must depart in haste. They were finally so impressed that they gave him the horses, and so failed to place the King's relay where they had been ordered. However they stayed at their post, and having supped went to bed.

At a quarter to eleven the berlin reached the entrance to the town and drew up with a sudden jolt which awakened the Queen; she looked out of the window expecting to see the relay, but there was no one in sight, and no sound, not even Valory. He had arrived about fifteen minutes before and finding no one where he expected to see the relay, had gone in search of it, or at any rate of the people in charge. He looked about, he even called – nothing – the whole town was asleep. He returned to the road and there found the berlin with its occupants. The King got out and recognizing the post house from the description he had been given went to the row of small houses all shut up, and hammered on the door. From inside a voice called, 'Go on your way, we do not know what you want.' He returned to the coach and the Queen impatiently ordered Moustier to seek somebody sufficiently wide awake to direct them. On the right-hand side of the street was a large house, from which came a ray of light. He pushed the door, and felt somebody pushing from the other side; he pushed harder, he was a strong man – the door gave and he saw a man in a night-shirt and nightcap who asked what he wanted.

'I want you to show me the road leaving the town for Stenay. I am lost and don't know my way.'

'I will do that willingly,' said the other, 'but I will be done for if anyone gets to know about it.'

Said Moustier, 'You are too honest not to wish to help a lady.'

'We know very well who it is, it is not a lady,' replied the man. This remark so appalled Moustier that he broke off the conversation and returned to the berlin followed by the man, to whom the King wished to speak. The fellow had taken off his shoes to make less noise and the sight of him in his big nightcap frightened Madame Royale and made her cry. However he consented to take Moustier to the convent of the Cordeliers where the hussars were quartered and on the way he said that his name was de Préfontaine and that he was a Chevalier of St Louis; but although loyal he was so frightened, so pusillanimous, that he never ceased to swear Moustier to secrecy and silence. At the convent they found one soldier who told them that his Lieutenant – Rohrig, a young German – had ordered him to stay there till one o'clock only. Returning to the berlin it was decided that they would go into the town as far as the Auberge du Grand Monarque at its other end; if the relay was not there at least they could refresh the horses and perhaps persuade the postilions to continue with them to the next relay. The postilions refused to do this but consented to take them as far as the Auberge, and one of them, Arnould, remarked that while they had been waiting he had heard the sound of two horses near by, two post horses his trained ear had told him.

He was right, it was Drouet and Guillaume arriving hot foot to enter Varennes by a side road; dismounting they separated to explore the town for the berlin and the 'treasure'. It was very dark, but they could see vaguely, close to the wall, some carriages and people who were disputing with their postilions as to whether they would proceed. They went on into the town and found an inn still open, the 'Bras d'Or'. Entering they saw a number of young men of the town, Jean Leblanc, Joseph Pouait, Justin George with friends from neighbouring villages who had stayed up late talking politics, for they were all patriots. Drouet took the innkeeper aside and asked 'Are you a good patriot?' Receiving the answer, yes, he cried to them all. 'Alerte! there is a carriage in the town and in it I believe the King and his family'. A stunned silence followed his words and then a clamour of talk; it must be stopped immediately, quick; the postmaster rushed out to put up a barrier across the bridge while Drouet with a Varennais to guide him ran to wake the Procureur of the Commune, Sauce. Jumping from his bed, the latter put on a pair of breeches and a jacket over his nightgown and hastened into the street to wake his neighbour the tanner Pultier, who stood in for the Mayor when he was absent. This citizen woke his three children and told them to run through the town calling out, 'Fire'.

Out of breath they all tore back to the 'Bras d'Or' where they found the two brothers Leblanc, guns in hand; together they rushed to post themselves just where the road descending from the house of Préfontaine passed under the archway of the Church of Saint Gengoult. At this moment they heard the carriages approaching, slowly because the wheels were braked on account of the steep hill. First came a horseman, Valory, they let him come under the vault, then suddenly leapt at him. 'Halt, halt or we fire.' Valory jumped to the ground and the cabriolet stopped. The two ladies, Madame de Neuville and Madame Brunier, stepped out terrified, to see a big man with a lantern facing them. 'The passports quick.' 'They are in the second carriage,' they stammered. The two Leblancs went forward, amazed to see the huge vehicle and perched on top a mountain of baggage. Madame de Tourzel was peering anxiously from a window and behind the brothers could be seen the group of peasants armed with guns. 'The passports,' they insisted. 'Tell them to hurry up, we are in haste to be gone.' The voice was the Queen's. Madame de Tourzel handed the passports to Madame de Neuville, Madame Brunier was huddled against her, and both were pushed into the bar of the inn. Here were Drouet, Guillaume, Pultier representing the Mayor and a huddle of late drinkers who paid little heed to what was going on, except for one voice which said, 'The passport is perfectly in order.' Others then agreed, there was no need to keep the travellers any longer. But Drouet, furious, was not to be persuaded, he was sure it was the King. He shouted and cursed. 'If you let him go you will all be guilty of high treason against the State,' he yelled. Nobody knew what to do. The townspeople were afraid of the responsibility, and besides, who knew whether it really was the King, no one had ever seen him, how could they tell? Even Sauce, the grocer, who insisted on taking his torch and pushing it into the carriage, lighting up first one face and then another, could not be certain. But he would not let them pass for all that. Wait till tomorrow morning, he reiterated, and in any case the horses were not fit to leave. Now the King, losing patience, took a hand. 'Let us go on our way,' he cried. Immediately the guns were levelled. 'Not a step, or we fire.' Louis, leaning forward, could see a menacing crowd in the narrow road, the horses were held, from the town came the ringing of the tocsin, the sound of many feet, the cries of alarm; windows were lighting up, heads flew out. They were caught!

Where could they pass the night? Sauce, now very polite, showed the way into his simple house. The carriage door opened, they all stepped out, the people made way staring. Were these tired dusty travellers really the King and Queen? They had imagined them quite different. Everyone wanted to see, but the party were already within, only the two waiting ladies stayed in the bar room quite exhausted, leaning on the table. Outside the men armed with whatever they could find, spades, scythes, forks, mounted guard. All at once a cry was heard, 'The hussars, the hussars.' It was indeed the detachment of Lauzun with Choiseul and Goguelat at their head, the noise of the tocsin had finally guided them to Varennes.

At the entrance to the town they were stopped. 'Who goes there?' 'France, Lauzun Hussars.' 'No one can pass without order from the municipality.' Choiseul, furious, dispersed the crowd with blows from the flat of his sword and galloped into the town. He saw the cabriolet and a group in front of a house, and without a pause pushed his way to the stables, where he was informed that his hussars were all over the town without an officer. Retracing his way he rejoined his men, who were drawn up in front of the Town Hall. He harangued them, telling them that it was the King, the Queen, and the Dauphin whom they must free or die. Alas, he had forgotten that they were all Germans who could hardly understand a word of French, 'der König, die Königin', that was about all. And now appeared Sauce, who had suddenly recollected that there was a man in the town who had been in Versailles and had certainly seen the King: he could tell them whether the unknown traveller was the monarch or not. Run, fetch Monsieur Desier. Returning with him the two men passed Choiseul and his soldiers and they too held a speech. 'You are all good patriots, we believe the King is in this town, but you will not aid his escape.' The same blank faces were turned to them, but Choiseul, outraged, commanded 'Pas Quatre' and the charge swept the street bare of passers by.

Within their sordid room the Royal Family heard the sound of the horses and a ray of hope entered their weary souls; could it really be a rescue, at this last moment? The door opened and the two men on the threshold saw three silent ladies sitting and a man in a nondescript grey coat and a small round felt hat walking up and down. He turned and looked at them; it was indeed their King, Louis XVI.

There was a deathly silence, broken after a few moments by the King who went to Sauce and threw his arms around his shoulders. 'Yes, I am your King,' he said and then proceeded to embrace all the others present at this extraordinary scene. He included the members of the Council of the Commune and the municipal officers, becoming himself more and more moved as he went. It must have been the sudden relaxation after a day of fatigue, terror, hope and disappointment, together with the feeling that he had always had, that he was the father of his people and in his own words 'wished to be loved'. The Queen too, though less moved, showed her agitation, and most of the onlookers were in tears. Louis explained that he had only left Paris because of the constant insults to which he was subjected, that he had no intention of leaving the country, but would stay among his faithful subjects. He spoke the truth, for having always loved history he had employed the time in the prison of the Tuileries by reading English history and had formed the opinion that the cardinal fault of James II lay in leaving England and that Charles I was beheaded because he had made war on his own people. He was firmly decided to do neither.

It was a curious scene; the King, very calm now, talking, while the Queen barely hiding her anxiety was seated with Madame de Tourzel nodding beside her. In the background the three guards and the two ladies brought from the 'Bras d'Or', Madame Elisabeth the silent onlooker, while outside the growing multitude sounded as a crowd always does, with the vague growling noise of many voices together. Now came Choiseul and Goguelat to pay their respects, and Damas with six of his dragoons. Drawing Louis aside they proposed a daring scheme, the King should mount a horse with the Dauphin in his arms, the Queen equally with Madame Royale (it must be remembered that they were excellent riders), and with Madame Elisabeth mounted too their men would take the two ladies, and surrounded by the rest of the troop they should with a sudden sally get away. But the King had too much sense to accept the proposal. What if a chance shot should wound or kill the Queen or the Dauphin, he said. No, it was better to wait; the municipality had promised to send them on to Montmédy if they waited till daylight, and at any moment Bouillé might appear.

Now with the rising sun the crowds, augmented by peasants from the surrounding villages – news flies quickly in the country – flocked to Varennes and soon the little town took on the appearance of a fair. The bakers were busy, the inns were full. Everyone talked at once, everyone had his own version of the story; those who had seen the King described him to those who had not, and among the crowds wandered the soldiers, mostly drunk. At three o'clock the lawyer Mangin left the grocer's where he had been in conference. He was on his way to Paris to take the orders of the Assembly. The mass applauded him. Until now they had been good-natured, excited no doubt, but there was no violence. But suddenly the rumour that Bouillé was on his way stiffened the atmosphere. Bouillé, he would come to take away the King, to massacre any who resisted, the patriots were in danger, and the town too, it might be burned. One knew this Royal Allemand, they were foreigners who could have no interest in good patriots or the Revolution.

Marshal Bouillé, having waited in vain for the arrival of the King in Stenay, had gathered his troops and after a gruelling passage through mountainous country had indeed arrived in the neighbourhood of Varennes. He sent an officer, Monsieur Deslon, to the King to ask what were the orders, what could he do, and the King sent back the dispiriting response, 'I am a prisoner, I can give no orders; tell M. de Bouillé that I am afraid he can do nothing for me, but I ask him to do what he can.'

But now the temper of the mob was changing, a voice cried, 'He came from Paris, let him go back there.' It was taken up and passed along. In the Town Hall the officials could not reach a decision; would it be *lèse majesté* to prevent the King from proceeding to Montmédy, ought he not to go back to Paris? In the middle of all this at 5 a.m. two horsemen presented themselves at the entrance to Varennes; they were Bayon and Romeuf. Worn out and choked with dust, hardly able to speak, they were taken to the grocer's and Sauce showed the way into the room where Louis XVI was sitting, his family grouped around him, the two children asleep in the corner. Choiseul and Damas were still there, and the former describes the scene. Romeuf, when he saw the

Queen who passed him every day at the Tuileries, halted and let Bayon go in first. Fatigue and emotion tightened his throat. 'Sire,' he stammered, 'Sire, Paris has gone mad, our wives, our children are threatened . . .' The Queen took his hand and pointing to the Dauphin and his sister said, 'And am I not also a mother?'

'Now, what do you want?' this from the King.

'Sire, a decree from the Assembly.'

'Where is it?'

'My comrade has it.'

He opened the door and Romeuf could be seen leaning on the balustrade sobbing. He had a paper in his hand, which he presented to the King. Marie Antoinette spoke:

'What, it is you, I could never have believed it.'

Louis XVI took the paper and read it aloud. 'Order to all functionaries to arrest all the individuals of the royal family.' He looked at his Queen and said slowly 'There is no longer a King in France.' So saying he laid the paper on the children's bed. Marie Antoinette snatched it up, exclaiming 'I will not allow it to soil my children.' The onlookers murmured and Choiseul, fearing an explosion, lifted it and put it on the table.

Earlier in the night the grandmother of Sauce, an old peasant of nearly ninety, had made her way into the town having heard that the King and his son were there. She was old enough to remember the Great King, she had known no other France, they let her go up to the room where the King was. She saluted him with a profound reverence and turned to the sleeping Dauphin, the Child of France. All her faith, all her respect and veneration were in her gesture as she dropped to her knees beside the couch to bless the sleeping child; she could not, and hiding her wrinkled face in her hands she sobbed bitterly.

Now the King, having recovered his habitual coolness, drew the two envoys of the Assembly aside and implored them to allow his party to wait at any rate till eleven o'clock; they seemed to agree, but Bayon on leaving the room went into the street telling the mob that the King wished to await the arrival of Bouillé and inciting them to ever louder cries of rage. He was successful. 'Let them depart; to Paris, to Paris, we will drag them by the feet into their carriage,' they yelled, surging, trampling, half in anger against the King, half in fear of what Bouillé might do to them when he came. They were insensible to the pleas of the municipality, who were forced to go to the King and entreat him to depart. The Queen was in a dreadful state and went so far as to beg the grocer's wife to help them, but the woman only answered: 'My goodness Madame, your position is very annoying, but my husband has the responsibility, and I do not want him to have any trouble,' and went on preparing the breakfast which the King had asked for in the hope of gaining a few more minutes. He ate slowly, pretending to be overcome, and slumped in his seat; then Madame de Neuville, really worn out, fainted. This gained a little more time, for Marie Antoinette refused to go without her. And all the time the noise outside grew louder and more menacing, the first troops had been seen in the woods. Sauce, appalled by the disaster but frightened for his own safety, listened while the King implored him to go to the carriage and to bring away a small coffer which contained papers which must be destroyed. Marie Antoinette pictured for him the horrors which they had sought to evade in leaving Paris, the constant fear of death, and the danger to them all if on their return Orléans and his party should get hold of these documents. At last the grocer weakened, he went hurriedly to the carriage and returned with the papers and the whole royal party threw themselves into the work of destroying them; they tried to burn them, in vain, and finally they threw them in tiny fragments out of the window where the wind took them up and blew them away.

It was now seven o'clock and the carriage was in front of the house. The King was forced at last to give the order to leave. The three bodyguards were on the box, and the hussars who should have saved them all mingled with the crowds crying 'Vive la Nation'. Then the door of the little room which had seen so much tragedy, so much despair, opened. The King descended the stairs followed by the Queen supported by the arm of Choiseul, then Madame Elisabeth with Damas; Madame de Tourzel and the children were the last to appear. They got into the berlin, the crowd, quieted for a moment, cried 'Vive le Roi' as well as 'Vive la Nation'. Choiseul closed the door. 'Do not leave us,' said the Queen in a broken voice, but the berlin lurched forward and he was thrown off. He felt an inexpressible anguish, and a witness who caught sight of Marie Antoinette's face with its expression of unbearable fatigue and suffering wrote that he had never in his life felt what he felt in that moment. Outside the carriage the people were exulting, they ran alongside and many even meant to accompany it to Paris, where they pictured even greater glory and triumph.

They were little people in a little unimportant village, they could not know to what an extent they had played their part in history, nor what the future could hold for them of suffering, calamity, glory, and pain. The next twenty-five years would teach the French many lessons, but do nations ever learn any more than the human beings who compose them? When the King came down those stairs they saw a man very like themselves, rather stout and ordinary looking and some of them may have even felt sorry for him and ashamed. But for him France and himself were one and inseparable; although he was vacillating and weak he was not stupid, and as his brother-in-law had said, his business was royalty, without it he was nothing, with it he was the sixteenth Louis. His ancestors had made the nation, it was theirs and he belonged to it. It could give him up, he could never renounce it. As for Marie Antoinette, she had never had much opinion of the French, even as a child she had commented on their frivolousness, their capacity for sudden change of mood. To this she had now added a profound disgust; but her son was the Dauphin and till it was no longer possible she would fight for him. She would never leave, never accept security for herself alone, she would take unflinching whatever was in store for her, but she would endure with them till the end.

One quarter of an hour after their departure, one little quarter of an hour, General Bouillé arrived on the other side of the river facing the town, so near that he could even see the berlin slowly climbing the hill outside it. If he had only known that a little further on the road passed to the right hand side of the river, he could have cut off the cortège there and rescued the prisoners. But helplessly he sounded the retreat from the village of Ratantout,* a fatal name it seems.

A crowd of six thousand men and women accompanied the coach, raising a cloud of dust in the gathering heat. After about an hour a body of dragoons were seen in the distance and the crowd panicked, fearing that it would be a rescue party. On the contrary, they were the soldiers who had defected from the command at Clermont the previous evening. They had elected another officer

* Everything lost.

in the place of Damas and accompanied the National Guard of Clermont, and the town council sent to meet the King. Devillay, the President of the district, approached to harangue the King and to express the alarm of the citizens at the thought that their monarch was leaving them. Louis replied shortly that he had not intended to do so, the Queen and the children 'appeared sick, and worn out with fatigue', and the cortège moved on into the town. It was ten o'clock. An enormous crowd was gathered in the narrow streets, the berlin could only move at a snail's pace and on every side rose the cry, '*Vive la Nation*.' Sunk in bitter reflections, silent, the royal party were forced to hear the applause which greeted their retreat. Only the Varennais were uncertain, faced with the results of their actions, moreover they feared for their town, the rumour spread that it was in flames; better to go home and leave the future to take care of itself. After giving up the passport in the name of Madame de Korff to the Clermontais, Sauce led his fellow townsmen home.

From now on the journey was a real Way of the Cross for the unfortunate family. The heat was suffocating and even more the dust raised by the thousands of feet. It was like a fog, it permeated everything, the Queen's clothes were white with it; as soon as some villagers left, having gazed their fill, others equally curious took their place. The vast plain spread in front of them and smouldered in the sun, as the day wore on, a furnace of heat. The windows of the carriage were open and through them came an unending bombardment of insults. At Sainte Menehould the Mayor met them and led them to the Town Hall, where they were regaled with a lunch. The King was speechless, the Queen and Madame Elisabeth were grey with dust, the Dauphin could hardly keep awake. They were served with distinction, etiquette still held, the Queen pleased the onlookers by the attention she paid to her little son; he had not been undressed for a day and a half and she feared for him. The Mayor offered them the hospitality of his house, which the Queen accepted at once, and their departure was postponed till dawn next day. But the mob had other ideas. Doubtless the relentless heat affected them too, for cries were heard, 'We are betrayed, they are waiting for Bouillé, to Chalons, to Chalons.' 'Very well, very well, let us go,' said the King with resignation.

As he was about to descend the stairs he saw, through a grating which was between the Town Hall and the jail, the prisoners looking through; taking from his purse a piece of ten louis to which the Queen added five, he gave it to the Mayor to be distributed among the captives and continued on his way sadly, without saying a word. They all remounted the carriage.

At three o'clock they left, among a crowd of wretched men and women in such a state of ferocious excitement that the magistrates of Chalons who had come to receive them despaired of ever reaching the carriage and returned without even seeing it. Through village after village they went, always surrounded, always insulted, speechless, worn out, with what thoughts we may imagine, till at last they reached Chalons. At the entrance to the town Marie Antoinette could see the Arc de Triomphe which had been erected to welcome her on her journey from Vienna; the cavalcade, so different from that which had met her then, stopped at the Prefecture and at last the tortured party could leave their carriages and hope for a little respite; they had not slept since their departure from the Tuileries. But even now they did not dare to relax. The authorities of the town were loyalists to a man, they even proposed to the King that he should escape by a hidden staircase and rejoin Bouillé, but this would have meant leaving his wife and children, and he refused. They counted on the arrival of the National Guard from Rheims, and these men, if they were of the same opinion as the Chalonais, would protect them. Louis XVI was sure that his 'good Rémois' would be on his side. He would wait, it would gain time. At half past two in the morning they went at last to bed and Marie Antoinette could enjoy a troubled slumber.

But when the 'good Rémois' arrived they proved to be nothing more than a motley crew of the dregs of the city, who were determined that the King should leave immediately for Rheims, there to be exhibited to all who wished to see him. His Majesty acquiesced, only asking that he be permitted to go to Mass and afterwards to dine. This was conceded and at ten o'clock he appeared and went to the chapel, but hardly had the office begun than the crowd forced the soldiers who had guarded him aside and broke into the building yelling, 'Capet is fat enough for what we have in mind,' and 'We will eat their hearts and liver.' It was more true than one can believe, the people were mad with a rage which they themselves could not have explained, they were like wild beasts unthinking, driven on by their own seething passion, a terrifying multitude. The King and his party, giving up all thought of food, sought the shelter of the berlin, under strong guard. Only at midday was the cavalcade again under way, protected by the City Guards, who forced a road at a foot pace. But at the village of Malougues a runner from Chalons brought the news that the town was being sacked, shops and houses were pillaged, help must be brought, and the Guards turned and abandoned the Royal Family to the Rémois. At Chouilly the inhabitants, gathered to see the King, could hardly believe that the spectacle that met their eyes was possible. The sun poured down an unremitting blaze, the carriage was almost lost under the mass which surrounded it. A man leapt to the step and spat directly into the King's face. Louis, saying nothing, wiped off the spit with a trembling hand, the Queen and Madame Elisabeth wept tears of complete resignation to misery, and the Calvary continued on its way to Epernay.

Here they stopped 'for refreshment' and a pathway was managed for them between the ranks of madmen. One of the guards carried the Dauphin high above their heads, and the little boy finding himself separated from his mother shrieked with fear and wept so that his tears wet the cheeks of the man who carried him to his mother, who had found refuge in an adjoining room. Her dress was torn, and was mended by the weeping daughter of the house. The King was cleaning himself when one of the Epernassiens said to him 'this is what one gets when one wants to travel'. Louis replied that he had not wished to leave France, but he could not stay in Paris where his family was in danger. 'Oh yes, sir, you can!' was the cynical response. But another voice was heard while they were dining, 'They seem to be good folk all the same,' it said.

After one hour it was time to go and they returned to the berlin guarded by a strong escort of National Guards. Madame de Tourzel was hoisted nearly fainting into the carriage and when the Queen appeared, a woman shrieked at her, 'Well my dear, you will see a lot more of this.' It was true. From then on Bayon, who was commanding the guards, lost all authority, and the few decent people in the crowds were of the opinion that they would never reach Paris alive.

Their torment continued until they reached the farm of Chêne Fendu, on the banks of the Marne. Here they were met by the three deputies sent by the Assembly, Pétion and Barnave who were of the moderately advanced party, and their colleague Latour-Maubourg who was of the right. They had left Paris at four o'clock that morning and had had an agreeable drive through the country which the royal party had seen a few days before. At the village of Dormans where they halted to dine they were met by conflicting rumours which decided them to hasten, and from there on they saw the gathering crowds of country people, who from fear of the expected troops of Bouillé were gathering on the roadsides.

At seven o'clock a distant rumour and an immense cloud of dust announced the approach of the berlin. They waited, it slowly drew up, a path was carved through the compact mass of people and the carriage door opened. A confused sound met them. 'Ah messieurs, messieurs,' came from Madame Elisabeth, and the Queen holding out her hand echoed it 'Ah Monsieur de Maubourg, thank God.' They were almost speechless, could only stammer through their tears, while the King with sudden volubility declared to anyone who would listen that he had never meant to leave France. Pétion, who was, or affected to be, the more brutal of the three, interrupted the 'cackling' to read the Assembly's decree which gave the three commissioners full powers. He climbed on the box-seat and read it twice, emphasizing the fact that they must be obeyed. He then descended and indicated that they would seat themselves in the berlin. At this Latour-Maubourg decided that he would ride with the ladies in the cabriolet and Pétion and Barnave once they had entered the carriage saw how little room there would be for two more persons. 'Sire, we will make you too uncomfortable,' they said, 'We will find some other place', but the King insisted that they could manage; the Queen took the Dauphin on her knees and Barnave seated himself between her and the King. Pétion took the seat between Madame Elisabeth and Madame de Tourzel, while Madame Royale stood in front of her governess.

Now here were these strangely assorted people who would travel two days in this close proximity, seeing every gesture, almost hearing every thought, learning each of them to know beings so different from themselves in birth, in tradition, in belief and yet still all six human beings. Pétion, thirty-eight years old, robust, popular, of bourgeois origin, was amazed to see how simply the royal family bore themselves. The Queen dandled her son on her knees, he saw the King in his dirty clothes, and what a natural person he was. 'One would think that this mass of flesh is insensible,' he recorded later, 'but one would deceive oneself. It is very seldom that he speaks without sense.'

The Queen at first disassociated herself from them all; she pulled down her veil and remained mute. Gradually, however, she was drawn into the conversation while her little boy sitting so close to Barnave got down and stood against his knee. From there he kept up a running fire of questions, in the manner of lively and inquisitive children, and at last wishing no doubt to show off his learning he took to spelling the motto on the deputy's coat buttons. '*Vivre libre ou mourir*',★ he repeated, 'Listen Maman *Vivre libre ou mourir*, look, look, on all of them, *Vivre libre ou mourir*.' Marie Antoinette made no reply. But she set herself to speak of her ideas for education, and a lively discussion ensued. The cortège ground slowly on, it was now night and cooler, the moon rose, the children slept, Madame Royale with her cheek against the sleeve of Pétion, they were almost one family. Barnave spoke quietly with the Queen, the King dozed, and at last they came to Dormans, where all was illuminated and shouts of '*Vive l'Assemblé, Vive la Nation, Vive Barnave, Vive Pétion*', met their ears.

They entered the Hôtel where they would stay the night, the guards were set, the table with their supper was ready, and Pétion without thinking sat down but was pulled up by Barnave refusing politely to seat himself with the royal family, who were always served alone. Their night was hardly a tranquil one. The National Guards sang, drank and shouted beneath their windows and the poor little Dauphin awoke sobbing from a bad dream in which he was in a forest pursued by wolves, and Maman Reine was in danger. He could not be quieted till he was taken to his mother. At seven o'clock next morning they were on their way again; it was Friday 24 June and the sun was already high and burning. Pétion this time took his place between the King and Queen, Barnave between Madame Elisabeth and Madame de Tourzel. The deputy, thirty years old, handsome and of a better family and upbringing than his colleague was by this time becoming more interested in the Queen and she in him. The King, immersed in his Itinerary and his maps which he had studied

★ Live in freedom or die.

throughout the journey, paid little heed to Pétion, who endeavoured to give him a lesson on the beauty of the country which he had thought to leave. 'How lovely it is,' he said. 'There is no country in the world that can compare with it.' The Queen on the other hand was very talkative, saying that what was most important in the education of children was that the character should be developed. 'One must have character until the very end,' she announced, throwing a piece of the pigeon she was eating out of the window, which she insisted on closing with the curtain in spite of the protests of the clamouring crowd. 'Show us your face 'Toinette,' they shouted, and they also insisted that the Dauphin should cry '*Vive la Nation*', which he did with good grace, not having the remotest idea what the words signified for him.

At La Ferté-sous-Jouarre they stopped for dinner at about two o'clock. The Mayor had offered his house, an elegant building with balconies and a terrace overlooking the Marne, a delicious retreat after their miserable journey. Here the ladies could repair their toilettes and the men stretch their legs. The beautiful calm river delighted them all, and the King, relaxed and happy, invited all to dine with him. The children played, the dinner was served simply but well, says Madame de Tourzel, and the mistress of the house Madame Regnard de Lisle would not sit down as the King wished but stood behind the Queen's chair. 'Are you the mistress of this house?' asked Her Majesty. 'I was until you came Madame,' was the loyal reply. At the end of dinner when they all regained the terrace, Monsieur Regnard de Lisle came up to Barnave and said 'If you permit, we will cry, *Vive le Roi*.'

At five o'clock Dumas gave the signal to depart, and the journey continued to Meaux where they arrived at eight o'clock; here the narrow streets were already full of a waiting mob reinforced in their vicious hate by some of the dregs of Paris. The guard with difficulty forced a way to the Episcopal Palace where the party spent the night in the immense cold unfurnished rooms. The King slept, but the Queen, already agitated, tried to find out something of the feeling in Paris; she was particularly anxious about their bodyguards, the three men who had accompanied them on their flight; even Barnave at first had believed that the figure on the box was that of Fersen in disguise, and though this was not true, they were all three in great danger, the crowds having already almost murdered them.

At six o'clock next day they were en route once more, under a brassy sky, the forerunner of a furnace-like day. Barnave seated himself once more between the King and Queen, Pétion opposite and the Dauphin between Barnave's knees. This was the most dangerous, the most frightening part of the journey: it lasted thirteen hours. The King, very much at his ease, ate and drank, and Pétion followed suit, pouring wine for himself and Madame Elisabeth and then holding out his glass for her to replenish. The Queen and the two ladies took nothing, but the Dauphin was constantly thirsty. By ten o'clock they were descending the steep hill leading to Claye, with what reflections we may imagine. Here Paris was close, and the angry mobs grew louder. Now by midday it was Bondy where they met a detachment of the Paris Guard. The grenadiers escorting them refused to make way and there was a tussle during which a group of ferocious women, always the worst, forced their way under the bellies of the horses to the carriage, screaming the most filthy threats at the Queen. 'She has a nerve showing us her boy,' they shouted, 'everyone knows he is not fat Louis' son.' The little boy, terrified, hung on his mother's neck, and Pétion saw Marie Antoinette's tears.

At three o'clock they arrived at Pantin, here La Fayette awaited them with a completely silent crowd; the word had gone out, heads covered, no cries, no noise. In this fantastic silence the berlin, completely submerged beneath the men who hung on every available finger space, made its slow way. Past the barrier of Villette, along the walls which surrounded the city, up to the barrier of Monceau where the King, to give himself courage, demanded a glass of wine which he swallowed at a gulp; down the long hill of the Champs Elysées always guarded by a hedge of National Guards keeping back the masses, across the Place black with people and silent as the grave.

At the terrace of the palace of the Tuileries the six deputies from the Assembly sent to receive the King arrived just in time. It was a critical moment. How were they to make the few steps necessary to gain the refuge of the palace? Already the crowd, mad with blood lust, demanded the lives of the three unhappy guards, still sitting scarcely protected on the box. Dumas tried in vain to command; his hat was lost, his belt torn from him, Moustier fell, he disappeared in the tumult, no, he was saved and dragged half dead into the vestibule, the second, more fortunate, managed to gain the shelter without wounds. La Fayette rallied his troops, they made a hedge, the deputies appeared and the mob took breath, and suddenly there was a silence. The door of the berlin opened, the King appeared, and he walked calmly into the palace followed by the Queen who stepped down and was quickly seized by M. de Noailles and the Duc d'Aiguillon, two men whom she detested, and rushed into the palace. They mounted the staircase which led to their apartments, the valets were there waiting and the other persons in their service, they might have arrived from a hunting party except that Pétion had been pushed about by the crowd, and saying that he was half dead with thirst demanded that Madame Elisabeth should pour out a drink for him. This she did smiling, thinking perhaps that this would be the end of her trials. The King disappeared into his private apartments, he seemed to be quite happy to be back again, nobody would have believed what he had been through, such was his phlegm. Suddenly the Queen cried out, where was her son? She had last seen him beside the carriage, how did he come to be separated from her, what was being done with him? There was a moment of frightful suspense, but it was quickly over when she found that two deputies had carried him, tired out, to his own rooms. Marie Antoinette controlled herself, and approaching La Fayette who stood there waiting, she offered him her keys of the coffers left in the berlin. He refused to take them, protesting that no one dreamed of opening her private coffers. With a disdainful gesture she threw them into the hat which he was holding and when he said that it would be difficult for her to take them back again since he would not touch them, she replied, with irony 'Oh I shall find people less delicate than you!' It was in small actions such as this that she let her disgust and resentment be seen, but when one considers what provocation she had suffered, it was perhaps justified. La Fayette had his own justification; the King, still imperturbable, having written some letters and feeling himself once more a prisoner, told his valet to show them to the General before sending them away. La Fayette protested vehemently that he was not a spy, and asked what orders His Majesty had for him. 'It seems,' said the King laughing, 'that I am much more obliged to take orders from you than you from me.' And indeed it was he who set the guards before leaving with the three deputies who went to the Assembly to make their report.

On the next day three new deputies waited on the King to take his deposition, and that over, wished to see the Queen. Word was sent that she was at the moment in her bath but that she would see them on the 27th, the next day. And when they appeared she offered them armchairs while she herself took a simple seat, another gesture of cynical resignation which was doubtless not lost on them. Her declaration was not well received by the Assembly, that of the King was better; he was already being forgiven while she was still regarded as the chief culprit. She knew it and when the day after one of her women complimented her on her good looks she simply took of her cap and showed her hair, grown quite white 'like that of a woman of seventy years'.

The King however entered in his diary 'I took some milk', and doubtless he enjoyed a sound sleep.

7

History Marches On

HAVING seen the berlin with its precious passengers disappearing in the distance, Axel de Fersen prepared to set out for Mons where he arrived at six o'clock two days later, to find the town in an effervescence of joy. Monsieur had arrived bringing the news of the flight, all the French emigrants were jubilant and Fersen noted in his carefully kept *Journal* that a monk asked him in the street if the King was saved. At this precise moment, six o'clock, at Varennes, Romeuf and Bayon presented the King with the Assembly's decree. Axel wrote his father a short note telling him the news and saying that he was preparing to join the Royal Family at Montmédy. He noted in his *Journal* that he took a carriage and left at eleven o'clock, without wasting any time in rest, passed Namur still early, for the road was one of the best in France, and next day gained Arlon, where at the posting house he ran into Bouillé. What was the General doing in Arlon? The King is arrested – stupefaction! The wretched Axel was speechless. How could such a thing be, what had happened to the soldiers, were they late, who was to blame? He was so stunned that all he entered in the *Journal* were the two words *'reposé là'* (stayed there).

Before leaving at 4 a.m. he wrote two letters, one to the King of Sweden, the other to his father. The first said 'Sire, everything is lost! The King has been arrested at sixteen leagues from the frontier and taken to Paris. I am going to see Monsieur de Mercy.'

The second, 'Everything is lost my dear father and I am in despair. The King has been arrested at Varennes. . . . Judge of my pain and be sorry for me, it is M. de Bouillé who is here, who has brought this news. I am leaving at this moment for Brussels to hand to the Comte de Mercy the letter which the King has given to me.' Riding hard he arrived in Brussels at two in the afternoon. For five days and nights he had hardly rested, what matter, he could not rest, and he noted in the *Journal*, 'Everything is in disorder here, everyone seems mad, thousands of rumours, all false.' Only on the 28th did he receive accurate tidings, worse than all the rest, of the King's entry into Paris with Barnave and Pétion in the carriage, and commented 'Horror, no applause.'

He had found his friends Crawford and Madame Sullivan in Brussels, so he was not without consolation. He saw Marie Antoinette's sister the Archduchess Marie Christine, the Comte de Provence and his wife, and the Comte d'Artois with Calonne, his inseparable companion and mentor, arrived. At last Fersen received his first word from Marie Antoinette. On 5 July he wrote to his sister, 'I have decided to sacrifice myself for them as long as there is a ray of hope. It is this idea alone which sustains me', and he told her that he had decided to go to Vienna as the Governor, Marie Antoinette's sister, had suggested. On the 30th he wrote to Marie Antoinette the same thing and on the following day he had her first letter, written during her return to Paris: 'Be reassured for us, we are alive. The heads of the Assembly seem to wish to modify their conduct. Speak to my relations on the subject of possible action.' Next day came a second letter:

I exist. . . . How anxious I have been on your account, and how I pity you in having no news of us. Heaven grant that this arrives. Do not write to me, it would be dangerous and above all do not come here, on any pretext whatever. It is known that it was you who brought us away from here; everything would be lost if you appeared. We are watched day and night. Be calm, nothing will happen to me. . . . Adieu . . . I cannot write you again.

It was true, this time they were really prisoners. The courtyards were full of soldiers, right under their windows, probably for fear, says Madame Elisabeth with some humour, that they would try to jump out! At every door was a sentinel, and even on the roof-tops. All their apartments had been thoroughly gone through by La Fayette, who went so far as to send chimney sweeps to examine the chimneys – for the same reason? Even in the Queen's chamber two National Guards were stationed day and night, with orders not to let her out of their sight; she was obliged to get up, to perform her toilet, and to dress with their eyes upon her. Since the chapel was considered too far from their apartment to be serviceable, another was installed nearer to them, and even here they were under surveillance. When the Queen visited her son she was escorted by two officers; she found the door closed and was obliged to announce herself before it could be opened by the guard within.

Weber recounts an incident which is not without its humorous side. One night when she could not sleep she lit her candle and began to read. The guard seeing this, opened the curtains of her bed and said, 'I see that you cannot sleep, let us talk together, that's better than reading', and seating himself on her bed he proceeded to do so. She controlled her indignation and made him understand that his presence was not acceptable at that hour.

Under these conditions their life regained its normal dull routine; they rose, they went to Mass, they dined, and because the King could no longer take his exercise in hunting they played billiards after each meal. The Queen never went out but stayed and played with her children, finding in them her usual pleasure. At seven in the evening they received their entourage and at eleven they went to bed. In these circumstances she had plenty of time for thought, and her habitual energy returned when she began to reflect upon the problems which faced them all.

In the first place she considered the King, and she was forced to admit, after the intensive study she could make of the last few days, that owing to his lethargic nature and his good-natured ability to compromise in any situation, he would be practically unable to take drastic action for their safety. Mirabeau had said of him, 'Imagine some billiard balls slippery with oil which you vainly seek to hold together.' This was what she had to do. She considered the forces ranged against them; first her known enemies of whom the chief was the Duc d'Orléans. This vile creature whom she had once offended had for years worked against her, his was the press which disseminated the poisonous news-sheets and lampoons, it was from the Palais Royal that the propaganda blackening her character was sent out. He had his centres in every province and town in France through the Freemasons of whom he was the Grand Master. The Jacobin Clubs were widely spread, and Orléans had close ties with them also, and further to the left and still more violently opposed to the monarchy, there were the Cordeliers, the Society of the Rights of Man and the Citizen, who immediately after Varennes expressed themselves in favour of a Republic. The new men were in this group, Danton, the peasant from the Champagne, huge, loud voiced and ugly. 'Nature has given me an athletic frame and the rough features of Freedom,' he declared. Then Camille Desmoulins, the orator, fiery and excitable, Marat, bitter, ruthless, the Friend of the People, and finally Robespierre, green-eyed, icy, arrogant, and convinced of his own infallible rectitude, the incorruptible. What chance had she against such men? But she would fight, and since she was a woman, she must fight with a woman's weapons, charm, deceit, flexibility, and a hopeless courage. In this fight she would show herself as a most exceptional woman.

Her last and perhaps most difficult enemies were her friends and relations, the émigrés, those who had left her in her trouble and now from safety thought to dictate her line of conduct. Over and over again she must insist that she and the King were the sole judges of what was expedient in their situation. Her words went unheeded. 'They think themselves heroes,' she said ironically. 'Fine heroes! What will they do, these heroes, even with the King of Sweden at their back?' Another time she exploded, 'If my brothers-in-law are successful in helping us, our gratitude will be a heavy burden for us and we will have them as masters, the most demanding of all.'

As we have said, the spies and agents provocateurs of Orléans had been busy. Their object was to keep the populace in a ferment and on 17 July the citizens were convoked to a mass meeting on the Champ de Mars to sign a document, put together in the most insolent terms, calling for the King's abdication. An enormous crowd gathered, the National Guard was called in, they were stoned and the Mayor, Bailly, ordered a burst of fire. No one was hurt and the mob refused to disperse, on which Bailly read the martial law, and hoisted the red flag. A second burst of fire shook them, they fled, and the place was cleared. The immediate result was that the firmness on the part of the authorities created a certain pause in the inflammable public situation and this was felt in the Tuileries.

Added to this the Constitutionals were now clear as to the designs of the extremists in the Assembly, and the understanding which Barnave in particular had achieved with the Queen influenced them in seceding from the Jacobins and founding the Club of the Feuillants. They feared anarchy, the populace was going too far and some steadying force must be introduced; this was the basis for the growing relations between the Queen and the Triumvirate, Barnave, Alexandre Lameth, and Duport. The Queen on her side was not fully convinced of the sincerity of their cooperation: she could not but be suspicious of these men who had until so shortly before been her enemies but she had no better contacts. From this uncertainty stems the contradictory nature of her subsequent policy.

From her conversations with Barnave during their journey to the capital, she had come to realize that the only hope for the King lay in his recognition of the Constitution which was being prepared; though faulty, it represented the ardent desire of the nation and thus it was out of the question for him to think of a reinstatement of the *ancien régime* with its absolute monarchy. In these circumstances she had to continue her contact with Barnave who through his deep and ardent republicanism had much influence in the Assembly, and was personally sympathetic to her. In the early days of July she wrote to the General de Jarjayes, the husband of one of her women, the following:

I wish that you should try to see 2-I [her code for Barnave] for me, and that you should say that, struck by his character which I recognized during the two days which we spent together, I very much wish to hear from him what we have to do in the situation in which we find ourselves. Having thought deeply since my return about the strength, the means, and the spirit of the man with whom I conversed, I felt that there was nothing to do but to establish a sort of correspondence with him, reserving for myself however as a first condition, that I will always say quite frankly what I think, that I praise what I think good and condemn what I think bad. This condition accepted, our correspondence can begin at once. I will number each paper; my paper shall be returned to me with the answers dictated to my agent. Thus there will be no danger from writings discovered and recognized.

She added that he could count on her discretion and her character, which for the general good would always know how to temporize when it was necessary. They could not simply do nothing, it was certain that they must do something. But what? It was for this that she addressed him. She insisted on her good faith, but at the same time she wrote to Fersen that she would keep all this correspondence for him and that a committee of five persons had been formed to advise together, and she gave the names: Barnave, Duport, Alexandre Lameth, d'André, and Dumas.

This agreed, the five recommended their plan. First, the King should approve the new Constitution. This done, various actions should be insisted on – the return of the Princes and the émigrés, recognition by the Emperor of the Constitution, and a declaration by him of his friendly and peaceful intentions towards France. The King and Queen must do all in their power to implement these aims, for the spectacle of the first European monarch dethroned could only encourage a revolutionary movement in all nations. The first duty of the Princes and the émigrés was to seize the moment when they could return with honour for their own advantage, for that of the King and for a peaceful France. This tied in well with the Queen's own thought; she had insisted from the beginning that there should be no invasion, that civil war was of all things the most to be avoided, a point she underlined again in a letter to her brother on 30 July. When Lameth and Duport showed uncertainty as to the Queen's capacity for consistent thought, the pressure of day to day events forced them to admit that unless they held solid behind the monarch the Republican party would succeed in deposing him, and Barnave in the Assembly declared that 'when the nation is free, when all French men are equal, to ask for more would be the moment when they would begin to be less free and to become culprits'. And even Robespierre could not disagree.

As a result the King was declared to be 'suspended' until he could approve the new Constitution with which the Assembly was in travail. Marie Antoinette had ended her letter to Leopold by saying that she thought the King might find in the disposition of the nation, once calmed and at ease, more deference and loyalty than he could hope for from those French who were actually outside the kingdom. As for them, the essential thing was to keep them quiet, and to do this they should return to France. But since, on 9 July, the Assembly had voted to sequester their properties she also pointed out to Barnave that it was not quite a happy moment to ask them to listen to negotiations. However the Constitutionals now sent two men on missions, one, the Chevalier de Coigny, to Coblentz, the headquarters of the Princes, and the other, the Abbé Louis, to Brussels where he would see and confer with Mercy. Before leaving the two had an interview with Louis XVI and Marie Antoinette, and the King in the presence of Ministers gave M. de Coigny a letter for the Comte d'Artois, and another, sealed, for Monsieur and M. de Montmorin. In the first the King advised his brothers to return to France, writing that the Constitution had the faith of all the nation behind it and it was impossible to fight it. In the second, he added that the Princes should only consider the well-being of France without regard to his personal advantage, and that they could have complete confidence in de Coigny. When he arrived in Coblentz and the Princes had read this they asked de Coigny if this could be the real desire of the King, to which he replied that as far as he could judge, somewhat equivocally, the King wished for the safety of himself, his family and all those faithful to him. This accorded so well with what they wanted themselves that buoyed up by the support of the King of Sweden, they were all the more determined on action.

As for the Abbé, before leaving for Brussels he had a long interview with Marie Antoinette in which he detailed the three courses open to her; either she could support the Princes, or she could throw in her lot with the democratic party, or she could gain time and wait till the people had come to their senses, and endeavour by her behaviour to make the royal family once more acceptable to the nation. It was the third alternative which she favoured, and the Abbé proposed that as a sign of her preference she should endeavour to persuade the Emperor, as the most involved of the Powers, to affirm his alliance with France, to withdraw from the émigrés and thus to help his sister to modify the distrust of the people. She led the Abbé to believe that she agreed with him and gave him a letter to Mercy, which urged him to return to Paris, for she badly needed his advice and help; in reality she was full of suspicion and was playing a double game. Her correspondence with Fersen proves this. Axel during all these weeks had been in Brussels and had constituted himself the clearing house for all the correspondence between the Powers, the émigrés and finally the King and Queen. It was the ideal spot for him; the Regent of the Low Countries was Marie Antoinette's sister, the Archduchess Marie Christine; Mercy was there, as were Metternich, representing Austria, and the Baron de Breteuil, who since his departure from France in 1789 had been Louis XVI's secret agent abroad, all of them determined for one reason or another to save the Royal House and support the counter-revolution.

Their aims were completely opposed to those of the Princes and émigrés: they were disinterested while the Coblentz conspirators were pre-occupied with their own advantage. Under the sinister influence of Calonne they were determined to defeat the Revolution by force if necessary and all the Queen's insistence on the danger from such a policy went unheeded. She told them that the army was helpless, with no money and no arms, and that the people on the other hand possessed arms and determination and would fight any invasion to the death.

During these weeks Marie Antoinette had another, more personal anxiety; she had no news of Fersen, did not know even where he was, or whether he was safe. She had written on 28 June and followed this by another letter on the 29th as we have seen, and on 4 July she wrote:

I can tell you that I love you, and have hardly time even for that. I am well. Do not worry about me. I wish I could know that you are the same. Write to me in a cipher by the post; the address to M. Browne . . . a double envelope to M. de Gougens. Let your valet write the addresses. Let me know to whom I can address whatever I can write to you for I cannot live without that. Adieu, the most loving and the most lovable of men. I embrace you with all my heart.

This was the letter discovered by M. Lucien Maury and published for the first time in the *Revue Bleue*; it has been taken by biographers as final proof that Fersen and Marie Antoinette were lovers, but this also is open to doubt.

It is very difficult to believe that the man who was quite openly the lover of Madame Sullivan should share his favours between her and the Queen. Everything he wrote to Marie Antoinette and everything he wrote about her breathes respect and admiration; for her he was the one true friend to be trusted above everybody, and it seems unimportant whether they had been or were lovers in the physical sense of the term compared with this deep relationship. But the public loves above all things a scandal, and so this unfortunate woman has been exhibited to posterity as a shallow lubricious royalty unworthy of the state she enjoyed.

Now, in her precarious situation she knew it was essential to seem to trust the Triumvirate, and she even admitted to Mercy that she appreciated their honesty and their desire for order restored through the royal authority. But she continued, 'Whatever good intentions they display, their ideas are exaggerated and can never suit us.' Indeed, would she not be a fool to trust these people who still gathered beneath her windows, who menaced her life, and subjected her to the most humiliating supervision? For her they were monsters and traitors and although the King might be forced to make concessions to placate them, he would always do so with reservations and wait till the day would come for his revenge.

Between the émigrés whom she execrated and the Constitutionals whom she could not wholly trust, she lived in a fever of doubt, but in her mind a plan was forming and on 11 July she wrote a long letter to Fersen which surprised him very much. She began by saying that the King considered that open force would be an incalculable disaster, for the people who were fully armed would in flying from the invading force turn against all those who for the past two years they had considered their enemies. The King desired that his captivity should be recognized publicly by the Powers, and that through the efforts of his relatives, friends and the other sovereigns some sort of Congress should be called where negotiations could be undertaken, with of course the backing of a sufficient force to support it, but which should be kept always in the background in order that there should be no danger of crime or massacre. She continued that it had been announced that the Constitution would be presented to the King within two weeks; everything which had taken place during the past two years must be considered null and void as far as the King's real will was concerned, at the same time it was impossible to change the will of the people at that time; their whole endeavour must be to change it imperceptibly by their conduct.

This plan differed from that of the Constitutionals, who wished the Powers to remain completely inactive, and from that of the émigrés, who wished for armed action: it was this last which she most feared. She was quite aware that both in Brussels and in Coblentz the King was regarded with little respect, and in Coblentz it had even been stated that when his brothers had *given him back his throne* his power should be so limited that he could neither name his ministers nor dismiss them. D'Artois was completely dominated by Calonne, who hated Marie Antoinette, it was the Versailles life of favourites and their intrigues transplanted. Marie Antoinette had through her ordeal passed beyond all that, she was considering the situation in its bitter reality; life and death had taken on a heightened meaning, terror was a present shadow.

Immediately on his arrival in Brussels, Fersen had applied himself to the formation of plans to save the royal family, and the first of these, approved by the King of Sweden, was to send Crawford to London in the hope of persuading the King to contribute towards another flight, while Axel himself would go to Vienna to speak with the Emperor. Crawford had an interview with Pitt, who made it quite clear that there was nothing to hope for in that quarter, while Fersen in Vienna was equally disgusted with the town and the Emperor's attitude, for Leopold, after having written gushing letters to Marie Antoinette before the flight to Varennes, now procrastinated and showed complete indifference to the plight of the King and Queen. 'He is a true Florentine,' commented Fersen in his *Journal*. Leopold had just signed an alliance with Prussia, he had made peace with Turkey and his affairs in Brabant, which had been in insurrection, were now quiescent. A few weeks later Leopold, Frederick William of Prussia and the Elector Palatine met in the château of Pilnitz and concocted the Declaration which bears its name.

It was an elegant elaboration of nothingness, and Marie Antoinette commented unfavourably on it. She wrote to Mercy on 12 September:

They say here, that the two Powers state that they will never permit the new French Constitution to be established. There are certainly some points which the Powers have the right to oppose; but regarding the internal laws of a people, *each can adopt that which it thinks right for itself. They are therefore wrong to demand otherwise* and everyone can see in this the intrigues of the émigrés, which will lose them even what is right in their cause.

In this tangled web of plot and counterplot it is sometimes hard to reconcile one letter of the Queen with another, but when what she does or writes is summarized it comes always to the same thing, she wished that the Powers, backed by a strong force which they however must not think of using, but only as support for their arguments, should demand the freedom of the King, so that in this freedom he could make what reforms were needed for the good of his people. And she deemed it essential that he should in consenting to the Constitution seem to do it in all good faith and of his free will, and for this she was willing to lead the Constitutionals on, for they were the only deputies capable of confronting the '*enragés*' of the extreme left. She felt no guilt in cheating them, for were they not also revolutionaries, only once removed from those other intransigents? They would all perish, for like Chronos eating his children the Revolution would dispose of them all.

The end of her letter is no less amazing than what we have quoted:

Well, the die is cast, the main thing at present is to shape one's course as circumstances direct. I wish that all the world would direct its course as I do mine; but even in our own circle we have great obstacles and great quarrels to be fought. Pity me; I assure you that it takes more courage to support my condition than if I found myself in a real battle; all the more because I do not deceive myself and I see only misfortune in the lack of energy of some and the bad faith of others. My God, how is it that, born with a certain character and feeling as well the blood which runs in my veins, I should be destined to spend my days in such a century and with such men? But do not believe for all that that my courage will fail me. Not for me, but for my child, I will persevere, and I will fulfil until the end my long and painful career. I can no longer see what I am writing. Adieu.

And some days after she wrote to Esterhazy that 'it was not necessary to trouble themselves about her personal safety but only for the benefit of France'.

No, Fersen's adoration for her, which he held till the end of his life, was in our opinion of quite a different order; it was a profound and tender love, which, because as he said at the beginning, it could never be satisfied, was all the more sensitive. For him she was '*Parfaite*'.

But this question is unimportant in comparison with the

difficulties and dangers which surrounded her. She was almost completely alone, for as she wrote more than once to the Triumvirate, she could only communicate with Barnave by letter, and all writing was open to incomprehension. During the whole month of August, while the Assembly was terminating its labours on the Constitution, their correspondence continues, and one senses in it the desire for certainty on both sides for each other, and the uncertainty which arose from their mutual knowledge of the other's background. After the unhappy incident of the Champ de Mars, the Queen was profoundly shaken, seeing that the populace still hated the throne, and that the extremists in demanding an abdication were as dangerous as the King's brothers who would be satisfied to see Louis XVI and his family perish so long as the monarchy could be saved. In these circumstances she was forced to appear at any rate to follow the reiterated advice of Barnave.

He promised to send her the revised version of the Constitution, and promised her also that in following the advice of M. de Montmorin in considering this document she could again become the Queen of France; not as she once had been, sovereign and absolute, but surrounded by a numerous society and the homage of an immense people, enjoying the effects of peace. But the days passed, the revised document did not arrive, and her suspicions awoke again. They had said that the Constitution was very monarchical: was it really so? She and the King were determined that all who had been their devoted followers and servants should not be sent away from them, and anything which took from the monarch his veritable rights of governing would be equally unacceptable. To which Barnave replied that it was his party alone which had influenced the direction of affairs in a way which without them no one would have dared to undertake.

The Triumvirate enumerated in a long letter the advantages which the King would gain in accepting the Constitution, they recommended the terms in which he should couch his speech to the Assembly and also urged the Queen to write to them a letter which would demonstrate the nobility of her character and which would paint for history a portrait of her person. They were convinced that all difficulties would disappear when the King did this; it would disarm those who were against him, except the extremists and his enemies among the émigrés, for he would extend an amnesty for those who had been accused at the moment of his flight, and would invite all parties to reunite for the general pacification of the kingdom. It seems so reasonable, they were so certain when they wrote that the roots of his power rested in the Constitution, that one wonders why Marie Antoinette did not accept what was after all a *fait accompli*. But she was under constant bombardment from Fersen who as a rabid monarchist encouraged all her doubts.

She refused to write to the Assembly, for said she, the King and she were completely united, he spoke for both of them, and moreover all her acts and wishes had been for the benefit of the kingdom, they spoke for themselves. She thought that the King's discourse should be short and to the point, that which had been proposed was too long:

Why enter into so many details? Is it to inspire confidence? Anything which is said at this moment is useless; it is only by consistent conduct and firmness that one can prove the truth of one's feelings. Is it to persuade the Assembly? Fifteen pages will not produce a better effect than one. The wise people who desire order are already persuaded, the others will never be. Is it for the people? They will never read such a long paper, and would understand it even less. So I consider it is essential to modify this communication.

She wished only that their future action should not run the risk of lack of conformity with their present statements. The deputies agreed with her, and it was modified.

On 13 September the King's letter was read to the Assembly and evoked applause from the majority. When Louis XVI went on the 14th to sign the Constitution and to swear to it, he too was received with a certain amount of enthusiasm. It is true that he had been imprudent enough to order the gates of the Tuileries closed, and the public who had gathered there to show its pleasure at the acceptance demonstrated their wrath at being shut out in no uncertain manner. Marie Antoinette wrote to Fersen, 'The People is what it always was, ready for every horror. They say it is on our side, I do not believe it, at any rate not for me.'

The Constitution, which seems to us a moderate and sensible document, gave very considerable powers to the monarch. He could exercise his ancient right of veto, he could appoint his ministers, his ambassadors and his generals. He could not declare war on his own account, but neither could the Legislative Assembly without asking his consent. It set the cost of the right to vote at two hundred francs in the towns and seventy-five in the provinces. It was limited but might be effective given good-will and trust on both sides. But for Marie Antoinette, who by tradition, birth and upbringing was used to regard a nation as the property of the monarch, it was 'a tissue of insolence and imprac-ticability'. This to Mercy, and later she wrote: 'It is not possible to exist like this. There is nothing for us to do but to disarm them and make them trust us, in order to circumvent them afterwards.' Barnave had written earlier that there was but one moment for the Queen to choose her path: she chose now, and she chose wrong.

The sitting of the Assembly was a painful experience for both the King and the Queen; while His Majesty took his oath the deputies remained seated, and they did not rise during his speech. Seeing this, he took his seat too. And when the unfortunate couple returned to the Tuileries, he threw himself into a chair and bursting into tears lamented, 'Was it for this that I brought you to France, you have been a witness to this humiliation.' Marie Antoinette wrote to Fersen:

It might have been more noble to refuse the King's acceptance, but it was impossible in the circumstances. I wished that it might be more simple and shorter, but it is our misfortune to be surrounded by traitors. . . . I believe that the best way to disgust [the public] with what is happening is to seem to acquiesce completely; that will soon show them that nothing will work. Besides, in spite of Pilnitz I do not believe that help will come so quickly from outside. It may be a good thing, for the more we advance the more these wretches will feel their miseries, perhaps in the end they will wish for the foreigners. . . . You cannot know how much everything that I do now costs me, and still more this villainous race of men who have never done us anything but harm and are so mad with hate at this moment . . . it is their conduct which has brought us to the pass where we are. . . . I have only one cause for happiness, it is to see all the gentlemen who were imprisoned because of us set at liberty.

Less pessimistic than she, the public, beside itself with joy, believed once more that the Revolution was finished. Two days later the Constitution was proclaimed from the Champ de Mars in the presence of an immense and jubilant crowd; the cry '*Vive la Nation*' rose from the throats of three hundred thousand men and women; laughter, tears, embraces on all sides, banners waved, bands played, the days of peace and – one hoped – plenty, were come. In the evening Paris was illuminated, the King, Queen and Dauphin drove around till eleven in the evening and even cries of '*Vive le Roi*' were heard. But every time a stentorian voice replied, 'No, don't believe them, *Vive la Nation.*' The Queen was terrified, it was the Revolution proclaiming itself not finished with yet. On re-entering her apartments she said sadly to Madame de Tourzel, 'What a pity it is that something so beautiful should leave in our hearts only a feeling of sadness and disquiet.'

But they must all the same have enjoyed their unaccustomed freedom – a Te Deum, games and shows in the public gardens, and finally, the Comédie Française, where their reception was 'inexpressible', and a few days after at the Italiens it was no less warm. 'But,' wrote Madame Elisabeth who enjoyed it all even more than her elders, 'It remains to be seen how long this enthusiasm will last.' However on 30 September the Assembly voted itself closed in the presence of the King, and La Fayette, radiant with success, left for his property in Auvergne declaring that the Revolution was over.

When the news of the King's acceptance of the new Constitution arrived in Coblentz, the Princes and the émigrés lost no time in declaring that they regarded it as null and void, for he could not have given it freely. He had written them a touching letter in September urging them to return to France and to renounce their plans for armed invasion; he knew better than they to what extent the nation regarded the Constitution as the charter of their freedom. Marie Antoinette too added her entreaties, she wrote to the King of Sweden urging him to use his influence with the Princes. Unfortunately the King had only a short time in which to do anything either one way or the other, for he would be shot by a Swedish 'patriot', Ankarstrom, and would interfere no more in the affairs of France. Coblentz indeed was alive with hate and rebellion. Daily the *Journal des Princes* published libels on the Queen, calling her '*démocrate*' and worse. Madame Elisabeth's friend and correspondent, Madame de Bombelles, wrote 'How can the Queen ever trust M. d'Artois, she who knows what infamous things are said in his circle against her and the King? . . . If she knows as much as I do she will never allow her fate to depend on people who owe her so much and who are her mortal enemies.' She exempted Artois from the worst of the scandal but added that he was ruled by those surrounding him.

Coblentz did not stop at scandal, the Princes had established themselves as a Court, with ambassadors to the Powers, and all the paraphernalia of royalty, and all the weakness too. So far the Powers had not been of much use to them. Catherine made promises, England insisted on neutrality and Leopold preached patience and temporized; he was facile and indiscreet, wrote Fersen. As for the Count himself, he had recovered from his first horror, for Marie Antoinette had convinced him that her correspondence with those whom she called 'enragés', who were in reality her best and wisest friends, had been simply a ruse. Reading the correspondence between Barnave and the Queen one is struck by the wisdom of so much of his advice. It was he who advised the King to write his letter to his brothers before the Constitution was signed, for, said he, it was necessary to defeat any bad intentions on the part of the public while the circumstances were favourable and not to lose an instant in doing so. In a revolution success comes when not only is action good but when it occurs at the right moment. This was something that the King might have taken to heart, for his well-intentioned actions rarely fulfilled this desired requisite.

For some time both the Queen and her 'counsellors' had felt the necessity for a meeting; the difficulty of a complete understanding through letters was too great. But how to arrange such a meeting, how were the Triumvirate, already suspected by the extremists of a too monarchical tendency, to arrive without danger to themselves, and how could she evade her constantly watching guards? However, on 1 October she wrote to Barnave that she had decided to see 'ces Messieurs'.

However, when at last the Assembly had finished its work and dissolved itself the Triumvirate were no longer so afraid of any loss of influence if it became known that they were in correspondence with the Queen, and a meeting was arranged; it would take place on 1 October at half past seven in the evening and Barnave and Lameth would be met at a certain spot and taken by a trusted agent to the Queen's study. The evening came, Madame Campan was stationed at a small door to let them in. Here she waited three quarters of an hour without result and at the end of that time went to the Queen. It appeared that the two deputies, when they got to the courtyard of the palace were frightened by the daylight and by meeting various persons who knew them. They did not dare to seem to be entering, but went straight through the gardens and away. The Queen scribbled a short note saying that she knew what had happened and that she would try to find a more secure rendezvous. To which Barnave replied that for them it was not only a question of life or death if they were discovered, but they would no longer be of any use to the monarch. They must find a safer way of meeting. This they finally did and since the military guard on the royal family had been replaced by civilians they were less rigorously watched and the meetings, particularly with Barnave, were frequent.

Even before the Constitution was signed there had been questions of the replacement of ministers. Montmorin the Foreign Secretary had resigned and was replaced by Moustier, the King's choice but not acceptable to the government, for he was an aristocrat. The post of Minister for War had been even more difficult to fill. M. de Ségur, having at first accepted, refused the post when he saw the reception given by the Assembly when his name was submitted. Barnave acknowledged the nuisance value of the republicans in the new government, all the more he insisted ought the King and Queen to profit by the favourable atmosphere in the provinces; they should do everything possible to increase their personal popularity. With the approach of winter and the probable scarcity of wheat they should support abundant charity through the municipalities, they should let themselves be seen informally, so that if the government made mistakes they would not incur the blame. At this moment the Assembly did indeed perpetrate a gross error. They passed a law condemning to death all émigrés who had not re-entered France by 1 January. Now even the King sought Barnave's advice. How could he condemn his own brothers to death, and on the other hand would his veto be respected? Barnave replied promptly. The King should exercise his veto but he should recommend at the same time strong measures to force the Princes and émigrés to return, and a notification to the Powers that there should be no assembling or arming the dissident French on their part.

For in Coblentz plans were openly afoot for an invasion, which all assumed would be successful. Lists were being prepared giving the date of each aristocrat's emigration, so that each might have his due share of the spoil. The German Princes pressed their claims to properties in Alsace, arms were being hammered out in Liège, horses collected from Germany, cavalry and foot soldiers enrolled and trained, especially among the defecting troops from France. All this the Queen knew, and to add to her fears Fersen wrote on his return from Vienna, asking inconvenient questions. Was she sincerely on the side of the Revolution, did she wish to be helped or should all negotiation with the Powers cease? Had she a plan, and if so what was it? Yes, she had, and it was one which she hoped would circumvent both the discontented at home and the violent abroad. She demanded that the Emperor should take the initiative in calling a Congress at Aix-la-Chapelle, it should be attended by all ambassadors. There the interests of European equilibrium should be considered, together with the rights of the German Princes in Alsace and the guarantees of the treaties with France which were compromised by the establishment of a new régime. The presence of a considerable armed force should give to the more reasonable members of the Assembly a means of countering the unreasonable demands of the 'factions'; any discussion of the Constitution should be rigorously avoided, so that no excuse could exist that the Congress was interfering with the internal affairs of France. And a summons should go to the government demanding that the King be free to leave the capital and go whither he would. This she thought would give the French people time to breathe after so many shocks, so that they could resume their habitual life, and consider what they themselves thought necessary for the future. On his side the King would do all that he could to regain their confidence, and by working strictly with the Constitution let them see for themselves wherein it was lacking. If this was done and the Powers declared it done, they would give the decent people a point for reunion and would frighten the 'factions', and the King, being free, could join the Congress and from there act as mediator between France and the Powers. She wrote to Mercy:

It is the only role which suits him, both from the love he has for his subjects and for the necessity for impressing the émigrés, who by their plots would plunge the monarchy into a new slavery. The whole of the sensible part of the nation could join with the King in pressing reforms. The Revolution would thus be achieved within the nation itself, it would be made through the threat of war and not by war itself.

Marie Antoinette, with her indomitable optimism, believed that this plan could succeed, and in order that it should, she condemned herself to an unending correspondence which continued until the outbreak of war made its success impossible. After some persuasion, Mercy and Fersen agreed to it and the latter sent her voluminous letters recommending this or that prince to whom she should write, and in what form she should do it. So now the poor woman had two sets of advisers, for Barnave did not cease his efforts to sustain the monarchy, and Fersen urged her to press the Emperor to constitute the Congress without delay. During the months of November and December his letters did not cease to give her lessons regarding her approach to the various Powers.

It is essential that one should try to picture the life of Marie Antoinette at this time, which was one of terror. Twice this woman had undergone the most ghastly trial, the two drives to Paris from Versailles and Varennes. Surrounded by a howling mob for hours she had learned that death was not a word but a fact which stared her in the face; at any moment she, or worse still her children, might have been torn limb from limb as others were before her eyes. We must ask ourselves how did she support such an agony, not once but twice, and what did it make of her? For when it was over the danger still remained. They were constantly on their guard against poisoning, so much so that knowing that the *Chef Patissier* had been in the employ of the Palais Royal they decided that the King and Queen should only eat meat, and Madame Campan was deputed to bring cakes to them secretly which she bought in one shop or another. They ate alone with a small bell to call the service, and they hid the cakes under the table in case they should be noticed.

Towards the end of the year the Duc d'Orléans paid a visit to the King and seemed to have repented of his evil ways and to wish sincerely to help the monarch. Or so the King in his good nature believed. Whether it was true or not, the Duke's endeavour went for nothing, for on his way out of the palace he was set on by the crowd of royalist courtiers and hangers on, who even spat at him as he descended the staircase from Marie Antoinette's apartment. He left the palace in a fury, and understandably vowed never to return, for he believed that the insults had been instigated by the Queen. Another opportunity was missed for conciliating an enemy, the unfortunate pair were pursued by an inexorable fate. Now the Queen sat writing, writing; her light burned until far into the night, her letters were in a particularly difficult cipher, and then she had to decipher those immense screeds which Fersen sent telling her exactly how to proceed.

First she must write to the Emperor asking him to use his influence with the Empress Catherine of Russia, then to the Empress herself, with a little flattery to begin with. Then to the other monarchs of Spain and Sweden, and the King should write to Spain too. Pages and pages of advice, of dictation, even of remote details. He watched as well what was happening in these other Courts and informed her that her brother was most indiscreet, he let it be known that she corresponded with him and when his dislike of any definitive support was seen, evil-minded people put it about that it was because the Queen wrote to ask him not to intervene:

Your enemies have availed themselves of this means of suggesting that you are against any enterprise, that you prefer to abide by the Constitution and to make use of the factions rather than to acknowledge to the Princes and the émigrés the re-establishment of your authority; that you would rather lose the kingdom than that authority, and all sorts of similar tales, one more ridiculous than the other.

Poor Queen, whatever she did it was misunderstood by somebody; but she was a diligent pupil, on 3 December 1791 she wrote to the Empress, on 4 January 1792 to the Queen of Spain, a little later to the King of Portugal. The replies were dishearteningly vague. The King had written in November recommending his wife's plan to his representative in Coblentz, de Breteuil. He followed this up by letters to the King of Prussia in December, and to the Kings of Spain and Sweden at the beginning of the year. While waiting for replies they were obliged to agree that events in Paris and the country were not going their way. A new Mayor of Paris had been elected. Who should it be but Pétion. Montmorin, the Minister for Foreign Affairs, had not been replaced, for M. de Ségur persisted in his refusal, but the new Minister for War was the Comte de Narbonne, thanks largely to the intrigues of Madame de Staël, whose lover he was. With this appointment this extraordinary woman enters our story; it is not the place to enlarge upon her, but no account of the times would be complete without a reference to her. Necker's daughter had returned to Paris some months earlier and had joined the salon of Madame de Condorcet, the wife of the philosopher and mathematician who occupied a leading place in the reconstituted Assembly. Her nose for political intrigue was unerring and it took her no time at all to realize that war was in the air and that whoever held the ministry for war would have a key post. The Queen, to whom Madame de Staël and La Fayette were equally objectionable, at first opposed his nomination. 'Rather perish', she said, 'than be saved by La Fayette and the Constitutionalists', but she was persuaded to agree to his appointment by a letter from Barnave. She therefore urged her husband to nominate Narbonne immediately and on 6 December the Comte was installed as Minister for War.

The Queen wrote to Fersen on the following day a letter which would be taken to him by a sure hand, that of the Bishop of Pamiers. In it she alluded to the *'volume de correspondance très curieux'*★ which she would keep to show him in happier days, evidently the letters from Barnave. Their position was a little improved, she said, for all those who called themselves Constitutionals were banded together to defeat the Republicans and the Jacobins who at the moment were perpetrating every atrocity they were capable of. They were supported only by traitors and brigands, but, said she, it might only be for the moment, for in this country everything could change from one day to the other. She had never lost her first impression of the French as a light-minded and inconsistent people, it seems. On the following day the King was due to deliver his address to the Assembly against the law concerning the priests. This was one of the things on which Louis XVI was really determined; he could bring himself to accept everything but the civil constitution of the clergy, it offended his pious heart. She continued, 'The Comte Louis de Narbonne is at last Minister for War; what glory for Madame de Staël and what a pleasure for her to have the whole . . .' the following words have been scratched out, but one can readily imagine that they were 'army at her disposal' – for the multitude and variety of the lady's lovers was well known. He could be useful, she said, for he had sufficient authority to rally the Constitutionals and to impose on the armed forces:

★ The very curious volume of correspondence.

But do you understand my position and the role that I am obliged to play all day; sometimes I cannot hear myself and I am obliged to think whether it is really I myself who is speaking; but what can one do, it is all necessary and I believe that we would be even lower than we are if I had not adopted this role at once, at least we gain time with it, and that is what we most need. What happiness if one day I can become free enough to be able to prove to all these wretches that I was not their dupe.

She finished the letter by assuring him that she was better in health than she could have hoped, only she suffered from a prodigious spiritual fatigue, the result of the lack of change of scene, for there were so many persons whom she must see, and time must be found for her children, her only joy: 'When I am very unhappy I take my little boy in my arms, I kiss him with my whole heart, and that consoles me for a moment. Adieu once more.' The last line of the letter has been scratched out. It has been rightly inferred from this letter that the Bishop of Pamiers had informed Fersen about the Queen's relationship with the Triumvirate and through them with the Constitutionals. She seems to apologize and to clarify her position and this explains a note in Fersen's *Journal* some months previously when he was in Vienna, when he comments on the malicious rumours which were current there. The town was full of spies, of whom de Noailles was one, he says, although all the Archduchesses were on the side of Marie Antoinette. The Emperor was more and more indiscreet and people were saying that the Queen was led by Barnave and even that she slept with him. Whether Fersen believed this rumour we cannot tell, for the letters in which it might have appeared were among those destroyed, but some biographers have taken this entry with its lack of comment to prove that Fersen, being one of her lovers, could accept the fact that she might have others and would merely feel jealousy and not disgust! Nothing in the correspondence between the Queen and Barnave suggests such a possibility. Both of them asserted their good faith in their transactions and they had respect for each other, but their good faith was limited by their different goals. Marie Antoinette was fighting for the monarchy in the person of her son, who for her was France, Barnave regarded the monarchy as a weapon in his struggle with the Republicans and the extremists; he too was fighting for France, but one which should be new and free to decide its own laws and government, a monarchy yes, but a very limited one.

Now war seemed really nearer, the Queen wanted it less perhaps than others, but she was gradually beginning to accept it as their only hope. If her brother Leopold could fuse the hesitant Powers into one fighting force he might save her. The Girondins wanted war to further the Revolution, and La Fayette and the other returned American revolutionaries wanted war for their own glory and to reform the army. Madame de Staël, who must not be left out, wanted war for the benefit of Narbonne and he wanted it for the same reason. The Assembly voted twenty millions for the army and he promised that within a month 150,000 men would stand ready for action. And finally the émigrés wanted war because they were convinced that they would win and then everything would go back to normal, the old régime would be reinstalled and the King's brothers would – perhaps – be in their rightful place, with their favourites, Calonne at the head, around them.

In February Axel de Fersen paid his last visit to the woman he was never to forget. He arrived and as he noted in his *Journal* managed to enter the Tuileries by his accustomed route. He stayed all day with her and in the evening saw the King. He had a plan, a new escape: the King would not hear of it, they were too closely guarded and besides he had given his word not to fly, 'truly he was scrupulous, having often promised to stay where he was, for he is an honest man'. Louis XVI was indeed honest. He acknowledged that he had failed through weakness and irresolution but he had found himself in an extraordinary position. He had missed his moment, now it was too late: 'I have been abandoned by all the world.'

At half past nine Fersen left the Tuileries. He stayed a week in Paris, hidden by Madame Sullivan without Crawford's knowledge. In his *Journal* he notes this with amusement; in the evening when her lover was away Elenore ordered her supper, which Fersen ate, and when his friend returned he was regaled with what was left. A truly amoral situation, and apparently isolated in Fersen's mind from his devotion to the Queen, though Madame Sullivan shared his devotion to Marie Antoinette.

He left on 23 February and through the intense cold drove over the frontier without hindrance, and on his arrival in Brussels reported to Gustave III.

During the four last months of the monarchy all parties had the firm impression that events were leading to a crisis. In the country things were chaotic, the winter was bitter, food was scarce or unobtainable, and now the armies which La Fayette and Narbonne were gathering needed money which could not be obtained from taxes, and even when it was, consisted of half worthless paper. The rumours of war alarmed the country towns and brigands took advantage of the general unrest to be active everywhere. Housewives barricaded their homes at night, and the men armed with whatever weapons they could find, knives, scythes, and staves, stood guard or rushed into the woods and fields looking for imaginary invaders. And in Paris the Assembly argued, passed decrees, listened to endless speeches by Robespierre, or Marat or Brissot, all advocating a different point of view, all full of suspicion and hate. The Queen was fully aware of all this and as she wrote to Mercy, hate, suspicion, and insolence were the three activating forces in the country. They were insolent through excessive fear and because they believed that nothing would happen from without. She was certain of this, because when they believed that outside power threatened them they became quiet. So she had come to believe that really the only solution for the troubles of the monarchy was war, and to Mercy's excuses for the dilatory Emperor and to the extended plan which he submitted to her she replied that it was too late for anything but action. For Narbonne had returned from his inspection of the forces and made his report to the Assembly, and at the end of it Brissot had risen and moved that unless Austria disavowed the declaration of Pilnitz★ by 1 March France was to consider herself at war with her, and the Assembly rose in applause.

★ In which the Austrian Emperor and the King of Prussia called on Europe to re-establish Louis XVI in his former authority.

8

The Storm Gathers

MERCY, who had done his duty as Austrian Ambassador in defending his Emperor, had not hesitated to point out to Marie Antoinette one fact; if the French were threatened by war from without they would immediately forget their differences and draw together in a common determination to defeat the enemy. She replied that they need not fear, that if only the Emperor would show himself at the head of the other Powers everyone would tremble in France, for it was the French who were provoking the war. She was convinced that the persons of the King and his son were necessary to those she called traitors, and that they would be safe. Nothing was worse than to do nothing; only the first moments would be dangerous. Like a prudent housewife she was considering the placing of their money and consulting her banker Laborde; she thought England the best and safest place. Among all these fears and displeasures she enjoyed from time to time an echo of her former life. On 20 February she went with her children to the Italian Opera to see *Les Evénements Imprévus* by Grétry, and when the Valet and the Chamber Maid had their duo, Madame Dugazon, as royalist as her husband was Jacobin, bowed to the Queen when singing 'Oh comme j'aime ma maîtresse' (Oh how I love my mistress). This was a signal for a tempest of shouting, 'Pas de Maître, pas de Maîtresse, Vive la Nation, vive la Liberté', from the Jacobins in the stalls, 'Vive le Roi, vive la Reine', from the royalists in the boxes.

The whole house was divided, blows and cuffs were exchanged and tufts of hair flew about. But the royalists had the best of it. The National Guard restored order and the duo was repeated four times, the last time when Mme Dugazon sang '*Il faut les rendre heureux*' (We must make them happy) the audience cried '*Oui, oui.*' 'This is a funny nation,' wrote Madame Elisabeth to her friend Madame de Bombelles, 'one must admit that they have charming moments.' The Queen retained her calm throughout and was warmly applauded when she left. It was her last visit to the theatre.

Fersen had returned to Brussels fairly content with the success of his visit. It seemed that the Queen was now converted to the inevitability of war, and the King consented to allow the Powers to act. And they too were ready. Prussia and Spain joined with the Empress of Russia and the King of Sweden in asserting the necessity and even the Emperor appeared more disposed to bestir himself; suddenly an unexpected event arrested their design. On 1 March Leopold died after an illness of only two days. In spite of her differences with her brother Marie Antoinette was deeply shaken by his death. But she had little time for grief or tears, for as she wrote to Mercy on 2 March, every day brought its calamity and aggravated their troubles. The Emperor had accused her of wishing to drive Austria alone into a 'holocaust for the benefit of France'. She protested against such a thought, for had she not from July, almost at the moment of their arrest, asked her brother to unite with all the Powers to extricate them from their position? He had not even answered her. And since then had she ever asked for anything else? But now that she had renounced all hope of a peaceful solution, of negotiation, the ordeals through which she had passed had not weakened her resolution nor dampened her spirit, and she urged the utmost haste, not a moment must be lost. She sent to the new Emperor, her nephew Francis II, the Baron Goguelat, under the assumed name of Daumartin, bearer of credentials from herself and from the King who wrote 'I am in absolute agreement with your aunt, and I have the same confidence. Louis.'

The paper he brought was written by Breteuil in Brussels and told the Emperor the horrible news that the extremists appeared to dominate the country and that they had a plot to separate Marie Antoinette from the King on the grounds of nineteen accusations of which the chief one was that she had urged the late Emperor to form a confederation in favour of the royal prerogative. It underlined again the need for speed. 'There is no time to be lost,' said Marie Antoinette, 'for they lose no time who are against us.' She was to be spared nothing it seemed, for on 16 March her most fervent supporter King Gustave of Sweden was shot dead by an assassin at a masked ball. Verdi in his famous opera has told us the story. There were three conspirators of whom one, Count Horn, pointed out the King to the murderer by placing his hand on Gustave's shoulder and saying '*Bon jour, beau masque.*' Ankarstrom shot at once. When the dreadful news was brought to the Tuileries the King and Queen were shattered. They had lost their chief support; almost Gustave's last words were that one of his regrets in quitting this life was knowing that his death would injure their interests. Madame de Tourzel coming into the royal apartment found Marie Antoinette with her weeping little daughter in her arms. 'Who can know,' sobbed the Queen, 'if we may not suffer the same end.' Who indeed, for in the kingdom the rejoicing was great. 'Here is a blow which will gladden the Jacobins,' said the monarch when he was hit, and he was right. Ankarstrom and his associates were called Brutus and Mutius Scaevola, and the poniard was held up as the ultimate weapon of the people. This last blow seemed to have robbed Louis of all his resistance, for he lapsed into a sort of coma. For days he did not speak a word, neither the caresses of his children nor the entreaties of his wife could move him; it was not until she implored him on her knees to remember that if they were to perish they should do it with honour and not wait till they were smothered on the floor of their apartment, that he somewhat recovered from his torpor.

The news-sheets outdid themselves in scurrilous disrespect for the Queen's sorrow. 'The death of the Emperor has had its effect,' wrote one, 'Elisabeth went to confession the same evening, and Marie Antoinette, who is reputedly a strong woman, has had a stroke.' 'Leopold is dead; but the most redoubtable of our enemies is full of life and lives among us. The defunct is in his tomb: he has left us a sister.' And on 10 March in a stormy session of the Assembly Verniaud cried:

From this tribune where I am speaking to you can be seen the palace where perverse counsellors mislead the King whom the Constitution has given you, forging the irons which will deliver us bound to the House of Austria. I see the windows of the palace where they prepare the counter-revolution, the means which will plunge us again into the horrors of slavery, after having forced us to pass through all the disorders of anarchy and the furies of civil war. The day has arrived when you can put an end to so much insolence . . . let all there know that our Constitution gives inviolability only to the King. Let them know that the law can reach the culprits without distinction, and that there will not be a single head, condemned as criminal, which will escape the knife.

A terrible speech and a terrible thing for Marie Antoinette to hear, for it confirmed what in her heart she knew, that she was already condemned without hope of a hearing. When it was told her she was overwhelmed and wept, and she who had longed for peace saw nothing but misery and war unless help came from somewhere; from outside, from those near her, or from the monarchists, the men of goodwill who still existed in this torn and unhappy France.

And yet, when their last chance of survival did arrive, she could not bring herself to accept it, so strong, so inborn had her suspicions become. On 16 March General Dumouriez was called on to replace Lessert as Minister of Foreign Affairs. The General had been one of the secret agents of Louis XV; he was not only a soldier but a diplomat, witty and supple beneath a seemingly rough and brusque exterior. Louis immediately liked him, but since he had been put in by the Girondins he was suspect to the Queen. In vain he employed all his arts of persuasion – for he saw himself as a second Mirabeau – in vain he implored her on his knees to let herself be saved; she was adamant. He insisted:

Madame believe me, I abhor as you do anarchy and crime. But I am better placed to judge of events than is your Majesty. This is not a popular movement which will pass, it is the spontaneous resistance of the whole nation to deep-seated wrongs. The King and the nation must remain united, everything which leads to their separation will ruin them both.

He was right when he said that the abuses by the Paris mob did not represent the feelings of the whole people, who at this time were still firmly monarchist, as were indeed many of the deputies. If the King had been firm, if the Queen could have trusted him, they might have been saved. But what was Marie Antoinette to think when on the very next day she heard that he had spoken in the Assembly praising Robespierre?

The end of March saw the arrival of Roland into the Ministry, a curious man, who in himself was of impeccable honesty but limited by his very virtue. He was chosen to represent the government at the Tuileries, for the Girondin party was now in full power. Unfortunately Roland had a wife, pretty, ambitious and viciously partisan where he was weak; she loathed Marie Antoinette with all the loathing of a woman of the middle classes for an aristocrat. In 1789 she had written to an associate, 'You are nothing but children, your enthusiasm is like a fire of straw, and if the National Assembly does not put in action the trial of two illustrious heads you are all F. . . . .' Her salon became the seat of government, in rivalry with that of Mesdames de Staël and Condorcet, from whence issued a sickening flood of enmity. Easter fell in the first week of April and the Queen had chosen a confessor, who because he was non-juring could not fulfil his duties publicly. At five o'clock in the morning she arose and in the darkness, accompanied by Madame Campan, she slipped into her chapel and heard her Mass. She stayed a long time, says the faithful follower, and only left when day was breaking.

Even though she was tormented day and night by sinister reflection on what the future months might bring, Marie Antoinette always found time for her children; the Dauphin, now seven years old and a most enchanting child with his blue eyes and his long fair hair, should now be given a preceptor and the choice of this man was causing both his parents grave concern. He was so loving, so trusting and above all he adored his mother. The dreadful events which he had witnessed did not seem to have altered his natural gaiety and friendliness, and they feared like all parents that all this might be destroyed by the wrong choice. Above all if he were given to the charge of the men the Assembly had suggested, Pétion, Sièyes, Condorcet, atheists all, what would become of his religious belief? On 18 April the King, taking his courage in both hands, wrote to the President putting forward the name of M. de Fleurieu; this had the effect of discontinuing the Assembly's interest and in fact the appointment was never made. If the unfortunate parents could have foreseen what the future education of their lovely child would become, they might have thought that even death would be preferable.

On 15 April Paris enjoyed a fête. It was the return of the Swiss convicts who had been sentenced to the galleys after the mutiny of Nancy. They had been liberated and were welcomed by a crowd of dancing, shouting citizens. The Assembly met them with full honours and in the evening Paris was illuminated. It was the fête of indiscipline, of theft and of assassination, and the greasy red caps which they wore became the honoured sign of the Revolution, like the trouserless suits of the 'sans-culottes'.

On 26 March Marie Antoinette had written to Mercy:

M. Dumouriez, who has now no doubt of the decision of the Powers to move their troops, has a project to begin here by an attack through Savoy and another through Liège. It is La Fayette's army which should make this last attack. This was the result of yesterday's Council. It is just as well to know about this in order to be on our guard and to take whatever measures seem proper.

This is the letter which is the basis for the accusation that the Queen betrayed her country to the enemy, and it is irrefutable. But one can see it in whichever light one prefers; either she was a traitor, or she was a woman who had over and over again been openly threatened with the murder of herself and her children, and possibly the King, reduced through the failure of all her efforts at negotiation to calling on any help she could find. The argument continues to this day.

Be it as it may, on 20 April the King went to the Assembly and in the flat dull voice of one performing an unpleasant duty declared war on the King of Hungary and Bohemia, the pretext, the presence of Austrian troops on the frontiers under the command of the Duc de Condé. France was at war. The ultimate moment feared by all had arrived. On 30 April 1792 the Queen wrote to Mercy:

War is declared. The Viennese Court must do its utmost to keep the greatest possible distance between its own cause and that of the émigrés; it must say as much in its Manifesto, at the same time giving it to be understood that it might use its ascendancy over the émigrés to modify their claims, persuade them to have more reasonable ideas, and finally join forces with all those who are defending the King's cause. It is easy to imagine the ideas which must constitute the basis of the Manifesto of Vienna, but in calling on the world to witness the efforts for the preservation of peace, the ever-constant desire to come to an agreement, the indisposition to uphold particular pretensions or certain individuals against the nation, too much talk about the King, the idea that it is he who is being backed and defended must be avoided.

Such implication would be embarrassing, compromising, and in order not to seem to be conniving with their nephew, the Court would be forced to exaggerate the importance of its activities, which would be degrading, or might even give a wrong impulsion to public opinion. Equally important is to avoid wishing to seem, firstly, to interfere with home affairs, and secondly, wishing to force an issue. Attempts have already been made to thwart Leopold's good intentions by spreading a rumour that he sought to promulgate an arrangement between all our parties. It is no doubt desirable that the course the Viennese Court takes should incite the French to do the same, but this design must be very hidden for it would be impossible to carry out if it were revealed beforehand. The French would always reject any intervention by foreigners in their affairs, and their national pride is so solidly attached to this idea that the King cannot possibly set it aside if he wishes to restore his Kingdom.

Three weeks later a confidant of their friend Malouet, like him a determined upholder of the Monarchy, Monsieur Malet du Pan, was charged to go to the Powers and enlarge again on this plan. Above all he was to insist on the necessity for the Princes and the French émigrés, in the words of Rocheterre, 'not to lose the actual struggle by making the sort of war waged by one Power on another'. And it was not less important that the Allies in the Manifesto they were to address to France should endeavour to separate the extremist Jacobins from all classes of the rest of the nation, to reassure all those who were likely to repent their errors, all those who, though not approving the present Constitution, feared a return to the grave abuses of the past; all those whom bewilderment, the contagion of example, and the first intoxication of the Revolution have been caught up in this criminal cause, and who, guilty only of mistakes, exaltation or weakness, show themselves to be disarmed and repentant if they are presented with an issue comporting neither ignominy nor personal danger. ... Finally the Allies must introduce fundamental truth that they have no intention of interfering with the integrity of the nation. It was essential not to impose any one mode of government, but to declare that they were arming for the restoration of the monarchy and legitimate royal authority according to the wishes of His Majesty himself.

This was his mission and it proves once more that Marie Antoinette was determined by every means in her power to avert a war which she was certain would be disastrous to the King's cause and to France. She wrote again on 4 July that their position became daily more critical, there was nothing but rage and violence on one side and feebleness and inertia on the other. They could count neither on the National Guard nor on the army, they did not know whether to stay in Paris or to try to go elsewhere. Everything would be lost if it were not possible to stop the extremists by the threat of future punishment; they were determined on a republic, and in order to achieve it would even go so far as to assassinate the King. But she had not lost her courage, Mercy could count on that as she counted on his attachment; this was the moment to show it, and she adjured him by the memory of her mother, and what he had felt for her, 'Now is the time when you can give me the proof by saving me and mine, if there is still time.'

War had been declared, both sides had known that it was inevitable, but when it came to the point neither side was ready. The Powers had yet to assemble their troops, and when they did it was impossible to know whether they would march for they were riddled with Jacobin spies preaching sedition. The French could have reached Brussels with ease, but they too were in difficulties, they had lost their best generals and many soldiers had deserted to follow their chiefs. The whole army was disorganized, Théodore Dillon's corps assassinated their general, Biron's regiment was set in flight by a corps of Uhlans, and Rochambeau resigned. In this crisis La Fayette chose to leave for Paris. Why? Did he think at this late hour that he could save the monarch – would it be worth his while? Certain it is that he did propose a plan whereby the Royal Family, sheltered by his troops, should leave Paris for Compiègne where they could still be guarded by the King's detachment of the Swiss guards and the National Guards. But the King refused and the Queen, who as usual would not take any initiative without his consent, refused also. A sad decision, if anything which came from this vacillating man could be given such a name.

He was of course accused of being the cause of the first defeats of the national army, and the public believed that there was at the Tuileries an Austrian committee bent on the destruction of the patriots even if it meant a new St Bartholomew's massacre. Rumour succeeded rumour in the city, accusation accusation in the Assembly. Pétion announced the probability of a projected flight of the King and made it the excuse for the doubling of the guards around the Tuileries. Then came a more serious affair. The King had bought up, contrary to the Queen's wish and knowledge, the latest libellous edition of the *Memoirs* of Madame de la Motte, of necklace ill fame, and had given it to M. de la Porte to hide. The latter, fearing a perquisition by the Assembly, when the papers might be found, had taken it upon himself to dispose of them, had loaded them on to a cart and sent them to the porcelain factory of Sèvres with orders to burn them all. A big fire was lit in the presence of two hundred workmen, who were expressly forbidden to approach, and the smoke belching from the chimneys could be seen by all. The workmen lodged a de-nunciation, the director of the factory was called to the bar of the Assembly and in spite of his protests it was immediately assumed that these were the papers of the 'Austrian Committee'. Jacobins and Girondins combined for once to denounce the plot and the result was that the King was deprived of his Constitu-tional Guard. The unfortunate prisoners in the Tuileries were now without defenders and the Constitutionals who had made a last unsuccessful attempt to save him, abandoned him. Barnave, asking only one last favour, that he might kiss the Queen's hand in parting, left for the country, from which he would not return until he too was tried and met his end on the same scaffold which she had ascended before him.

But the Assembly was not disarmed and on 26 May it decreed the deportation of all non-juring priests who might be denounced by a group of twenty citizens. Its next step was to decree the formation of a camp of twenty thousand men drawn from the provinces and the country round Paris, a 'federated' army at the gates of the City. Ostensibly for the celebrations of the fête of the Federation on 14 July, this decree, with the one before it, affronted the King's authority, and His Majesty vetoed both and dismissed his Girondist Cabinet. The three Girondist ministers, Clavière, Servan and Roland had unceasingly persecuted Louis and on 10 June the last named had presented him with a letter, written by his wife it was understood, which outdid all that had gone before in insolence and invective. It was too much for the normally unresisting King and was the reason for their dismissal. Dumouriez, for whom the King had a measure of respect and trust, was charged with forming a new ministry but the General refused to remain unless the King rescinded his two vetoes. Louis let himself be persuaded with regard to the camp, which Dumouriez agreed should be formed at Soissons instead of at the gates of Paris, but he was inflexible on the deportation of priests. The General then gave in his resignation and departed for the army of Lukner. On 19 June the King formally upheld his veto for the two decrees, of which one would destroy the right of individual conscience proclaimed by the Constitution, and the other would be a continuing menace to good government. For once he was determined, his own conscience could not allow him to offend the conscience of others; on the same day he wrote to his confessor: 'Come to me, I have never had so much need of your consolation. I have finished with men; my eyes are now fixed on heaven. Great troubles are expected tomorrow, I will have courage.' He was a man of personal integrity, but weak when he should have been strong, and obstinate when he might have compromised.

The 20 June, the anniversary of the Tennis Court Oath and the flight to Varennes, dawned cloudy. All night the crowds had been gathering; in the Quartiers, egged on by Danton and Santerre, their rage was growing against the man who had dared to contradict the Assembly, and at eight in the morning they set themselves in motion. The plan for the day had been elaborated in Madame Roland's salon; by midday a compact mass of people were in the rue St Honoré and moving towards the palace where the only protection was the gates, which had been shut. Led by Santerre and Legendre the butcher and dragging the Tree of Liberty on a cart (this was the pretext, to plant the Tree on the balcony of the Feuillant's clubrooms) they soon broke the frail defence and overflowed the Riding School and the forecourts. The Queen with Madame de Lamballe, Madame de Tourzel and her other ladies, was watching with apprehension behind the window curtains, while in the King's apartment a small group of brave men were hurriedly making a barricade with benches in front of the window behind which Louis could stand. Shouting 'Down with the Veto, *Vive la Nation*', the mob precipitated itself through the corridors. Marie Antoinette heard its heavy growling and suddenly a great noise; it was the cannon which they had dragged to the first storey. With their red caps and their pikes they presented a terrifying spectacle. A man outside the door yelled 'I will have the Queen, dead or alive.' Her women pushed her through the passage to the Dauphin's room. He was not there, his servant had carried him to his sister. Quickly, breathlessly, the Queen rushed in pursuit, at least she could have her two children in her arms, and they hid themselves in the little passage through which the King had escaped the year before. Now Marie Antoinette had only one idea, to join the King. If she appeared the mob would take its revenge on her, it was her life, her blood they wanted, but with the King she might be spared. But an officer barred the way and dragged her to the Salle du Conseil, which was still empty. Here they persuaded her to place herself with the children behind a heavy table in a corner of the room and three rows of the regiment of the Filles de St Thomas drew up before her.

By this time it was not only the Queen who was threatened, the whole palace resounded with the cries, '*Vive la Nation, à bas le Veto*', and the roaring crowd mounting the staircase had discovered the cannon; it was enough, they were persuaded that it had been placed there by the defenders of the palace to threaten them; in this moment the lives of all the family were within a hairsbreadth of being sacrificed. Fortunately the sappers were ordered to take it below, and there it remained for the rest of the day. The King was in the Oeil de Bœuf, only a door separated him from the raging mob. Some of his gentlemen, a few National Guards and the battalion of the 6th legion, this was all his defence. Already they were hammering at the door, the panels were giving when the King gave the order to open; a hussar obeyed, the mass poured in. One of his faithful officers, who had implored him to show himself to the people, shouted, 'Citizens, here is your King, respect him as the law commands. We will all die rather than permit him to suffer harm.' This so surprised the foremost in the mob that there was a moment of confusion, during which his friends drew Louis into the bay of a window and placed benches in front of him with three rows of the grenadiers. One of them said to him, 'Sire, do not be afraid.' 'My friend,' replied the sturdy monarch, taking the grenadier's hand and placing it on his chest, 'my friend, put your hand on my heart and see whether it is beating more rapidly.'

But now the hall was filling and the cries were redoubled, '*A bas Monsieur Veto.*' The King tried to speak but the noise was so great that 'even Jupiter tonans could not have been heard', said a witness. In the forefront of the mob was an individual by name Soufin, who had won glory by having washed and put on the pikes the heads of Foullon and Berthier at the taking of the Bastille. Other such patriots filled the hall, shouting, gesticulating, breaking the furniture, and the mirrors, stealing and smashing precious ornaments, and behaving as if the palace were besieged – as indeed it was. Now the butcher Legendre forced his way to the front. 'Monsieur,' he began, 'listen to us, it is your business to listen to us. . . . You are perfidious, you have always deceived us, you are still deceiving us. But take care, the measure is full; the people are tired of being your toy.' 'I will do simply what the Constitution and its decrees order me to,' calmly replied Louis XVI.

One of the Municipals, Mouchet, took from a man who carried it on a stick one of the red bonnets and gave it to the King, who put it on his head. The idiot crowd applauded; '*Vive la Nation, Vive la Liberté*', they screamed, and even here and there '*Vive le Roi*', and one of the grenadiers heard an aside, 'He has f . . . well had to put it on, for we would have seen what would have happened if he had not.' Then a glass of red wine was offered him; taking the glass he raised it, 'People of Paris, I drink to your health and to that of the French nation.' But Madame Elisabeth was seen in one of the window seats where she had been standing half hidden. 'There is the Austrian! We will have the head of the Austrian.' 'It is not the Queen,' shouted her equerry. 'Why undeceive them,' said the generous princess, 'their mistake might have saved the Queen.' At last the Mayor of Paris arrived, it was six o'clock. 'Sire, I have only just heard of the situation in which you find yourself.' 'That is remarkable,' replied the King with justified irony, 'it has been going on for hours.' However Pétion, carried on the shoulders of two soldiers, succeeded in calming the mob and the King announced, 'I have given orders to open the State Apartments, it may amuse the people to see them.'

The rabble streamed slowly past led by a man carrying on a pike the bloody heart of a calf with the words 'heart of an aristocrat'. At the same time, another band had gone up to the Dauphin's apartment where they hoped to find Marie Antoinette. The child had gone and the disappointed people, among them a horde of women, tore open cupboards, stuck their knives into the couches and beds, swearing to find her, dead or alive. Having been held back from joining the King the poor mother, half inarticulate from crying, had implored her attendants to save the children, but the little Dauphin, terrified, could not be parted from her. At last she was persuaded to go to the Salle du Conseil and to take refuge of a sort behind a large table in a corner of the room; it was there that the wretches found her, surrounded by her friends and a few grenadiers. The first to enter was Santerre: approaching he said, 'Madame, do not be afraid, no one will do you any harm.' 'I am not mistaken nor deceived,' replied the Queen, 'and I am not afraid; no one is afraid if they are with good people.' And she held out her hand to the guards who were with her who seized it and kissed it with fervour. The horrible procession began, one man carried a sheaf of whips 'For Marie Antoinette', another a gallows from which dangled a doll, 'Marie Antoinette to the lamp post', and another a guillotine with the legend 'National justice for the tyrants, down with Veto and his wife.' Santerre played the part of compère. 'Look,' he said, 'here is the Queen, here the Crown Prince.' Someone gave her a red cap saying, 'If you love the nation put this on your son's head.' She took it and did so. The heat was frightful and the poor child was so suffocated that even Santerre was moved to pity. 'Take it off,' he said, 'the child is too hot'. Now a woman leapt in front of the Queen, 'You are infamous,' she screamed, 'We will hang you.' 'Have I ever done you any harm?' replied the unfortunate woman sadly. 'You are deceived, I have married the King of France; I am the mother of the Dauphin, I am French; I was happy when you loved me.' The woman was touched in spite of herself by the sight of so much pain and sorrow. 'Pardon me,' she muttered, 'I did not know you. I see that you are good.' 'The woman is drunk,' said Santerre, it did not suit him that anyone should sympathize with the Queen and he pushed her away. Sitting there in the suffocating heat, the waves of insensate hatred mounted round her like a foul miasma; the people brought with them their dirt, their hunger and degradation, all the sufferings of years were being avenged in a welter of feelings which they did not understand and could not control. Driven on by men who knew very well what they were doing, the unhappy flood moved past the woman who symbolized for them all that they had undergone. and yet she had only to speak and she could have conquered them, But it was too late and leaning back she murmured to her friend, 'It is too much; it is beyond what anyone can bear.'

But at last it seemed that the worst was over, the crowd moved past more from curiosity than from rage. Santerre and the officers of the National Guard managed to get rid of the last stragglers, who went off muttering that they had come there for nothing, but they would return and next time they would get what they wanted. And Santerre, who had helped to engineer the whole rising grumbled that the coup had failed, it had been too difficult to manipulate, but they would return and then they would get the King out. At ten o'clock the palace was empty, and the royal family could regain their ravaged apartments. The Queen, broken by all that she had undergone in silence, and by the suffering of her daughter who was old enough to understand the ignominy which they had been forced to support, could not stay her weeping: she threw herself into her brave husband's arms but when he reproached himself for having brought her to such misery, she grew calm, and went to her own rooms. To her friend the Princess de Tarante, who admired her self control, she said, 'I have never felt more tranquillity, more freedom, or a colder courage.' She had passed into a state beyond what anyone could do to her, she had faced the threat of immediate and brutish death, and surmounted it.

On the same evening Pétion with his supporters celebrated the 'Great warning' which the French people had given to their masters. And Madame Roland in her salon, with her friends, was full of admiration for the 'Just lesson' which the Queen had had. 'How I would have loved to see her long humiliation; and how much her pride had to suffer.' One can only say that when she came to mount the scaffold she bore herself with very much the same pride.

'I still exist, but it is a miracle,' Marie Antoinette wrote next day to Fersen. 'The day of the 20th was frightful, it is not only I whom they wish to kill, it is my husband's life they want, they do not hide this any longer.' And again on the following day, 'your friend is in the greatest danger, her sickness is making frightening progress, let her relatives know of her situation.' The veiled language is easily understood. The anguished appeals follow one after another during the month of July, and it is hard to understand Fersen's replies which insisted that she should remain in Paris and that after a few weeks assistance would come. How could he reply so to these lamentable appeals? 'The moment presses and it is impossible to wait, tell M. de Mercy that the King and Queen are in the greatest danger, every day produces incalculable terror, the horde of assassins grows daily.'

The French people were indeed in the throes of a mass madness, uncertainty augmented by terror reigned over the land; they were menaced by the invasion in which the unhappy Queen now saw the only chance of survival, and it is impossible not to have some feeling for both sides in the upheaval.

The populace filled the gardens of the Tuileries, it seemed an amusement to go there and insult the King and Queen; and the despairing couple faced the ever present threat of assassination. On 23 June Louis XVI had written a proclamation which expressed in noble terms all that he felt; after denouncing the excesses to which they had been subjected he added:

The King has only opposed the menaces and insults of the factions with his conscience and his love for the public good. He does not know how long they will continue but he feels the necessity for telling the French nation that no matter how long this violence continues to carry it to extreme ends, they will never drag from him anything which he considers contrary to the public interest. . . . As the hereditary representative of the French nation he has serious duties to fulfil, and even if he must sacrifice his peace and quiet, he will never renounce his duties.

It was an heroic gesture, and if it had been left to the people themselves the hereditary love and respect which they bore their kings might have triumphed. Seventy Departments wrote condemning Pétion, twenty thousand signatures protested against the crime of *lèse majesté*, and on the 28th La Fayette arrived in Paris and in the name of the army demanded from the Assembly the suppression of the Jacobin Club, and vigorous measures for the protection of the King. The Right applauded him, the Left listened in silence, and when it came to the point his proposals met with nothing but coldness. He left on the 30th having discovered to his dismay that his influence was waning.

For in the Assembly the demands for assassination were no

longer veiled but absolutely open. Brissot in a violent speech announced that to strike the Court of the Tuileries was to strike all the tyrants at one blow, while Marat thundered against the palace where a perverse Queen dominated an imbecile King, and opened all doors to tyranny. And as a seal for all this, Pétion, who had been suspended, was reinstated on 13 July. It was now impossible for the Queen and her children to walk in that part of the Tuileries gardens which had been reserved for them, their ears were assailed by shouted threats, pamphlets with the most sordid insults were waved in their faces, verses were sung

Madame Veto a promis
De faire égorger tout Paris★

and at night they could hear the footsteps of those who slunk around the palace, so that their sleep was unquiet and full of alarms. Madame Campan was told to make a cuirasse, a waist-coat of many thicknesses of felt which might give some protection to the King, for they feared that on 14 July all these threats would take a practical shape. They tried its use, when it was finished, and found with joy that it resisted stiletto blows, and even pistol shots bounded off it. The faithful woman wore it as a petticoat for three days before the King could find an opportunity to try it on without being found out. When at last he did it was in the Queen's bedchamber. He drew Madame Campan aside and said that it was only to satisfy his wife that he consented to wear it, for they would not assassinate him, they would take his life in another way. When he had left the Queen asked Campan what he had said and on being told commented that she had feared it, for the King passed his time reading about Charles I of England in order not to make the mistakes of that monarch. An she added that she feared a trial for the King, for herself she no longer cared, but what would become of their children?

Now the dreaded 14th was near and from all over France men were taking the road to Paris for the Federation festival, the great rally in the Champ de Mars, after which, some thought, they might disperse to Soissons and there form the camp of Federates which the King had vetoed. They were all bringing with them petitions to the Assembly, mostly that the King be suspended or deposed, and the only money they had had been wrung out of

★ Madame Veto has promised to slaughter the whole of Paris.

their local Jacobin Clubs. And as they walked they heard the rumours that Brunswick was almost ready to move, with eighty thousand men it was said, Prussians, Hessians, and the émigrés all itching to be at them. And what army had they to oppose such an invasion, for an invasion it would be. All Marie Antoinette's entreaties for negotiation, for peace, had gone by the board, and what she predicted would come to pass, France would arise, would forget its quarrels; and on 11 July the Legislative Council decreed 'that the country is in danger'. And now the marching men know why they are going, and Barbaroux who had asked Marseilles to send him 'six hundred men who know how to die' will know that they are on their way; and Marie Antoinette knew it too, for she wrote Mercy that six hundred assassins were coming to Paris. They brought with them a new song to fire their blood and raise their spirits and join the 'Ça ira' in fame – it was the *Marseillaise*.

Since the Queen, who slept on the ground floor of the palace, found it almost impossible to find any repose, the King insisted that she should change her room, which she did under protest, for she disliked giving any sign of weakness. She therefore took the room of Madame de Tourzel where at least she would be above the constant provocation from the crowd in the gardens. A little dog was also installed who would by his barking alert the guard if anyone tried to enter. The Dauphin was the best pleased by this arrangement, which placed his room beside his mother's. All day he ran from one to the other kissing her, and saying sweet things which rejoiced her heart. Her health strangely was better than it had ever been.

The dreaded 14 July drew near, the groups arriving from the provinces were received with acclamation by the Jacobins, lodged for nothing, given wine and weapons. The best of them left for Soissons where a force was being formed to support La Fayette's army; the worst remained in the capital, swelling the crowds who found their daily occupation in vituperation: 14 July dawned and in the event passed off better than expected.

From her place on the platform in the Champ de Mars the Queen's eyes followed her husband as he made his way to the Altar of the Fatherland, and Madame de Staël commented: 'My eyes followed his powdered head amid all those dark-haired heads; his coat, embroidered as in times past, contrasted with the clothes of the populace which was pressing around him. From that day the people did not see him again except on the scaffold.' And she added: 'The expression on the face of the Queen will never be effaced from my memory. Her eyes were ruined with weeping; the splendour of her toilette, the dignity of her carriage contrasted with the cortège by which she was surrounded; only a few National Guards separated her from the populace.'

It is true that many devoted friends made plans for their safety, among them the Princes of Hesse, of whom Prince George came to France expressly for this purpose. Marie Antoinette refused to take the risk of leaving and wrote a long letter to her childhood's friend the Landgravine; she could not leave her husband, her children and all those who had shown them devoted service. She ended, 'They have taken everything away from me except my heart, which is still mine to love you. Never doubt it, it is the only unhappiness which I could not bear.'

A more important proposal was that of Madame de Staël, for it offered the safety of all the royal family; but again the reply was the same. They refused, but not for the same reason; how could they trust a woman who had displayed such rancour and was besides too intimately associated with the 'Patriots'?

But Malouet, back from his mission, was not discouraged; in common with Montmorin, Lally-Tollendal and Malesherbes he addressed the Duc de Liancourt who commanded at Rouen and who consented to send the four regiments under his orders to Pontoise where they could meet the royal family, escorted by the Swiss. At Rouen a yacht would await them and take them to Le Havre or even to England. But when the King read Malouet's letter he was so agitated that the Queen noticed it, and was told of the plan, but that it was too hazardous. Louis could not permit so dangerous a project, Varennes had been a lesson. The Queen said nothing, but when Montmorin heard the reply he exclaimed, 'They must make up their minds; we will all be massacred and it will not be long now.' But to make up his mind was just what Louis xvi could hardly ever do.

The last attempt was made by La Fayette, and here the American Ambassador, Morris, was drawn into the affair. The Fête de la Fédération was near and on the day after, profiting by the inattention of the crowded city, the King and his family should leave the Tuileries surrounded by the faithful Marshal

Luckner and La Fayette and one hundred devoted horsemen in daylight. The National Guard would protect their departure and the Swiss would guard the route to Compiègne. Once there, well supported by an efficient army and cannon, the King should offer himself as mediator between the Powers and France, and having thus reassumed his authority, should revise the Constitution. At first the King seemed disposed to accept this plan, which his Council of Ministers supported, when suddenly the preparations which had already begun were called off; he would not leave Paris, he was afraid that this departure would lead to civil war. Why had he so suddenly changed his mind?

The blame as always was laid to the door of Marie Antoinette, and still today she is accused of having ruined the monarchy, for the sake of her personal antipathy for La Fayette. It is true she did not trust him; how could she when he had returned from insurgent America, inflamed by his success and proclaiming loudly the cause of Liberty? His conduct since had seemed to her highly suspect: he wished, it is true, for a limited monarchy but with himself in the chief seat of power. Thus, she said, rather perish than be saved by M. de La Fayette and the municipals. And her friends Mercy and Fersen constantly warned her not to call on M. de La Fayette but rather on the faithful provinces such as Picardy.

On 25 July the Duke of Brunswick launched his famous manifesto, threatening instant reprisals should Their Majesties be harmed; the Allies had not the faintest idea whether they could ever carry them out. But Fersen in far-away Brussels approved of it and wrote that the Duke would pass the frontier in five or six weeks, for he was about to move, and was only eight or ten days from the frontier. If anything was needed to force the French to rally this was it. And in this crisis Fersen employed himself with the formation of a Court and a Ministry and even asked Marie Antoinette to furnish him with blank procurations so that the men whom he proposed could be formally accredited! This was too much for a woman daily and hourly in terror for her life. She wrote with remarkable forbearance that in such danger it was difficult to think of the choice of ministers, for the moment it was more important to study how to avoid the daggers of assassins and to foil the plots of conspirators who surrounded a throne which was ready to disappear: 'We have to consider how to gain twenty-four hours, and I need not repeat that if no one arrives [she means the Powers] only Providence can save the King and his family.'

Now the family was occupied in disposing of all papers. Madame Campan burned the greater part of those belonging to the Queen, who put in a portfolio her family documents and the letters from Barnave and her replies which she had copied, for she judged them important for the history of the Revolution. The King possessed a prodigious quantity of papers and unfortunately had the idea of putting them in a strong-box constructed by a locksmith whom he had known for ten years and trusted. It was hidden in a secret place but the locksmith later betrayed the secret to the Assembly, and it was found. At every moment they awaited an irruption from the Quartiers and did their best to arm themselves against it. Marie Antoinette hardly slept at all, and on occasion the King watched so that her sleep should not be disturbed. She had given orders that her shutters and curtains should be left open, and one day when the moonlight was streaming into her room she remarked to Madame Campan that in a month she would not see this moon again without being free. She still alternated between hope and despair, without knowing that Danton and his Cordelier associates had decided on 10 August as the day when the monarchy would be finally destroyed.

It is extraordinary to think that while all this was going on, life in the city continued on its accustomed way; the theatres were open, people ate and drank, married and died, and Marie Antoinette, lulled into a false security, felt a faint rebirth of hope when she received her last letter from Mercy saying that in a month they would be saved. But on 3 August Pétion presented himself before the Assembly and demanded the King's abdication; the Insurrectional Committee sat permanently and the section of the Théâtre Français under the presidency of Danton declared itself in a state of insurrection. The Marseillais, the most turbulent of the newcomers, were brought from the distant barracks to the centre of the capital, they were incorporated into the revolutionary battalions and given unlimited wine and money. Every violent man on whom the leaders could rely was given arms, and at the same time the regular troops were sent to the provinces or the army, and the Assembly ordered that the guard at the palace should be composed each day of citizens from the Quartiers. With the lack of discipline, the strangers who camped wherever

they could find shelter and roamed the streets singing and shouting, the filth, the walls covered with placards all of the same
bloody colour, the town presented a revolting spectacle. The
Assembly sat helplessly by while rumour said that the Queen
would be put in an iron cage and taken round the city while the
King would be imprisoned, and a woman very near to the revolutionaries said publicly, 'It will rain with blood; I do not
exaggerate.'

On 7 August the few remaining faithful, Malesherbes, Morris,
Lally-Tollendal presented to the King their last attempt to save
him. They would take him to Pontoise or Compiègne, under
guard of the Swiss and grenadiers of Aclocque and inform the
Assembly that he had gone there in conformity with the Constitution. He refused, and Madame Elisabeth insisted that the
insurrection would not take place, for bribed by the Queen,
Pétion and Santerre had promised to support her party with the
Marseillais. This was an ultimate despairing attempt on the part
of Marie Antoinette. Conflicting emotions fought in her, she
had looked at death, had recognized and accepted it, uppermost
was this personal resignation. Her disgust and dislike of the
French arose from what was left of her sturdy decent Germanness;
her energy was still alive, she was thirty-six and in full possession
of her mental and physical powers, in fact any physical disa-
bilities seemed to have passed away – as she said, nerves were for
happy women. But if she still fought it was for the monarchical
principle embodied in her husband and her son; once they were
destroyed it would disappear completely. In fact she was right,
as she so often was: the brief interludes of Louis XVIII and
Charles X prove it.

On the night of 9 August the palace was comparatively
quiet. The King had played billiards after dinner with Madame
Elisabeth and the Princess had written to a friend, 'This day which
should have been so terrible is the most calm possible.' The
Queen however was uneasy and strayed from room to room,
but that was all.

At midnight the tocsin began to sound and soon the beating
drums could be heard as well, the Quartiers were awake and
preparing to march. The Tuileries was defended by about nine
hundred Swiss, a small number of gentlemen and some companies
of the still loyal National Guard. They were commanded by

Galiot de Mandat, an energetic officer who knew his business, and had disposed his small army to the best advantage. The family were all awake, the Queen with the devoted Madame de Lamballe went from window to window; suddenly the tocsin stopped, the silence was heavy and full of dread; the Marquis de Mandat had been called to the Municipality and murdered on the steps of the Hôtel de Ville. His body was thrown into the Seine, and the palace had lost its defender.

Now the Queen, who appeared to be the only person with sufficient energy to take any action, pressed the King to show himself to those who would defend him. He hesitated but then went to the balcony in his suit all crumpled from having slept in it and with untidy hair. The Queen, his children, Madame Elisabeth and Madame de Lamballe were with him and warm *Vivats* greeted them all. Passing through the great gallery he was hailed by those of his gentlemen who were prepared to perish with him, and the battalion of the Filles de St Thomas, to whom the Queen spoke with all her accustomed grace and warmth. It was an affecting scene, for none of them knew where they would be by the end of the day. Those about to die saluted him! When he came to the vestibule and was on the point of going into the courtyard he sent the group back for safety, although the Queen insisted that their presence might protect him. It proved to be an unwise decision, for the further he went on to the terrace the more hostile became the cries. From 'We will defend him to the death', they became '*à bas le Veto, Vive la Nation*'. He was so closely surrounded that it seemed like a swarm of flies, says one commentator, and the further he went the worse it became. He was obliged to return to the ¦palace, and the Queen observed to Madame Campan that all was lost, it had done more harm than good.

But a young man who observed the scene, a certain Lieutenant Bonaparte, wrote to his brother Joseph that if the King had taken his horse and put himself resolutely at the head of his troops, he could have chased all this rabble off the place. This officer learned something which he would later employ with exactly that effect.

But the King was no Napoleon; he hesitated and was lost. The municipals who were there seemed more occupied in destroying order than in keeping it; they exhorted the defenders only to fire when they were fired upon, but at seven o'clock in the Place

Vendôme, which was full of people going towards the Place du Carrousel, they tried to argue with the crowd and were answered by the cry 'Abdication or death'. Now the municipals, thoroughly demoralized, went to the palace to endeavour to persuade the King to seek refuge with the Assembly. Roederer, the Procureur Général, had already tried the same thing during the night and been answered by the Queen with indignation; it was she who again protested that to leave the palace where they had some defence and go to the Assembly which had never lifted a finger to help them would mean their defeat. At half past seven Roederer tried once more, he wore his scarf of office and brought with him the Directeur. 'Sire,' said he, 'Your Majesty has not five minutes to lose, there is no safety for you but with the National Assembly.' 'But,' replied the King, 'I have not seen many people in the Place du Carrousel.' 'Sire, there are twelve cannon and an immense crowd which is coming from the Faubourgs.'

Marie Antoinette's blood was now boiling: turning to her faithful servants she said, 'You can nail me to the wall before I consent to leave them,' and then to Roederer 'Monsieur, we are not without defenders.' 'Madame, all Paris is on the march, action is useless, resistance impossible. Will you be responsible for the massacre of the King, your children and of yourself, in a word, of these faithful servants who are round you?'

'Would to God that on the contrary I could be the only victim!'

'Sire, time presses, this is no longer a request which we make to you, nor advice which we take the liberty of giving you; we have only one thing to do at this moment, we ask permission to take you away.'

The King lifted his head and looked long and earnestly at the Procureur. 'Come,' he said, 'since we must, let us give this last mark of devotion.'

'Yes,' said the Queen, 'it is the last sacrifice, but' – and she gestured towards her husband and son – 'You see the reason.'

Then to Roederer, 'You guarantee the person of the King and of my son?'

'Madame,' he replied, 'we will die at your side, that is all that we can guarantee.'

The King rose and said, 'Let us go', and at about half past eight the tragic cortège started. First walked the King, wearing a hat which he had taken from one of the guards. The Queen took the arm of de Molleville, Minister of the Marine and held the Dauphin by the hand; the little boy amused himself as they went by scuffing up the fallen leaves in the garden. Then came Madame Elisabeth and Madame Royale, Mesdames de Lamballe and Tourzel, and some other nobles, the Comte de la Rochefoucauld among them, and other ministers. Everyone was weeping to see them go. 'We will come back.' said the King, and the Queen echoed him, but they had little hope, and for Marie Antoinette it was the end. All her resistance had been in vain; deserted by her brother, betrayed by her émigré friends, unsupported by the one man who loved her, she was indeed alone. But Roederer wrote 'The Queen in that fatal night showed nothing of affectation or romance; I saw nothing in her of excitability nor of spirit of vengeance; she was woman, spouse, mother, in peril; she feared, she hoped, was afflicted and reassured.'

In the palace, emptied of its royal occupants, those who were left debated whether they should leave or stay, but the Marquis de Milly – he was eighty-four years old so had not much to lose – considered that to die sword in hand was the fitting death for a gentleman and he proceeded to organize a defence. This was to be one of the accusations brought against the Queen at the time of her trial, that she had given the order to fire upon the people.

She had still some agonizing moments during their slow progress towards the Riding School with the mobs shrieking and hurling insults at them; at one point a huge grenadier seized the Dauphin and held him up, she gave one frantic scream, a terrible cry of alarm, and the man reassured her and the little boy who was also in tears. The Assembly which had been sitting since two in the morning sent a deputation to meet them; suddenly a deputy darted out and, seizing the King's hand shouted 'Give me your hand, I will take you in, but not your wife, she shall not enter, it is she who is the bane of France.' Roederer pushed a path through and managed to lead the royal party to safey amid a rain of threats which would daunt the bravest heart.

The King took his place beside the President and his family behind him. The grenadier who carried the Dauphin put him down beside the secretaries, the child tried to run to his mother. Instantly shouts were heard, 'No no, he belongs to the nation; the Austrian is unworthy of the confidence of the nation.' Now the King spoke: 'I have come,' he said, 'to prevent a great crime; I know of no better place than among you.' And Vergniaud replied, 'You can count, Sire, on the firmness of the Assembly, the members have sworn to die in defending the rights of the people and the constitutional authority.' But by law they were forbidden to debate in the presence of the King, and it was decided that Louis and his family should be accommodated in the small tribune of the Logographe. It was ten feet square, exposed to the hot sun, and so low that one could hardly stand upright. Here they would stay for the next eighteen hours, forced to listen to the debate which would decide their fate.

Suddenly the sound of firing was heard; the Swiss had retired into the palace and viewed with anxiety the arrival of the insurgents. A shot sounded, immediately answered by a volley from the Swiss; it was enough, the battle had begun. The prisoners in the Assembly were left in no doubt as to its progress, as messengers arrived constantly to tell the news; from his narrow cell the King, determined that no more blood should be shed, sent to tell the Swiss to surrender. Obediently they laid down their arms, it was the signal for a massacre. The gallant Marseillais threw themselves into the palace, killing as they went, breaking everything, pillaging, swearing, drinking, and particularly possessing themselves of the Queen's belongings. Soon they appeared before the tribune bearing their spoils, and Marie Antoinette saw in their bloody hands her jewels, her silver, her dresses and the correspondence found on her table. And they brought too their prisoners, miserable Swiss who were on their way to the prison of the Abbaye. All this she saw without uttering a word, she listened – her heart frozen within her – while the deputies debated two measures. First, the French people is invited to form a National Convention; second, the head of the Executive Power is provisionally suspended from his functions. Marie Antoinette spoke only once throughout the agonizing day; it was when there was a question of a governor for the Dauphin; she implored several deputies to try to evade this decision which for her would be the worst of all. They were the more successful because the Assembly, which proposed the establishment of a republic, cared little what happened to the heir to a lost throne. The little boy was asleep on his mother's knee and she tried to wipe his face, wet with sweat in the suffocating heat. Her handkerchief was soaked, and M. de la Rochefoucauld lent her his, red from the blood of the brave defenders of the palace.

At about two in the morning the royal family was transferred to the near-by convent of the Feuillants where they were allotted four small cells; half dead with fatigue they walked across the garden lit by smoky torches which showed in a macabre flickering light the faces of the brutes who never ceased to vilify them. The ferocity of the people of Paris in this tragic time was indescribable, and can only be explained by the memory of all that they had suffered in past years, suffering which they attributed entirely to these sad victims. What harm had she ever done them, said the King when their shouts demanding the Queen's head reached the cells which were given to them. What indeed? But their minds had been so indoctrinated by enemies and zealots that they were unable to do anything but vent their wrath on the nearest and most helpless object.

Now the august captives were in their four little rooms; at the end of the corridor was the prison with its barred window-slits from whence the convicts could see them and taunt them with horrid cries and curses. And the poor little Dauphin cried, 'Maman has promised that I can sleep in her room tonight because I was so good with those bad men.' They got a meal of some sort, which Marie Antoinette could not touch, and were comforted by the arrival of some friends who had managed to slip through the guards. But the Queen was restless and woke unrefreshed to another dreadful day. Madame Elisabeth dressed the children and took them to their mother, who sighed 'Poor children, it is cruel to have promised them such a fine future and now to be forced to say, look what we are leaving to them. Everything comes to an end with us!' At half past seven they regained their wretched box, their torture recommenced, and during three days they were forced to listen while the Assembly heard delegations all demanding their death, awarded a prize to the heroes of the Tenth and ordered the statues of Kings in Paris to be overturned. Every day they were taken back to their cells by guards who prevented assassination but encouraged invective. One evening a young man thrust his fist under Marie Antoinette's nose and hissed, 'Beastly Austrian, you wanted to bathe the Austrians in our blood, you will pay for it with your head.' She made no reply, she had gone beyond it.

The Assembly had decided that they should be transferred to the Luxembourg but changed their mind, the Luxembourg was not safe enough; the Commune sent Manuel to inform them that this new master had decided on the Temple. When the Queen heard this she shuddered, and turning to Madame de Tourzel whispered, 'You will see, they will put us in the tower and make it into a real prison. I have always felt horror for this tower and besought the Comte d'Artois to destroy it, it was certainly a presentiment of all that we will suffer there.'

On the next day the King had a long parley with the Assembly as to the number of servants they might take with them, he wanted twelve, they were given six; when the moment came for them to bid farewell to all those who had followed them the Queen was in tears, they had nothing, neither clothes nor money; these devoted friends put on the table whatever they had of money or assignats, the King pushed it away saying, 'Messieurs keep your purses, you have I hope longer to live.'

On 13 August at six in the evening they mounted two enormous carriages, and drove at walking pace through the pullulating streets, escorted by Manuel, Procureur of the Commune, and Pétion. When they arrived in front of the old palace they found it brilliantly illuminated; candles and torches flared in all the windows, and an enormous dinner had been prepared for them. The King, whose appetite nothing could spoil, ate with gusto, the Queen could touch nothing. But who would dare tell them that their lodging would not be in the palace but in the donjon? No one knows, but at one o'clock in the morning Marie Antoinette could at last reach the medieval tower whose occupant, the archivist of the records, had been summarily evicted to make room for the family. And as she ascended the staircase a song reached her from the street:

> *Madame à son tour monte*
> *Ne sait quand descendra.*★

She went, as she was used to do, and saw her son asleep and then, saying 'Did I not tell you so?' to Madame de Tourzel, she drew herself up and with her accustomed calm busied herself with the arrangement of the apartments.

★ Madame goes up into her tower
She does not know when she will descend.

9
Prisoners

THE Temple, where the royal family now found themselves
virtually prisoners, was not in fact a prison. The medieval castle
with its four pepper-pot towers had been a residence of the Duc
d'Artois; it had been erected by the Order of the Knights Tem-
plars at the time of the Crusades and with its small turreted tower
beside it had dominated the quarter where it stood for hundreds
of years. The small tower into which Louis xvi and his family
were now introduced and which would serve them until the
larger one had been reinforced as a prison, had a little door so low
that the head must be bent to enter. It comprised four floors,
each with two rooms and a tiny closet placed in the turret, and a
winding stair led to the platform of the roof. The Queen occupied
the second floor while the King had the apartment above. The
walls were hung with the indecent engravings of the previous
occupant; Louis commented that they were not fit for his daughter's eyes and had them removed. Madame Royale had a little
bed in her mother's room, while Madame de Tourzel slept in
that of the Dauphin. Madame de Lamballe was worst off of all
for she had only a connecting passage for her bed. In the turret
which connected the rooms was the wardroom for the soldiers
and the watching municipals.

The whole was sparsely furnished and dirty, but the energy
and resourcefulness of the Queen next day established some kind
of order. The family used her room as a meeting place, alas,

without the consolation of being alone there: a municipal who was changed from hour to hour was their constant companion. To them, says Madame de Tourzel, they behaved with such courtesy and gentleness that many of these men, suspicious as they were, felt themselves won over. At about five o'clock in the evening they all went down into the garden for a breath of air and so that the faithful Hue, who had followed them into confinement, could clean and adjust their rooms, but here they found little repose, for the crowds who constantly infested the place amused themselves by fabricating ever new insults, and were completely unrestrained. But as long as the children could play, their mother and father bore it; at least they were protected from assassination, and Marie Antoinette could breathe a little more freely after the terror in the Tuileries, and watch daily their larger prison being fortified. Her respite was short-lived. On 19 August two municipals presented themselves and in spite of anguished protests, took away Madame de Tourzel and her daughter and Madame de Lamballe. In vain the Queen wept and implored; they were inexorable – the last friend was gone. The days wore on, the King gave his little son instruction in Latin, geography, history, while the Queen taught her daughter music, drawing, and religion. Madame Elisabeth mended and kept their clothes in order – the King had but the one suit. They were not allowed to receive any news, but Hue by hoisting himself on to a window-sill could catch what was being shouted in the street below and it was thus that they heard of the Allied victories at Longwy and Verdun. In his memoirs Hue recounts a long conversation with the Queen in which she emphasized once more their determination not to admit any dismemberment of France and implored him to support the King in this determination, for said she, 'I am sure that I will be separated from the King.' On 2 September they noticed an unaccustomed tumult in the streets around when they took their usual turn in the garden. The guards made them re-enter quickly to avoid the stones thrown at them. A little later a municipal rushed into the room and addressed the King, 'Monsieur, you do not know what is happening, the tocsin has sounded, the drums been beaten, the émigrés are at Verdun! If they come we shall all perish but you will be the first.' The monarch replied mildly, that he had always done what he could for his people, the Dauphin terrified ran crying to his mother, and the man, turning to Hue, arrested him and took him away.

No one could sleep that night, and in the morning the noise around the tower increased. The King wished to go into the garden but was prevented by the guards, and at about three o'clock the hubbub was intense, frightful shrieks and uproar, louder and louder, ear-splitting, terrifying in its menace. The ruffians, who had murdered the unfortunate Madame de Lamballe, had outraged her body and had dragged it from the prison of La Force to the Temple. One brute held her chemise covered with blood and dirt on a pole like a flag, another had her genital organs tied to a pike, while a third more vile, more malignant than all, wore her pubic hair as a moustache. And above them all rose the head of their victim, its long lovely hair streaming, which with a refinement of horror they had carefully dressed. They had brought these trophies of their night's work to show 'the Austrian' and they demanded that she show herself.

She and the King were playing tric-trac when this clamour was heard and the valet Cléry rushed into the room pale with fright, followed by a municipal who ordered the curtains drawn. The King asked what was wrong, and was told that the crowd, believing that he was no longer in the tower, had come to see for itself, but they (the municipals) would not allow it. But the shouting redoubled and one assassin was climbing up to get at the window. Now came more municipals of whom one insisted that the King and the Queen should go to the window. 'No do not go,' cried another named Menessier. The King asked again why not. 'Well, Monsieur, if you must know, it is the head of Madame de Lamballe that they want to show you. I advise you to show yourself if you do not want the crowd to come up here.' At these words the Queen fainted dead away; her daughter wrote long after that it was the only moment when her resolution failed her, and the King turning to their tormentor said, 'Monsieur, we are prepared for anything, but you might have spared the Queen this frightful news.' The man turned and left the chamber. They were perhaps spared the full knowledge of the atrocious massacres going on in the prisons on this ghastly 3 September 1792, which history has never forgotten; a bestial madness had entered the soul of the people of Paris, who were urged on by organized assassins and terrified by the threat of oncoming invasion.

The Duke of Brunswick's manifesto had threatened France with military occupation and Paris with 'total destruction', and Marie Antoinette's prediction that this would forge the nation into unity against a foe was justified indeed. The reply was 'To Arms citizens' and everywhere men were arming and marching. Since 10 August the Assembly had been virtually powerless, the militant Commune was in full charge, the Revolution was entering a new stage, and Danton and the Men of the Mountain were its masters. Robespierre was there and Marat, risen a long way from his stable-boy state; they had their agents all over France. In the Town Halls, in the market places and everywhere they preached resistance, against royal 'traitors' and against foreign invaders, and everywhere France gathered and armed. Now Dumouriez and Kellermann had their army and on 21 September they met Brunswick advancing along the valleys of the Argonne. At Valmy they defeated him and forced him to retreat. Goethe was there and said that with this battle a new era was beginning and the future of France and of Europe was decided.

And on 20 September the new National Convention with Pétion as President met to propose and pass its decrees. The corner-stone of the new Constitution should be the Sovereignty of the People, it should be accepted by the nation or be null, the people should have new judges and finally after various other decrees, royalty from that day should be abolished in France. At four o'clock that afternoon Lubin, who had seconded Collot d'Herbois in this proposal, went with four mounted gendarmes and read the decree beneath the windows of the Temple. It could be heard clearly in the Queen's room, and Hébert, the writer of the infamous news-sheet *Père Duchesne*, was at that moment on guard in the Queen's room. He watched Their Majesties with curious and malignant eyes during this trial. The King who had a book in his hands read on imperturbably, the Queen kept her usual calm dignity; they gave their opponents no sign over which they could exult. That evening Madame Elisabeth told the Dauphin's valet Cléry to write in future when making his requests 'It is necessary for the service of Louis XVI, of Marie Antoinette, of Louis Charles', etc.

With what despair must Marie Antoinette have received all

these blows, enough to have shaken the bravest woman, but with each shock her superhuman courage returned fortified by her pride and resolution never to give in. Nor did hope die, until the very end there were plans for escape and the devotion of those serving them to comfort her. Of these the chief was M. de Turgy; he had been in the King's service since 1784, and when they arrived in the Temple he managed to insinuate himself into the tower. It was he who did their shopping once or twice a week so cleverly that he was never suspected. The King, when he left for his execution charged his valet Cléry, another faithful friend, to tell Turgy how thankful he had been for his service, that he gave him his blessing and commended him to the family. Another friend was M. Hue, miraculously escaped from the massacre of the Tuileries, who would be indefatigable in sustaining communication with the world outside.

A great comfort was the valet Cléry; between them they invented a sign series which could convey the news without words, for they were watched night and day. The fingers placed in certain ways on the cheeks or nose or mouth would tell what they wished to know. Another was Toulon, one of their guards whom at first they distrusted, he was so brusque and rude, but he proved so trusty that they gave him the name of Faithful. On the 29th six municipals came and removed all paper, ink, pencils and any other means of communication, and in the evening of the same day they returned with Hébert at their head and read the decree removing the King to the Great Tower. All protest was hopeless, and the King, visibly affected, took leave of his weeping wife and children. The apartment, newly made, was hardly ready for him and in the morning he prepared to breakfast with his family; this was refused. When Marie Antoinette was told that they were separated her gloom increased, she could eat nothing, and when Cléry came in to fetch books for the King – there was a library of about 1,200 volumes in the tower – they were all in a hopeless state. The Queen implored the municipals who accompanied Cléry to allow them to be together at least for their meals, and their dolorous cries touched even their hard hearts. They were allowed to dine together 'just for this one day', but they must only speak in good French and with loud voices. The order for their separation was finally rescinded, for when Santerre came in the evening he too was touched by their grief. 'These bitches of women make me want to cry,' he said.

But one more trial was in store for Marie Antoinette, when in October the women were also transferred to the larger tower. For the hatred against her was as strong as ever, and doubtless her tenderness and loving care for her little son had aroused the desire to torment her afresh. At the end of October they announced that it was time that the son of Louis Capet should be removed from the hands of women and join his father, both day and night. He might only see his mother during the short repose of his father every afternoon, and without even telling her what was happening, the child was removed.

The prisoners' life in their new quarters took up its routine, the King rose, prayed, ate, gave his son lessons – all under the eyes of the prying guards – while the Queen taught her daughter, embroidered with her sister, and the children played as best they could in the confined space. They were watched all the time, the guards were always with them and the constant surveillance must have frayed their nerves to breaking point. The news which reached them could not have been worse from their point of view: all hope of aid from without was fading fast. In the country the elections had been held and contrary to Paris the provinces remained conservative, though men hesitated to say openly that they were royalist. But in Paris the Commune had won. Out of seven hundred and fifty members one hundred and fifty-five were Girondins. They sat on the right and facing them on the left were the Mountain with Danton, Camille Desmoulins and Fabre d'Eglantine, the most fanatic of all. Between the Gironde and the Mountain sat the Plain, *Le Marais*, which watched both of them; they were prudent and hoped to gain from the competition of the other two. And further to the left again sat the *Enragés*, the extremists, who wanted common ownership of goods, what we would today call Communists.

The Girondins who had been guilty of so much disorder were now becoming the conservatives, and the whole convention was split into factions. They were ambitious, argumentative and even hated each other personally but they were united by one common idea, that of a France free and equal. And the citizen army, which had been welded into a superb fighting force, was giving them something to be proud of. For the Allied armies were in a rabbled flight. The poet Goethe gives a horrified account of the scene:

Self-preservation in so monstrous a press knew no pity, no respect of aught. Horse and foot endeavoured to escape from the narrow laborious highway into the meadows; but these too were rained to ruin; overflowed by full ditches, the connection of the footpaths everywhere interrupted. . . . That under such circumstances one saw, in ditches, in meadows, in fields and crofts, dead horses enough, was natural to the case; by-and-by however one also saw them flayed, the fleshy parts cut away, sad token of the universal distress.

And among the rabble the magnificent carriages of the nobility moved along like the rest, but with their haughty manners undisturbed, so that the people who served them in the inns reported how insupportable these Frenchmen were. High in honour at the head of the table, says Goethe, you observed with your own eyes not a Seigneur, but the automaton of a Seigneur fallen into dotage. A miserable picture indeed!

Dumouriez in Paris was fêted and adored, he had occupied Belgium, the Austrians were routed at Jemappes, and on 15 November he was in Brussels, on the 28th at Liège. He showed himself benignant, returning the keys of the city to the Brussels dignitaries and assuring them that France sought no conquest of territory, but only desired friendly states surrounding her. The Convention announced that it would grant brotherhood and help to all people who sought their freedom. The generals were to abolish feudal rights wherever they were victorious. But when the French arrived in Antwerp the English began to show interest in what was happening, perhaps a little late.

The month of November had passed sadly for the prisoners. On the 14th the King had fallen ill, but was denied a doctor until he took a turn for the worse, when one of his old attendants was permitted to enter after having been searched and warned never to speak softly. Following this the little Dauphin confined in his father's room had whooping cough; his mother pleaded earnestly to be allowed to remain with him at night, but the request was brutally refused and the poor woman, a prey to every anxiety, was forced to return to her own rooms where she found little repose. Now the whole of the family succumbed to the malady and even the faithful valet Cléry caught it, so that it was the turn of the young prince to run between the sick beds. He was a

Barnave

Danton

Mirabeau

Robespierre,
engraved by
Geoffroy

gentle loving child, looking always for any sign of kindness in his guards. A harpsichord had been placed in Marie Antoinette's room and this gave the children great pleasure when their mother played and sang to them. But on 7 December Cléry had terrible news; in four days' time the King would be called to appear before the Convention for his trial, and early in the morning of the 11th Marie Antoinette heard the drum beginning to beat the Générale. At nine o'clock Louis mounted the stairs to his wife's room for the last time. They breakfasted together – with what death in their hearts one can imagine – no word could be spoken, only a look could tell what they felt. The King regained his chamber with his son, who all unknowing demanded a game of cards. He was unlucky, and complained, 'Every time I get nearly sixteen I can't get any further.' The King's glance flickered but he said nothing. At eleven o'clock two municipals entered and ordered the child to follow them; the King exclaimed but they insisted, his father kissed him and he was taken to his mother. At one o'clock Louis XVI left the Temple escorted by the mayor of Paris and others, at six o'clock he returned and asked to see his family. It was refused and during the next six weeks Marie Antoinette never saw her husband.

The three women had passed the day in the most dreary uncertainty. The Queen tried to persuade herself that now that France was a republic the King might either be set at liberty or exiled; some of the press had even written that a king without a country has no friends while a king killed awakes sympathy. But one may point out that it seems nearly impossible that there could have been any other result from the trial than a verdict of death. Step by step, through the Legislative Assembly to the Constituent and on to the Commune, the Revolution had taken its way. At the beginning still royalist in its ideas and supported in them by the majority of the citizens of France, the extremists had become more and more insistent. Revolution never breaks out violently, it simmers for a long time with periodic revolts brutally suppressed, or it may be averted by menace from without or victorious and successful adventure; the people can be called out to shout for the glory achieved by their masters. But glory will not fill their stomachs nor clothe their children, nor put a roof on their homes. Suddenly, the cup is full, finally death is no more hideous than life, nothing more can be lost or suffered; this is the moment when the men with ideas see their chance, the two states work together and the revolution is there. And once it has started nothing can stop it, it must run its course, until at last the ultimate victim is found on whom all the fury can be expended, the hate and malice purged. Then only can the people be appeased, and wiser counsels prevail.

On the King's return Marie Antoinette had demanded that he should be allowed to see his family; the mayor, Chambon, did not even take the trouble to answer her. Madame Royale recorded, 'My brother passed the night with her, he had no bed and she gave him hers, all night she was up, in such misery that we could not leave her, but she forced us to rest, my aunt and myself.' Everything that could be thought of to make their captivity insupportable was done; the guards were doubled, and they never knew whether one of the municipals who were now their warders would be a little more kind-hearted than another, and allow them a moment's respite from the constant watching. All objects which might cut or scratch had been taken from the family, their pockets had been searched and even the knives for cutting their food were suspect. The Queen with one of her gusts of irony suggested that their needles should also be taken 'for they prick very sharply.' Needlework was their only occupation during the endless hours of waiting; inaction was not the least of their tortures.

On 12 December Marie Antoinette demanded afresh that she should be allowed to see the King, and Louis on his part did the same. Both received the answer that the Convention was considering the case. Seeing that the municipal whom he questioned was more conciliatory than most, the King asked him to tell the Princesses that he was well, and to inquire after their wellbeing, but he also told Cléry to take the Dauphin's bed up to his mother's room. On the valet's objection that he should wait for the decision Louis replied, 'I do not count on any consideration from them, nor on any justice. But we will wait.' Unfortunately the Convention left to the Commune the details of the day-to-day life of the royal family and the Commune had no mercy on them. While the Convention sent a deputation to inform the King that he might have a defending lawyer, the Commune decreed that he might keep his children with him, in which case they would leave their mother completely. Considerate as ever, Louis refused to deprive his wife of her sole consolation, and remained alone except for his devoted attendants, until his trial was ended.

He chose to defend him Target, one of the principal authors of the Constitution and if he was not available Tronchet, a lawyer. On the 13th the deputation returned: Target was unable to accept because of ill health but the King had the joy of hearing that the Convention had received many letters asking for the honour of defending him, of which the most urgent and touching was from the venerable Malesherbes. He wrote that having been twice a member of the Council when that post was coveted by all, he deemed it right that he should render the same service when it was a function which many men would think dangerous. The list of those offering to defend their late master is too long to give here, but we must mention the letter which the poet Schiller, that lover of real liberty and brotherhood, sent to the Convention. The King accepted with emotion the offer of Malesherbes, and asked him to confer with Tronchet. On their arrival the following day, Louis welcomed the illustrious philosopher with tears in his eyes, and drawing him apart after a brief conference said to him, 'My sister has given me the name and address of a non-juring priest who could help me in my last moments. Go and see him from me and tell him this, persuade him to help me. This is a strange commission for a philosopher, is it not?' 'Sire,' replied Malesherbes, 'there is no hurry about this.' 'Nothing is more pressing for me,' replied the King, giving him the note with the name and address.

The Abbé Edgeworth was the son of an Irish vicar who had settled in Toulouse following his conversion to the Catholic Church, and his name has gone down in history as that of a brave and selfless man who worked among the poorest in the city and who had a special gift for the cure of souls. When he received the King's message which asked him as a favour, but did not insist, for Louis knew the danger as well as the Abbé, the common opinion being that whoever performed the melancholy task would not long survive, the Abbé considered only his duty to his sad parishioners, and that his King had the right to be considered above all. He therefore answered that 'whether he lived or died I would be his friend to the last.' He received orders to remain in Paris and not to leave his house until he saw what turn affairs would take.

On 11 December the King appeared again before the Convention. The Queen had been suffering not only from the thought of the lonely man in the rooms below but from the ignoble efforts to torture her. Written on the walls where she could see them opposite her prison were such slogans as 'The guillotine is permanent and waits for the tyrant Louis XVI', or a caricature showing her husband 'spitting into the sack'. It was a penetratingly oppressive Christmas for the little family but for her above all; she hardly ate and grew daily thinner and more silent. The harpsichord, which a kindly municipal had tuned for her, felt her touch no longer, all she lived for was the slight news which Cléry could surreptitiously communicate about the progress of the trial.

The advocates had been frightened by the enormous number of documents of accusation which it was necessary to examine one by one, and more so when they heard that the King would appear for the last time before the Convention on the 26th. Malesherbes, who was old and deeply affected by the weight of responsibility, proposed that he should be replaced by a younger man and Monsieur de Sèze was accepted by the King, who remarked with humour 'The doctors are numerous when the danger is great. You prove to me that you despair of a cure, but I will show you that I am a good patient.' De Sèze was accepted by the Convention and the three defence lawyers met regularly for the remaining days. Throughout this trying time Louis XVI showed himself as always unselfish, thinking more of others even to small acts of kindness for his servants, and towards the municipals who watched him. The faithful Cléry managed to give him messages from Madame Elisabeth which they both hid with the ingenuity born of necessity. He talked with his guards and astonished them by the breadth of his knowledge and the common sense of his observations, and above all by his calm courage. On Wednesday 19 January when Cléry brought his dinner, Louis remarked, 'You were up earlier on this day fourteen years ago,' and then to the listening municipals, 'fourteen years ago my daughter was born; door child, today is her birthday and I cannot see her.' His eyes were wet, and even the jailers were silent before the father's grief.

The work of the lawyers continued; the justification was long and difficult, for as Louis said, it was the labour of Penelope, the Convention would undo all they did. On Christmas Day he had written his testament, that magnanimous document in which he recommended his children to his wife, asking her to continue to bring them up as good Christians, knowing that the honours of this world are perishable and dangerous, only in Eternal Truth lies real glory. He prayed his sister to continue her tender love for them if they should have the misfortune to lose their mother. And he asked his wife to pardon all the ills she suffered for him, and the pain which he might have given her in the course of their union, just as she might be sure that he kept no memory of anything against her if she thought that she might have anything to reproach herself with. In his last hours this man, down to ultimate truth, surveyed their whole lives together and found in his heart an understanding which transcended all petty thought and superficial difference. They had lived together, suffered together and now they would die, still together. And when, on 20 January, Marie Antoinette heard the men calling under her window, 'The Convention decrees that Louis Capet is condemned to death. . . . The execution will take place twenty-four hours after the notification to the prisoner', she would know it too.

The 19 January dawned; the King fearing that the Queen would be awakened if she heard the sound of the drums had asked that this shock might be spared her, and when the deputies arrived to conduct him to the Chamber he took his coat and hat and calmly went down with them. It was pouring with rain and he asked that the windows of the coach might be closed, but this was refused on the grounds that the waiting crowd would suspect something wrong. There was evidently great anxiety that an attempt at rescue or flight might be attempted. During the long slow drive from the Temple to the Riding School the King talked peaceably with his companions, discussing with them the ideas of Seneca and Titus Livy with a phlegm which amazed them. It is obvious that he had already said his adieux to this world and could not be disturbed. Arrived at the vestibule he found his lawyers, and he was talking with them when a deputy Treilhard, hearing them address him as Majesty and Sire, furiously demanded what gave them the audacity to dare to pronounce a name which the Convention had proscribed. 'Contempt for you, and contempt for life,' replied Malesherbes.

The trial wound its expected course to its tragic end. The King spoke declaring that he was not afraid of public inquiry into his actions, and that speaking for probably the last time he felt his conscience clear, and his defence would speak nothing but the truth. At five o'clock he returned to the Temple and though his lawyers still maintained that there was hope, he said:

This day has finished everything for me, the struggle is over. They have sent me back to give the appearance of a judicial measure to their decision, already arrived at. I have only asked them like Charles 1 by what authority I appeared before them, but like my predecessor I say, for a long time now they have taken all things from me, except those which are dearer to me than life, my conscience and my honour.

On 20 January, the King, having heard his death sentence, asked the Convention to allow him three days to prepare himself to appear before his Maker and to see his family. The vote had been taken and his cousin Equality Orléans, true to his vile self, had cast his for death; nothing had been spared this unhappy man. But one of the principal persecutors left this remarkable witness to his greatness:

I wished to be one of those who would be present at the reading of the sentence of death of Louis. He listened with a rare sang-froid to this reading. When it was finished he asked to see his family, a confessor and all which was necessary for the comfort of his last hour. He put such dignity, such nobility, such grandeur into this demand that I simply could not stand it. Tears of rage sprang to my eyes and I was obliged to retire.

These were the words of the murderer Hébert.

The respite having been refused the King prepared himself for the final farewells, and in the evening of the 20th his family heard that they might see him for the last time. The Queen had passed the day in unspeakable anguish; Madame Elisabeth who with her heavenly nature had thought more of her sister's sorrow than her own, was equally unnerved, but they hurried down the narrow stairway under the inquisitive glances of the municipals, who seemed for this day to be chosen from among their bitterest enemies. Louis had taken the greatest care in arranging the poor room for their reception, even asking Cléry to bring a glass of the Queen's special water in case she needed it. She came in first, leading her son by the hand, followed by Madame Elisabeth and Madame Royale, and threw herself into her husband's arms. No one could speak; in the silence only their sobbing could be heard. When at last they were seated they spoke tenderly together.

The King gave them an account of his trial where Orléans had been among his judges. For a majority three hundred and sixty-one votes were needed and this was the exact number which were cast. If Equality had not voted for death the King might have been saved. He spoke with infinite love and compassion to his two children, asking them to promise never to seek revenge for his death, but to pardon those who offended them, as their religion taught them. And then, taking his little son on his knee, he said, 'My child, you have heard what I just said to you, but since an oath is something much more sacred than mere words, swear to me with your hand uplifted that you will fulfil the last wishes of your father.' Madame Royale wrote, 'My brother, bursting into tears, obeyed him, and his goodness moved us all profoundly.'

He then gave them his blessing and at a quarter past ten rose, and when Cléry entered he saw the Queen in an agony of tears imploring her husband to see her once again. She had wished that they might all spend the night together, but he had refused, saying that he had need of tranquillity to prepare for the ordeal which faced him. Now she pleaded for one last look, one last embrace and he agreed for eight o'clock next morning. 'Why not at seven?' she demanded. 'Well then, at seven,' he replied. Once more he set his son upon his knee and made him swear with hand upraised, never to avenge himself upon the men who had condemned him, and then it was the terrible moment of adieu. His young daughter fainted, and was raised and taken from the room by Cléry. The little boy cast himself on the floor before the municipals begging them to let him ask the gentlemen of the sections of Paris to save his father, and Marie Antoinette, with a deathly pain at her heart, took a speechless farewell of the man whose life she had shared for years. All this was heard by the Abbé Edgeworth, who had gone into the little turret room after his interview with the King. He recorded it, saying that it was the most agonizing scene possible to imagine. To end it, the King tore himself from their arms and went into his room.

Marie Antoinette ascended the stairs and after putting her son to bed threw herself on her couch and spent the night shivering and wretched, waiting for the dawn. Worn out with grief she heard a distant clock strike five and steps in the room below. It was Cléry lighting the fire. During the night the Abbé had been engaged in obtaining from the Council permission for Louis to hear Mass, which had eventually been granted on condition that it was over by seven o'clock, for at eight punctually the King must leave for his execution. This was announced with as little emotion as if he were going on a picnic. A little later the heavy bolts on the Queen's room were drawn. She started up, but it was only a guard asking for Madame Elisabeth's missal for the Mass, and the door clanged to again. Soon a cold and foggy light crept into the apartment, and the noise of troops assembling and the usual sounds of a multitude rose from the street beyond. The Queen was pressed against the door, which did not open, hoping against hope that she might see him once more, but Louis XVI had said his goodbye to this world and all he loved in it, had made his peace with God, and with a clear conscience and a mind at rest was wiser than she as he stepped forth to his end.

Then the Queen heard the trumpets beneath the window and the roll of drums further and further away. He was gone, all they could do was to wait. Turgy brought the meal, she tried to persuade the Dauphin to eat, but he refused. Slowly the hands of the clock reached half past ten and at the same time the guns roared. It was over, a tempest of weeping shook them all, while beneath their prison the drums of the Temple guard beat, and the sentinels cried '*Vive la République*.' The Queen stretched on her bed sat up, a memory stirring in her paralysed mind. She rose, there was no cry, '*Le Roi est mort, vive le Roi*', as from the balcony of Versailles so long ago, but she went to her son and saluted him as King.

On the next day Marie Antoinette had sufficiently recovered her calm to demand mourning clothes for herself and her family, also she hoped that the faithful Cléry would be allowed to continue the service he had given the dead King for his son. She hoped that through him she might have some account of her husband's last hours. She was told that the Commune would decide. The 21st was long and sad, the fog had thickened over Paris and the people seemed to awaken to the full horror of the act which they had performed. In the cafés in the evening, says Prudhomme, the men who had planned the act shook hands and congratulated each other; by the next day they began to understand what they had done. The streets were silent and deserted, people avoided each other, in the Temple the long hours passed heavily, and when evening came only the children could sleep. The Queen and Madame Elisabeth watched the little boy. 'He is now,' said his mother, 'the same age as his brother when he died at Meudon: they are happy who have gone on first; they have not been present at the ruin of our family.' Late into the night they were awake, and the jailers Tison and his wife, always on the watch, came to their door to spy on them. 'For pity's sake,' said Madame Elisabeth gently, 'let us weep in peace.' They were ashamed for once and went away quietly. Next day when Louis Charles awoke his mother took him in her arms and said, 'My child one must think about God.' 'Maman,' replied the boy, 'I too have thought about God, but every time I call Him it is my father who comes to me,' at which their tears flowed afresh.

On 23 January the Commune allowed them their mourning garments, but refused to let Cléry continue his service. On the other hand the prisoners were happy to have the visit of one of the ladies of the bedchamber to Madame Royale, a Mademoiselle Pion, who came to adjust the dresses which fitted badly. They could not of course speak freely before their guards, but the Dauphin managed in playing to ask the questions which they did not dare to put. She saw how woefully the Queen had aged, how thin she had become, how wretched was their life in spite of a slight relaxation in these last days. Their guards were less virulent, and two of them, Toulan and Lepitre, had even been captivated by Marie Antoinette's charm and kindliness to a worship which led them into some danger. They managed to be on guard together, and generally on Sunday, and on 7 February Lepitre brought a song which he had composed and Madame Cléry set to music, and had the pleasure of seeing the young princess sitting at her harpsichord with her mother beside her holding her son in her arms and teaching them both the words which commemorated their father's death. The young voices rose and the rough guards had tears in their eyes.

It was not long before they showed their devotion in a more practical way, for Toulan, who had been an extreme revolutionary and implicated in the attack on the Tuileries, now conceived a plan for the escape of the royal family. The plan was ingenious and took account of the fact that the Temple was not as inviolable as the authorities believed, while it was possible to count on the help of the few royalists who had remained in Paris in the hope of aiding their late masters. The chief of these was the Chevalier de Jarjayes, the husband of one of Marie Antoinette's ladies in waiting, who had already proved his fidelity. On 2 February he was surprised by a visit from Toulan bearing a note from the Queen: 'You may rely on the man who will speak to you from me and give you this note. His feelings are known to me; for five months he has always been dependable.' But Jarjayes still doubted and asked if Toulan could possibly help him to see the Queen; the audacious Toulan assured him that he could, and announced to Her Majesty that the Marshal would soon visit her, on which she wrote again, 'Now if you have decided to come here it would be best if it could be soon. But, my God, take care not to be recognized and above all not by the woman who is confined with us [Madame Tison].'

Now Toulan persuaded the man who came every evening to light the lamps to lend his costume to a 'patriot' friend who was dying to see the Queen 'in irons'. In this disguise Jarjayes got into the tower and the plot began to take shape. Two other accomplices were added, Turgy and Lepitre, who has left his account of the whole thing. Jarjayes ordered for the Queen and Madame Elisabeth two men's costumes which Toulan and Lepitre spirited into the apartments under their own clothes. Miraculously, they were not suspected, in spite of their increased girth. Wearing these with tricolour scarves and cockaded hats the women would resemble municipals. For the children it was more tricky, but even this the ingenious Toulan managed. Every evening the lamplighter was accompanied by his two children, of about the same size as Louis Charles and his sister. These two would be dressed in ragged clothes like those worn by the lamplighter's offspring and the different groups would take the two cabriolets waiting for them. Once out of the Temple, Lepitre optimistically arranged the flight to the coast, and he reckoned that it would be five hours before their flight would be discovered and the pursuit organized. He had been given 200,000 francs but took so long in making the arrangements that in the intervening time events had occurred to make the whole plan more uncertain.

Europe, horrified by the crime of the King's execution, now united against France, and the Mountain, dominated by the extremists Robespierre and Marat, seized upon the excuse and set up the Revolutionary Tribunal and the Committee of Public Safety. The Gironde and its leaders, Danton, Buzot and others who had hoped to save the old régime were helpless to prevent it.

Unfortunately on 7 March, the day before the escape was planned, an unusual panic spread throughout Paris due to the bad news from the armies. The French had been obliged to evacuate Aix-La-Chapelle and to raise the siege of Maastricht; worse, the Austrians had retaken Liège. As a result all the barriers were closed and all passports for exit forbidden. The project in these circumstances had to be given up.

Undaunted, the intrepid friends Toulan and Jarjayes set about a new enterprise. They were determined at least to save the Queen, who was most vulnerable. Their one fear was that she would never decide to leave her children and sister. They argued, they implored and Madame Elisabeth joined her entreaties to theirs, pointing out that she would still be there and would care for the young ones like a mother. The Queen listened and seemed at last to consent, and the day for the escape drew near. On the night before the little boy was asleep, but Madame Royale heard the conversation which she later recorded. Marie Antoinette walked up and down, up and down, still uncertain. Suddenly she exclaimed, 'It is impossible, impossible.' And next day, when Toulan arrived excited and joyous she said, 'You will not forgive me, but I have thought it all over. It is too full of danger, it is better to die than to regret.' And she gave him a letter for Jarjayes:

We have had a beautiful dream. That is all. But we have gained much through discovering through this trial a new proof of your entire devotion. My trust in you is complete. You will always find in me firmness and courage; but my son's need is the sole guide. What happiness could I find far from here? I cannot consent to separate myself from him. I could not enjoy anything without my children, and this thought fills me with not a single regret.

'I shall die unhappy,' she said to Toulan 'if I cannot prove my gratitude to you.'

On 12 March General Dumouriez was accused of treason and denounced by the sections, and on the 13th the Vendée, still royalist in feeling, revolted. Civil war seemed inevitable but instead of taking a conciliatory attitude to avoid it, the Mountain redoubled their repressive measures. The family in the Temple, although they were ignorant of what was happening, were naturally disturbed by the sounds of excitement which reached them from the surrounding streets, and equally naturally feared that it might bode them ill. But the entry of Toulan reassured them, and more; he had found a means of abstracting from the King's room, where Cléry had left them sealed up, the precious objects which Marie Antoinette had so longed for, the wedding ring, the small amulet which Louis had always worn, and tresses of the children's hair. The ring was golden and when opened it showed the engraved inscription *M.A.A.A. 19 Aprilis 1770 jour des fiançailles de Marie Antoinette, Archiduchesse d'Autriche et de Louis August, Dauphin de France.* The Queen, overjoyed, wept when she saw them, but decided that to keep them would be too dangerous. She therefore decided to send them by Toulan to Jarjayes with letters to her brothers Provence and Artois. The Marshal would tell them by what a miracle these precious souvenirs of the being who was dear to them all had been preserved and would give them news of the prisoners.

With these she sent another packet carefully made up with the message: 'The sealed packet is quite a different thing. I desire that you should send it to the person whom you know came from Brussels last winter to see me, and you say to him that the motto has never been more true.' It was a pigeon flying – one of Fersen's emblems which Marie Antoinette had made her own. The bird was surrounded by a motto '*Tutto a te me guida*' – everything leads me to you. Her thoughts and her heart must often have gone out to him in these dark days.

In the country things were not going well for the French, and the treason of Dumouriez was a crushing blow for the government. Already in February Fersen in far-away Brussels had a notion that some sort of understanding was being reached between the general and the invaders; on the 24th the Allies reentered Brussels and on 18 March Mercy announced the *entente* which was signed by Dumouriez and the Princes at Cobourg. Fersen had been so pessimistic in his letters to his sister, so disgusted by the lack of feeling shown by the Counts of Provence and Artois when they heard of Louis XVI's execution, that his satisfaction over this happy turn in events was all the stronger. 'The rebels have lost their best general,' he wrote and indeed for the Gironde it was the kiss of death. He had been their man, his loss was the signal for a violent campaign against them instigated by the Mountain. On 27 March Robespierre demanded the banishment of all the Bourbons with the exception of Marie

Antoinette, who would be arraigned before the Revolutionary Tribunal and the 'Capet son', who would remain in the Temple. The attempt failed for the time being, but it seemed as if the Commune had some wind of the plots for escape, for the precautions were redoubled again. Another wall was built round the garden, uselessly it seemed, for Marie Antoinette had not entered it since her husband's departure; she could not bear to pass his door, nor to take the risk of seeing Santerre who had behaved so brutally to him. Tison and his wife, who also could not leave the prison, revenged themselves on the unhappy prisoners by every means in their power and finally denounced them to the Council, with the result that there were again searches in their rooms. The last, which the brutish Hébert undertook in person in the middle of the night, lasted five hours. Everything was turned upside down, every stitch of their clothing tossed and shaken, the drawers rifled, all to no purpose. Nothing incriminating was found, no correspondence with the world outside, only a few poor personal things, a little red purse containing a pencil without lead, and from Madame Elisabeth a stick of sealing wax half used. From Marie-Thérèse an amulet of the Sacred Heart, and a prayer for France. The infuriated Hébert forced them to sign a receipt and went away cursing. Three days later they came back, this time they discovered under Madame Elisabeth's bed a felt hat which she had kept as memento of her brother. All this had one disastrous result, the suspension of Toulan and Lepitre from their duties.

If the prisoners could have known it, the King's death had thrown both the parties at home and the Allied forces without into confusion. In Paris, on the evening of the King's conviction one man avenged him. Lepelletier de St Fargeau, entering a café was accosted by a young man. 'Are you Lepelletier?' he asked. 'Yes.' 'You voted in the King's affair?' 'I voted death.' 'Traitor, take that,' cried the young man. He ran his sword deep into the murderer's side and disappeared. St Fargeau lingered two days, died and was given a public funeral, all parties walking in solemn procession after the body borne high on its bier. It was the last thing they ever did in common. Roland, long disgusted with the turn which revolutionary affairs were taking, sent in his resignation. England asked the Citizen Ambassador to leave the country within eight days, Spain declared war, England too, and Danton thundering in the Convention might well shout 'The Kings in coalition threaten us; we hurl at their feet as a gage of battle, the Head of a King.'

It was one thing to declare war, another to wage it. There was dissension in Coblentz, in Frankfurt and in Vienna too. In Coblentz Monsieur was occupied in assuring for himself the regency, for although they neded Dumouriez they could not be sure that the price of his aid would not be a pretension to govern France. Fersen wished to push Vienna into supporting the Queen's right to the post; on 5 March he wrote in his *Journal* that he feared no longer for the Queen, so certain was he that when Dumouriez with his fifty thousand men marched on Paris the revolutionaries would be defeated and nothing would remain except for the right person to be there to instruct the Queen on the course she should follow. He had heard of a proposal to set Orléans on the throne but could not believe it. A council of regency would be formed in which the influence of one party would be balanced by the other, the princes by Dumouriez and Monsieur by the Baron de Breteuil. 'You must write to the Emperor, the Kings of England and Prussia,' he advised the Queen, 'they have been sympathetic to you, and you must also write to the Empress [of Russia] . . . in any case until the moment when you are recognized as Regent and you have formed your Council you must do as little as possible and reward only with compliments.'

Poor fellow, his wonderful dream of a re-established monarchy where he also would have the reward for his devotion was doomed to disappointment; it was only a matter of days before he heard that Dumouriez had lost control of his army and was in full flight towards Mons with his whole staff.

In the Temple tedious day succeeded day, never alone, spied on by the odious Tison and his wife, without news, without exercise, without interests, the prisoners made what they could of their solitude. Even the little Dauphin, lately so gay and playful, was restrained lest some chance word should make him suspect to his guards. They could not know that in the city and the country they were still remembered, that the victims of the guillotine died with their names upon their lips, acknowledging with their last breath the child whom they honoured as their King. The bad air, the confinement was telling on them all and in the beginning of

May Louis Charles fell ill. His distracted mother, fearing the worst, sent a message by one of the municipals to the Council, asking them to allow Brunier, the doctor who had attended the first Dauphin, to visit him. The Council responded by commissioning M. Thierry, the doctor to the common prisons, to go to the Temple, their excuse being, 'For it would attack the idea of equality to send any other.' Thierry, a kindly man, examined the young patient and on Marie Antoinette's request consulted with M. Brunier, and followed his advice with good results.

Since they were still alive hope, which never completely dies, stirred sometimes in their hearts, and outside the persistent Baron de Batz was still plotting their escape. In June he had succeeded in forming a group of thirty royalists and some National Guards who were to enter the Temple disguised, and placing the prisoners in their midst, force their way out. In this plot they were helped by Michonis, the administrator of the prisons, and on the night of 21 June Michonis really found himself in the Queen's room, with his men below and a further group waiting in the street. Suddenly bells rang, cries were heard, it was Simon, commissioner of the Commune, who had received an anonymous letter 'Take care, Michonis will betray you this evening.' He sounded the alarm, Batz managed to escape, but the plot had failed.

Worse was to come. The public was divided by the dissensions of the Factions and constantly made uneasy by the reports from the provinces; the armies, always on the point of an outbreak, were only matched by the quarrels of the deputies themselves. That devious patriot Robespierre suspected a design for the deliverance of the young King, and pushed through laws condemning any émigré putting his foot on the soil of France, any patriot convicted of having helped an émigré, or anyone having a passport showing that he had sworn allegiance to Louis XVII. And well he might, for everyone was conspiring, or trying to; all those who had suffered themselves or through those dear to them, all who had felt the horror of rebellion and the cruel reprisals, all who hated the rulers and their laws. Every man distrusted his neighbour and most of the plotting was centred on the figure of the young King. Therefore it does not surprise us that on 3 July the doors of Marie Antoinette's chamber suddenly opened and six municipals appeared. It was ten o'clock, the little boy was asleep but the other members of the family were peaceably employed, Madame Elisabeth and Marie Antoinette mending their threadbare clothes, and the young girl, Marie Thérèse, reading from the *Semaine Sainte*, a quiet prelude to their repose. On seeing the guards they started up, what could this mean? 'We are come,' said one of them, 'to bring the order of the Committee, which decrees that the son of Capet shall be separated from his mother and his family.' Horrified the Queen stammered 'Take away my son, no, no, it is not possible.' Elisabeth and Marie Thérèse listened speechless while the unfortunate mother tried to convince the immovable men before her. The Committee had made this decision, they insisted, and it must be obeyed. Now the Queen who until then had by a superhuman effort controlled herself, broke down, and the two others seeing that the little boy had awakened stood in front of his couch shielding him with their outstretched arms. In vain. 'What is the use of all this caterwauling?' said one of the men, 'nobody is going to kill your child; give him to us, or we will know how to take him.' And now the child added his cries to theirs, clutching his mother's skirts he wept, 'Don't leave me Maman, don't leave me.' She held him to her, kissing and soothing him, she *could* not let him go, until one municipal threatened to call the guards. 'For God's sake,' murmured Madame Elisabeth, 'do not do that, have pity, at least let him stay this night, give us time to breathe, we must accept what you order, but let the child sleep tonight, tomorrow he will go to you.' No answer; and then his mother. 'At least let us see him every day, for his meals perhaps.' And one municipal, 'You think you are unhappy because you have to give up one child; what about us, what about us who see our children destroyed by the enemies whom you have called to our frontiers.' To which the Queen replied in her usual gentle way, 'My son is too young to fight for his country, but I hope that one day, if God wills, he will be proud to consecrate his life to it.' While she spoke she began to dress the child, taking as much time as possible over each article of clothing, while the men stood there stony faced. It was perhaps not because they were particularly brutal, at times even they showed feeling of a sort, but they had passed through a hard school of suffering themselves and for them this family, and especially this woman, embodied all that endangered their hopes for change. As long as this residue of monarchy existed they were not safe.

At last the painful moments had passed, the last touch of the clothes so carefully mended and cleansed, the last caress of his frail neck and shoulders had been given; his sister and aunt embraced him for the last time and his weeping mother rallying all her love and fortitude placed him before her and blessed him, telling him always to be honest and good and to remember his father who would bless him from heaven. The poor little boy clung to her for the last time and was forced away by his jailers. 'My son, we must obey, we must,' said Marie Antoinette, while one of the men answered her, 'Don't bother yourself, the Nation, always just and generous, will look after his education.' 'We have been patient too long,' said another, and they slammed the door behind them. Then indeed the three left behind broke down. This was the most dreadful blow: not only were they losing their one solace, the only ray of sunshine in their sad lives, but they feared the worst, for Louis Charles was to have a keeper, that very Simon who had shown himself the most disgusting, the most hateful of their warders. For the next few days they heard the child crying almost uninterruptedly. His despair was so profound that Simon did not dare to let anyone see him and it began to be said that he was no longer in the Temple. The Committee of Security, intent on scotching these rumours, sent a deputation to the prison to see for themselves. It was headed by Drouet, the man of Varennes, not by any means an impartial witness. They saw the royal child who with the greatest courage demanded by what law he was separated from his mother, and they interrogated Simon, who, as a fanatically devoted patriot, believed that his duty was to make a *sans culotte* out of this sprig of nobility. But it would appear that the deputation made him aware, in an oblique fashion, that the intention of the revolutionary government was quite other. Simon asked, 'Citizens what have you decided about the wolf cub? He is insolent but I know how to curb him. All the worse if he succumbs, I won't answer for it. After all what do you want – to deport him?' 'No.' 'To kill him?' 'No.' 'To poison him?' 'No.' 'What then?' 'To get rid of him [*S'en défaire*]!'

The child's fate was sealed. From then on Simon employed the utmost brutality in breaking his spirit, and the unhappy mother who spent hours watching through a small crack in the wall as the pair went up to the tower, suffered the daily agony of seeing the gradual perversion of her son's mind. Soon he cursed like his mentor, he was dirty and coarse, he blasphemed, he suffered on those days when because of bad news the fury of his keeper was vented in blows and insults. Thus when the Austrian Army took the town of Condé he was reproached with his Austrianness, and when Simon's patron Marat was assassinated on 14 July, he was put into mourning for the 'friend of the people'. But when on 1 August Paris was alerted by the taking of the fortified town of Valenciennes the result was far more momentous for the prisoners of the Temple. This success left the route to the capital open, it seemed only a matter of days before the invaders would be outside the walls of Paris.

Marie Antoinette was awakened by the augmented street sounds, the beating of near-by drums and nearer still the loud trampling of many feet in the prison itself. Hanriot, the commander of the city army was conducting an inquiry into the further strengthening of the fortress and its guards. The poor mother, now so worn by her sufferings that she seemed only the shadow of herself, had still the questionable joy of seeing her child from time to time from her narrow hiding place; and together the prisoners could remember happier days and comfort each other. And the warder Tison, moved perhaps in spite of himself, brought news of Louis Charles, seldom good, but at least he still lived. Now Simon's treatment had become so vicious that Madame Elisabeth begged him not to tell her sister, but on this day Simon, infuriated by the bad news, exceeded himself. The Queen at her watch-post saw them both, the little boy wearing the red cap, his head bent, his feet dragging, sick and hopeless. Marie Antoinette, her heart torn, in an agony threw herself into her sister's arms. 'My presentiment did not deceive me,' she moaned, 'I knew that he suffered, if he were a hundred miles from me my heart would tell me if he were ill. For the last two days I trembled, I was agitated, the tears of my poor child fell on my own heart. I care for nothing; God has forsaken me, I do not dare even to pray.' But then, repentant, 'Pardon my God, I feel myself menaced by some new misfortune.'

She was right; on that day Barère made a great speech in the Convention, he enumerated the misdeeds of the Allies, the English fleet before Marseilles and Toulon, the Republican Army defeated in the North and the West, anarchy fomented by agents throughout the land, Spain on the South, Bourbon in the Midi, the exchequer empty. He spoke of Pitt, 'That young slave of a mad King', of Burke, the enemy of the Republic. 'Is it that we have forgotten the crimes of the Austrian, is it our indifference towards the family of Capet which encourages our enemies? *Eh bien!* it is time to extirpate the remains of royalty.' Thus he cried, and the National Convention made haste to adopt the following measures. It was fear which dictated their act, fear for their persons, for the Republic in which they believed, right or wrong, and terror which for months had reigned in the city spreading everywhere its evil fumes:

1 Marie Antoinette to be sent to an Extraordinary Tribunal, and transferred to the Conciergerie.

2 All the individuals of the Capet family to be deported from the Republic, with the exception of the two children of Louis Capet, and those who are beneath the sword of the law.

3 Elisabeth Capet not to be deported until after the sentencing of Marie Antoinette.

4 The expenses of the two children of Louis Capet to be reduced to what is necessary for the maintenance of two individuals.

5 The tombs and mausoleums of former Kings, in the Church of St Denis or in other temples or places, in the whole of the Republic to be destroyed by 10 August next.

No time was lost; at two o'clock next morning the Queen was awakened and the decree was read to her. She listened in complete silence. Madame Elisabeth and Madame Royale implored permission to accompany her, but it was refused. The municipals stood there watching while she dressed and made a little packet of her few clothes. They insisted that she turn out her pockets, she did it, and they took the small unimportant contents, leaving her nothing but a handkerchief and smelling salts 'in case she should feel ill'!

'My mother,' says Madame Royale, 'embraced me tenderly and told me to take care of my aunt and to obey her, my aunt whispered a few words to her, and then she left us without looking at us again – for fear of losing her self-control I think.' She stopped a moment at the foot of the tower, for the municipals had to dictate a document stating her discharge. She stood mute, carrying her small parcel. Finally, the regulation complied with, she was pushed towards the exit to the garden and here she forgot to bend her head beneath the low portal. Michonis, seeing her hit her forehead, asked if she had hurt herself. 'No,' she replied, 'nothing now can do me any injury.'

She mounted the first of the waiting carriages and was borne swiftly away from the palace which she had entered a year ago, when she had still been treated as a Queen. Now she was a fragment of human flotsam, a wreck in the sea of time, she had lost everything except herself and that which she had said on a more hopeful day one must preserve until the last, her 'caractère', in other words her self respect, her inner fortitude.

Arriving at the Conciergerie she was conducted to her new prison, a small damp room with a window hardly above ground level. It had been occupied until a few hours previously by the General Custine, and Madame Richard, the wife of the concierge, and her servant had hastily furnished it with a bed and two mattresses, a bolster and a coverlet. To these they had added a kind of cupboard, and a washing bowl. There were also a table and two straw-bottomed chairs. This was to be her last abode, to this had the daughter of Maria Theresa, the Queen of France, descended.

10
The Victim

DURING the month of July Fersen in Brussels had not ceased to follow with varying emotions the progress of affairs. He had one desire which transcended all others, the safety of the Queen, and he was not sparing in his detestation of the revolutionaries who were tormenting her, and the Allies who were losing every chance of saving her. There had been moments when she really might have been rescued, there had even been projects such as the exchange of the royal family against the Commissioners whom Dumouriez had given to Austria. But every attempt had foundered on the rocks of intrigue and apathy; there was no organization, no vision; when in July Danton was criticized in the Convention for his conciliatory attitude and as a consequence withdrew on Robespierre's joining the Committee of Public Safety, an attempt might have been made. It was hinted even that he had been offered a bribe, but this too came to nothing. And when on 9 August Axel heard of the transference of Marie Antoinette to the Conciergerie he was in despair. He pictured to himself her hopeless case, the degradation of this last imprisonment and saw no chance of her survival but in a determined effort from the Allies to reach Paris. The road was open and the troops could find all the farms well provisioned. But when he visited Mercy he found no encouragement; the Ambassador had given the Queen up for lost and that was all there was about it. And Fersen was further enraged when in the evening he saw the whole of the French colony at the theatre with their wives!

It was three in the morning when the Queen entered the wretched cave where she would spend her last days. Still frozen with shock she hardly looked round, but took the little gold watch which she had brought from Vienna as a child, and which had never left her, hung it on a nail in the wall, stretched herself on the miserable bed and lapsed into a sort of sleep. With the first light of dawn however her tormentors were there, two gendarmes took up their station, she would never be out of their sight. An old woman had been found to serve her, but proved too kindly and was replaced by a younger servant, the wife of a man employed in the secret service, a more reliable spy, by name Harel. The Queen took an instant dislike to her and in future hardly spoke to her. She was better served by the young servant of Madame Richard, Rosalie Lamorlière, a pretty girl, with a kind heart, who has left a touching account of the royal prisoner. A dilapidated screen had been stretched across the room, which gave her a little privacy for her toilet, but the guards lived their life behind it, drinking, smoking and doubtless spitting or retailing coarse jokes after their kind – though they were not ungentle and sometimes brought her flowers

Shortly after her arrival she was able to have ink and paper and wrote to her daughter that she was well, calm and would be tranquil if she could know that her poor child was well too. She asked for some silk stockings, a coat of cloth and a petticoat. The letter was confiscated but Michonis succeeded in procuring for her some chemises, two pairs of black silk stockings, a mantle, three fine linen fichus and a pair of easy shoes 'which she badly needed', for those she was wearing were destroyed by dirt and damp. She also had some water for her teeth, a box of powder and a swansdown puff. All this seems rather ridiculous in the light of her predicament, but women will know that it is by these simple means that they preserve their individuality and self-respect. So this fallen royalty, when she rose at seven in the morning and had taken her cup of coffee or chocolate, brought by Rosalie, made a meticulous toilet. She brushed and parted her hair and tied it back with an end of ribbon given by Madame Harel, powdered it lightly and covered it with her large widow's bonnet – out of which she later made two. She managed her further toilet while Rosalie made the bed, and then put on one of her two dresses, the white or the black; she was ready for the long long day, empty except for her thoughts or the few books which Hue or Montjoie succeeded in procuring for her – she preferred travel stories, Cook's *Voyages* was amongst them 'with the most frightening adventures' she said when asked. Like her husband, she had always enjoyed such books.

The Queen was well fed, she had soup, chicken, vegetables, for her dinner at two o'clock and cutlets, pigeon or duck for her supper, and since she had never drunk wine and had been supplied in the Temple with water from Ville d'Avray, two of the bottles were sent daily to the Conciergerie. Soon her jailers, won over by her gentleness, were doing their utmost to distract her. Madame Richard brought her little boy of about the same age as the Dauphin to see Her Majesty. The poor woman smothered him with kisses, played with him and could not be stopped from talking about her lost child, it was almost too much for her. She wore concealed under her corset the portrait of Louis Charles and a little yellow glove which he had worn, and said Rosalie, 'I could not help noticing that she often hid herself in her bed to hold these things and speak to them.' One could speak to her of her situation, of her troubles, without her showing any emotion, only when she mentioned her children did her tears flow.

At the Conciergerie at this time political prisoners were all mixed together with common thieves, murderers, and other criminals, in fact the jails were too full for discrimination. All over Paris and in the country too suspicion was the order of the day, friend was denounced by hidden enemy, colleague by colleague, and the guillotine swallowed them all. In the Terror which brooded over France the really republican patriots were witnessing the failure of their aspirations, men like Pétion, Buzot and Barbaroux, honest ministers like Roland, philosophers like Condorcet, however opposed they had been to the monarchy, were appalled by the tyranny which Paris, 'that vile multitude', exercised over the rest of the country. The Girondins were finished, blotted out by the extreme left with Robespierre, the icy incorruptible image presiding over all. They had wished for a united France, and could possibly have been persuaded at first to accept a limited monarchy; they saw the danger of centralization and Buzot even wrote when he was wandering through the country, a hunted prescribed fugitive, 'the Terror is the *real* counter-revolution

– total centralization means despotism or tyranny – the freedom of the press is the saviour of all liberties.' And Danton, sickened by the slaughter going on in the capital and the provinces, said to Desmoulins, 'The Seine is running with blood, go back and ask for clemency. I shall support you.' Alas, his days were numbered too.

But for the men who confronted her the idea of monarchy was in itself a crime. In the words of Hébert, under his pseudonym Père Duchesne:

I suppose ... that she might not be guilty of all these crimes ... but was she not a queen? This crime is enough to condemn her, for what is a king or a queen? Is it not that which in all the world is the most impure, the greatest traitor? To reign, is it not to be humanity's mortal enemy? The counter-revolutionaries whom we strangle like mad dogs are worthless enemies, nothings. But kings! Their race are born to do us harm. In being born they are destined for crime like the plant which poisons us; it is as natural for emperors, kings, princes to oppress and devour mankind as for a tiger to devour his prey. They care no more for their subjects than we care for the insects which we crush with our feet without notice. It is the duty of every free man to kill a king, or those destined to become kings, or who have shared the crimes of kings.

The Queen, in her narrow cell which looked out on the vast Courtyard of the Women, could catch sight of the men separated by a grille but able to converse and even to take their meals in common. Death was so near to them all that a sort of light-heartedness prevailed, when nothing more is to be hoped for one can laugh equally at life and extinction; love affairs were begun, friendships formed, hatreds too were remembered, the fine mingled with the coarse, the lady with the woman of the gutter. And under such conditions it was easier to have some connection with the outside world, however closely she was watched. So Michonis allowed a certain Mademoiselle Fouché to enter her cell; this was a young girl from Orléans who with the Abbé Magnin, a refugee from Autun, visited the Conciergerie frequently. At first the Queen refused to notice the visitor to her solitude, but before her departure she replied indifferently to the question whether she might return, 'As you like.' The second visit was more successful and Mademoiselle asked whether the Queen would like a priest to visit her. 'Do you know of one who has not taken the oath?' asked the prisoner. On being told of the Abbé Magnin she assented and with Michonis he visited her for an hour and a half. Now there in the prison an Abbé Emery who was able, at a short distance from the Queen's cell, to say Mass, to confess, and to give Communion, to whom the holy wafers were brought clandestinely by some refractory priests in the town. In the immense crowd of prisoners awaiting their execution it was impossible for the guards to keep all under constant observation, and in fact when the members of the Tribunal had withdrawn for the night the jailers, more kindly than they, permitted the Abbé Emery to pass the night with the condemned in the 'waiting room'. In 1824 the Abbé Magnin wrote – and swore from his chair in Church and before the altar, that he had twice confessed the Queen of France and given her the Holy Communion. This must have been an immense solace for her; not only would she die in the communion of the Faith but she could talk with him about the fears which beset her, and even find some interest in discussing the future, for it cannot have been unknown to her that there were still friends who plotted her escape. Besides, Michonis had constituted himself, not without remuneration, a sort of guide to persons who desired to see that rarity, a Queen of France in prison. Several painters, such as Kucharsky, did her portrait and even one Englishman, who paid twenty-five louis, was permitted to carry her a jug of water.

Under these circumstances it was not surprising that Michonis could communicate with Turgy and Toulan in the Temple and give them news of the 'person' which they could by signs convey to the two lonely women there. The greatest circumspection was necessary, however, and the two princesses threw away everything incriminating and wrote with gall and the juice of almonds. Richard and his wife, like nearly all those who came into close contact with Marie Antoinette, were gradually won by her sweetness and grace, her lovely voice and manners, but were all the same far from conniving at her escape. Various plans were made which came to nothing and ended with the important and famous 'affair of the carnation'.

Among the faithful adherents to the monarchy who still hung around the Conciergerie hoping to help the Queen was one de Rougeville, a Chevalier de St Louis, who had been at the sacking of the Tuileries and who had taken the Queen to the Council

Chamber to save her from the mob. He managed, through friends of both, to approach Michonis and the two were soon in accord. On 28 August Michonis accompanied by Rougeville appeared in the cell; the stranger was a small man of about thirty-five, simply dressed and wearing two carnations in his buttonhole. At the sight of the Queen he was shocked, was this the lady whose beauty he had admired, this old shrunken white haired woman? Tears were in his eyes. She paid no attention to him at first, then seeing him more clearly she started and was so overcome that she fell into the chair, while the blood rose in her cheeks. He went nearer to her, and signed that she should take the flowers from his coat; she did not comprehend in her emotion and he let them fall behind the stove and left the cell with Michonis.

By this time the Queen had rallied her wits and with an astonishing quickness had signed to Gilbert, one of her guards, that she wished to speak to Michonis, she had a complaint to make about her food. And while he turned to the window to recall the administrator she had the time to pick up the flowers which contained a little note. Soon Michonis and Rougeville reappeared and from now on the accounts of what actually happened are extremely difficult to disentangle. We will endeavour to give shortly what seems to be the truth, for both the Queen in her two interrogations and Michonis in his answers during the trial which resulted in his condemnation to death contradicted themselves. Historians have debated whether the administrator was implicated in the plot, and it would seem that he must have been, for in this second visit of Rougeville a quarter of an hour after the first, he held the gendarmes in conversation while the Queen and her visitor were able to confer behind the screen.

With scarcely concealed excitement she entreated Rougeville not to run into such danger. He answered that he had arms and money and even the men, that he would let her have money to bribe the gendarmes. 'Does your heart fail you?' he asked. 'It never fails me,' she answered, 'but it is profoundly affected', and putting her hand on her heart she added, 'Even if I am weak and cast down, this is not.' As soon as they left the cell the Queen read the note concealed in the flowers – Harel's wife, her inseparable attendant, was playing cards with one of the gendarmes and for once not watching her – which confirmed what Rougeville had said, and she immediately tore it into tiny pieces. Now it was necessary to reply and having neither ink nor pen she pricked with a pin the following words on a fragment of paper.

> *Je suis gardée à vue*
> *Je ne parle à personne*
> *Je me fie à vous. Je viendrai.**

This paper, which can still be seen in the National Archives, is unreadable today. A specialist, M. Pilsinski, has asserted that these are the words, but the researches of M. Costalot lead him to believe that only the last line has any value, for of the two others the first was well known to Rougeville, and the second was inexact. We shall see later how the Queen dealt with this in her interrogation.

What seems true is that while the woman Harel was out of the room to fetch water, the Queen went to Gilbert, the gendarme who had already shown himself sympathetic to her, and bracing herself for the effort, said 'Monsieur Gilbert, see how I am trembling. That gentleman was a Chevalier de St Louis, engaged in the armies, to whom I am grateful for not having abandoned me in my trouble.' This Gilbert asserted during his interrogation and continued: 'Michonis went out with the person, and it was now that she showed me a note which she had pricked and on which the holes formed two or three lines of writing, saying to me, "look, I do not need a pen to write".' She added that it was her reply to be given the following Friday to the person who had given the note in the carnation.

Gilbert left the cell and went in search of Madame Richard to whom he gave the paper; she later asserted that she had given it immediately to Michonis but he testified that he had received it on the Thursday or Friday. It is the proof that at first Gilbert was implicated in the plot. Rougeville returned on Friday 30 August, he later said under a different disguise, and gave the prisoner money in louis d'or and assignats.

The project of escape was fixed for the night of 2 September, and it is easy to imagine the Queen's state of mind during the intervening days. During his last visit Rougeville had been struck by her extreme weakness, and on the next day the Lieutenant in charge had written twice to the Public Prosecutor, Fouquier-Tinville, informing him that the woman Capet had been ill twice

---

* I am guarded and watched / I speak to nobody / I trust you. I will come.

during the evening. Hopeless for so long, she had borne her sorrow with stoicism; now the chance of a reprieve made her heart beat with frightful intensity. She paced her cell with more than usual energy, or threw herself on the palliasse in the effort to sleep away the hours. It depended on so many people, on so much audacity, could it succeed? And then the moment arrived. At about eleven o'clock the door suddenly opened, Michonis was there to transfer her to the Temple – this was the pretext – the Queen with the two gendarmes following left the cell and walked rapidly down the corridor, passed the control wicket, and only the gate of the street remained when one of the gendarmes, whom Rougeville had bribed with fifty louis, stood in their way. They were lost, it was over!

Rosalie Lamorlière accused Madame Harel of having given the plan away, but it seems fairly certain that it was Gilbert, for on the next day he sent a report to Colonel du Mesnil denouncing Rougeville, telling about the carnation and the pricked note, but of course not mentioning his part in the affair. Rougeville disappeared without trace, but Michonis was taken on the 4th, Richard and his wife were also imprisoned and two deputies from the Convention arrived in the prison to interrogate the Queen. Marie Antoinette had had time to control her anguish, with extraordinary lucidity this remarkable woman parried all the questions put to her, with the firm intention to incriminate none of those who had tried to help her. She denied having seen a flower, she denied having recognized any Chevalier de St Louis, there were many people who came to her cell she said, it was possible, given the state of her nerves, that she had at some time been agitated but she did not know by whom or when. The inquisitors had little success with her nor with Madame Harel and Michonis. They went away dissatisfied, having pinned the incriminating note to their report, which gave it two more holes.

But this was not the end; Michonis on being interrogated for hours contradicted himself, confessed to some parts of the affair, sought to save himself by every possible means. Finally the deputies appeared again in the prison and in this second interrogation the Queen was forced to admit much of what she had previously denied. In the intervening days she had been able to find out from the gendarmes what they had done. She implored Gilbert with tears to tell her if Rougeville had been arrested, and not to divulge what she had said to them. Now she was occupied in trying to shield Michonis – her loyalty was admirable. She admitted the visit of Rougeville, and her note to him but when asked, 'Did the administrator Michonis make certain propositions to you?' she said, 'Never.'

'Why were you so interested to see him again?'

'Because his honesty and humanity had touched me.'

'It would seem that that interest arose from the fact that he brought to your apartment a man who would offer to help you.'

'It is likely that Michonis himself did not know the man.'

The interrogation went on until late at night; never did she falter, nor lose her head. Only when she had to sign the *procès-verbal* did she hesitate. She was ashamed of having lied, it wounded her pride, lowered her in her own eyes, and she stipulated, 'If she had not told the truth at first it was because she did not wish to compromise the man and preferred to harm only herself.'

But the Convention had been alerted to the danger of an escape in spite of their precautions; the lesson had been learned, their victim should not have a second chance. On 10 September the police visited the cell and took away the last few treasures which the unhappy woman had kept: her two little rings which contained hair, a medallion with the Dauphin's hair. They turned everything inside out and took away her underclothes. In future she only received one chemise every ten days. And on the 11th they took steps to make the prison even more secure. She must be moved and they chose the abode of the pharmacist, a miserable hole which they further fortified with bars and bolts and locks so that almost no air and very little light could enter it. Into this wretched place the Queen was put, she would leave it only for her trial. No more women around her, watched night and day, with sentinels outside her 'window'. Nothing to do but read by the feeble light, or pray for those she loved and for herself. The accounts of the pharmacist give proof of the state of the Queen's nerves after this misadventure, she was prescribed calming potions, lime tree water, orange flower water and refreshing soups. Her food was light and nourishing, it is curious how her jailers cared for the pleasures of the table, and truly French. Or they wished to preserve her for something worse, her trial.

The new concierge, whose name was Bault, had been brought from the prison of La Force and beneath a very Jacobin exterior hid a compassionate heart. It was Hue who had, through his relations with the Administrator of Police, Dange, succeeded in having him appointed. Rosalie Lamorlière, who had not been thrown out with the Richards, reported the first morning after the Queen's arrival in her new prison:

When Bault appeared for the first time before the Queen I was with him, and I brought Madame the soup which was usual for her dinner. She looked at Bault, who, in accordance with the custom of the time wore the waistcoat and trousers called carmagnole. The collar of his shirt was open, but his head was uncovered; with his keys in his hand he stood near the door against the wall. The Queen took off her night-cap, took a chair and said to me in her sweet voice, 'Rosalie, you will make my chignon, my hair today.' When the concierge heard this he ran forward, took the comb and pushing me away said, 'Leave it, leave it, it is for me to do it.' The princess, astonished, looked at Bault with an air of such majesty that it is impossible to describe it. 'I thank you,' she said and rising at once she gathered her hair and put on her bonnet. Then the Queen took the white ribbon with which Madame Richard had always tied her hair and gave it to me with an air of sadness which penetrated my heart. 'Rosalie,' she said, 'take this ribbon and keep it always in memory of me.'

Rougeville wrote three versions of the carnation affair. Taken prisoner by the Austrians as a spy he was interrogated by Fersen. Five months later he sent a memoir to Count Metternich and lastly he sent one to the Five Hundred. Fersen in his diary speaks of him as a man who was slightly mad, very much in love with himself, and thinking of himself as a person of great importance but certainly not a spy and meaning well. He was probably all this, and if his plan had not been defeated by a matter of minutes he would be remembered as a hero. But as Marie Antoinette herself felt, she was unlucky.

There was one person whose devotion never wavered. Fersen in his letters to his sister and in his *Journal* shows his desperation. On 22 September he noted that he had received the brochure written by Madame de Staël, *Reflections on the Trial of a Queen*: he thought it useless and insignificant, and indeed it was more an appeal to the emotions than to justice, and had little bearing on the case of Marie Antoinette. He suffered more than he could express, sometimes he wished that all could be decided one way or the other, but then again he felt that if he lost her he lost all that he had in the world, three sovereigns who were his benefactors and friends, how could he live on? His hatred of the revolutionaries was matched by his disgust for the Allies; here they were within marching distance of Paris and they did nothing to rescue her, and when one day chance put in his way the man Drouet, who had denounced Louis XVI at Varennes, he felt a delicious revenge in feasting his eyes on the prisoner, in irons, exposed to the curiosity of the populace. Another officer taken with him had said that the Queen was not treated badly, that she had all she needed. 'The traitors, how they lie!' exclaimed Axel.

In fact Bault, her new jailer, republican though he was, could only feel some pity at the sight of his prisoner, for now she was ground down into the dust. Her poor clothes were in rags, she had but two dresses, one white, one black, they hung on her thin frame and the daughter of the concierge was constantly occupied in sewing the tatters together. Her food was limited now and under these unendurable conditions she was taken with frightful haemorrhages which further depleted her strength. The guard in her cell was separated from her by a screen it is true, but the one outside the window could and did see in at any time, so that her most intimate life was open to him. In such unimaginable degradation nothing remained of what she once had been; beauty was gone, power gone, friends too, husband and children were lost. Yet while she lived there still flared in her some trace of the old spirit, breeding and training had not been for nothing, she still charmed her warders and her mind was, when necessary, clear and subtle.

One more escape was planned and like the others failed, and by the end of August even Mercy was writing to Cobourg that posterity would not understand that such a crime could be accomplished without the victorious armies of Austria and England attempting at least an effort to prevent it. But Cobourg preferred to take up winter quarters. An extenuating word might be said, in that his English, Hanoverian and Dutch troops were deserting him after the taking of Valenciennes, in favour of the siege of Dunkirk. Whatever his reason, the blame for it will always rest on the government of Austria and its Emperor, the Queen's nephew.

Meanwhile the Revolutionary Tribunal in Paris seemed to be taking its time over the trial of Marie Antoinette. A sort of lassitude had come over the judges, though they dispatched their daily quota of victims to the guillotine; only the Public Prosecutor Fouquier-Tinville was busy with his preparations for the trial. This squat ill-favoured creature, devoured by hatred and a splenetic rage, was finding it difficult to discover factual evidence, and on 2 December the Committee of Public Safety held a sitting to discuss the matter. Hébert cut short their arguments crying, 'I have promised the head of Antoinette, I will go and cut it off myself if you do not make haste to give it to me. I have promised it on your account to the *sans culottes* who urge me without ceasing to get it.'

On 3 October Billaud-Varenne demanded an immediate trial and Fouquier Tinville was working madly to compose his case. But as he informed the Convention on the 5th, he had received the order of the Convention but as yet had no documents relative to Marie Antoinette so that it would be impossible to obey the order. At the Temple the abominable Simon was busy preparing his victim, the young Louis XVII, to furnish them. The child had been progressively brutalized, until he was almost unrecognizable, but there still glowed in him an unquenchable courage, and a devotion to the memory of his mother. The two unhappy women confined in the tower had also suffered from a tightening of their imprisonment, their food was restricted, they could never leave their narrow room, they had no light but a candle, and no news from the outer world, but they could comfort each other, while the child was completely given over to his tormentor.

On 6 October, Hébert, Pache and Chaumette appeared at the tower of the Temple to interrogate Louis Charles, already prepared for his torture by a mixture of blows and brandy. Half drunk and subdued by three hours of questioning, they at last succeeded in wringing from him the answer which they sought to the most revolting suggestion which could be made by a child against its mother, that of debauching her son's innocence in incest. They began by asking the eight-year-old boy what persons had visited Marie Antoinette in the Temple, to which he replied Lepitre at first, 'who spoke more familiarly with her than others', and continued with naming Michonis, Jobert, Moëlle, Vincent and Leboeuf, and said he, 'during these conversations I was sent away'. They continued their questions for hours and finally the exhausted little boy admitted 'that having been surprised several times in his bed by Simon and his wife they found him committing acts

The widowed Marie
Antoinette, by Kucharsky

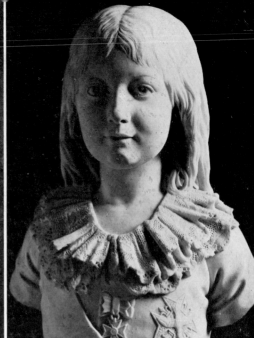

Bust of the Dauphin,
Louis XVII

La Fayette, by Deboncourt

Sketch by David of Marie Antoinette on the way to the guillotine

harmful to his health and he said . . .' On the following day they
returned with the Commissioner Danjou and the painter David,
and having again interrogated the child Capet who persisted in
his statement and said again and again 'yes it is true', they wrote
on their report 'That by the way the child spoke he gave us to
understand that when his mother was in bed with him she . . .'
Not content with this they brought his sister to substantiate the
accusation. Madame Royale wrote later:

> Chaumette asked me a thousand vile questions about my mother
> and my aunt. I was dismayed by such a horror and so indignant that,
> in spite of the terror which I felt, I could not help saying that it was
> infamous; in spite of my tears they insisted; there was much which I
> could not understand, but what I did understand was so horrible that
> I wept with indignation.

Then they brought in her brother, and for another two hours
sister and brother were submitted to the same villainous questioning. Finally, worn out, the two unhappy children signed their
name in trembling hands to the verbatim documents, and were
taken away. This was not all however. Madame Elisabeth was
then brought down, but here they found another person entirely;
they could not extract from this noble creature any equivocal
phrase which would bear out the half ignorant replies of her
young charges, and they were forced to let her go.*

On 12 October it was terribly cold. The compassionate Bault
had already asked for another coverlet for Marie Antoinette's bed,
and had been threatened by Fouquier-Tinville with the guillotine
for his impudence. So the Queen had gone early to bed, aided by
Rosalie, who brought her nightdress hot from her own kitchen
and covered her shivering limbs with what care she could.
Suddenly she heard heavy footsteps, the door was burst roughly
open, and she was told to rise and dress; a huissier and four gendarmes had come to take her to be interrogated. Quickly she put
on her black dress and followed them through corridors, up and
down steps, till she found herself in the great Hall of the Parlement, a hall which she had known in happier days for it was there
that the King's *lits de Justice* were held. Now the famous tapestries
had given place to the placard of the Rights of Man, and the busts

* The full extent of their report is so filthy that we follow the example of
successive historians and leave the words to the imagination of our readers.

of Marat, Lepeletier and Lucius Junius Brutus graced the walls. She was given a bench to sit on and the interrogation began. She gave her name as Marie Antoinette de Lorraine-Autriche, and was immediately accused of having had political contacts with the King of Bohemia and Hungary, contacts contrary to the interests of France, a country which had heaped favours on her. The President, Herman, a creature of Robespierre, reviewed all the complaints against her, the sums of money sent to her brother, the contact with the Princes since the war, the so-called Austrian committee of the Tuileries and the King's veto. He said, 'It was you who taught Louis Capet the art of dissimulation with which for so long he deceived the French people.' She replied, 'Yes, the people have been deceived, cruelly so, but not by my husband nor by me.'

By this time the Queen had called to her aid every atom of intelligence which she possessed. She knew that she would need her wit, her complete balance, she must not give way to anger, nor be betrayed by sorrow, she must fight, fight, fight, till the end. She must have known herself vulnerable, nor could she be sure how much evidence they had accumulated against her; she was sick and cold, but not beaten.

The questions continued; had she not ruined the finances by her incredible extravagance? To this she answered that she knew that she had been accused of this but she loved her husband too much to ruin the finance of his country; and here she was on safe ground; for she had not spent *public* money, and did not say that the King had given her personally vast sums. It went on; since the Revolution had she not plotted with the Powers against Liberty? The answer was important and it was not true: 'Since the Revolution I have forbidden myself all correspondence with the outer world and I never meddled with the interior.' Had she forgotten the letters to Mercy, the correspondence with Barnave? But she insisted to the further question: 'whether she had employed secret agents in order to correspond with foreign powers', '*Jamais de la vie.*' – Never in my life.

Herman was infuriated by these answers, for although Fouquier-Tinville had not the documentary proof, it was known that the Queen had intrigued with Barnave, and certainly she had done all in her power at the end to contact the Powers. But as we have said before, this was in her eyes no treason; in saving the monarchy

she believed she was saving France itself, and considering the
excesses of the Revolution who can contradict her? Now came
the questions about Varennes. Was it not she who had planned the
coup, had she not with her own hands opened the doors for the
King's exit? Her reply was witty. 'It does not follow because one
opens a door that one directs the policies of a person.' The President cried, 'You have never ceased from wishing to destroy
liberty, you wanted to reign no matter what the cost, even if you
remounted the throne over the corpses of patriots.' And the retort
'We had no need to remount the throne, we were already there.
We never wished for anything but the happiness of France; whatever made her happy, if she really were, we would have been
content.'

Now Herman made a mistake. He asked whether if she really
wished this she would not have kept her brother from making
war, to which she could with justice reply that it was France
which had declared war, and insisted that the King had only
consented after the reiterated demand of the Council.

Next came the affair of the dinner of the Swiss Guards at
Versailles, when it was asserted that the tricolour was trodden
under foot and the white *cocarde* worn. To this also she replied
with skill, 'That can only be a mistake, no one can believe that
loyal people would treat with disrespect the emblem which the
King himself was wearing.'

Then came rapid questioning. She must have been tiring but
her dexterity did not leave her.

'What interest have you in the armies of the Republic?'

'The happiness of France is what I desire above all else.'

'Do you think that kings are necessary for the happiness of a
people?'

'An individual cannot make a decision on such a subject.'

'Without doubt you regret that your son should have lost a
throne on which he might have sat if the people, at last enlightened
as to its rights, had not destroyed that throne?'

'I shall regret nothing for my son if his country is happy.'*

* On a conversation with Mr John Paget, Arthur Garfield Hays, the celebrated
American defence lawyer, once said to him: 'If I set a trap for a witness, if it is a
man, I can be pretty sure of the way he will answer, but with a woman it is quite
different. She will, in a very subtle way see, or rather feel the trap and will answer
in a way dictated by her intuition, which will evade the danger.' This seems true
of Marie Antoinette, and also of Jeanne d'Arc, another Lorrainer.

341

Seeing that he could not trap her, the President turned first to 10 August when the Swiss were accused of firing on the people, and then to the affair of the carnation. The questioning was deftly parried and at the end she was asked if she had a lawyer, to which she retorted that she knew no one. And the citizens Chauveau-Lagarde and Tronçon du Coudray were appointed. After which she was taken back to the Conciergerie and a new guard was appointed, an officer of the gendarmerie who did not leave her again.

It was a remarkable sitting, and if the judges had not been so convinced of the justice of their cause and of the guilt of the woman they had before them, they must have been struck by the dignity and presence of mind of this Queen, who after so much trial, so much inflicted sorrow and shock, could yet impose respect. But it was impossible that the two parties should understand each other, each regarded the other as traitors to the national cause, one or the other must be destroyed, and since the accusers were in power and since there were no means to which they would not stoop to achieve their end, the Queen was doomed.

Chauveau-Lagarde was in the country when he got the summons; he left at once and arrived at the prison on the evening of the 13th with his associate. He entered the cell with tears in his eyes and his knees trembling – he was only twenty-eight and has left the record – and the Queen received him with 'a majesty full of sweetness'. He sat down on one of the two straw chairs with the two gendarmes on his left and their conference began. Hearing that she had not yet seen the act of accusation he went to the Registrar whom he found in the process of copying the act, and received one of the copies he was making for the judges. He was appalled by its volume. The Queen regarded it with an indifferent eye and made various observations which might have displeased the gendarmes. More upset than she, he pleaded the immensity of the work and the shortness of time, and insisted that there must be a delay; she asked from whom should she demand it, and when he replied that it should be from the National Convention she exclaimed brusquely 'No, no never', her pride and her dignity as a widow refused to ask a favour from those who had condemned her husband to death. But when he insisted that she owed it to the memory of that husband and to her children to make the best case she could, she gave in and with a sigh signed the note which follows:

Citoyen President, Les citoyens Tronçon et Chauveau, que le tribunal m'a donnés comme défenseurs, m'observent qu'ils n'ont été instruits qu'aujourd'hui de leur mission, je dois être jugée demain et il leur est impossible de s'instruire dans un si court délai des pièces du procès et même d'en prendre lecture. Je dois à mes enfants de n'omettre aucun moyen nécessaire pour l'entière justification de leur mère. Mes défenseurs demandent trois jours de délai; j'espère que la Convention les leur accordera.*

It was sent and was ignored, and was found later beneath the bed of the defunct Robespierre, *together with the King's testament.*

On the morrow, long before the trial was to commence, the huge hall was filling up. Paris would not want to miss so exciting a spectacle. Everything that was hideous, the grey faces, the villainous expressions, the raucous voices issuing from their hoarse throats, the rags, the dirt which made the air stink even in the early morning, all contributed to give the place a hellish air. The travesty of justice was continued with the assembling jury: who were they? Fouquier-Tinville had chosen them carefully. The ex-Marquis Antonelle, Renaudin, the most atrocious of an atrocious band, Fiévée, Besnard, Thoumain, Desboisseaux, Baron, Sambat, Devèze, the surgeon Soubervielle, who wished to excuse himself, for he had attended the accused, the musician Lumière, Chrétien, misnamed indeed, the printer Nicolas, and the cabinet-maker Trinchard. The noise grew, the Judges entered, it was nearly eight o'clock, the knitting women were there in the front row, the most malignant of all, dead to feeling, sluttish and bitter.

Just before eight o'clock the Lieutenant de Busne and the gendarmes opened her door; she was ready. With what indefinable feminine feeling it is difficult to say, she had taken more trouble than usual over her poor toilet, had twisted a fragment of black into her linen bonnet and a piece of black crêpe like a small veil.

* Citizen President

Citizens Tronçon and Chauveau whom the Tribunal has assigned to me as defenders tell me that they have only today been instructed on their mission, that I shall be judged tomorrow and it is impossible for them to understand such a mass of documents in so short a time, or even to read them through. I owe it to my children not to omit any means towards the justification of their mother. My defence ask for three days' delay; I hope that the Convention will accord them this.

It was an insistence on her widowhood, and for the expression of her majesty she had as always her bearing, the carriage of her head, and the ravaged beauty of her face. When she entered the hall a murmur arose, the people could hardly recognize in this ageing woman the lovely vivacious Queen they remembered; she seemed old, old. They had put a chair for her so placed that all might see her. Nevertheless during the interrogation the women screamed that she should stand when answering so that they might better feast their eyes on her. Her lawyers were near her, and facing her the President with the Judges beside him. She remained standing while the witnesses gave the oath and then was told that she might sit.

And now the Reader Fabricius will read the act of Accusation, a most extraordinary document which Fouquier-Tinville had put together, a tissue of half-truths mixed with a varnish of erudition and reality which would be ludicrous if it were not tragic. Antoine Quentin Fouquier-Tinville shows that from the examination of the documents given to the Public:

It would seem that like Messalina,* Brunehaut and Frédégonde and Médicis, who were once called Queens of France and whose names forever odious will never be effaced from the pages of history, Marie Antoinette widow of Louis Capet has been since her arrival in France the curse and leech of the French people; that before the happy revolution which has given the French people their sovereign freedom, she had contacts with a man called the King of Bohemia and Hungary, that these contacts were contrary to the interests of France; and that, not content, in agreement with the brothers of Louis Capet and the execrable Calonne, then Minister of Finance, she had dilapidated in a frightful manner the finance of France, fruit of the blood and sweat of its people.

He then proceeded to enumerate the various charges against her and finished with the frightful accusation torn from the unwilling prisoner in the Temple, the accusation of incest. This said, the Public Prosecutor summed it all up in three main accusations, and he called the first witness.

Marie Antoinette, as the news-sheets of the day attest, listened to it all with calm, and no sign of emotion, not even when she

* Messalina, wife of Claudius and mother of Britannicus was notorious for her licentiousness. Narcissus, the freedman of Claudius persuaded the Emperor to put her to death because she publicly married a Roman youth during the absence of Claudius in Ostia AD 48.

heard her son's atrocious accusation did she blench except for a movement of disdain. She sat there immobile, except when her fingers strayed over the arm of her chair as if 'she were playing the pianoforte'. The first witness was Lecointre, the man from Versailles, where he had been in the National Guard, and who had sent in 1789 an address to the King beginning, 'Sire, one of your most faithful subjects comes with confidence to lay at your feet his respect and homage.' Now he was one of their most inexorable enemies. He enumerated all the expenses incurred for fêtes and entertainments between the years 1779–89 as witness to the ruin of the finances; at the end Herman asked the Queen whether she had anything to say, to which she replied that she knew nothing about the greater part of his allegations and as far as the 'orgy' of the Swiss officers was concerned, it was true that she and the King had gone round the tables but no more. Then followed questions about the famous secret meeting in the Tuileries on 23 June when the King's address was modified and when the next day in his meeting he refused to separate the three orders. It was on this occasion that the King spoke with a paternalistic firmness and Herman asked, 'Did not your husband read the speech to you half an hour before entering the hall, and did you not urge him to speak with firmness?' She replied, 'My husband had great confidence in me, and that is why he read it to me; but I did not permit myself to make any comment.'

Then came questioning on the events of 12 July 1789, and the troops placed under the orders of the Marshal de Broglie and Besenval. 'You were without doubt not ignorant that there were troops in the Champ de Mars.' 'I did not know at all for what reason.'

'But if you had the confidence of your husband you must have known the cause.'

'It was to ensure public calm.'

'But at that moment everything was quiet, there was but one cry, that of liberty.'

As we may remember, on the contrary, it was a moment of great confusion, at any rate for the monarch. Necker had just tendered his resignation which the public greatly resented and attributed to the Queen and to d'Artois, so much so that Besenval was forced to retire to Versailles with his men. In fact the Queen had called the minister on the 10th and had implored him to resume his office. She was in a period of extreme sadness owing to the death of the Dauphin, and given this and the vacillation of her husband she might be forgiven if she had advised the concentration of troops around the palace as she said, for security. But they only served to inflame the passions of the crowd, and the taking of the Bastille was the result.

Her next response was less fortunate. She was asked 'For what did you employ the vast sums which had been given you by different controllers of the finances?'

'I was never given vast sums; those which were given to me were used to pay the employees who were attached to me.'

'Why were the family of the Polignacs and many others covered with gold?'

'They had positions at the Court which entitled them to riches.'

Then came a certain Lapierre, Adjutant General in the service at the Tuileries on the night of the flight to Varennes, who testified on this account; followed by Roussillon, a surgeon who deposed that he had seen on the night of 10 August 1792 'under the Queen's bed many bottles, some empty some still full, which indicated that she had given drink, both to the officers of the Swiss and to the Chevaliers du Poignard, who filled the palace.' He also testified that the accused had contributed to the plight of France by sending large sums to her brother for his war against the Turks and also his war against France; he had this information from a 'good citizen who had been formerly employed at Versailles' under the 'ancien régime' and to whom a favourite at the Court had told it in confidence.

The good citizen turned out to be a former maid of the chamber who asserted that she was told this by the Comte de Coigny; apart from the fact that de Coigny was a duke and not a count, which she might certainly have known, it was highly unlikely that a nobleman would have imparted to such a person such a piece of information.

However Fouquier sent immediately to fetch this eminent witness. And the knitting women, themselves intrigued, loudly insisted again that Marie Antoinette should stand when answering. The Queen murmured, 'Will the French people never be satisfied with my fatigue?'

The witnesses continued, with nothing of any great importance emerging and a complete absence of proofs. Their evidence implicated other famous names as much as that of the Queen; Lafayette, Bailly, Pétion, all were mentioned in equivocal situations, but now came a sensational witness, Hébert. He began rather vaguely; he had found counter-revolutionary articles among the personal effects of the Queen; he suspected the guard Toulan of being too sympathetic towards his prisoner. And then he affirmed:

The young Capet whose constitution deteriorated daily was surprised by Simon in pollutions bad for his temperament; and when Simon asked who had taught him such things he replied that it was his mother and his aunt that he thanked for such fatal habits. From the declaration which the young Capet had made in the presence of the Mayor of Paris and the Procureur of the Commune it appeared that these two women made him often lie between them, and that so he committed the most disgusting acts of debauchery; that there was no reason to doubt, after what the son of Capet said, that there was an incestuous act between the mother and son.

Imagination balks at such a villainous accusation; that it could be thought of, much less spoken publicly, gives us the measure of the men who were conducting this inquiry. The Queen sat transfixed, and when asked by Herman if she had anything to say she replied in a trembling voice that she knew nothing of the facts reported by Hébert. And even the President seemed to wish to evade the subject for he turned to other issues. Was it not true that after the death of Capet she and her sister had given the head of the table to her son and had treated him as King, he had precedence and was served first? The Queen turned to the witness and asked if he had seen this. He retorted that he had not seen it but that the whole Municipality would confirm it. Suddenly a voice was heard, 'Citizen President, I beg you to draw the attention of the accused to the fact that she has not yet answered the charge made by the citizen Hébert, on the subject of what has passed between her and her son.' The President, rather unwillingly perhaps, repeated the question.

The Queen arose, 'very much moved', this is the verbatim report, and said, 'If I have not answered, it is because nature refuses such an insinuation made to a mother,' and turning towards the crowded hall she cried, 'I appeal to all such who find themselves here.'*

Faced with this sublime cry a sort of magnetic current ran through the mass. Even the knitting women were shaken by it, for a moment they might have applauded; there were cries, and the tribunal was forced to call for order and for some minutes the sitting was suspended, some women even fainted and had to be carried out. Marie Antoinette, in revealing her true nature, had without meaning to scored a victory, almost her last. It was nearly two o'clock and soon the sitting was adjourned; as the Queen left the Chamber she heard a woman murmur, 'Look how proud she is.' She held herself so straight, her head so erect among all these draggled creatures, that even her enemies were impressed. But the whisper agitated her. 'Do you think I put too much dignity into my answers?' she asked her lawyers, and what did they think of her chances? She went through the evidence with them. Chauveau-Lagarde wrote after all was finished that her observation showed that she still hoped, and it proved too that in the clearness of her conscience she must have felt mistress of herself, since for all the agitation of her spirit she heard all that was said around her, and that she sought in the attempt to support her innocence to regulate both her silence and her words.

And it also proves we think, that those who have written and thought of her as flighty and vapid were wrong and that her earliest preceptor Vermond, who attributed to her an intelligence beyond her years, was right. And as she said, one must have 'du caractère' until the end. By character she meant firmness, fortitude, principle and self-respect. Can it be denied that these were hers?

Her lawyers reassured her. No proofs had been found or brought, the witnesses were cancelling each other out, half of what they said had no value. 'In that case,' said she, 'I fear only Manuel.' But she was wrong, for when the sitting resumed at about five o'clock he was the first witness, but his deposition was a compound of personal griefs, and that of Bailly who succeeded

* When Robespierre, dining that evening with Saint-Just and Barère, heard of this, he broke out in a rage at the imbecility of Hébert, who had given the Queen such an opportunity to engage public sympathy. It is probable, says one of the jury who recorded this, that it was at this moment that Robespierre determined to rid himself of so compromising an associate.

him was the same. Now the Prosecutor had found his 'good citizen' Reine Millot, a domestic in the café of the 'Couronne d'Or' who added to her wonderful story of the Comte (Duc) by telling the court how the Queen had conceived the design to murder the Duc d'Orléans and had for that purpose concealed two pistols under her dress, and how the King finding them had condemned her to two weeks' confinement in her apartment. She had no proof of course and the Queen listened with a cold disdain, and interpolated, 'It is possible that I received such an order from my husband but not for such a reason.'

After some time spent in considering the affair of the carnation the sitting terminated at eleven o'clock and Marie Antoinette left the Chamber. Tired, hot, thirsty she asked for a cup of water. There was no one to give it to her; only de Busne, the officer who guarded her, was brave enough to offer it. He helped her faltering feet down the narrow stairs to her cell. 'I think I am ill,' she whispered, 'I cannot see.' She held his arm for guidance.

The morning of the 15th dawned cold and rainy, it was the fête of St Theresa, her mother's name day and that of her daughter. Once more she made the journey from her prison to the Chamber, through the draughty corridors, up and down the steps, surrounded by the guards; frozen in her ragged garments, but still upright, she arrived before her judges and the people.

The first witness was the late Admiral d'Estaing, who complained that the accused had by her intrigues prevented him from becoming Marshal of France, but when interrogated on the events of 5 October he deposed to having heard her say, 'If the Parisians come here to assassinate me they will find me at the feet of my husband; I will not fly.' It seemed more a homage than an accusation. Then came the two La Tour du Pin brothers, of whom the elder had been Minister in his time. Asked whether he knew the accused he replied with a courteous bow, 'Ah yes, I have the honour to know Madame.' As a reward for their courage all three men would be guillotined on 28 April 1794. Herman, disappointed in his witnesses, turned then to the extravagance of the Queen – had she not spent immense sums on Trianon? He resuscitated the affair of the necklace – was it not then that she had known Madame de la Motte, who had been her victim? The Queen denied it. 'You persist in denying that you knew her?' thus the Prosecutor. 'I am not denying anything, I am speaking the truth and that is what I shall continue to do,' was the response.

'Did you not force the Ministers of Finance to deliver to you large funds, and when they refused did you not visit your indignation upon them?'

'Never.'

'Did you not ask Vergennes to send six millions to the King of Bohemia and Hungary?'

'No,' and fundamentally she spoke the truth, for this had been a political decision, though the public as usual laid it at her door.

All accusations, but without one single proof. Now however Fouquier-Tinville believed that he held a trump card; rising, the President asked

'Did you not sign bonds on the Civil List to be honoured by the Treasurer?'

'No.'

But here was the witness, a spy named Tisset, who deposed to having had in his hands a number of notes of payments made by the Treasurer, Septeuil, among them two bonds for eighty thousand livres signed Marie Antoinette. They had been left with Garnerin, the late Secretary of the Committee of Twenty-Four, which unfortunately no longer existed. And here *was* the late Secretary of the Committee to testify that he had seen a bond of eighty thousand livres signed Marie Antoinette for the benefit of the Polignacs; this had been left with Valaze, a member of the Commission. This brought the Queen to her feet. At what date had these bonds – which Garnerin now reduced to one – been given, she asked. Tisset hesitatingly replied that one was dated 10 August 1792, the other he did not remember. And the Queen:

'I have never given any bond, and in any case how could I have given a bond on that day when we left the Tuileries at eight in the morning to go to the National Assembly?'

And so the accusations went on. In all her answers the Queen's endeavour was to absolve those who had tried to help her from any shadow of blame, and this is one of the reasons why in some cases her answers seem to be disingenuous; as when confronted with Lepitre, accused of having brought her news from the outer world, she insisted:

'I have never had conversation with the witness, and for another thing I had no need for news to be brought me, I could hear it well enough from the bearers of it who cried every day in the street of the Corderie.'

A harder test was the opening of the packet taken from her when she went to the Conciergerie. Here were the pathetic souvenirs of her husband and children, the little tresses of their hair, the small pocket-book with a piece of paper covered with numbers.

'What is this?' asked the President.

'It was to teach my son to count.'

The portraits of women, who were they?

'Madame de Lamballe, and two friends of my childhood, the ladies of Mecklenburg and Hesse.'

And a small piece of cloth on which was painted a heart transfixed with an arrow, the sign of the Sacred Heart, which Fouquier pretended not to know, and insinuated that it was a sign worn by many of the conspirators coming before the tribunal, a counter-revolutionary emblem. As if he were not wearing himself that very sign beneath his coat, as testified years later by his daughter.

On and on went the questions, dulling in their effect, wearing her down till at last at three o'clock the sitting was suspended and she was free for a few hours. She was not taken to her cell however, but brought a cup of soup by the faithful Rosalie, who had it snatched from her by a female ghoul, the friend of one of the guards, who wished to gloat over the fallen majesty. At five o'clock the jury and the Judges filed into the hall and the final agony began.

The night had almost fallen, in the vast hall only a few candles sent their scanty light into the gloom; two lamps behind the Judges were lit but what words can describe the scene? The crowd was there, the knitting women, all in their places, waited for the victim. The final verdict was certain, for who would dare to speak in support of this woman when all know in their stricken hearts that such support could only bring imprisonment and death? She entered and the dreary questioning went on. It was the turn of men who had been near her in her imprisonment, Michonis and Fontaine who recalled the affair of the carnation, of Tavernier who had been lieutenant of the guard at the Tuileries on 20 June, the painter Boze who had never spoken to the Queen but who had done a portrait of the late King. This earned him instant arrest. Then came one Michel Gointre, who accused her of having a press for the fabrication of false assignats, and finally Didier-Jourdreuil with a more important charge, that of having seen a letter from Marie Antoinette to d'Affry the Commander of the Swiss Guards saying, 'Can we count on your Swiss? Will they hold firm when the time comes?'

'I never wrote to d'Affry,' exclaimed the Queen, surprised.

Here Fouquier interpolated that when as director of the jury of accusation following the tribunal of 10 August he was in charge of the trial of Affry and Cazotte, he remembered seeing the letter of which the witness was speaking. But the Roland faction managed to suppress the tribunal and took away all the papers in spite of the protests of good republicans.

So again proof failed for the substantiation of the charge.

Now came President Herman. 'At the time of your marriage to Louis Capet did you not propose the reunification of Lorraine with Austria?' At the age of fourteen-and-a-half!

'No.'

'You bear that name.'

'Because one must bear the name of one's country.'

'Were you not occupied in sounding the opinion in the departments, districts, and municipalities?'

'No.'

But Fouquier rose, 'We have found in your desk a paper which proves the fact in the most precise manner, and the names of Vaublanc, Jaucourt and others are mentioned.' The accused persisted that she could not remember any such paper.

It must be remembered that the men who were trying her, the Girondins, who had at one time been regarded by the Queen as advanced republicans, were under suspicion or even arrested as counter revolutionaries, and in a month twenty-two of them would follow her to the scaffold, so rapidly did the glorious Revolution work. They would die singing the *Marseillaise*, in their various ways like herself, the offering to unshakable conviction; for her it was monarchy, for them freedom, for both it was their country's good.

There was little more that Fouquier could find. Herman asked if she had not taught her children badly after having promised to bring them up in the principles of the Revolution? For example, had she treated her son with the regard she considered due to one who might be one day the successor to his late father? To which she answered that he was too young to understand that, she had put him at the table beside her and had given him what she considered necessary.

Finally 'Have you anything to add to your defence?'

Marie Antoinette rose, and with an indescribable air of majesty said, 'Yesterday I did not know the witnesses. I did not know what they were going to say: well, no one has articulated a single positive fact. I will finish by observing that I was only the wife of Louis XVI and that it was necessary that I should be obedient to his wishes.'

The trial was over, and the Public Prosecutor began his summing up. He went through all the evidence in an interminable rigmarole from which he omitted however the hideous accusation of Hébert, and at the end declared the accused the open enemy of the French nation who had brought about all the troubles of the past four years, through which thousands of French had suffered.

Then came the turn of the defence and the two brave men Chauveau-Lagarde and Tronçon du Coudray, taking their lives in their hands, proceeded after *a quarter of an hour's* preparation to do what they could for their client. They acquitted themselves, says the verbatim report 'with as much zeal as eloquence'. The former dealt with the accusation of contact with foreign enemies, the latter with that of internal policy: both insisted on the lack of proofs. When they were finished the Queen leant over and murmured, 'How tired you must be, M. Chauveau-Lagarde, I am very aware of all your trouble.'

Her words were heard. Fouquier-Tinville stopped the proceedings and calling a gendarme arrested Chauveau-Lagarde. In spite of which Tronçon du Coudray pleaded with the greatest eloquence and bravery against the charges of conspiring for civil war. He was also detained and searched on the spot.

Now the President Herman took up the case. He opened with the words, 'Today a great example is given to the universe, and without doubt it will not be lost upon the people who inhabit it. Nature and reason, so long outraged, are at last satisfied. Equality triumphs.' One can hardly say that any lesson has been learned, perhaps the universe was not as impressed as he imagined. He at any rate, and what he did, have not been forgotten. He continued:

A woman once surrounded by the most brilliant prestige which the pride of kings and the baseness of slaves can imagine today occupies before the Tribunal of the nation the place which two days ago another woman filled, and this equality ensures for her an impartial justice. This affair, citizen jurymen, is not like those where a single fact, a single crime, is submitted to your conscience and your enlightenment; you have to judge the whole political life of the accused since she came to seat herself beside the last King of France. But above all you must give your attention to the manoeuvres which she never for an instant ceased to employ to destroy our newly-born liberty whether in the interior, or through her intimate liaisons with infamous ministers, perfidious generals, unfaithful representatives of the people, or whether outside the country by supporting the negotiation of the monstrous coalition of the despots of Europe, for which History will reserve the ridicule it deserves for its failure. Finally by her correspondence with the late emigrant princes of France and their unworthy agents.

Since after this diatribe he could only present accusations for which he could produce no proof, he was obliged to associate the Queen with Louis xvi, whose papers had indeed been seized and used as justification for his trial. Her high treason, for that is what it was if his charges were true, rested on her role as the 'instigator of the greater number of the crimes of which the last King of France was guilty'. She had agreed that she enjoyed the trust of Louis Capet, he said, and he was too good a lawyer not to feel embarrassed by the lack of concrete evidence; in consequence he was forced once more to enumerate the less important subjects – the white *cocardes* distributed at the 'orgy' of Versailles, the bottles as evidence of the Queen's debauching of the Swiss. But he avoided the infamous accusation of Hébert; it was too dangerous, and he only referred in passing to the affair of the carnation, saying that it was a prison intrigue not worthy to figure in such a grave cause. And in terminating his address he made a bid for popular acclaim by insisting that it was the French nation which accused Marie Antoinette, that the blame for all the political events of the past five years lay at her door. The souls of their brothers slain as a consequence of the infernal machinations of this modern Médicis cried aloud for vengeance. He then enumerated the charges:

1 Is it agreed that there had existed schemes and contacts with foreign Powers, enemies of the Republic, which were for the purpose of furnishing them with money and giving them entry into French territory and helping the course of their arms?

2 Is Marie Antoinette of Austria, widow of Louis Capet, found guilty of having cooperated in these manoeuvres and contacts?

3 Is it agreed that there had existed a plot and conspiracy to begin a civil war in the interior of the Republic by arming the citizens and setting them against each other?

4 Is Marie Antoinette of Austria, widow of Louis Capet, found guilty of such a plot and conspiracy?

To all this, as the news-sheets of the day bear witness, the Queen listened without a movement. Through the hours and hours of questioning and speechmaking her bearing did not alter. But her active mind missed nothing, and when she was led from the Chamber, following the exit of the jury, she can have had only a faint hope of reprieve, perhaps of exile or imprisonment, anything but death. For whatever the fortitude, the human mind, the healthy human mind, recoils from the fact of a horrible and violent end. One might imagine that after the torture she had borne for the last year, death would have been preferable, she may even have thought this herself, but not now. And among the crowd which hung about, waiting for the verdict in the dark cold hall, there were also some who thought she stood a chance. No one dared say much for spies were everywhere, but the feeling was there, and Madame Bault heard some whisper, 'Marie Antoinette will get herself out of it, she replied like an angel, she will only be deported.'

After the Public Prosecutor had summarized the indictment and the Queen had been led from the hall, the jury in their retirement kept up the formula of deliberation, although they well knew that the verdict was inevitable. And to us, with the knowledge which we have of the correspondence preserved in the Archives in Vienna and the letters to Fersen, it must seem the same. She had indeed corresponded with the enemies of the Republic and in the last resort had used any and every means to preserve the monarchy and the King's and her own life, though both had been firmly opposed to civil war. But at that time there was absolutely no proof of any of this; Fouquier-Tinville had been unable to produce any and legally the jury could not condemn her. We have tried to show that in spite of inconsistencies and sometimes downright lies she still felt herself innocent; it was her accusers who were guilty of treason, and not she. At four o'clock the jury had been out an hour, the early morning hour, dragging its slow way, when fatigue takes hold and the pulse is low. She heard in the distance the tinkle of the President's bell; it was here, the fatal moment; her heart nearly stopped and then beat frantically, what would it be, life – or death? She could vaguely hear Fouquier-Tinville speaking but could not distinguish his words as he insisted on the greatest calm and reminded the crowd that the law forbade any sign of approbation and that a person, 'no matter what their crimes, once sentenced by the law belonged only to sorrow and humanity', a hateful pretence at compassion coming from such a man.

A doorkeeper came to fetch the accused. Rising she walked slowly in and took her place, her defence counsel with their guards were brought back, all the travesty of impartial justice was gone through. 'Antoinette,' said Herman, 'here is the verdict of the jury.' Far away as in another world she heard their answers – Yes to all the questions – and Fouquier-Tinville asking for the sentence of death, in conformity with the first article of the first section of the first part of the second part of the penal code, and he read it. All she could hear were the words 'to death', condemned to death. This was where life had brought her, to this cold hostile people, to this terrible end, alone, all alone; and when Herman asked if she had anything to say all she could do was to shake her head. He turned to her lawyers and asked the same question, had they anything to offer against the application of the laws which the Public Prosecutor had read? Tronçon du Coudray replied, 'Citizen President, since the declaration of the jury was precise and the law is formal in this regard, I announce that my advocacy for the Widow Capet is finished.' Herman turned to the Judges who inclined their heads, and he spoke for the last time:

The Tribunal, following the unanimous decision of the jury acceding to the requisition of the Public Prosecutor, and following the laws which he has cited, condemns the said Marie Antoinette, called of

Lorraine Austria, widow of Louis Capet, to death, and declares in conformity with the Law of 10 March last, that her possessions if she has any in the French territory be forfeit for the benefit of the Republic, and orders that the judgment shall be carried out on the Place de la Révolution, and shall be printed and published throughout the Republic.

Now at last she could go, her dazed mind told her. Without a sign or a word she rose and walked through the hall to the barrier where even the knitting women were silent; there she straightened herself and with head erect she left the hall. Hat in hand de Busne walked beside her, and when she arrived at the stairs which led to the courtyard he heard her murmur 'I can hardly see to walk.' He offered his arm and thus helped she went across the slippery yard, while the prisoners with their faces pressed against the bars of their cells watched in silence her halting passage. She left behind her in the slowly emptying Chamber a collection of doomed men. The Prosecutor, the President and three of the Judges would fall under Sanson's knife, her lawyers were more lucky. Chauveau survived to write his memoirs, while Tronçon du Coudray was deported to the hell of Cayenne. Of the witnesses, fourteen were guillotined, some must have feared it even while they spoke there. Bailly and Valaze were Girondins and already without hope; within twelve days Valaze, hearing his death sentence, thrust a knife into his heart and died; but he did not escape the scaffold for his corpse was taken with the others and decapitated. Of the jurors five were guillotined and four deported; but on this night of 15 October 1793 most of them were cheerful, they had done their duty, the law was satisfied, France was justified, and they could sleep with a good conscience. As one of them, Trinchard, wrote to his brother, 'I'd like to tell you, old boy, that I was one of the jurymen who judged that ferocious beast who has devoured the greater part of the Republic, that one who they used to call the Queen of France.'

In Brussels her one true friend, the man who would love and reverence her until he too died a violent death, Axel Fersen, had given up all hope. On 13 October he wrote:

Although there is no proof against this unfortunate princess, how can one flatter oneself that these traitors, even if they have none, will not condemn simply on assertions and vague suspicions, no, do not let us deceive ourselves, we must resign ourselves to the Divine Will, her end is decided and we must prepare and gather enough strength to support this terrible blow. God alone can save her, let us implore His pity and submit to His decree.

On the 20th he received the news of her execution and was utterly overwhelmed. His resolution served him little, his despair was total. He vowed vengeance on the hellish brutes who had condemned her, and as it turned out he had not long to wait, the coming months would see their end. Her death was but the prelude to the real Terror which engulfed France and would not be appeased until the Revolution should have run its course.

She had not been taken back to her cell but put in the narrow cabin reserved for those condemned to die. Entering she threw herself upon the couch shivering with cold. After a short rest she rose and asked for pen and paper and sitting down began to write her last letter, to Madame Elisabeth:

This 16 October at 4.32 in the morning.

It is to you, my sister, that I write for the last time. I have just been condemned, not to a shameful death, that is only for criminals, but to rejoin your brother. Like him, I am innocent, I hope to show the same firmness in my last moments. I am calm, as one is when one's conscience does not reproach one. I feel a profound sadness in leaving my children. You know that I existed only for them; and you, my good and tender sister, you who have in your friendship sacrificed everything to be with us, in what a position I leave you! I learned during the trial that my daughter was separated from you, alas the poor child, I do not dare write to her, she would not receive my letter. I do not even know if it will reach you. Receive my blessing for you both; I hope that one day when they are grown older they will be reunited with you and enjoy completely your tender care. They must always remember what I never ceased to teach them, that principles and attention to duty are the foundation of life, that their friendship and trust will be its happiness. My daughter must think that since she is older she must always help her brother by the advice which her fuller experience and his love will inspire in her, that they may feel in whatever situation they may find themselves they are only really happy in their union, that they follow our example and remember how through all our troubles our friendship has consoled us, and in happiness we have enjoyed it doubly because we have shared it with a friend, and where can one find the most tender and faithful friends if not in one's own family? And my son must never forget his father's last words, which I now solemnly repeat to him, that he should never seek to avenge our death. I have to speak to you of something which much afflicts my heart. I know how much this child has wounded you, pardon him, my dear sister, consider his age and how easy it is to make a child say what one will, and specially something which he does not understand. A day will come I hope when he will feel more keenly what all your goodness and tenderness have been and what it has cost you. It remains only for me to confide to you my last thoughts. I wished to do this before the trial, but partly because they did not allow me to write and its progress was so rapid I really did not have the time.

I die in the Catholic Faith, Apostolic and Roman; that of my fathers, in which I was brought up and which I have always professed; having no consolation to hope for, not knowing if indeed there are still the priests of that Faith and if there were whether it would not be too dangerous to come even once to this place. I ask God's pardon for all the faults which I may have committed since I was born; I have no hope but in His goodness. I hope that in His mercy He will receive my last prayer and those which I have made so long, that He will receive my soul in His merciful kindness. I ask pardon of all whom I have known and in particular from you, my sister, for all the trouble which without meaning to I may have caused. Forgive all my enemies the evil they have done me. I say goodbye to my aunts and to all my brothers and sisters. I had some friends. The thought of being separated forever from them is one of the greatest regrets I have in dying. They may know at least, that until my last moment I have thought of them.

Farewell, my good and tender sister, I hope that this letter may reach you. Do not forget me. I embrace you with all my heart as well as my poor children. My God! how it tears my heart to leave them for ever. Farewell, farewell! I must now only think of my spiritual duties. As I am not free they will perhaps bring me a priest (having taken the oath) but I swear here that I will not speak one word, and I will treat him as an absolute stranger.

This is a very extraordinary letter for a woman only a few hours from death to write, and shows Marie Antoinette with the thought of her husband in mind and determined to face the coming ordeal with the same nobility and calm that he had displayed. And it is all the more remarkable because she had suffered far more than he, had been outraged in her feelings of woman, mother and Queen, had been brought down physically to the lowest ebb; spied upon in the intimate functions of her body, drained of her strength by frightful haemorrhages, and racked by cold and damp; but her spirit and energy still existed. She had wept in writing it, but it was for her children. When it was finished she folded it and gave it to the concierge Bault.

The accounts of the Queen's last hours vary. Rosalie, the servant of Madame Richard, wrote later an account which has been suspected of inaccuracy. If Marie Antoinette had been transferred from her prison to the death cell, how was it that she had a table to write on, and how did Rosalie manage to penetrate to her and serve her there? The Queen's latest biographer to whom we are indebted for his deep research does not mention the change of prison and relies on the account of Rosalie Lamorlière. We shall try to give what seem the essential facts.

The letter finished, she knelt and prayed a long time; then rising, she ate a little of the food which was brought her and once more, still fully dressed, lay down and fell into an exhausted sleep. From five o'clock the streets through which she would pass had been filling up, the drums beat and the thirty thousand troops began to take their places; cannon had been placed on the bridges and in all the squares, and behind the double row of soldiers and gendarmes the crowds were massing. Why was all this display of force drawn up against one poor woman, did the authorities think that even at this late hour an attempt might be made to rescue her; from whence could it come? From her friends, all those *ci-devant* aristocrats who now hid behind the frontiers, from her devoted Fersen in Brussels, half mad with rage and pain because he could not die with her? From the people of Paris where there were still a handful of royalists who might risk their lives in a useless attempt?

None of these – but there was a plot, a pathetic conspiracy. It was devised by a small group and on 17 January 1794 Fouquier-Tinville revealed this 'conspiracy to rescue the woman Capet from the national vengeance'. There were fifty-four witnesses and they all combined under the pressure of terror to accuse the chief instigators of the plot, the lacemaker Lemille and her son of fourteen and a number of other small shopkeepers.

At six o'clock the Queen was awakened and told that a priest from Paris was in attendance and asked if she wished to confess, but faithful to the promise she had made in her letter she refused, though he came in and insisted that if it were known that she died without the consolation of the Church it would be unfortunate. She kept her own counsel but let him see that she would not recognize a juror, for he was dressed in civilian clothes. Besides, she said, God in His mercy had provided for her. Rosalie Lamorlière had already brought a little warm soup for the Queen shaking with the cold, and the priest suggested that she should cover her feet with a pillow. She did this, lying down again and for the next minutes occupied herself with her thoughts and silent prayers. Towards eight o'clock she rose and Rosalie entered to help her dress. The poor girl was in tears, for Marie Antoinette had said to her, when she brought the soup, 'I need nothing now, everything is finished for me.' It was the last time she would help her august prisoner, the last time she would hear that gentle voice and be treated with the courtesy which showed in every movement. Marie Antoinette wished to go to her death in white, the royal mourning; she took a new chemise and spread it out and then went behind the bed and in the space between it and the wall slipped off her black dress while the young girl tried to shield her from the inquisitive eyes of the gendarme in the room. But he came towards them and the Queen said imploringly, 'In the name of decency, Monsieur, allow me to change my linen without a witness.' To which he replied, 'I don't know anything about that, my orders are not to let you out of my sight for a moment.'

Sighing, she slipped off her chemise all spotted from her loss of blood and put on the clean one. She assumed the white negligé which she wore in the mornings and rolling up the miserable soiled linen sought for a place where she might hide it away: finally she found a crack in the wall and pushed it in. She tied a white linen fichu round her shoulders pulling it up to her neck and put a white mobcap on her head. Then they waited and the priest, the Abbé Girard, tried timidly to exhort her. Her death would expiate, he began, when she broke in, 'Faults yes, but never crimes' and he was silent.

Now four men entered, Herman, two of the Judges Foucauld and Douze Verteuil, and Fabricius the Registrar. The last held a paper in his hand and the Queen who was on her knees turned to them.

'Pay attention,' said Herman, 'We will now read your sentence.'

The Queen rising, replied, 'This is useless, I know it already only too well.'

One of the Judges declared that that did not matter, it must be read a second time. The four, who all held their hats in their hands, seemed abashed by the majesty and poise of the prisoner, but the reading went on and hardly was it finished than a fifth man entered, Sanson the executioner. He was an enormous young man who had achieved the unprecedented record of a head a minute, and he growled:

'Hold out your hands.'

The Queen fell back, horrified, stammering, 'Are you going to tie my hands?' and when he nodded, she protested, 'But Louis XVI did not have his hands tied.' Sanson turned to Herman who said roughly 'Do your duty.'

'Oh my God,' cried the unfortunate victim, aghast.

At these words Sanson seized her hands and pulling them behind her back, tied them together very brutally with a length of cord; it hurt her as well as mortifying her but she mastered her tears and said nothing more. He then snatched her cap from her head and cut her thin white hair which he pushed into his pocket: it would be burnt after the execution. Putting the cap on again all askew, he pulled the cords tight and the Queen rose to leave the cell. It had been a horrible scene, without one mitigating moment; these men were fiends.

It was nearly eleven o'clock, outside the weather was cold and damp, a foggy miserable day; but this had not kept the good people of Paris at home. They had assembled in their thousands to feast their eyes on this grand show, fallen monarchy at its most tragic end. Every window was loaded with sightseers, the pavements solid with men and women and their children, for this was an historic occasion. There were executions every day, but not of a *ci-devant* Queen of France. Speculation too was rife, how would she die, like most of these damned aristos with her head high, proudly, or would she have given in at last? The women were the most interested.

The crowd was perhaps thickest around the Conciergerie, and its noise met her ears when she arrived before the gateway. The door opened and they saw her pale and with reddened eyes, but still noble with an air of ineffable disdain as she looked at the people over whom she had once reigned, who had welcomed and

applauded her. 'Do not awaken that great beast,' Richelieu had
said. Now it was awake – or was it living in a nightmare, from
which it would recover with horror at its past deeds?

And then she saw the wretched cart in which she would ride,
and fell back with a spasm of disgust. At least Louis XVI had gone
to his death in a carriage, this was the final insult. Nature was too
much for her, Sanson was obliged to untie her hands and she
bent down in a corner of the wall and relieved herself; then she
offered her poor hands again to the man and stepped forward.
She had put on as a last piece of coquetry shoes with very high
heels, they were called à la Huberty and set off her tiny feet. In
these she mounted the ordinary cart sent for the condemned,
dirty with mud, not even a truss of straw, but a plank for her to
sit on. Behind her stood Sanson with his assistant; they held their
three-cornered hats in one hand while with the other Sanson gripped the cords which bound the prisoner, taking good care to let
them be seen by all. She was going to step over the plank when the
man stopped her and made her sit with her back to the horse. It
was half past eleven. The cart started with a jerk and the onlookers applauded with cries of 'Vive la République.' The priest
stood beside her and from time to time sought to exhort her by
pious words, saying that this was the moment to arm herself
with courage, to which she replied with her accustomed spirit
that she had made that apprenticeship for so long that it would
not be credible that she should lack it today. When he continued
she reprimanded him sharply, she was not of his religion but
that of her husband and she would not forget the principles which
he had always taught her. The priest fell silent but when it was all
over he testified to her courage and integrity. Meanwhile the
lugubrious cortège continued on its dreary way, the old horse
clopped heavily over the bridge, turning left into the rue St
Honoré, and the crowd was mercifully silent for the most part.
But, arrived in front of the Church of St Roche, the atmosphere
suddenly changed. Here had been massed on the steps and around
the church a multitude who greeted her with shouted insults
and seemed to have forgotten all natural feeling; in their hardened
hearts reigned only resentment, not alone for her but for all that
she represented. She was so used to their delirious infamy that
she was able to preserve a haughty silence. And yet–this was such a
familiar road for her, here she had passed so many times, saluted by

all who saw her in her carriage with its six white horses, laughing as she looked from the windows on the adoring populace, the young Queen in her silks and satins like a ray of sunshine in a harsh world. The rue St Honoré seemed as if it would never end, the old horse stumbled on his way, the workman who led him swore and encouraged him alternately; when the cart jolted she was nearly thrown from the plank, but through it all she preserved her unalterable calm. Among the crowds were many who if they had dared to speak would have greeted her, but even a whisper would bring death; fear and suspicion brooded over the city, it was given over to brutality and evil. Around the cart caracoled the actor Grammont, encouraging the furies of the mob. 'Here she is, my friends,' he would cry, 'the infamous Antoinette; she is F ...' and laughter and cheers greeted his sallies. She did not even show that she had heard, she was impassive, she would not give them the satisfaction they craved, to see her weep or even tremble before their vociferations. But she was not unobservant, for a few yards further on was the headquarters of the Jacobins, with an inscription over its door 'Committee Room of the Republican arms to destroy the tyrants'; here she seemed to ask the priest a question. For answer he held an ivory cross before her eyes, and she relapsed into silence. Still a little further on stood a sad group, the men who had hoped to raise a force to deliver her; there they were, a handful of small shopkeepers and workmen and hairdressers and the little street cleaner of fourteen who had said, 'You must go to the rich merchants, who will want to take her from the executioners.' They had failed and would pay later for their temerity.

Now it was nearly twelve o'clock and the wretched procession turned into the Place de la Révolution, where a still denser crowd was massed. To the right lay the palace of the Tuileries, and as she turned her head and saw it, she grew visibly paler. Here she had come in 1773, the radiant child, to be acclaimed by 'two thousand lovers', and to feel her loving heart go out to them, the 'poor people' so generously welcoming her; and here she had left that same weathercock people in 1792, pursued by their yelling voices prophesying her ruin. Here her children had played in the gardens and she heard again their cries of pleasure, and heard too her little son's terrified weeping and felt his frail arms around her neck. No wonder she shrank; but her weakness was momentary, she mastered her emotion, and as the tumbril stopped she descended and mounted the steps of the scaffold quickly and unaided; so quickly, says a witness, that she lost one of her little shoes and stepped inadvertently on Sanson's foot. With her accustomed graciousness she murmured, 'Pardon Monsieur, I did not mean it.'

Her last words! Four minutes later she was dead, and the assistant, holding the head streaming with blood and the lips still twitching, paraded round the scaffold, greeted by jubilant cries of '*Vive La République*'. It was finished; she had paid with her life for all the mistakes, the extravagance, the incomprehension of her times, she had trodden the road her mother had set her on to the end. But she died as a daughter of the Caesars should, head high to the last. She had entered History.

The remains were loaded into the cart and dragged to the cemetery of the Madeleine where the executioners found that neither coffin nor grave had been prepared, so they threw the corpse on the ground with the head between the knees. Two weeks later the gravedigger Joly made a grave and having noted his expenses presented the bill to the Revolutionary Tribunal.

The Widow Capet, for the coffin	6 livres
For the grave and diggers	25 livres

It was the last entry on the books kept 'For the service of the Queen of France'.

It is not without a certain satisfaction that we note that her worst enemy, Philippe d'Orléans, was guillotined a bare three weeks after her. If she had wished for revenge, which she never did, in his death she was avenged. Another more unfortunate victim was the *ci-devant* Comtesse Du Barry who from her retreat in England had generously aided many an émigré, and had even written to the Queen offering what help she could give. The guillotine was not nice in its choice of victims, and Du Barry was shortly followed by a very different woman, Madame Roland. She had had so little mercy on the Queen that she had gloated over her defeat. Now she too stood on the scaffold and her last words might be the epitaph of the epoch, 'Oh Liberty, what crimes are committed in thy name!'

HOUSE OF BOURBON

LOUIS XV (1710-74)
King of France 1715-74
m. Marie Leszcynska

Unnamed (1730-31) duc d'Anjou

7 daughters

Elisabeth (1740-94)

Clotilde (1759-1802)
m. Charles Emmanuel IV of Sardinia

CHARLES X (1757-1836)
Comte d'Artois
King of France 1824-30
m. Thérèse of Savoy

LOUIS XVIII (1755-1824)
Comte de Provence
King of France 1814-24
m. Louise of Savoy

LOUIS XVI (1754-93)
King of France 1774-93
m. MARIE ANTOINETTE
of Austria (1755-93)

LOUIS (1729-65)
Dauphin

m. (1) Teresa of Spain (died 1746)

m. (2) Maria Josepha of Saxony

Marie-Thérèse (1746-48)

LOUIS (1751-61)
duc de Bourgogne

Louis (1753-54)
duc d'Aquitaine

Marie Thérèse (1778-1851)
m. Louis Antoine
duc d'Angoulême

LOUIS XVII (1785-95)
King of France 1793-95

HOUSE OF HABSBURG

MARIA THERESA (1717-80)
Queen of Hungary and Bohemia 1740-80
m. Francis Stephen of Lorraine (1708-65)
Grand duke of Tuscany 1735-65
Emperor FRANCIS I 1745-65

Maximilian Francis (1756-1801)
Elector of Cologne

MARIE ANTOINETTE (1755-93)
m. LOUIS XVI of France

Ferdinand (1754-1806)
m. Beatrice of Modena

Maria Caroline (1752-1814)
m. Ferdinand of Naples-Sicily

LEOPOLD II (1747-92)
Grand duke of Tuscany
1765-90
Emperor 1790-92
m. Marie Louise of Spain

Maria Christina (1742-98)
m. Albert of Saxe-Teschen

JOSEPH II (1741-90)
Emperor 1765-90
m. (1) Isabella of Parma
m. (2) Maria Josepha of
Bavaria

Zephyrine (1750-55)

Maria Amalia (1746-1804)
m. Ferdinand of Parma

Arnaud-Bouteloup, Jeanne: *Le Rôle politique de Marie-Antoinette* (Paris, 1924).

Barker, Sir Ernest, ed.: *The European Inheritance*, 3 vols. (by various authors). Edited by Sir E. Barker, Sir George Clark, Professor P. Vaucher (Oxford, 1954).

Behrens, C. B. A.: *The Ancien Régime* (London, 1967).

Bertin, Georges: *Madame de Lamballe d'après des documents inédits* (Paris, 1888).

Besenval, P. J. V. de, Baron: *Mémoires*, 4 vols. (Paris, 1805).

Boufflers, S. J. de, Marquis: *Correspondance inédite de la Comtesse de Sabran et du chevalier de Boufflers 1778–1788* (Paris, 1875).

Bouillé, F. C. A. de, Marquis: *Mémoires sur la Révolution française* (Paris, 1802).

Bourgoing, Jean F. de: *Vœux et conseils du vrai peuple français à l'Assemblée nationale* (1790).

Bright, J. F.: *Maria Theresa* (London, New York, 1897).

Burke, Edmund: *Reflections on the Revolution in France* (London, 1790).

Campan, J. L. H.: *Memoirs of the Private Life of Marie Antoinette, Queen of France*, 2 vols. (London, 1823).

Campardon, Émile: *Madame de Pompadour et la cour de Louis XV* (Paris, 1867); *Marie-Antoinette à la Conciergerie* (Paris, 1863).

Carlyle, Thomas: *The French Revolution*, 2 vols. (London, Everyman's Library, 1906).

Castelot, André: *Marie-Antoinette* (Paris, 1953).

Choiseul, E. F. de, Duc de Choiseul et d'Amboise: *Mémoires du duc de Choiseul . . . 1719–1785* (Paris, 1904).

Du Barry, Marie Jeanne, Comtesse: *Lettres originales de Madame la Comtesse Du Barry* (London, 1779).

Du Bois de Beauchesne, A. H.: *Louis XVII. Sa vie, son agonie, sa mort: captivité de la famille royale au Temple*, 2 vols. (Paris, 1852).

Duchesne, Gaston: *Mademoiselle de Charollais, procureuse du roi* (Paris, 1909).

Du Deffand, Marie: *Lettres de la Marquise du Deffand à Horace Walpole (1766–1780)*, 3 vols. (London, 1912).

Eckard, Jean: *Fragments historiques sur la captivité de la famille royale à la tour du Temple recueillis par M. de Turgy, pendant son service, du 13 août 1792 au 13 octobre 1793, et publiés par M. Eckard* (Paris, 1818); *Mémoires historiques sur Louis XVII* (Paris, 1817).

Egret, Jean: *La Pré-révolution française, 1787–1788* (Paris, 1962).

Falloux, F. A. P. de, Comte: *Louis XVI* (Paris, 1840).

Fay, Bernard: *Louis XVI ou la Fin d'un monde* (Paris, 1955).

Fersen, Hans Axel von, Count: *Lettres d'Axel de Fersen à son père pendant la guerre de l'indépendance d'Amerique publiées avec une introduction et des notes par le Comte F. V. Wrangel* (Paris, 1929); *Diary and Correspondence* translated by K. P. Wormeley (London, 1902).

Fleischmann, Hector: *Madame de Polignac et la cour galante de Marie-Antoinette* (Paris, 1910).

Girard, Georges, ed.: *Correspondance entre Marie-Thérèse et Marie-Antoinette* (Paris, 1933).

Goncourt, E. and J.: *Histoire de Marie-Antoinette* (Paris, 1858).

Gontaud, Armand Louis de, Duc de Biron: *Un Amant de Marie-Antoinette. Le 'divin' Lauzun et ses mémoires* (Paris, 1911).

Gooch, G. P.: *Maria Theresa* (London, 1951).

Hanet-Cléry, J. B. A.: *Journal de ce qui s'est passé à la tour du Temple pendant la captivité de Louis XVI* (Paris, 1816).

Heidenstam, O. G. von: *Marie-Antoinette, Fersen et Barnave. Leur correspondance* (Paris, 1913).

Herold, J. Christopher: *Mistress to an age. A life of Madame de Staël* (London, 1959).

Hüe, François, Baron: *Dernières années du règne et de la vie de Louis XVI* (London, 1806, Paris, 1816).

Jobez, Alphonse: *La France sous Louis XVI*, 3 vols. (Paris, 1877–93).

Kayser, Jacques: *La vie de La Fayette* (Paris, 1928).

Khevenhueller-Metsch, J. J., Prince: *Aus dem Hofleben Maria Theresia's* (Vienna, 1859).

Klinckowström, R. M., Baron: *Le Comte de Fersen et la Cour de France* (Paris, 1877).

La Rocheterie, Maxime de: *Histoire de Marie-Antoinette*, 2 vols. (Paris, 1890; London, 1893); *Lettres de Marie Antoinette, recueil des lettres authentiques de la reine, publié pour la Société d'histoire contemporaine, par Maxime de La Rocheterie et le M. de Beaucourt*, 2 vols. (Paris, 1895–6).

Leitich, Ann Tizia: *Augustissima. Maria Theresia – Leben und Werk* (Zürich, 1954).

Lenôtre, G.: *Le Drame de Varennes, juin 1791* (Paris, 1905).

Lévis, P. M. G. de, Duc: *Souvenirs et Portraits 1780–1789* (Paris, London, 1813).

Ligne, C. J. E. de, Prince: *Lettres et Pensées* (Paris, London, 1809).

BIBLIOGRAPHY

Lockroy, Édouard: *Journal d'une Bourgeoise pendant la Révolution* (1881).

Maria Theresa, Empress of Austria, and Marie Antoinette, Queen of France: *Briefwechsel* ed. Paul Christoph (Vienna, 1952). See also Girard

Marie Antoinette, Queen of France: see Girard; von Heidenstam; La Rocheterie; Maria Theresa, Empress of Austria and Marie Antoinette, Queen of France; Söderhjelm

Maurois, André: *A History of France* (London, 1949).

Michelet, Jules: *History of the French Revolution* (London, 1847, 1848).

Moelle: *Six journées passées au temple, et autres détails sur la famille royale, qui y a été détenue* (Paris, 1820).

Moreau, Jacob-Nicolas: *Bibliothèque de Mme la Dauphine* (Paris, 1770); *Mes Souvenirs* (Paris, 1898–1901).

Nolhac, A. M. P. G., de: *Marie-Antoinette, dauphine* (Paris, 1898); *Le Château de Versailles* (Paris, 1898).

Pétion de Villeneuve, Jérôme: *Mémoires inédits de Pétion et mémoires de Buzot et de Barbaroux . . . Précédés d'une introduction par C. A. Dauban* (Paris, 1866).

Pfister, Kurt: *Maria Theresia, Mensch, Staat und Kultur d. spätbarocken Welt* (Munich, 1949).

Sagnac, Philippe: *La Fin de l'ancien régime et la Révolution américaine, 1763–1789* (Paris, 1947).

Scudder, E. S.: *Prince of the Blood. Being an account of the illustrious birth, the strange life and the horrible death of Louis-Philippe-Joseph, fifth Duke of Orléans* (London, 1937).

Ségur, P. M. M. H. de, Marquis: *Marie-Antoinette* (Paris, 1920).

Sénar, Gabriel Jérôme: *Révélations* (Paris, 1821).

Söderhjelm, Alma: *Marie Antoinette et Barnave: correspondance secrète* (1934).

Taylor, Ida A.: *Life of Mme Roland* (London, 1911).

Tourzel, Duchesse de: *Mémoires*, 2 vols. (Paris, 1883).

Tschuppik, Carl: *Marie-Thérèse* (Paris, 1936).

Turgy, M. de: see Eckard

Viel-Castel, H. de: *Marie-Antoinette et la Révolution Française* (Paris, 1859).

Voltaire, F. M. A. de: *Candide and other romances, Letters*, translated by Richard Aldington (London, 1927).

Vuaflart, A., and Bourin, H.: *Les Portraits de Marie-Antoinette, Étude d'iconographie critique* (Paris, 1909).

Walpole, Horace: *The Letters of Horace Walpole*, 9 vols. (London, 1891).

Wanderuszka, Adam: *Das Haus Habsburg. Die Geschichte einer europäischen Dynastie* (Stuttgart, 1959).

Weber, Joseph: *Mémoires de Weber, concernant Marie-Antoinette*, 2 vols. (Paris, 1922).

Woodgate, M. V.: *The Abbé Edgeworth*, 1745–1807 (Dublin, 1945, New York, 1946).

Wurzbach, Constant von: *Biographisches Lexicon des Kaiserthums Oesterreich* (1856).

Young, Arthur: *Travels in France* (London, 1892).

Zweig, Stefan: *Marie Antoinette* (London, 1952).

INDEX

INDEX